Ksenia Menshikova

RUNES & GODS

ANCIENT KNOWLEDGE
IN MAGICAL SYMBOLS

Rune Department of the Menshikova School

More about the Menshikova School:

Copyright © 2024 Ksenia Menshikova
English Translation Copyright © 2024 STUDIO LABYRINTH Sp. z o.o., Poland
All rights reserved.

ISBN: 9798332112416

CONTENTS

THE FUTHARK

Fehu
Uruz
Thurisaz
Ansuz
Raidho
Kenaz
Gebo
Wunjo
Hagalaz
Nauthiz
Isa
Jera
Eiwaz
Perthro
Algiz
Sowilo
Tiwaz
Berkana
Ehwaz
Mannaz
Laguz
Inguz
Othala
Dagaz

INTRODUCTION

Hearing I ask from the holy races,
From Heimdall's sons, both high and low;
Thou wilt, Valfather, that well I relate
Old tales I remember of men long ago.
(The Poetic Edda[1]. Voluspo)

Having mastered the Elder Futhark, linking all the runes into a single chain, the rune Fehu connected with the rune Dagaz, and all 24 runes began to work independently, transforming consciousness every minute through the sequential transformation and reassessment of all data, connections, causes, and effects. The foundation was the task set by each individual entering the process of transformation through the runes: who to become? How to change oneself to change reality?

The Futhark is arranged in such a way that every transformation performed by a rune provides the basis for each subsequent one to activate its special processes. But, by linking the runes into a chain, the transformation becomes continuous; the correlation happens constantly with each introduced change — everything transforms.

This connection brings consciousness closer to the northern tradition, making it ready to receive the ancient sacred

[1] All passages from the Poetic Edda are given in Henry A. Bellows translation. The passages from the Prose Edda - in the translation by Rasmus B. Anderson.

knowledge about the gods and worlds, about norse magic and its secrets. On the pages of this book, we will embark on a journey into the mysterious world of the birth of magic and try to understand what the gods wanted to tell us. They left us sagas and legends, tales of their deeds and defeats. Without hiding the truth, they opened up a space for comprehension before their descendants — that which is not said but needs to be understood.

All who have passed through the Futhark note an unprecedented increase in inner strength and the power of the mind. Confidence in feeling oneself, confidence in one's abilities — this is the least the runes give, but such sensations are natural because these are the feelings of a warrior. Runes are a warrior's tool.

ᛊ ᛞ

The power that has touched the mind is quite tangible, but it is not yet personified: who is it? What is it? Does it have a name? Which god does it belong to? What does it mean for the future? But it is very important to understand it. Very. It is precisely the understanding of the minds of the ancient norse gods that is the goal of further work.

To know means to understand. After all, runes are not only a tool that changes something in consciousness but also a force that truly affects the external world. And this is a completely different level of mastery and a different level of responsibility. When you understand this, it becomes obvious that responsibility implies greater knowledge. Including the laws of this world. Including the nature of the force that will guide you.

The impact of magical signs on reality can be very significant. Runes always work, even if it seems to you that they do not. To see and understand this, one must first and foremost obtain comprehensive knowledge about consequences and causes, about actions and results — and their reflection in magic.

To change one's inner world, a person's intention and will are sufficient. But to change the outer world, one must learn to align their actions with the forces that created and sustain the world, and therefore bear a certain responsibility for it. Thus, knowledge of these forces, their principles, and their laws becomes an essential necessity for the practicing mage. When one's own intentions align with the vectors of reality's intentions, the effect becomes significantly greater. Otherwise, a situation may arise that leads the weaker one to a sad outcome.

ᚹ ᚠ

In this book, the basic and mandatory laws will be presented. We will thoroughly examine the forces that permeate this world through their connection with the pantheon of norse gods. We will learn to write runic formulas and use them correctly. We will study those staves that bring real and tangible results and try to understand exactly how they work.

There are various ways to study runic magic. Usually, people who use runes for the first time do so to solve basic everyday problems: healing themselves, helping loved ones, attracting money, summoning love — in short, everything that is close to the heart and necessary for the body. No one says that this is trivial, unworthy, or wrong — we all engage in this and will continue to do so, including in the pages of this book. But primarily, those studying runic magic are interested not so much in everyday effects but in personal transformation. One can learn ordinary witchcraft anywhere and achieve very tangible results in this matter; and although it is indirectly related to magic, it also has its place. My students are more interested in magic and personal magical transformation, which means that we will have to study the issue both deeper and wider. We need additional strength and additional knowledge to understand not only how a magical formula or intention works but also why.

Practicing mages — erilar[2] — have long noticed that runic formulas and staves work much better and more precisely if they are bound "on the channel." This term means the mind of the mage coming in contact with the mind of a specific god. In the process of such a connection, the mage becomes a conduit for the force and will of the god with whom he has established

---

2 Erilar — a mage in the Scandinavian tradition who possesses the magic of words.

ᛊ ᛞ

contact, and everything that is bound on this channel is bound not only in his own name but also in the god's name.

Such an effect can only manifest in a magical consciousness, whereas it is not available to ordinary sorcerers and people. A force like the mind of an ancient god is more likely to manifest in a consciousness that can conduct this force without distortion. To bring one's mind in line with these mandatory "technical characteristics," preliminary runic transformation through the Elder Futhark was required.

Each force carries its own requirements. To reliably understand them, one must delve into the study of primary sources, in our case, the myths of the northern tradition: sagas, eddas, legends, and tales. These are the main sources of information for both beginners and the most experienced erilar, for everything is recorded there. How to read it correctly? How to hear it? How not to err in understanding?

The answers to these questions will be the solution to the task we set here.

This book consists of two parts: theory and practice. I highly recommend that you begin to practice using runic formulas and staves only after you have studied the runes themselves, let the energy of each pass through you, and allowed it to transform your mind to a different range of possibilities. There are enough sources of rune knowledge, and my book "Runes Reveal the Mysteries of the World" is regularly published. Remember that sequential transformation of the mind "from simple to complex" will give a better effect than trying to master everything at once.

The study of runes awakens specific qualities of personality in the mind, allowing the force that transforms *simple* nature to be constantly present in consciousness. This means that the process of inner transformation will never be completed:

ᚹ ᚨ

what has been achieved will never be sufficient, and what is learned now will generate many additional tasks, opening the way for new opportunities in the future. But magical force never comes into the seeker's consciousness just like that, and this should always be remembered. Force dictates its own rules and requirements; it teaches one to make the right actions, take timely decisions, and leave the correct traces behind; it certainly controls what is being carried out.

Runes are a magical tool, which means they possess their own consciousness. This consciousness has a predisposition to identify its own and others, ensuring only the former remain. Correctly interpreting primary sources and understanding their hidden meanings will help every seeker attract the forces that will guide them further along the thorny but beautiful path of the magical current.

Each deity in the Scandinavian pantheon, which we will study, operates on its own frequency, its own channel, its own primal essence, and accordingly will activate those mental capabilities that resonate with this power. If the force is *yours*, you will feel it immediately. If not, even more so. It is very important for every practitioner to find their god(s), their channel, their frequency, their force.

The search will bring its own results and effects into the seeker's life. The search itself is a process of learning, comparing results, and understanding the hidden. During this process, you will inevitably encounter a situation where the channel of a certain god expands the mind to unimaginable widths, awakens, and gives unseen power, while another channel, on the contrary, either changes nothing or, at worst, closes the mind, making it small and insignificant. This effect is explained by the fact that you have matched the carrier frequencies of one god's emanations, but not others. The power of the divine mind is incomparably stronger than the mind of one person or even all humanity. Therefore, the mismatch suppresses the person, despite all their willpower—there simply aren't enough basic strengths.

The search for magical power can follow different paths. We can conditionally distinguish two methods used by seekers in their quest for power. Some live within this power, as in a mother's womb, and perceive it as it is. Others hunt for it, viewing magic as legitimate prey and attempting to conquer it. It cannot be said that one method is right or wrong, useful or harmful, bad or good. It is either effective or it isn't. Problems arise when the seeker begins to use a method that isn't their own. Only you and your magic can determine which method is yours. But to understand your natural force and grasp the correct mechanism for interacting with it, you need to immerse yourself in worlds where magic exists, where it has already established itself, where, without hiding, it has shown its presence and demonstrated its power over reality. This is the realm of Myth.

YGGDRASIL TREE

When studying the runes during the first stage of learning, you have already begun to immerse yourself in the realm of myth. Indeed, by understanding each rune of the Elder Futhark, it is impossible not to touch upon the myth that follows each rune, like a thread follows a needle. However, a full entry into the realm of myth is achieved only when this entry begins with the very first step, from which the gods themselves once started — the myth of the creation of the worlds.

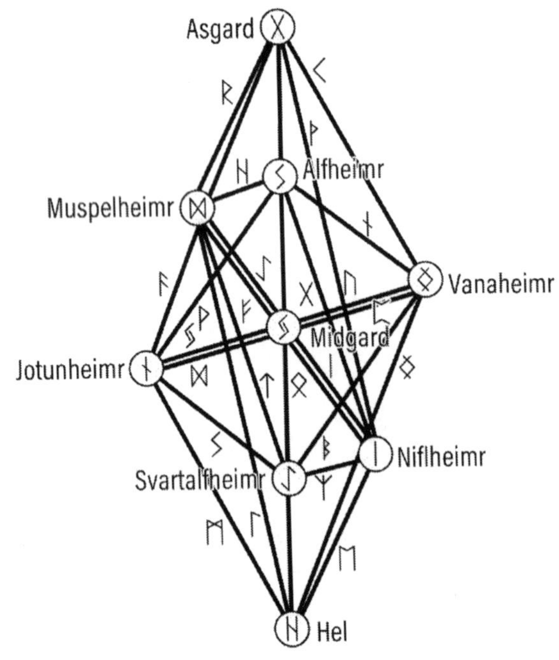

ᛊ ᛞ

An ash I know, Yggdrasil its name,
With water white is the great tree wet;
Thence come the dews that fall in the dales,
Green by Urth's well does it ever grow.
(The Poetic Edda. Voluspo)

The Yggdrasil tree is the structure of the system, the description of the Universe of gods and humans in the Scandinavian tradition.

Three roots there are that three ways run
'Neath the ash-tree Yggdrasil;
'Neath the first lives Hel, 'neath the second the frost-giants,
'Nealh the last are the lands of men.
(The Poetic Edda. Grímnismol)

The three roots represent three sources of nourishment:
Hel — the source of primordial matter, chaos.
Frost giants — Niflheimr, the world of the jötnar.
Humans — Midgard, the world of time.

The Yggdrasil tree system will exist as long as it has nourishment.

But the viability of the entire system depends not only on the sources of nourishment. The Yggdrasil ash is constantly subjected to the influence of external forces, intending to kill it, destroy the creation of the gods, and thwart their plan.

Four harts there are, that the highest twigs
Nibble with necks bent back;

ᚹ ᚨ

Dain and Dvalin,
Duneyr and Dyrathror.

More serpents there are beneath the ash
Than an unwise ape would think ;
Goin and Moin, Grafvitnir's sons,
Grabak and Grafvolluth,
Ofnir and Svafnir shall ever, methinks.
Gnaw at the twigs of the tree.

Yggdrasil's ash great evil suffers.
Far more than men do know;
The hart bites its top, its trunk is rotting,
And Nithhogg gnaws beneath.
(*The Poetic Edda. Grímnismol*)

The nine worlds are connected by runic channels, and each channel operates on a specific frequency. This frequency corresponds to a certain rune of the Futhark, which you have already learned and internalized.

The nine worlds and 24 runes. There are reversible runes and irreversible runes. There are exactly 9 irreversible runes, one for each World.

Each irreversible rune on the tree performs two functions: it simultaneously acts as both a connection between the worlds and a key to a specific world. Meanwhile, reversible runes serve only as connections.

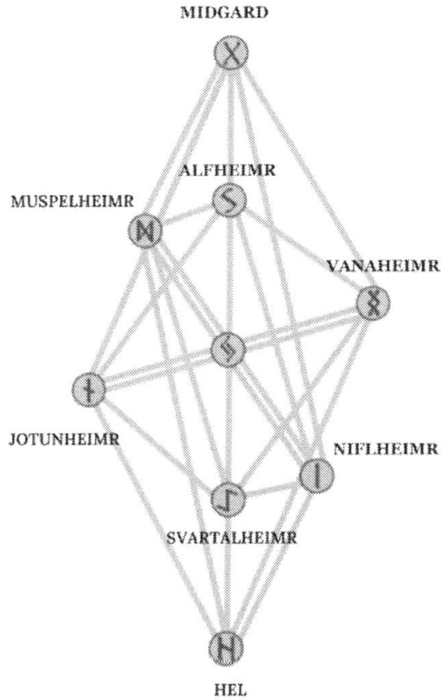

Mostly, the irreversible runes pertain to the second aett — it revealed the qualities of consciousness necessary for the development of natural powers (the first aett). This "disproportionate" distribution of keys among the aettir (houses) is not accidental and indicates that a person's mind will have the ability to shift between worlds only when they develop the necessary and sufficient qualities to correctly perceive and retain information different from their direct worldview. Otherwise, they are doomed to be conduits of others' will without understanding and awareness. If you recall your journey through the runes of the Elder Futhark, you will agree that the second aett was the most challenging to master. The greatest revelations occurred precisely there.

All the qualities of consciousness that were honed in the second aett, against the backdrop of the irreversible key runes, developed self-awareness as an individual. This was a very difficult task, paradoxical as it sounds: to separate oneself from the human mass, to refuse to retain any quality that would make one an integral part of the crowd, granting a false sense of security — doing this proved more challenging than it initially seemed.

The revelation obtained when encountering the key runes in the second aett is based on a deeper understanding of the powers and rights that the mind comprehended and brought to the surface in the first aett.

The first aett spoke of the powers embedded in every person, the rights granted to them by birth. But upon entering the second aett with all this power, we see that these rights are not granted forever. They are merely initial capital, and if they, the rights and powers, are not protected and developed, losing one's capital is easier than ever.

The shock that the mind experienced from this fact is comparable to a child's revelation in the harsh world of adults, where the childish illusions of "everyone owes me" crumble to dust. Because from now on, one has to fight for their rights. To struggle. And only the ability to defend one's own values will determine the results that can be achieved in the third aett — the path to achieving real life outcomes. However, there will be no results if one does not fully realize themselves as absolutely separate from the mass, does not understand their natural, fundamental, inherent loneliness, and does not accept it as a guarantee of future success — only those unburdened by anything have a chance to reach the result faster than those laden with the baggage of connections, habits, and obligations. Only in this case can one achieve their own results in the third aett —

those needed solely by the individual; those that do not require sharing with everyone else.

Understanding one's individuality is challenging. It is much easier to say, "I am a human" and thereby associate oneself with the society of people on the simple grounds that you belong to a single biological species. It is easier to define oneself as "I am a woman" or "I am a man" and immediately limit oneself by all the rules and norms that automatically follow such definitions. It is easier to find an acceptable classification that somehow equates you to everyone else or at least to a group of similar individuals.

And how much harder it is to say to yourself, "I am as I am," and feel it to the fullest extent. To understand that there is no one else like you and that searching is pointless, even though you still belong to the human race, you are still a man or a woman, still a father or a mother — but all that is no longer the main thing. The main thing now lies elsewhere — in something that has no analogy in the entire world (and beyond). And in this, find your great sorrow and your great joy.

Sorrow because from now on, there is absolutely nothing to lean on, and there is no longer a standard with which you can compare yourself in any way. For an immature consciousness, this is a catastrophe, the collapse of the world, a loss of bearings. But happiness in that, from now on, there are no longer any barriers that prevent you from independently creating such standards. For yourself and for others, as well.

The entire path traversed in the Futhark and the realization of oneself as an individual was an important and necessary step for magical initiation and further study of the Nine Worlds system. Only by breaking away from the mass does consciousness cease to be inert, thought becomes light, and the speed of information processing increases manyfold. Only such a consciousness gains the ability to freely move between worlds, enriching itself in each of its journeys.

In the system of the Nine Worlds, the place of humans is defined in the middle world of Midgard. If you look at the location of Midgard on the tree, it is easy to notice that many connections extend to the human middle world, but these connections are not with all worlds, but only with certain ones. What are these worlds, and why do they influence our world directly, while all others do that indirectly through them? The answer to this question is hidden in the cosmological myths of the northern tradition.

The Origin of the World. The Birth of the Gods

Almost all religious systems, when touching upon the question of the birth of our world, indicate that the gods were born together with it. The northern tradition does not contradict this information either. The legend says that:

Many ages before the earth was made, Nifheim ha d existed, in the midst of which is the well called Hvergelmer. Still there was before a world to the south which hight Muspelheim . It is light and hot , and so bright and dazzling that no stranger, who is not a drizzling rains and gusts . But the south part of Ginungagap was lighted up by the glowing sparks that few out of Muspelheim . As cold and all things grim proceeded from Nifheim, so that which bordered on Muspelheim was hot and bright , and Ginungagap was as warm and mild a s windless air.

(The Prose Edda)

Thus, the reason for the emergence of the world system was the existence of two opposites, two forces diametrically different from each other. Sooner or later, they had to come into contact, meet in the expanses of the Universe, for here works the first magical principle: nothing can be static, development occurs only in motion. The principle of the necessity of this movement is embedded in the physical and psychological laws of the world: opposites attract, like positively and negatively charged particles. And so it happened.

The force lines running from north to south awakened the world of ice and mists, and the great union—the creation of the Universe—began.

ᛊ ᛞ

And when the heated blasts from Muspelheim met the rime, so that it melted into drops, then, by the might of him who sent the heat, the drops quickened into life and took the likeness of a man who got the name Ymer . But the Frost giants call him Aurgelmer.

(The Prose Edda)

Two opposites, merging with each other simultaneously in endless struggle and unimaginable attraction, will always result in a third force—the result. This is the second magical principle, which states that force (energy) does not disappear but is transformed under the influence of information.

From this point on, in our biological life, the physical world, and its psychological projection, this principle is valid always and everywhere: energy merges with information and ultimately produces a material, tangible world. At the same time, neither energy nor information ceases to exist on their own, but their union creates a third entity, independently existing and ready for further self-projection.

A man and a woman, combining their biological nature, give birth to a third entity—their child—while they themselves continue to exist.

Here's how it's described in Voluspo:

I remember yet the giants of yore,
Who gave me bread in the days gone by;
Nine worlds I knew, the nine in the tree
With mighty roots beneath the mold.

Of old was the age when Ymir lived;
Sea nor cool waves nor sand there were;
Earth had not been, nor heaven above,
But a yawning gap, and grass nowhere.

ᚹ ᚨ

Then Bur's sons lifted the level land,
Mithgarth the mighty there they made;
The sun from the south warmed the stones of earth.
And green was the ground with growing leeks.

The sun, the sister of the moon, from the south
Her right hand cast over heaven's rim;
No knowledge she had where her home should be,
The moon knew not what might was his.
The stars knew not where their stations were.

That same day, under Ymir's left arm, a boy and a girl appeared, and from his feet, the six-headed giant Thrudgelmir was born. Thus began the lineage of the giants, the Grimthurses, who were as cruel and cunning as the ice and fire that created them.

The firstborn of Heaven and Earth, the Titans, the Primordial, the Immortals—they have countless names and appear in all myths and religious systems. They embody the primordial principles and elemental forces that require development and understanding. The Poetic Edda ("Vafthruthnismol") tells of this event as follows:

Othin spake:
Vafthruthnir, hail! to thy hall am I come,
For thyself I fain would see;
And first would I ask if wise thou art,
Or, giant, all wisdom hast won.

Vafthruthnir spake:
Out of Ymir's flesh was fashioned the earth,

ᛊ ᛞ

And the mountains were made of his bones;
The sky from the frost-cold giant's skull,
And the ocean out of his blood.

Othin spake:
Fifth answer me well, if wise thou art called,
If thou knowest it, Vafthruthnir, now:
What giant first was fashioned of old,
And the eldest of Ymir's kin?

Vafthruthnir spake:
Winters unmeasured ere earth was made
Was the birth of Bergelmir;
Thruthgelmir's son was the giant strong,
And Aurgelmir's grandson of old.

Othin spake:
Sixth answer me well, if wise thou art called,
If thou knowest it, Vafthruthnir, now:
Whence did Aurgelmir come with the giants' kin,
Long since, thou giant sage?

Vafthruthnir spake:
Down from Elivagar did venom drop.
And waxed till a giant it was;
And thence arose our giants' race,
And thus so fierce are we found.

Othin spake:
Seventh answer me well,
if wise thou art called,
If thou knowest it, Vafthruthnir, now:

ᚹ ᚨ

How begat he children, the giant grim,
Who never a giantess knew?

Vafthruthnir spake:
They say 'neath the arms
of the giant of ice
Grew man-child and maid together;
And foot with foot did the wise one fashion
A son that six heads bore.

Othin spake:
Eigth answer me well, if wise thou art called,
If thou knowest it, Vafthruthnir, now.
What farthest back dost thou bear in mind?
For wide is thy wisdom, giant!

Vafthruthnir spake:
Winters unmeasured ere earth was made
Was the birth of Bergelmir;
This first knew I well, when the giant wise
In a boat of old was borne.

The Younger (Prose) Edda continues:

The next thing was that when the rime melted into drops, there was made thereof a cow, which hight Audhumbla. Four milk-streams ran from her teats, and She fed Ymer. Thereupon asked Ganglere : On what did the cow subsist ? Answered Har : She licked the salt-stones that were covered with rime, and the first day that she licked the stones there came out of them in the evening a man's hair, the second day a man's head, and the third day the whole man was there. This man's name was Bure; he was fair of face, great and mighty, and he begat a son whose name was Bor. This

Bor married a woman whose name was Bestla, the daughter of the giant Bolthorn they had three sons, the one hight Odin, the other Vile, and the third Ve.

But nothing is eternal in this world, even stars fade, and gods are mortal. The old must make way for the new, and the second magical principle applies here as well: everything transforms, but nothing disappears. Thus, the progenitor of the old gods, Ymir, became the foundation upon which the new gods built the first reality.

The god brothers did not like the world in which they lived and did not want to endure the rule of the cruel Ymir. They rebelled against the first of the giants and, after a long and brutal struggle, killed him. Ymir was so enormous that the blood gushing from his wounds drowned all the other giants and even the cow Audhumla. Only one of Ymir's grandsons, Bergelmir, managed to build a boat on which he saved himself along with his wife.

Now, nothing stood in the gods' way of arranging the world according to their desires. They made the earth from Ymir's body in the shape of a flat circle and placed it in the middle of a vast sea that formed from his blood. The gods called the land "Midgard," which means "middle country." Then the brothers took Ymir's skull and made the sky from it, made mountains from his bones, trees from his hair, stones from his teeth, and clouds from his brain. At each of the four corners of the sky, the gods placed a horn and put a wind in each horn: Nordre in the north, Sudre in the south, Vestre in the west, and Austre in the east. From the sparks flying out of Muspelheim, the gods created stars and decorated the sky with them. Some stars were fixed in place, while others, to mark the passage of time, were arranged to move in a circle, completing it in one year.

ᛊ ᛞ

Having created the world, Odin and his brothers thought of populating it. One day, on the shore of the sea, they found two trees: an ash and an alder. The gods cut them down and made a man from the ash and a woman from the alder. Then one god breathed life into them, another gave them intelligence, and a third provided blood and rosy cheeks. Thus, the first humans came into being: the man was named Ask, and the woman, Embla.

The gods did not forget the giants. Across the sea, to the east of Midgard, they created the land of Jotunheimr and gave it to Bergelmir and his descendants.

Over time, the number of gods increased: Odin, the eldest of the brothers, had many children, and they built a country high above the earth and called it Asgard, calling themselves the Aesir.

Thus, as the story goes, from the primordial matter, from the body of the giant Ymir, the gods created the worlds. But not all at once, only those they deemed necessary.

Each world was created from the primordial substance—Ymir. The gods dismantled him into parts, where each part carried some unique and inimitable properties of the progenitor. The gods assembled these isolated parts into a new scheme, and this scheme, which we now know as the "Yggdrasil Tree," is also Ymir, but in a different form. The progenitor divided chaotically, filling all space—without meaning or purpose, merely by the fact of his existence, he filled everything. The gods decided otherwise and did otherwise: now each world is bounded and self-sufficient in its unique property, but by interacting with each other, they begin to develop not randomly, but according to a goal, according to the task set by the gods. Ymir, a spawn of chaos and essentially chaos incarnate, when disassembled into parts and reassembled in a different sequence,

ᚠ ᚨ

transformed into Yggdrasil, the Tree of Nine Worlds. Chaos became order.

The Worlds of the Yggdrasil Tree

Thus, the human world of Midgard is situated between four fundamental informational and energetic structures:

Muspelheimr - the world of primordial fire.

Niflheimr - the world of Earth, the world of basic constants.

Jotunheimr - the world of memory and the accumulation of informational packets.

Vanaheimr - the world of nature, manifested reality, the world of life and death.

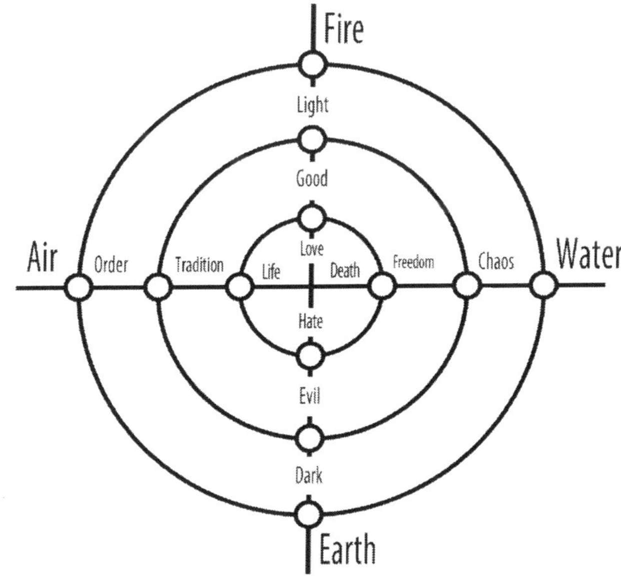

The other worlds on the Yggdrasil's Tree do not influence our world directly but rather indirectly through the worlds with the direct connection. These surrounding worlds include:

Asgard - the world of law (Order),

Helheimr - the world of Chaos,

Alfheimr - the world of the Light Elves (elves), the world of Good,

Svartalfheimr - the world of the Dark Elves (elves), the world of Evil. This world act as governors and correctors, but the system is designed so that their influence can only occur through a primary cause. There are nine worlds, eight of which are functional, and the ninth world—Midgard—is the applied world. Our world is the focal point of all processes that occur in other worlds under the governance of the laws of Asgard.

Now, let's discuss each world in more detail.

Muspelheimr, the World of Primordial Fire

Muspelheimr is an unimaginable world of energy that provides the impulse for any development and the initiation of any system. The rune **Dagaz**, which is the key to this world, describes the qualities of primordial fire — transformation, transition. It is a force capable of bringing about change and creation. This is the fire in the forge, the fire of the Titans, the fire of Prometheus, the primal substance of creation, the Grail of the rejected.

In Snorri Sturluson's Prose Edda (in the version known as the Uppsala Manuscript), it is said:

ᛊ ᛞ

Of the runes of the gods and the giants' race
The truth indeed can I tell,
(For to every world have I won;)
To nine worlds came I, to Niflhel beneath,
The home where dead men dwell.

(The Poetic Edda. Vafthruthnismol)

In the magical system of the three circles, the world of Niflheimr corresponds to the proto-foundation of Dark.

Asgard, the World of Law

This world did not form immediately but rather when the young gods, led by Odin, decided to embark on their own project.

Many theories have been proposed by researchers and scholars of myths attempting to pinpoint the geography of Asgard. Various opinions have been voiced. Some suggest that this world is related to the lost civilization of Mars or Venus or that it is located millions of parsecs away from our planet in an entirely different galaxy. There were opinions that the young gods of Asgard are Aeneas and his company, who survived the destruction of Troy. Some equated the world of Asgard with the legendary Avalon, the isle of the blessed. Some believe that Asgard is located on one of the many islands of Sweden. All of this is both true and not true. Asgard is an informational structure and exists both here and not here, in another space, in another time. But our reality is encompassed within it, like the

ᚹ ᚨ

yolk in an egg, like a seed in an apple, like the brain in a human body.

It is everywhere and nowhere. It is a world that permeates all worlds and can influence every one of them.

In the Poetic Edda, there are few direct mentions of Asgard. Only indirect references to it are made, as of an already established world. The Prose Edda expands much more on the topic of Asgard. However, it should not be forgotten that the Prose Edda (the Younger Edda) is more recent and emerged during the era of the Christianisation of the northern lands. For this reason, it has a noticeable biblical influence, making it very difficult to extract the true meaning from it.

Here is what is written in the Prose Edda regarding Asgard:

In the next place, the son s of Bor made for themselves in the middle of the world a burg, which is called Asgard, and which we call Troy. There dwelt the gods and their race, and thence were wrought many tidings and adventures, both on earth and in the sky. In Asgard is a place called Hlidskjalf, and when the earth w ith the foam from his bit . The horse on which Day rides is called Skinfaxe, and with his mane he lights up all the sky and the earth…

Then said Ganglere: What did Alfather do when Asgard had been built ? Said Har 'In the beginning he appointed rulers in a place in the middle of the burg which is called Idavold, who were to judge with him the disputes of men and decide the affairs of the burg. Their first work was to erect a court, where there were seats for all the twelve, and, besides, a high-seat for Alfather. That is the best and largest house ever built on earth, and is within and without like solid gold. This place is called Gladsheim. Then they built another hall as a home for the goddesses, which also is a very beautiful mansion, and is called Vingolf. Thereupon they built a forge; made hammer, tongs, anvil, and with these all other tools. Afterward they worked in iron, stone and wood, and especially in that metal which is called gold .

All their household wares w ere of gold. That age was called the golden age, until it was lost by the coming of those women from Jotunheim[4].

Asgard is the place where the gods reside. Each god who has influence over events in all Nine Worlds has their own hall in Asgard. Having a hall symbolizes the right to rule and participate in governance.

In modern terms, Asgard is the control centre of the system, representing power and law. Asgard in the system of 12 proto-foundations embodies the principle of Order. Here, foundational principles (not rules, but principles) are established upon which the entire system of created reality is built and operates. The key to the world of Asgard is the rune **Gebo**, the rune of the law of balance, connections, and proper partnership.

Odin rules not only in Asgard. He has a throne in a special realm called Valhalla, which means "Halls of the Slain" (Einherjar).

They shine with gold, and eternal happiness is destined for their inhabitants. Valhalla is surrounded by a river, separating the living from the dead, and the entrance to the halls is through special gates. In front of the gates is a grove called Glasir. All the leaves on its trees are made of red gold, shining and sparkling so brightly that it hurts the eyes to look. It is the most beautiful forest among gods and men.

Odin closely monitors the course of every battle. All who fall gloriously in battle are his adopted sons. They all go to Valhalla. If Odin needs help, 800 warriors will come out of each

[4] The women who came from Jotunheimr are the Norns, the goddesses of fate, who will be discussed in due course.

ᛊ ᛞ

door of Valhalla, and there are 540 doors. The great lord Odin commands a vast number of warriors.

Every day, as soon as the rooster Golden Comb crows, the Einherjar wake from their sleep, don their armour, and go out to the field. There, they fight and kill each other. This is their entertainment because, afterward, they all come back to life and return together, joyfully and peacefully, to the halls.

But how ever great may be the throng in Valhal, they will get plenty of flesh of the boar Sahrimner. He is boiled every day and is whole again in the evening. But as to the question you just asked, it seems to me there are but few men so wise that they are able to answer it correctly. The cook's name is Andhrimner, and the kettle is called Eldhrimner. A she-goat, by name Heidrun, stands up in Valhal and bites the leaves off the branches of that famous tree called Lerad. From her teats runs so much mead that she fills every day a vessel in the hall from which the horns are filled, and which is so large that all the einherjes get all the drink they want out of it. (The Prose Edda)

There Valgrind stands, the sacred gate,
And behind are the holy doors;
Old is the gate, but few there are
Who can tell how it tightly is locked.

Five hundred doors and forty there are,
I ween, in Valhall's walls;
Eight hundred fighters through one door fare
When to war with the wolf they go.

Five hundred rooms and forty there are
I ween, in Bilskirnir built;
Of all the homes whose roofs I beheld,

ᚠ ᚠ

My son's the greatest meseemed.
(The Poetic Edda. Grimnismol)

In Asgard, there are the halls of the gods, which are named Folkvang, Noatun, Sokkvabekk, Thrymheim, Idavellir, Breidablik, Landvidi, Glitnir, Brimir, Bilskirnir, Himinbjorg, Valaskjalf, which will be discussed further.

Jotunheim, the World of Memory

The world of ancient giants—wise and powerful, beautiful and terrifying, much like human memory. In the magical system of three circles and twelve proto-foundations, it corresponds to the proto-foundation of Tradition. Here, all information from the past is accumulated and preserved without division into good and evil, right and wrong. This is one of the oldest worlds at the dawn of time.

The inhabitants of this world are the Jotnar, giants, long-lived bearers of "long memory." Despite the apparent enmity between the Aesir and the Jotnar, the latter are kin to the Aesir—as all Ancients descended from the primordial ancestor Ymir and the frost giants. Therefore, the significance of this ancient world should not be underestimated, as their presence plays an important role in the narratives of the northern tradition.

The gods (and the all-wise Odin himself) constantly turn to the Jotnar for advice and help. But being an "outcast," they do not always receive a warm welcome in Jotunheimr. Therefore, to obtain the necessary information for building their laws and new reality, the gods often have to resort to cunning, flattery, and force. The Poetic Edda and Vafthruthnismol tell about this:

Othin spake:
Counsel me, Frigg, for I long to fare,
And Vafthruthnir fain would find;
In wisdom old with the giant wise
Myself would I seek to match.

Frigg spake:
Heerfather here at home would I keep,
Where the gods together dwell;
Amid all the giants an equal in might
To Vafthruthnir know I none.

Othin spake:
Much have I fared, much have I found,
Much have I got from the gods ;
And fain would I know how Vafthruthnir now
Lives in his lofty hall.

Frigg spake:
Safe mayst thou go, safe come again,
And safe be the way thou wendest!
Father of men, let thy mind be keen
When speech with the giant thou sleekest.

In essence, the world of Jotunheimr is a vast memory. Everything that has happened is accumulated and stored here, and the Jotnar themselves are genetic carriers of such a comprehensive memory. They are unaware of good and evil,

ᛊ ᛞ

not distinguishing past information as necessary or unnecessary.

The gods used the power of this world, and not only Odin but even the beautiful Freyja, when she needed to find information about the lineage of her favourite human, Ottar, sought help from none other than her Jotnar friend Hyndla[5].

It is from the world of Jotunheimr that the god Freyr chose his wife, and the beautiful giantess Skadi, though briefly, was the wife of the ancient sea god Njord.

So, the descriptions of the Jotnar as terrible troll-like creatures are not entirely accurate. Later narratives, including descriptions from astral travellers through the worlds, tell of the inhabitants of Jotunheimr as gods with completely diverse appearances: they can be incredibly beautiful or horrifically ugly. Extremes do not frighten them—for they know not of good and evil, and the nature of the Jotnar, reinforced by memory, insists that there is a place for everything in the worlds of Yggdrasil, including any past, any history.

The key to the world of Jotunheimr is one of the nine irreversible runes, **Nauthiz** (Naud). In the human world and mind, this rune acts as the rune of need. But as a key to the world of Jotunheimr, it gives us a broader understanding—memory, history, the need for information—any kind, without censorship or judgment.

The wisdom then of the giant wise
Forth did he fare to try;
He found the hall of the father of Im,
And in forthwith went Ygg.

---

[5] The ancient saga "The Poem of Hyndla" tells us about it.

ᚹ ᚨ

Othin spake:
Vafthruthnir, hail! to thy hall am I come,
For thyself I fain would see ;
And first would I ask if wise thou art,
Or, giant, all wisdom hast won.

Vafthruthnir spake:
Who is the man that speaks to me,
Here in my lofty hall ?
Forth from our dwelling thou never shalt fare.
Unless wiser than I thou art.
(The Poetic Edda. Vafthruthnismol)

Intellect and wisdom are the main qualities of the world of ancient Jotnar. But they do not share their knowledge with everyone. The sagas tell us about the trials that the bearers of memory put to all who ask questions. And it doesn't matter to the Ancients who stands before them—a powerful god or a weak human.

Vanaheimr, the World of Nature

The world of spirits and gods of nature, forces of life, and prosperity. It wasn't created by the gods but was somehow "woven," integrated into the overall system of Yggdrasil, as a reaction to the emergence of the Tree itself. The strength and power of the Vanir differs from the might of the Aesir—they are different. The legends tell of long wars between the Aesir and the Vanir for the right to rule and manage the entire system of the Tree. These same legends say that there was no clear winner in these wars and that the warring sides were forced to come to an agreement:

The beginning of this was, that the gods had a war with the people that are called vans. They agreed to hold a meeting for the purpose of making peace, and settled their dispute in this wise, that they both went to a jar and spit into it. (The Prose Edda)

The Aesir faced the task of conquering the world of fertility, and this was evidently a struggle for resources—any world-building requires energy.

Originally, Vanaheim was an independent and self-sufficient world of nature, harmonious within itself. Integrating it into the Yggdrasil Tree required a global rearrangement of all systems and rules of this world, and such changes are always associated with a global restructuring and war in one form or another. Nature always resists changes that it does not generate or that occur according to external, alien algorithms. This is what the myth refers to under the image of "war."

In the system of 12 prot-foundations, the world of Vanaheimr is represented as the proto-foundation of Freedom. The key to this world is the irreversible rune **Inguz**, the rune of fertility, the rune of real and visible results.

Alfheimr (Ljósálfheimr), the World of Good

The world of Light Elves (álfar). In the system of 12 proto-foundations, it corresponds to the proto-foundation of Good. This world was created simultaneously with its counterpart—Svartalfheimr—from the body of the giant Ymir.

The symbol and key of Alfheimr is the rune **Sowilo**, the rune of victory. The gods rely on the world of Light Elves when there is a need to influence other worlds and manage them from there. In sagas and legends, the Light Elves are mentioned as "servants of the gods," and after the war, the world was given to Freyr, indicating that the world of Light Elves is the domain of the Vanir, the world of nature.

Here is what the Prose Edda says about Alfheimr:

Then said Ganglere: Great tidings you are able to tell of the heavens. Are there other remarkable places than the one by Urd's fountain? Answered Har : There are many magnificent dwellings . One is there called Alfheim. There dwell the folk that are called light-elves; but the dark-elves dwell down in the earth, and they are unlike the light-elves in appearance, but much more so in deeds. The light-elves are fairer than the sun to look upon , but the dark-elves are blacker than pitch.

Svartalfheimr, the World of Evil

Unlike Alfheimr, much more is said about this world in the sagas and eddas. In Svartalfheimr, not only the dark elves live, who are rarely mentioned in the sagas, but also the dwarves-dvergar, masterful craftsmen who provided the gods with the

ᛊ ᛞ

most marvellous magical artifacts, enchanted items, and animals. The "Voluspo" lists all the clans of dvergar and tells about the origin of the dark bloodlines.

Then sought the gods their assembly-seats,
The holy ones, and council held.
To find who should raise the race of dwarfs
Out of Brimir's blood and the legs of Blain.

There was Motsognir the mightiest made
Of all the dwarfs and Durin next;
Many a likeness of men they made,
The dwarfs in the earth, as Durin said.

Nyi and Nithi, Northri and Suthri,
Austri and Vestri, Althjof, Dvalin,
Nar and Nain, Niping, Dain,
Bifur, Bofur, Bombur, Nori,
An and Onar, Ai, Mjothvitnir.

Vigg and Gandalf, Vindalf, Thrain,
Thekk and Thorin, Thror, Vit and Lit,
Nyr and Nyrath, — now have I told—
Regin and Rathsvith — the list aright.

Fili, Kili, Fundin, Nali,
Heptifili, Hannar, Sviur,
Frar, Hombori, Fraeg and Loni,
Aurvang, Jari, Eikinskjaldi.

The race of the dwarfs in Dvalin's throng
Down to Lofar the list must I tell ;

ᚠ ᚨ

The rocks they left, and through wet lands
They sought a home in the fields of sand.

There were Draupnir and Dolgthrasir,
Hor, Haugspori, Hlevang, Gloin,
Dori, Ori, Duf, Andvari,
Skirfir, Virfir, Skafith, Ai.

Alf and Yngvi, Eikinskjaldi,
Fjalar and Frosti, Fith and Ginnar;
So for all time shall the tale be known,
The list of all the forbears of Lofar.

The dark elves (svartálfar) are by nature closer to the jötnar than to the Vanir, unlike their light elf brothers. They are just as steadfast, just as mindful, and similarly not very fond of outsiders—neither gods nor heroes.

In Celtic mythology, light elves are known as the "Seelie Court," and dark elves as the "Unseelie Court." In magic, these two worlds correspond to the proto-foundations of Good and Evil, respectively. The key to the world of Svartalfheimr is the rune **Eihwaz**.

Dvergar not only possess rich underground resources but also masterfully utilize them. Being inherently reclusive and having a very rigid caste system, they equally hate both humans and their "relatives," the elves. Only to the gods and giants, recognizing their victory and supremacy, do they pay due respect.

Helheimr, the World of Hel

The key to this world is the rune **Hagalaz**, the rune of destruction and limitation. The key describes the main functions of this world: to destroy the unnecessary, return everything that has come out of chaos but is no longer needed back into it, and to restrain the currents of chaos until the proper time.

According to the rules of the Yggdrasil system, the law introduced by Odin, everything that is not considered good by this law goes to the world of Hel. For humans, this rule was projected as the tradition of a proper departure from life: those who died with a weapon in their hands and Odin's name on their lips are deemed worthy to go to Valhalla and become an einherjar—a warrior of Odin.

All the others: women, children, those who died from illness, accidents, or other reasons, must go to Hel. Logic suggests that with such a strict selection, the world of Hel will eventually become very overcrowded, and the gates of Helheimr will open, releasing currents of chaos into the world. Ragnarök is inevitable.

In the Yggdrasil system, the world of Helheimr is essentially the mirror opposite of Asgard, where Asgard represents Order and Helheimr represents Chaos. Asgard embodies principles of development, while Helheimr embodies principles of destruction. However, this is not a complete and accurate description, and the essence of Helheimr can only be understood through the power and intellect of its ruler, the goddess Hel, which will be explored in due course.

ᛊ ᛞ

Midgard

It would be a mistake to associate Midgard specifically with our planet; this is fundamentally incorrect. Such a misconception has led many seekers to make mistakes and draw wrong conclusions. Midgard is not here. Midgard is a present moment.

Midgard is the only world in the Yggdrasil system that does not have an obvious pair. It is bounded and finite, just as time in general and human time, in particular, are finite. The Midgard Serpent (Jörmungandr) encircles the human world and, like the Ouroboros serpent biting its own tail, acts as a timer, tightening the circle of time more and more. Everything has limits, and Midgard is the first world that depends on limits and deadlines, which people living in the here-and-now are well aware of.

The key to the world of Midgard is the rune **Jera**, the rune of time. However, understanding how this key works is only possible by considering it in conjunction with other worlds, as a point on the timeline Naud-Jera-Inguz, Jotunheimr-Midgard-Vanaheimr, which defines the present moment. Jotunheimr (rune Naud) represents the past, while Vanaheimr (rune Inguz) represents the future.

The creation of humans in the cosmology of the northern peoples is described as follows:

Then from the throng did
three come forth,
From the home of the gods, the mighty and gracious;
Two without fate on the land they found,

ᚹ ᚨ

Ask and Embla, empty of might.

Soul they had not, sense they had not,
Heat nor motion, nor goodly hue;
Soul gave Othin, sense gave Honir,
Heat gave Lothur and goodly hue.
(The Poetic Edda, Völuspá)

Created from natural elements and lacking long memories, humans live only in the present moment. The past is changeable, and the future is undetermined. However, by stretching their consciousness across worlds, each person can alter their destiny: reach out with your mind to the world of ancient memory, understand your need, and by the law of the pendulum, consciousness will reach the world of Vanaheimr, changing the future. Expand your consciousness to such an extent, and you will come to know good and evil. Experience multiple oscillations and repetitions, and life and death will be under your control. Know everything, and you will become akin to the gods, understanding the power of chaos and the foundations of order.

The structure of the tree itself is programmed with the possibility of human development within the system—balanced and evenly distributed. But for this opportunity, humans pay a high price—their time flows very quickly. This fact can also be observed in the Yggdrasil system if we imagine the tree not as a flat plane but as at least a three-dimensional image rotating around its axis at the point of the world of Midgard. The moment of rotation shows that the speed of rotation is maximum at the centre and minimum at the periphery.

Humans, being at the centre of the rotation, generate the momentum of time, distributing this vital resource to all the worlds. It's no coincidence that one of the roots nourishing the tree is situated in the human world: this nourishment is time.

All the worlds compete for this resource, trying to introduce their rules and laws into the Midgard system, which in turn affect the speed of time. However, humans, through the development of their minds, can influence the worlds that, according to their own algorithms, create these rules. After all, humans are endowed with nothing but their senses, reason, and the perception of life.

The runes that connect the world of Midgard along the temporal axis with the worlds of Jotunheimr (memory) and Vanaheimr (future) indicate the conditions under which a person can influence and impact the worlds of Yggdrasil.

The runes **Dagaz** and **Jera**, connecting Midgard and Jotunheimr, suggest the following: any memory of the past, any history, must undergo the test of time and transformation. This quality of consciousness is called analytical, meaning that a person must be capable of analysis. They should gather all past knowledge in their mind, in the point of "now," merge it together, highlight the main aspects, and send these main aspects into the future.

The power of the runes **Uruz** and **Perthro**, connecting the world of Midgard with the world of Vanaheimr, will allow the seeds to be sown into the ground, which will then weave the fabric of tomorrow's reality and change fate. The power of the final choice will shape your tomorrow, shape your future.

The process of connecting the world of Fire and the world of Ice, Muspelheimr and Niflheimr, once started, never stops. The abyss of Ginnungagap manifested itself in the system of the worlds, and now the two primordial forces have no other place to meet except in the world of Midgard. Dynamism and stagnation, change and constancy, stability and destruction — all of this now exists in the human world. Perhaps this is why human nature received a bit of madness from Muspel's sparks and a desire for stability from Nifl's ice. However, these two tendencies, colliding with each other, make humans so restless. Not all of them, of course, but for the most part.

The progenitor Ymir will sooner or later reassemble himself, gathering all the worlds and connecting them not through memory but through life. Then the boundary between worlds will disappear, and there will no longer be a need to separate one world from another by time and space. When this will happen is unknown even to the all-seeing völva. But that it will happen sooner or later is beyond doubt.

In the projection of the Yggdrasil Tree onto the system of 3 magical circles and 12 proto-foundations, the world of Midgard is seen in four proto-foundations: Life, Death, Love, and Hate—this is how mighty our world is.

* * *

All the worlds, connected into a system, form human life. By perceiving changes, a person initiates changes himself, which affects the other worlds. It is clear that such a process should not occur uncontrollably, "as the gods will." Therefore, the Yggdrasil system contains all the regulatory mechanisms capable of halting unnecessary and untimely actions and, conversely, initiating necessary ones.

Ratatosk[6], is the squirrel who there shall run

---

[6] Ratatoskr — "gnaw-tooth."

On the ash-tree Yggdrasil;
From above the words of the eagle he bears,
And tells them to Nidhogg[7] *beneath.*

And the Grimnismol echoes in the Prose Edda:

What is said about this place? Answered Jafnhar. This ash is the best and greatest of all trees; its branches spread over all the world and reach up above heaven. Three roots sustain the tree and stand wide apart.

The power of runic magic lies not so much in the ability to compose and read runic formulas and bindings, but in the precise and accurate manipulation of specific connections-channels between worlds through the runes, altering the world according to one's will and purpose. The power of the runes is immense. But even greater is the responsibility of the one who uses them in this capacity — because the processes affecting all worlds will be irreversible.

Runes none should grave ever
Who knows not to read them;
Of dark spell full many
The meaning may miss.

(Egil's Saga)

The god Odin brought the runes as magical tools, and each world received its runes from the All-Wise One. The power

[7] Nidhogg — the black dragon mentioned in stanzas 39 and 66 of the "Voluspo."

of the runes given to the inhabitants of the worlds of Yggdrasil varies for each world, depending on the degree of responsibility and the capabilities of that world. To humans, Odin gave a set of runes corresponding to the potential abilities of humans (the 24 runes of the Elder Futhark).

In the sagas and myths of the northern tradition, everything you have read above is recorded. But it is written in a completely different language—allegorical, encrypted with simplicity and the moment of "now." Our task is to decode the received information and uncover the hidden meaning of the gods' message. We need to free it from the shackles of primitiveness and find the universal key to understanding it.

The ancient people, conveying this message to us, recorded it in the Eddas and preserved it in sagas and tales. Having passed through the centuries and endured the crucible of Christian assimilation, it should have maintained the essence and invariability of what cannot be destroyed by fire, execution, fear, or oblivion. Details may be forgotten and distorted, specifics may be lost, and accents rewritten. But the essence, the key, the grain of truth must remain unchanged.

Cleansing the remnants and fragments of the once-powerful epic from the Christian overlay, restoring piece by piece the mosaic of meaning, we will attempt to find this hidden message—the commandments and guidance for us, the living, and for the young gods who have come to replace the Ancients. If our endeavour succeeds, we will restore and revive the program of the world of Yggdrasil, rebuilding the world according to the old designs but with the knowledge of all the mistakes made by our predecessors.

The world that the Ancient gods built is a world where the main human qualities and the primary strength of the gods were meant to be Valor and Honor. Precisely that, with a capital letter.

It is said that once, the One shattered himself into an enormous number of tiny parts and allowed these parts to develop independently. This is how the gods came to be. Each god then further divided themselves into billions of parts—thus, humans came into existence. Each god worked "in their own field," developing themselves in a specific way. The northern gods worked on creating a universal algorithm that would perfect the concepts of "valour" and "honour." Not only did humans become full participants in this process, but the gods themselves were actively involved. This is what the sagas tell us.

But the gods had not only helpers but also adversaries. Some, out of enmity, tried to hinder them. Others, out of friendship, attempted to do the same. What was the difference? The motive.

When everything is going smoothly, when there is no development, when in the joy of victory you do not notice the price paid for that victory, it is easy to stop searching, to be satisfied with what has been achieved, and ultimately to lose. A harmful friend will point out mistakes, push, and stimulate action. If you understand this, know that you have found an ally in your endeavours, someone who loves you sincerely—not with words, but with intention and action. But if you do not understand, the difference between friend and foe will blur, for you judge by actions (which is mistaken) and not by motive (which is correct).

The story passed down to us by the norse gods is a story of defeat. Yes, reader, do not be surprised. Boasting of non-existent victories is futile if you want your descendants to truly continue the work started, rather than just putting on a show for everyone. Descendants need to be told the truth.

ᛊ ᛞ

But not everyone is capable of accepting this truth. Those who live in the moment, "now," are unable to see the cause, effect, and consequence—they will only see the effect. The mind of such a person is small, but a small mind is not to blame for being the way it is. The narrative of the Ancients is constructed in such a way that the small mind, not seeing the key, does not touch it, only chiselling the edges of the story.

The ancient gods have passed down to us a story of delusions and mistakes that led to the downfall of the gods, leading to the battle of Ragnarök. The gods who survived the battle—the future creators of the worlds—will take the old eddas as technical documentation and, relying on them, will write new programs for the world, removing the causes of past mistakes, creating a new safe space for the life of all beings in all Nine Worlds.

The erilar, weaving the runes, fully participates in this process.

The story of each god in the Norse pantheon is a story of victory and defeat of a particular force, of a particular rule. Keys are woven into the narrative so that the seeker may find them and create a new worldview based on them, laying the foundation for a new reality.

But before embarking on changing the fabric of the overall world order, an erilar must understand themselves, study themselves, know themselves. Like the ancient Ymir, they must disassemble themselves into components and reassemble into a completely new personality, a completely new individual — a warrior-person, a warrior-mage. For this, the path through the Futhark, through the runes, was necessary: not just as a process of transformation but as a process of understanding.

The first step in studying the ancient tradition will be a deeper, mystical exploration of your nature, understanding the

ᚹ ᚨ

prerequisites of destiny, and realizing what changes need to be made to your personal fate to truly become an erilar and not be mistaken in this role. What lessons must be learned, what trials must be overcome, to gain the right to make changes not only to your destiny but also to the general program of humanity.

Every person is born with certain runes inscribed in them, and through these runes, some worlds will influence their life and fate more than others. This inherent preference determines a great deal, if not everything, in a person's life. This predestination is called the Individual Code of Fate. Some parts of this code can be changed by the person, while others cannot. We will begin the process of self-discovery by calculating this individual code, and having calculated it, we will try to understand: is it necessary to change something in it or not.

Practice 1. Individual Runic Code (page 355)
Practice 2. Individual Runic Amulet (page 418)
Practice 3. Amulets and Talismans (page 427)
Practice 4. Introduction. Magical Formulas (page 456)

THE NORSE PANTHEON

From this moment on, we will begin studying the pantheon of the Norse gods. It is important to note right away that a pantheon of gods is not the same as egregores. Egregores are created by human minds, based on the idea of a god (force). The pantheon itself, however, is a family of minds.

To understand what the gods tried to convey to us through sagas, myths, and legends, we must first turn off our critical thinking and remember that gods are not humans. Although they describe their adventures in a human-like manner. Each saga is an encrypted algorithm of actions that either leads the quest participant to success and victory or does not. In the latter case, the adept should not only feel disappointed for their "beloved hero" but also draw conclusions about why the action program of a particular deity was unsuccessful and what could have been done then (and now) to change it.

Each god or goddess, whose history and power we will study further, is not only a manifested mind but also an informational structure rich in methods for achieving results. The family of gods is not a random formation and should not be confused with the concept of "family" in the human world. If we are to draw an analogy, it is more accurate to think of the family of gods as a group of scientists and researchers working together on a specific task, developing specific algorithms for survival and management that are intended to exist always and to ensure the right. To ensure that the new gods and people, who by blood or spirit will be the descendants of these forces, that is, the continuators of tradition, the implementers of the idea.

The creation of such a person—a perfect human—exists in all mythologies. While it may not always be the central theme, it is clear enough for a researcher to see that the goal of the gods at a certain stage of their activity was to create such a human mind that could harmoniously incorporate all the algorithms developed by the pantheon gods. And through this, create such a human consciousness that would incorporate the algorithms of all pantheons, all gods, all systems. In other words, to become one who knows good and evil.

This task also touched the northern gods.

The Poetic Edda describes the process of human creation as follows:

Then from the throng did three come forth,
From the home of the gods, the mighty and gracious;
Two without fate on the land they found,
Ask and Embla[8]*, empty of might.*

Soul they had not, sense they had not,
Heat nor motion, nor goodly hue;
Soul gave Othin, sense gave Honir,
Heat gave Lothur and goodly hue.

Voluspo

The Prose Edda provides a more prosaic and detailed account of this story:

---

[8] Ask and Embla — the first humans on Earth, literally "ash" and "elm."

ᛊ ᛞ

"...As Bor's sons went along the sea–strand, they found two trees. These trees they took up and made men of them. The first gave them spirit and life; the second endowed them with reason and power of motion; and the third gave them form, speech, hearing and eyesight. They gave them clothes and names; the man they called Ask, and the woman Embla. From them all mankind is descended, and a dwelling–place was given them under Midgard. In the next place, the sons of Bor made for themselves in the middle of the world a burg, which is called Asgard, and which we call Troy. There dwelt the gods and their race, and thence were wrought many tidings and adventures, both on earth and in the sky."

This description shows us that the gods created "their" person not from just anything, but firstly from natural, living material; and secondly, they imbued them with particles of themselves. Importantly, they did this equally for both man and woman. They invested them with a soul, personality, and character traits. Clearly, they could only imbue them with what they themselves possessed: their breath, their temperament, their consciousness. Hence the ancient understanding that each person has the characteristics of the god(s) who oversee them (created them). They did not create the flesh (parents took care of that), but their soul, the foundations of their consciousness.

What personality traits are predetermined by the presence of northern gods in the mind of someone connected with them? First and foremost, these are the qualities of honour and valour, a warrior's character, and naturally, the right of the strong. It's enough to recall the classic depiction of a Viking, which has entered history and common memory, to understand what is meant. Especially if you know the rule of forming history: only phenomenal qualities and features remain in it, while the ordinary ones dissolve in the flow of time.

ᚹ ᚨ

This understanding of the phenomenon and its perception underlies the activity of the entire pantheon of northern gods—whether the character of the myth achieves victory honestly or not, nobly or basely; whether he is right from the standpoint of honour and what can happen if victory is awarded to someone not quite honourable (valiant).

It all seems simple, but only if what is described really pertains to humans. But no—the history of the northern myth concerns the gods, not humans. Whatever the god does becomes law for humans. If the god wins, humans will win if they act the same way. If the god loses, under the same circumstances, humans will lose too. No exceptions.

Each god in polytheism is a facet of the system. Conducting further practice within the Yggdrasil Tree system, passing the informational channels of the northern gods through yourself, you will be able to make your personal system of rights and values less dependent on those structures and systems that have no direct relation to you. Immersing your consciousness within the Tree of Nine Worlds will help you achieve this effect. Treat such immersion as a test space for honing results. Like a "cloud" where a new reality is created, which will be brought out and implemented into the overall system of multiple realities only when it is perfected. This will protect you from the mistakes that sagas unequivocally warn us about: when an unfinished and raw program, lacking survivability, without the necessary degrees of protection, childishly naive in its incredible power and boundless nobility, is brought into the world, this nobility is perceived by other, more "experienced" systems as foolishness. Inconsistencies in the system of meanings inevitably generate systemic conflicts, which for the stronger side will not necessarily end in victory.

The Nine Worlds system is highly suitable for learning to see and understand how numerous informational channels affect a point where realities converge (in this case, the world of Midgard) and how these channels change reality.

The entire pantheon of northern gods (as well as any other pantheon) is always a family with a complex system of blood ties and inheritance, with intricate, as is typical in a large family, internal familial and ethical relationships. But this is from a human perspective. It is enough to remember once again that gods are not humans but minds; their intricate relationships are nothing more than informational processes that generate specific effects when interacting. Remembering this, we immediately move from everyday gossip to science. More precisely—to magic.

However, what distinguishes a human from a mage is that a human, having simplified something for their own understanding and brought the god down to their semi-animal level, forgets to elevate it back and unpack what was understood not only in the human world but in the entire manifested reality. Mages do not forget. Thus, they see further and can do more.

Therefore, as we analyse the myths and legends about the northern gods, let us always remember that we are dealing with minds so ancient and powerful that all other modern religions are like infants before an ancient elder, like an acorn before an oak, like a fry before a school of fish, like a snowflake before an avalanche in the mountains. And like a human before the abyss.

It would be a grave mistake to treat gods as equals. Many beginners have stumbled over this crude mistake and have not achieved the desired result—power and knowledge. I would like to warn you against the wrong understanding—simplifying and belittling the gods. On the other hand, the minds of ancient pagan deities, the minds of the Ancients and the Primordials, do not perceive states of religious ecstasy and do not accept feelings of subservience and numinous states of mind. It is impossible to converse with them through prayer—memorized ready-made formulas whose meanings the speaker does not understand. They will not answer a kneeling and forehead-beating "slave" because the warrior northern tradition is not a slave system. The Ancients believed that if one must kneel before the highest, it should only be on one knee—rising from such a position is much easier.

The channels of the northern gods can be very strict but never humiliating to either themselves or the human in them. Northern morality understands the importance of a sense of self-worth. Therefore, remember that the two extremes—familiarity and obsequiousness—are equally bad and will not give the seeker what they seek. Dignity. Respect. The reverence of a student for a teacher. Caution in judgments and slowness in conclusions. The ability to admit your mistake if you realize you are wrong. The ability to go all the way if you know you are right. These are the qualities of personality that the gods love and will guide on the northern path.

The northern magical tradition (like any other pagan tradition) implies not the adoration of the deity but the striving to become a deity internally. It is not a personality to be blindly admired but an exemplar to be emulated.

The first god who will teach us "a different perspective" is the one-eyed god Odin, the supreme ruler of the northern lands, gods, and peoples.

ᛊ ᛞ

ODIN

I ween that I hung on the windy tree,
Hung there for nights full nine;
With the spear I was wounded.
And offered I was
To Othin myself to myself.
On the tree that none may ever know
What root beneath it runs.

(The Poetic Edda. Hovamol)

I know that I hung on the wind-swept tree for nine cold nights, astonished by the truth. (Wiligut)

Odin, the god of knowledge and the founder of Asgard, has the ability to connect everything with everything else, being both flexible and insightful, as well as firm and unwavering.

Odin is the foundation of the interconnected worlds. Without his deeds, neither our world, Midgard, nor humanity as we know it would exist. The first and primary god whose channel we will study and explore is, of course, Odin. He has many names (heiti[9]). Each heiti, each nickname reflects a facet of the god's character. It was believed that Odin had over a thousand names—he was indeed a multifaceted personality.

---

[9] Heiti in Old Icelandic poetry is a poetic synonym used to denote a name or object instead of a common word; a replacement of names, a renaming.

ᚹ ᚨ

However, in the interest of truth, it must be said that the original supreme god in the northern pantheon was the god of justice, Tyr (Tiu). But after certain events, which will be discussed below, Tyr was forced to step down and hand over the reins and leadership of the entire "Tyr's Justice" project to Odin.

What was so remarkable about Odin that he, and not Thor the Thunderer, Heimdall the White Aesir, or the beautiful Freyr, became the head of the entire northern divine family? This is what we need to figure out.

Odin's multifaceted nature shows that in all his manifestations, he left a visible mark on the fabric of reality. He could express himself in various forms without the slightest loss of integrity, and this versatility allowed him to absorb the victory and success algorithms of other deities, making him truly a god who knows good and evil.

It's no coincidence that Odin's name is strongly associated with the planet Mercury among occultists and mages exploring invisible connections, which in turn is linked in magic to the proto-foundations of Good and Evil in the system of magical circles of power. It should be noted here that in magic, these concepts are viewed somewhat differently than in the realm of human morality. More precisely, in magic, these two concepts have nothing to do with morality, as in the magical worldview:

Good means effective algorithms for achieving results, or simply—algorithms of victory.

Evil means ineffective algorithms, or—algorithms of defeat.

Odin possessed comprehensive knowledge of the "correct" ways to achieve victory, understood the prerequisites for defeat, and knew everything that could lead his team (family) to success and triumph among the pantheons of other deities.

ᛊ ᛞ

This is why Odin is called the god of knowledge, not just for the runes. Only those with access to these resources are worthy of developing civilization, building it "from scratch," advancing processes, and creating people—genetic and spiritual carriers of the program and the primary task of the project.

Therefore, it is Odin who stood at the head of the pantheon. He performed actions that helped him gain the missing knowledge and power that no other god of the northern family possessed.

Odin is the leader of the Aesir, a sage and shaman, the lord of runes. He is the patron of the military aristocracy, the master of Valhalla, a scholar and alchemist, a mage and sorcerer. He appeared to people under various names and in different guises, but in human memory, his blue cloak and wide-brimmed hat, which hides his wounded eye, remain most recognizable.

Odin's origin is the same as that of the other Aesir gods—he is from the frost giants. The concept of "Aesir" is not a designation of race or other blood origin. Aesir, Aesinya—is a status, a position, a rank in the hierarchy of worlds, but by no means a designation of nationality.

In the Prose Edda by Snorri, we read:

This man's name was Bure; he was fair of face, great and mighty, and he begat a son whose name was Bor. This Bor married a woman whose name was Bestla, the daughter of the giant Bolthorn; they had three sons,---the one hight Odin, the other Vile, and the third Ve. And it is my belief that this Odin and his brothers are the rulers of heaven and earth. We think that he must be so called. That is the name of the man whom we know to be the greatest and most famous, and well may men call him by that name.[10]

The mind of a magnitude like that of the god Odin should never be given a straightforward characterization as good or bad. He encompasses everything. Having a "personal relationship" with this god is to doom oneself to failure from the start: how can one have a "personal relationship" with the Universe? Especially if one's point of view is within it, not outside it.

However, to meet the declared requirements, Odin's own mind had to undergo the necessary transformation—essential and sufficient to fulfill his mission.

How did this happen?

At the very beginning of creation, the worlds were connected very loosely. There was no functioning system in this connection, and for this reason, the law of balance was severely violated. The worlds, which existed eternally, were not created by the Aesir—they existed long before the birth of Odin and his brothers. But the merit of the Aesir was that they managed to connect various worlds with a single logical essence, which was named Yggdrasil.

However, in fairness, it must be said that they were forced into system programming and some "legalization" of their work by circumstances, not by their own desires or well-thought-out projects with far-reaching plans. What was originally done—

---

10 Bölthorn — a frost giant. Bestla — Odin's mother, daughter of Bölthorn. Buri — the first man, who was licked out of the ice of Niflheimr by the cow Audhumla.

the worlds with different properties—was done by the gods for themselves, for play, for pleasure.

The legends describe it this way:

In their dwellings at peace they played at tables.
Of gold no lack did the gods then know,—
Till thither came up giant-maids three.
Huge of might, out of Jotunheim.

(*The Poetic Edda, Voluspo*)

Three giantesses from Jotunheim, the Norns—goddesses of fate and total control—pointed out to the gods the "inadmissibility of such actions," to use modern systematic language. Because anything created within the system of the Nine Worlds cannot exist independently but only in relation to everything else—this is the essence of any system. All processes occurring in one system will, to a greater or lesser extent, inevitably affect processes occurring in another, and therefore in all others—the System of Worlds is highly sensitive to changes.

Each world must and will be connected to any other world through specific ties. A properly constructed system of interdependence and internal regulation will allow for the adherence to the fundamental law of the universe, the fundamental magical law—the Law of Equilibrium. This means that such a system will live long, the worlds will be stable in relation to each other and to themselves, and, importantly, no external intervention for forced "alignment" will be needed.

However, the Norns only pointed out the error to the gods and provided the technical requirements, but did they give them the tools for this? No. The mechanisms of connection had to be developed by the gods themselves. They should not be stolen or "borrowed" from other systems, as the monotheistic projects did later. They had to be written in an original language with no analogues yet be readable by other worlds and understood by interconnected systems. The creator of such a programming language and the author of the "source code" was precisely the god Odin, and the connection tool was the runes he discovered.

The legend describes this discovery of the runes as a "sacrifice made by Odin" to himself—binding his consciousness to the Yggdrasil tree for nine long days and nights.

I ween that I hung on the windy tree,
Hung there for nights full nine;
With the spear I was wounded, and offered I was
To Othin, myself to myself,
On the tree that none may ever know
What root beneath it runs.

None made me happy with loaf or horn,
And there below I looked;
I took up the runes, shrieking I took them,
And forthwith back I fell.

Nine mighty songs I got from the son
Of Bolthorn, Bestla's father;
And a drink I got of the goodly mead
Poured out from Othrorir.

Then began I to thrive, and wisdom to get,
I grew and well I was;
Each word led me on to another word.
Each deed to another deed.

ᛊ ᛞ

Runes shalt thou find, and fateful signs.
That the king of singers colored.
And the mighty gods have made;
Full strong the signs, full mighty the signs
That the ruler of gods doth write.

(The Poetic Edda. Hovamol)

Odin was cut off from his usual sources of sustenance; he was self-sufficient during the initiation process. He became the Tree, and the Tree became him. The runes that the god Odin received were an absolute reflection of his self-sufficiency. Note the important point: Odin did not invent the runes—he received them from his ancestor, the jötunn Bölthorn, Bestla's father, as a familial gift, a right to bind worlds in the manner required by the gods.

Runes are codes and ciphers to databases of algorithms for forming realities. Each god and each being created by the gods has its own level of access and degree of ability to influence reality. This is further indicated in the "Hovamol": each world received different runes from Odin.

Othin for the gods, Dain for the elves.
And Dvalin for the dwarfs,
Alsvith for giants and all mankind,
And some myself I wrote.

The god Odin received much knowledge from his ancestor. However, this knowledge was not uniform for everyone; different types of runes were given by Allfather to different worlds, thereby determining that each world and each race would have a different degree of interaction with the system of the Nine Worlds. The Æsir had their own runes, the elves had theirs, and humans also had their own. It is important to recognize that the Yggdrasil Tree system is a complex, multi-level program that must be protected not only from external influences but also from internal ones, pre-emptively blocking the possibility of influence through known runes on all worlds. Odin, in his wisdom, gave each world its own keys, and these keys fit only specific locks. Odin's nine-night initiation on Yggdrasil was a way of obtaining these keys and algorithms for managing the Tree's informational structure. These keys became the runes.

To lead the system, one must understand it. Therefore, Odin had to internalize this system, to embed it within himself, feeling it with every nerve. The system of the Nine Worlds, in turn, had to perceive Odin's nerve as its own, not rejecting it but responding correctly.

The sacrifice mentioned in the "Hovamol" is the sacrifice of oneself, of one's old nature, of one's freedom from the upcoming mission, of one's right to choose otherwise. To embed the codes for managing the worlds within oneself is to make room for them, to overwrite the program of one's own consciousness. Odin became an integral part of the Tree, and the Tree became an integral part of him.

All the most valuable knowledge is stored in the world of Darkness. In the northern tradition, this world is called Niflheimr, and the keepers, the carriers of ancient knowledge, are the frost giants. It's important to emphasize that they are the carriers of ancient knowledge. The world of Jotunheimr and its inhabitants, the jotnar, are carriers of ancient memory, which is not the same. Knowledge is that which has been tested by time, filtered through centuries, even millennia of experience. These are ready packets of information, constants of past times and other worlds; these are ready codes and keys whose application does not require changes or modifications. In contrast, ancient memory is streaming information without rules for its application—it encompasses everything that is and everything that has been. The worlds were created from the constants of Niflheimr and the initiating impulses of Muspelheimr, and the entire Yggdrasil Tree is built on the constants of Niflheimr. This ancestral gift was received by Odin from his forefather, the giant Bölthorn[11] —nine songs for the nine worlds, nine true codes.

The runes of Midgard, which we know as the Elder Futhark, were given to humans for action in their own world. Runes help a person connect with other worlds, obtaining information from them to form changes, but they do not give a person the right to alter other worlds by their will or desire. Midgard is the central world, the mirror of the entire system. A mirror cannot wilfully affect the object it reflects, but it can show it the result, allowing it to see what is wrong with it.

But all this happened much later. Initially, as the legends tell, the supreme god of the northern pantheon was Tyr. The supreme god is like the project manager, setting the overall direction of development, forming the supreme idea: what is it all for? However, the story of how and why the supreme functions shifted from Tyr to Odin will be detailed in the chapter dedicated to the god Tyr: after certain events, he handed over the project management and the pantheon's supremacy to the

[11] Bestla is the mother of Odin himself, and Bölthorn, consequently, is his grandfather. He is a frost giant from the world of Niflheimr. A bearer of the ancient knowledge of the world of Darkness, which he passed on to his grandson. This is a very important point that should never be overlooked.

one whose strength and capabilities gave a chance to bring the project to a logical conclusion, possibly with a victorious result.

Using modern terminology, it can be said that the god Odin is the engine of the entire Yggdrasil Tree system. This system, created by Odin, is aimed at identifying the best qualities, much like any other systems that other pantheons of gods have worked with. Each system sets its own mechanism for evaluating what is best, but in the norse pantheon led by Odin, this mechanism is martial valour.

Everything described in the Eddas and sagas is an account of the development of such a system, presented honestly and without deception. Every god and every hero describes their algorithms for both victory and defeat as truthfully as the human mind can preserve and later reproduce this honesty.

What is embedded in the core of the system begins to develop the system in a strictly defined direction. When Odin, through self-initiation on Yggdrasil, closed the Nine Worlds system on himself, he gave an impulse for the system to function in a strictly defined manner. This key later became known as the "Fury of Odin."

In the system, each world, as an information block, performs its function. Some worlds within the system can fully express themselves, while others can function only to a limited extent, periodically, or not at all. The rules for interaction and functioning of the worlds within the system are set by the system's goal, describing its main task—why the system was formed.

From the moment Odin became the supreme god of the norse pantheon, the goal was clear—to win. In this program, the world of humans, Midgard, was given a very specific and limited mission, not the main one. The world of humans was meant to cultivate warrior-victors who, at the decisive battle of Ragnarök, the ultimate test of the system's strength, would stand shoulder to shoulder with the gods.

The Einherjar are the fallen warriors from the human world, for whom the gates of Valgrind—"the gates of the dead" or "the gates of those who fell in battle"—open, leading to the halls of Asgard.

There Valgrind stands, the sacred gate,
And behind are the holy doors;
Old is the gate, but few there are
Who can tell how it tightly is locked.

Five hundred doors and forty there are,
I ween, in Valhall's walls;
Eight hundred fighters through one door fare
When to war with the wolf they go.
(The Poetic Edda. Grimnismol)

There, the fallen warriors awaited the moment of the final battle, practicing in duels and feasting on the never-ending meat of the boar:

In Eldhrimnir Andhrimnir[12] *cooks*
Saehrimnir's seething flesh,—
The best of food, but few men know
On what fare the warriors feast.
(The Poetic Edda. Grimnismol)

---

[12] Andhrimnir is the name of the cook in Valhalla. Just like Saehrimnir (the name of the boar that comes back to life every time it is eaten by the inhabitants of Valhalla) and Eldhrímnir (the name of the cauldron in which this boar is cooked), it comes from the word "hrím" meaning "soot." (Translator's note)

ᛊ ᛞ

The god Odin was with them but never ate among the dead warriors; he only drank wine. The dead food of the dead was consumed by Odin's companions, the wolves Freki and Geri, "the greedy" and "the ravenous." Not only at the feast with the einherjar did the wolves eat "the portion of the dead," but they were also capable of destroying everything diseased and decrepit in the world system, ridding it of anything that could render it weak and sluggish from excess matter, as directed by Odin. The wolves also protected Valhalla from the intrusion of unwelcome guests.

Freki and Geri does Heerfather feed,
The far-famed fighter of old:
But on wine alone does the weapon-decked god,
Othin, forever live.
(The Poetic Edda. Grimnismol)

Valhalla is a very important hall. In the interpretation of the system as a program, the halls are considered separate databases that require preservation and enhanced protection. The gods we will meet later also have their own halls, provided that a god is functionally responsible for forming such a database. For Odin, Valhalla is the database of flawless warriors, comrades in battle. The wolves protect the gathered information, ensuring it is not used inappropriately or prematurely. Valhalla is part of the greater halls of Gladsheim ("abode of joy"). Another hall of Odin is Valaskjálf, with the throne Hliðskjálf ("watchtower"), from which the Allfather oversees all the worlds.

Exiting Valhalla is difficult, but entering is even harder. The gates of Valgrind are like an automatic control system, and

ᚹ ᚠ

the unworthy cannot enter: neither warriors nor women; those who died of illness or by accident — a very strict selection system. The right to enter the gates of the fallen cannot be bought or obtained through deceit. Those who died in their beds with a wooden sword in hand will not gain entry. The gates will not open for those who were wounded in the back on the battlefield or who died praying to the gods for salvation. This is strictly monitored by Odin's other aides — the winged Valkyries. They gather the fallen on the battlefield, bringing the best of the best to Valhalla, as recorded in Odin's special selection algorithm.

The spear Gungnir is an artifact acquired by Loki for his blood brother Odin. The spear is not only a symbol of supreme power but also a powerful tool of control. According to legends, it could strike without fail and hit any target it was aimed at. From a programmatic perspective on this myth, it can be said that this mechanism helps not only to accurately identify system vulnerabilities but also to block them, eliminating imperfections. Many artifacts were brought by Loki to the world of Asgard, but that will be told in due course.

Odin's companions, his helpers and allies, are the ravens Huginn and Muninn, "thought" and "memory." They collected all the information for Odin from worlds only these prophetic birds could penetrate. They helped Odin become all-knowing — one of his many names.

O'er Mithgarth Hugin and Munin[13] *both*
Each day set forth to fly;

[13] Huginn and Muninn are derived from "huga" ("to think") and "muna" ("to remember").

ᛊ ᛞ

For Hugin I fear lest he come not home,
But for Munin my care is more.
(The Poetic Edda. Grimnismol)

Wolves and ravens are considered chthonic animals[14] in many cultures. They are associated with the earth and matter, with the world of the dead, where the decayed flesh goes. Ravens and wolves are scavengers, which unambiguously points to their function under the supreme god Odin — to identify what is obsolete, unnecessary, and destroy it.

In the human world, Odin was recognized by his appearance — a wide-brimmed hat and a blue cloak. This calling card not only represents the visible appearance of the wandering god, the god-mage, but it also indicates status. In the era when the sagas were formed, the colour of clothing held significance. Blue belonged to mages, seers, those who could look beyond the veil.

The warrior god, after many centuries, became the god of those seeking themselves in magic. This did not happen then, but it has happened now. The entire history of Odin, the history of his victories and defeats, suddenly, unexpectedly, in our era, intertwined in such a new and intricate way that a new, previously unseen aspect of Odin emerged — the god-patron of knowledge, the patron of magic. The old tradition viewed Odin from one side, from the perspective of the formidable god-patron of warriors, the bearer of the "fury of Odin." The descendants saw more. They saw his other side — Loki. They

14 Chthonic (from the Greek χθών — "earth, soil") animals in many religions and mythologies are those who originally embodied the wild natural power of the earth, the underworld, etc.

ᚠ ᚨ

reassessed Odin's sacrifice — an eye in exchange for knowledge. They viewed his learning of seidr from the goddess Freyja differently (considering that in the old era, practicing seidr was considered quite shameful for a man). His ability to converse with the dead and his steadfastness to his path — all this is the path of a mage, the path of a seeker — this is how Odin was seen by his descendants.

Odin gained another strength in our era: the fury of Odin becomes the wisdom of Odin. His path is the path of the mage. His knowledge is honest, but only the worthy can still take it. But who is now considered worthy to enter the halls of the one-eyed god? What is now the criterion for selection? Let us now walk Odin's path, walk it completely. Let us try to understand and accept, to learn everything and experience everything, like the wandering god, to enter our own personal Ragnarök and undergo the very transformation of the world for which everything was started.

One cup for wisdom, your boon, to remain
When your vision at last fades to normal again.
One last cup I raise with you, to the Norns' skein
That binds us both to this gift won with pain.

Come to the Well, to the Well at the Tree
Come, look deep into its water, said He
And I'll drink with you if you'll drink it with me
And the more you drink of it, the more you will see.[15]?

15 "Come to the Well." Author: Michaela Macha.

* * *

If it is true that the god Odin is the Yggdrasil Tree itself, the entire system, and that each god of the northern pantheon is a part of this system, then it is also true that each god is a part of Odin. This does not mean that he has absorbed all the gods, but rather that they have become an inseparable part of him, connected to the foundation of the system by invisible neural links. If one can feel the full power of the universal presence of the Allfather, it will not be difficult to feel each divine consciousness connected to him.

The honesty with which a seeker enters into the knowledge of the northern pantheon will help not only to correctly see the descriptions of the gods' victories and defeats left for us by legends and sagas. It will also help to understand the true reasons for such successes and failures, to see things as they are, rather than as we would like them to be. This is precisely the essence of Odin's teaching: to solve this equation; the equation "in reverse," where the answer is known, but most of the elements that compose it are unknown. We must seek and find these elements: knowing the effect, we must determine the cause. To understand where there was victory and where there was defeat, where there was a false victory, and where there was a game of give and take. Who or what is truly responsible for the problems of the northern project; where the key to the mistakes made is really hidden.

This approach will be useful not only for the sake of understanding the northern myth but also for much more. Anyone who delves into the northern tradition takes on an honest internal obligation to neutralize and correct the system's identified errors, at least within themselves. This does not mean erasing, denying, or rewriting history to convince everyone that there were no mistakes — that it was all the work of enemies. It's not about that. All corrections must be made within oneself, reprogramming one's mind, identifying vulnerabilities in consciousness that justify powerlessness and betrayal, allowing oneself to be weak and dependent, bowing before foreign gods, forbidding oneself to challenge them, and forbidding oneself to fight for what is theirs.

Awareness and understanding resolve many issues, but action resolves even more. The northern tradition is a system for those who are capable of action, who can challenge fate, who can fight to the end. Awareness alone is not enough. One must act in accordance with this awareness, performing real deeds that can neutralize the causes of past mistakes, that can correct these mistakes.

Usually, when someone enters a magical or religious system, they expect help for themselves. They rarely consider not what the system can do for them, but what they can do for the system. In the northern tradition, this won't work: it will only help those who are ready to work for its success through their actions; those who are ready to reprogram reality, acting as a stalker, a progressor in this form of existence; correcting bugs in their own system and thereby correcting them externally as well. Strength is given precisely for this, not for the pleasure of the powerless. Understanding one's imperfections means correcting them, not standing on the advantageous position of "man is weak, man is frail"; one must perform real actions until the imperfect becomes perfect.

This is what the god Odin teaches us, and this is what all the gods of the Nine Worlds system will teach.

Practice 5. God Odin (p. 460)

Thor

The power of the gods, which we are exploring and will continue to explore, is inseparable from the main channel that the god Odin has opened before us—everything is included in him. However, this inclusion is always just a specific facet, a unique function that represents a special quality of the overall power, the main power. The specific power of the god Thor is also one of the facets of Odin, but at the same time, Thor himself is a completely independent, absolutely integral, and mighty force, whose might rivals that of any other god, even the supreme god Odin himself. This must be understood from the outset without reverting to familiar perceptions such as "older—younger," "superior—subordinate," "god—human," or "father—son."

The aforementioned point relates to the frequent description of Thor as Odin's son. If this familial terminology is taken literally, it can cause considerable confusion. This description of Thor's "belonging" emerged only when it became necessary to translate a multidimensional perception of reality onto the flat sheet of monotheistic description, with an unambiguous emphasis on hierarchy: who is related to whom. Ancient people did not need such flat thinking; they saw Thor as part of Odin and as a member of his family, using the term "son of Odin" without implying biological or legal parenthood. Odin is the head of the family; all other gods are family members. Here, the term "son" indicates clan membership, not direct genealogy.

Considering the pantheon of the northern gods as a global program for building reality allows for a more precise and clear understanding of each god's function within the "family"—as part of a large program, as a specific functionality. This understanding is impossible if one views mythology through the lens of human perception, seeing the gods as people and the myths as a family saga.

Thor is the strength and power of the northern pantheon. His origin is similar to that of Odin—he comes from the giants; he is a primordial force born of the Earth. His mother is Fjörgyn, or Jörð, Mother Earth. But even the goddess Frigg, Odin's wife, is called "the daughter of Fjörgyn," which shows their kinship with Thor and their common origin.

The god Thor is associated with the rune **Thurisaz**. The ancients would say of this rune: "The gods can rely on it." The same can be said of Thor: the gods can rely on him. Thor is absolutely loyal to Odin and the gods of his family. Even if he does not fully understand the depth of Odin's tasks, he always supports Odin—not necessarily his tasks, but Odin himself. In seeking to understand Thor, it is crucial to highlight that Thor is linked to Odin; he protects Odin and his interests. He does this consistently, even when Odin's interests change to the complete opposite—the gods can rely on him. If Loki falls within Odin's sphere of interest, Thor will protect Loki; if a human falls within Odin's sphere of interest, Thor will protect that human.

It is said that Thor is the best protector of humans. Understand this correctly: Thor is not a protector for the sake of humans, but for the sake of Odin and as long as humans are needed and interesting to Odin. Proper understanding not only helps eliminate unnecessary illusions but also allows a deeper and more truthful understanding of Thor's power, his might, and his functionality.

What qualities must a person possess to fall within Thor's sphere of interest? First and foremost, one must align with the idea of Odin, be his follower, and promote the northern system of world order. As long as a person aligns with this idea and remains a part of it, Thor will protect and defend him just as he defends anyone within Odin's family—not for the person's sake, but for Odin's. If a person is ideologically synchronized with Odin, then he is also synchronized with Thor.

Who cannot rely on Thor? Legends and myths tell us against whom Thor fought and who his systemic enemies were. Thor battled the serpent Jörmungandr, the world serpent. Jörmungandr was spawned by Loki and the giantess Angrboda, just as the goddess Hel and the wolf Fenrir were. The Æsir designated the ocean as the place for the world serpent, and it encircles the world of Midgard. This metaphor needs to be analysed separately.

Jörmungandr, the serpent, was not (he or she[16]) a personal enemy of Thor; this must be understood from the outset. Loki "spawned" three forces, three injections, meant to make the northern system stronger. The serpent is a function, a function of limitation, which in other myths might be known to you as the "Ouroboros," the serpent biting its own tail. Jörmungandr's purpose in the northern tradition is the same—limitation. One might say—a timer, limiting the time for action, the time for decision-making. From Odin's perspective—an obstacle, a temporary spur, a limiter of freedom; for Thor, for this reason—a definite enemy. The serpent is a function that hinders the system's freedom if we understand freedom as the right to unrestrained and uncoordinated actions.

---

[16] The gender of Jörmungandr is still a subject of debate.

The paradox of a superficial perception of the myth is that it prevents one from seeing the logic of the description: how can it be that Thor's mortal enemy, Jörmungandr the serpent, is Loki's child, while Loki himself is Thor's friend and inseparable companion? Thor tries to kill the serpent, yet this doesn't affect his friendship with its father? From a human perspective, this is impossible to understand, but everything falls into place if one stops perceiving gods as people and sees them as universal programs for building reality. Thor's function is to remove development obstacles in the system, while Loki's function is to introduce such obstacles to identify program vulnerabilities. The two inseparable travellers, Thor and Loki, perform different functions for a common goal—can they be enemies? Absolutely not. But this is utterly incomprehensible if one perceives gods as humans, because humans do not think this way.

The fact that Loki's children are planned injections for the northern system is a natural reaction of the Nine Worlds to the existence of Asgard. But this does not negate Thor's need to fight such injections and such reactions, because combating "undesirable phenomena" is Thor's function. This is paradoxical from the standpoint of human morality and logic, but completely normal from the standpoint of the functioning of reality-building programs. All mythological and legendary accounts of Thor's adventures are nothing more than descriptions of his function, his capabilities and limitations, his victories, and mistakes. Let us also look at the described functionality in this way.

The serpent is the force of chaos, a force opposite to the foundations of order symbolized by Asgard. Thor will fight any manifestation of chaos, so here in Midgard, those who are conduits of the chaotic power of the universe should not rely on Thor. These conduits are those called witches and sorcerers, also known as Loki's offspring. Thor helps those like himself,

defenders of Odin's plan, such is his nature, such is his function. The gods can rely on him.

Thor is a force acting in the present moment. He does not consider the past, nor does he look into the future. This function does not work with the concept of "yesterday," and there is no concept of "tomorrow" for it. What matters is what happens now. Thor is the battle against a threat to Odin's system in the present moment, not later. He does not assess the threat as useful or useless, does not calculate multi-step algorithms, his task is clear: the enemy must be destroyed. The gods can rely on him.

Bilskirnir[17] —Thor's hall, having, like Valhalla, five hundred and forty rooms. According to Snorri, Bilskirnir is located in a place called Thrudvangar (Fields of Strength), or Thrudheim (Home of Strength).

Mjölnir, Thor's hammer, is his formidable weapon, which Loki brought from the world of Svartalfheim. Made by the remarkable master dwarves, it became an inseparable part of Thor and possessed amazing properties. Here is what is said about it in the Prose Edda by Snorri:

"... Then he gave to Thor the hammer, and said that he might strike with it as hard as he pleased; no matter what was before him, the hammer would take no scathe, and wherever he might throw it he would never lose it; it would never fly so far that it did not return to his hand; and if he desired, it would become so small that he might conceal it in his bosom; but it had one fault, which was, that the handle was rather short."

---

17 Bilskirnir — Old Norse for "lightning striker with rays of light." Other possible translations are "illuminated only for a moment" and "indestructible." (Translator's note)

ᛊ ᛞ

Not everyone can wield Mjölnir—it is incredibly heavy. This fact signifies that such power and strength cannot be granted to just anyone. Even the god Thor had to acquire additional artifacts to fully utilize the hammer. His treasures include the belt of strength and iron gloves. He received these as gifts from the giantess Grid, the mother of the silent Æsir, Vidar. The belt doubled Thor's strength, and the gloves helped him grip the red-hot hammer. Grid is one of the goddesses personifying the strength and memory of the Earth. Thus, Thor is not only an original titan, a son of the Earth, but also blessed by it to fulfill his mission.

Mjölnir possesses another amazing property: it can revive dead flesh. This is described in the legends as follows: Thor has two goats, Tanngniost ("gnasher") and Tanngrisnir ("grinder"). Thor harnesses them to his chariot but can also dine on their meat. However, after collecting their bones in their skins, he consecrates them with his hammer, and the goats become alive and well again, provided that the bones are not damaged[18]. The names of these goats can be rephrased as "rage" and "anger." Rage and anger are driving forces for the god and his sustenance. He can always awaken this force within himself; he can always satiate his hunger with it. This too is a warrior-defender's trait: if he needs to evoke a strong emotion for battle, he will. Because the gods can rely on him.

All descriptions in the myth are symbols. They are instructions for the action of a reality-building program—instructions deciphering the algorithms of the gods. The absurd image of goats that Thor rides could have easily been replaced by a noble horse or self-guided chariots by later generations. But

---

[18] This story is described in the Prose Edda, in the tale of "Thor's Adventures."

ᚠ ᚨ

no. The image of the goats remains: dumb, lustful animals with fitting names—Gnasher and Grinder, Rage and Anger, as we might call these two states now. Renewable strength, natural lust—not an end but a means; it can become either a leading force or sustenance for the mind—it all depends on who controls it. Mjölnir, capable of restoring this force to life, severs it from the past, breaks the connection between yesterday's memory and today's day. A renewable resource, like the boar Sæhrímnir devoured by fallen warriors in Valhalla, is sustenance for today's rage, strength for the warrior, despite being "consumed" yesterday.

The hammer Mjölnir is mentioned in many sagas and legends, always depicted as a valuable and crucial tool for the god Thor's influence on reality. For example, in the multifaceted story "The Lay of Thrym," it is said that the giant Thrym stole the hammer from Thor while he dozed off after his righteous labours. In return for the hammer, the giant demanded the goddess Freyja as his bride. To retrieve the hammer, the inseparable pair Thor and Loki had to dress in women's clothing, with Thor impersonating the goddess of beauty herself and Loki acting as her maidservant.

It is important to understand the significance of a man dressing in women's clothing *in the human world* and the era of these events—it was not just a disgrace, but a profound dishonour. Wearing trousers with a hole in the backside might be tolerable, but covering the hole with a skirt was absolutely unacceptable.

Then Thor the mighty his answer made :
"Me would the gods unmanly call
If I let bind the bridal veil."
Then Loki spake, the son of Laufey:

"Be silent, Thor, and speak not thus;
Else will the giants in Asgarth dwell
If thy hammer is brought not home to thee."
(The Poetic Edda. Thrymskvitha)

And yet, the god Thor risked "public ridicule" to return the valuable artifact to Asgard. However, as the myth reveals, the giant Thrym wasn't really after the hammer, but this will be discussed further when we talk about the beautiful goddess Freyja and her power.

Thor teaches many lessons, but the main one is that victory is not permanent. Today's victory might need to be proven again tomorrow; it is not guaranteed over time. Thus, one must constantly rekindle anger and rage, "revive the goats," to enter the necessary battle state. A warrior must always be ready for this and should not assume that success and victory are everlasting. This principle extends to many aspects of life. For example, the glory of fathers does not necessarily extend to their children, who must prove themselves independently. Mistakes, like victories, are never eternal: everything can be corrected, and everything can be lost. Each new day is a new battle, not a continuation of the old one. This principle is vividly portrayed in the description of the einherjar's stay in Valhalla: every day resets and starts anew. In Valhalla, those who pass Odin's "natural selection" receive further training according to Thor's algorithm: only what exists now is real.

Such a life philosophy might seem simple and primitive, ascribed to Thor by superficial assessments, but this view of reality is exactly what a warrior needs to fulfill their mission—never relax, never rely on anyone, not even the gods; rely only on yourself. And then the gods can rely on you.

ᛊ ᛞ

Thor's motto is "Do what you must." If you feel you are right—act now, and Thor will help. Do not seek justification in the past or future; act now. A warrior is only a warrior if they have a weapon in their hands. If you do not have a weapon in your hands, it does not matter what kind of warrior you were yesterday.

Practice 6. God Thor (p. 476)

ᚹ ᚨ

ᛊ ᛞ

Týr (Tiw, Ziu)

When the Nine Worlds system began to operate within the framework prescribed by the Yggdrasil Tree scheme, the next step was to introduce planned injections into the project to test and check its resilience against external and internal cataclysms. Such injections are introduced into any project—this is how the programming process of any system and space works. They are necessary for developing additional algorithms, which ideally should turn inherent vulnerabilities into strengths or, at the very least, correct initial errors that are inevitable during the primary programming "from scratch."

In the project of the northern pantheon, the main injector was the god Loki, but we will discuss him later. However, it was his "creations" that posed the most complex challenges for the system; these were the challenges the gods had to overcome. This refers to Loki's children—the goddess Hel, the serpent Jörmungandr, and the wolf Fenrir. The responsibility of dealing with the Wolf fell to the god Týr.

To understand the kind of trials Týr faced, we need to closely examine the image of Fenrir and understand the function he was meant to fulfill. The answer to this question lies in his origin, specifically understanding the nature of the worlds that back him. Fenrir was born from the union of the god Loki and the giantess Angrboda from Jotunheim.

The giantess old in Ironwood sat,
In the east, and bore the brood of Fenrir;

ᚠ ᚨ

Among these one in monster's guise
Was soon to steal the sun from the sky.

(The Poetic Edda. Voluspo)

The nature of Loki stems from the fire and frost giants, while Angrboda's nature comes from the world of Jotunheim. Loki is the bearer of the primordial fire capable of melting the ice of Niflheimr, and his great spouse is the bearer of ancient memory—continuous, unending knowledge. These qualities, as primary genetic material, manifested in various forms in the children of this union—they all have access to ancient memory as well as the worlds of primordial forces, making them bearers of chaos magic. This is their nature, and they can only interact with the newly created system of order according to their own nature, not according to expectations, representations, or commands from above.

The gods assigned specific roles to each child from this union: the mistress of the dead, Hel, became the ruler of the realms of Helheim and Niflheimr, while the serpent Jörmungandr surrounded Midgard, swimming in the world ocean (thus also known as the "Midgard Serpent"). The wolf Fenrir was taken by the gods themselves. From this, it is clear that the injection-Fenrir was intended not just for the world of Asgard, but for its very core, the heart of the entire system, the fundamental principle. Fenrir was born for Týr.

The wolf was terrifying and instilled irrational fear in the hearts of the gods. He grew rapidly, and the only one who dared to approach him was Týr; the others did not risk it. The gods feared Fenrir because they did not understand him. Did Týr fear him? Perhaps. But unlike his fellow gods, Týr had a weapon—not against the wolf, but against his own fear. His weapon was valour and honesty, the core principles of the Asgardian system during Týr's rule. Likely, he too did not understand the nature of the wolf and could not comprehend it—such recognition algorithms had not yet been developed in the project. But Týr could overcome his fear, look into the eyes of the gods' killer, and approach this embodiment of both overwhelming love and hatred.

That wolf pup was entirely rational. He was not some wild monster with whom it was impossible to negotiate. But his strength was titanic, primordial. A kind heart in a terrifying body, wild love incapable of being tamed. Fenrir loved the gods, loved Týr—with wild, primordial love. By allowing Týr to feed him, he chose Týr as his leader, acknowledged his authority. The titanic strength of the unmanifest recognized the authority of Týr—not out of fear, but out of love. However, this strength frightened all the other gods because they lacked a system to restrain and manage it. The gods feared the unknown and uncontrollable. They decided to create such a system of restraint, and Týr was forced to agree with them. This was his first mistake.

In the primary algorithms for achieving results among the northern gods, there were no provisions for negotiation, for studying the unknown nature and finding mechanisms to manage it through such study. They had the capabilities of subjugation, destruction, and limitation. They had no other ways to cope with their fear except to destroy what they feared. This approach was applied to the growing threat—the gods decided to bind the wolf. Týr, as the supreme god, had to consider everything, including the fear of his fellow Aesir. The eternal conflict of any system undergoing its primary stages of development: the rights of one versus the rights of many. Týr made his choice.

ᛊ ᛞ

The gods forged a powerful chain named Læding, which means they created their own restraining algorithms. The wolf easily tore this chain to pieces with a simple swipe of his paw. The gods presented this as a game: "Let us bind you, and you can break the bonds." This presentation already contained a falsehood—they knew it wasn't a game. The responsibility for this falsehood lay with the supreme ruler, the head of the clan. And Týr remained silent. The gods forged another chain named Drómi and again proposed it as a game. Týr remained silent once more.

Realizing that they could not create a restraining program on their own, the gods decided to turn to the masters who knew how to make programs that no counterprogram could resist. These masters were the dwarves of Svartálfaheimr. They were the only ones capable of crafting the necessary artifacts, writing algorithms that would close vulnerabilities in the system and restore its wholeness, integrity, and functional independence.

To have such capability, the creator of the necessary unique addition must not only possess the skills but also have a special gift—to accurately determine what exactly the system lacks for completeness, to identify which program is failing, to detect the vulnerability and its true cause. Given the task by the gods to create a restraining program, to forge chains that Fenrir could never break, the dwarves first identified Fenrir's vulnerability. His immense strength was not something that could be restrained from the outside, but it could be restrained from within—by simply not allowing the wolf to manifest his strength. Therefore, the chains had to affect the wolf's inner essence, not its outward manifestation. And the dwarves made such a chain. This was Týr's second mistake.

This chain was not a chain at all. Soft and thin like a silken ribbon, Gleipnir was made from strange things: *a woman's*

ᚹ ᚨ

beard, a bird's saliva, mountain roots, the noise of a cat's footsteps, a fish's breath, and a bear's sinews. What were these? What were these components that were impossible to find in nature (at least, that's what the ancients believed)? And why were they the only things capable of restraining the wolf?

All the components of Gleipnir were things that **did not exist in nature** (as the ancients thought). In these kennings, they encrypted what could not be. Unreal. Illusions. Fancies. But this was identified by the dwarves as the only vulnerability of the wolf—his strength was powerless against a non-existent enemy.

The dvergar made chains that did not exist. Fenrir could not resist what did not exist. This "patch" simply looped his program back on itself, and all his strength went into forming new internal chains. The more he raged and struggled, the stronger these chains became.

The wolf, as previously noted, was not foolish. He was intelligent with his titanic mind. When he saw this delicate ribbon, he understood that something was amiss. All the previous shackles clanked like chains, looked like chains, and thus, they were chains. Against the obvious, the wolf had arguments. But Gleipnir appeared to be something non-obvious, named entirely differently from how it looked. Meanwhile, the gods continued to insist that the game continued, that it was merely entertainment and nothing more. Yet, Fenrir suddenly grew serious and demanded a pledge. "If this is a game," he said, "and you continue to claim it is a game, let someone place their hand in my mouth—there is nothing to fear, as it is just a game. If your intentions are honest, no one will get hurt." At that moment, all the fun instantly ended.

A spoken word must be fulfilled. It must be fulfilled by the one who bears responsibility for the entire family, the one for whom the wolf Fenrir was created—the terror of the gods, the offspring of darkness and chaos, the slayer of the weak. The god Týr placed his hand in the wolf's mouth. And he lost it.

Illusions are always born from ignorance. The mind tends to fill in the gaps of what it does not know, often taking the path of least resistance, filling these gaps with the simplest explanations that lie on the surface. Fenrir, the god of evil, the slayer of gods, was not dangerous to them until he was bound. Similarly, in consciousness, the ancient force of evil is a great help for those who do not fear it. But once this force is restrained by the bonds of one's own ignorance, fear, and the illusions born from these, the force of evil becomes an enemy.

The Prose Edda, in which the venerable Snorri vividly and artistically described this event, tells us that at the moment of binding the wolf with the Gleipnir bonds, the gods laughed. They had achieved their goal—the wolf was bound, and there was no longer any need to fear. They could continue to boast of their deeds at feasts, and at these feasts, they could display their bravery. They could now fight a known enemy and engage in familiar activities. Now, everything was possible, and the gods laughed. Only one of them did not laugh—Týr did not find it funny. He understood what had truly happened and what would come next.

The victory algorithm of the god Týr faced an internal programmatic conflict of application. Should honesty and truth extend to everyone and everything? Protecting the majority versus the truth of the minority. Family is paramount, but should one protect the family if it is in the wrong? Týr's choice favoured the family. Yes, he said, one must protect their own. By his choice, he saved the Æsir but invalidated the program of "honour and valour" within the core of the system. This is how Týr ceased to be the supreme god of the northern pantheon.

This is a story of perjury. A story of a fatal mistake, but not of ultimate defeat. The time of the final battle has not yet come—it will be when the Twilight of the Gods arrives, when Ragnarök occurs. In this battle, Týr will face his true enemy, and it will not be Fenrir. It will be the dog Garm, the third and final mistake of the god Týr. In the battle of Ragnarök, everyone will fight their true enemy. This is how the Norns have woven it; this is how the program of retribution manifests. Who is Garm, the true enemy of Týr?

Garm is the dog that guards the gates of the world of Hel. Garm is the personification of the fear of death, and it is he who manifests in the final battle as Týr's true enemy. It was the fear of death that forced the god of truth to commit perjury. It was the fear of death that made him lose power. But what fear are we talking about? Did he fear death when he bravely placed his hand in the mouth of the slayer of the gods? No, Týr did not fear for himself. Týr feared for his own. Their fear became his fear; he took on the responsibility for his comrades and protected them from the wolf—from the unknown threat. The fear of death for others proved stronger than Týr, the fear for his loved ones, the fear for their death, the fear of their fear. He committed betrayal not because he was afraid for himself but because he was afraid for those who feared more than he did. However, in the northern tradition, no noble motive can justify a dishonourable act. Truth, if it is unjust, loses the right to be called truth. Justice based on lies and deceit cannot be true justice. Truth and justice are only the strength of a king when none of this exists at the expense of another.

Why, despite everything, is Týr called the god of kings? Because his example is necessary for those who believe that supreme power and "good intentions" can justify everything and provide protection from all accompanying mistakes. The story

ᛊ ᛞ

of Týr tells us this is not so—but this is a lesson for kings. At the moment when loyalty to family became higher than loyalty to an idea, he ceased to be a king and became just a warrior fighting for his own. When someone else's fear becomes the reason for betrayal, when the fear of the powerless but close becomes the cause of breaking a royal oath. He ceased to be impeccable, and the symbol of the loss of this essential quality for a true king was his one-handedness—a clear defect that must be visible to all. A ruler is poor who stakes the entire country for the sake of his family. A ruler is poor who chooses his successor not by worthiness but by affection. A ruler is poor who indulges the weaknesses of his offspring. A ruler is poor who considers his family only his blood and flesh, not the land.

It should be said that in the legends that have reached us about the god Týr, not much is said. In the Poetic Edda, there is mention of the origin of this god—as with all, he is from the Ancients. His father is named the frost giant Hymir, and his mother is the fair-faced goddess, whom researchers of the Rökkatru[19] tradition attribute to the race of fire giants. The many-headed grandmother of Tyr unequivocally identifies his lineage from the ancient Thurs, from the Primordials.

There dwells to the east of Elivagar
Hymir the wise at the end of heaven;

---

19 Rökkatru (Rökkatru, literally "faithful to the Rökkr") is a branch of Northern Neopaganism, along with Asatru and Vanatru, whose followers worship the Rökkr (giants, Jötnar) of the Northern tradition. The name Rökkatru derives from the Icelandic words 'rökkur' ("twilight") and 'tru' ("faith, trust") and refers to a direction of Scandinavian paganism dedicated to working with giants and Jötnar—wild and elemental beings who possess significant wisdom. In this context, darkness should be understood as what lies beyond human perception, what is "unseen," while twilight represents phenomena at the boundary of the manifested and hidden world. (Wikipedia)

ᚠ ᚨ

ᛊ ᛞ

A kettle my father fierce doth own,
A mighty vessel a mile in depth."

The youth found his grandam,
that greatly he loathed,
And full nine hundred heads she had;
But the other fair with gold came forth,
And the bright-browed one brought beer to her son.

"Hail to thee, Hymir! good thoughts mayst thou have;
Here has thy son to thine hall now come;
(For him have we waited, his way was long;)
And with him fares the foeman of Hroth,
The friend of mankind, and Veur they call him.
(The Poetic Edda. Hymiskvitha)

The origin of Týr allows us to understand that he is not merely a god of justice but of true justice, the primal truth. He is a bearer of ancient memory and equally ancient constants of the world of darkness. This grants him great capabilities and immense power.

However, there are even older sources, predating written records and passed down orally, which describe Týr as a very ancient chthonic force[20]. This refers to a period of existence when the true king could only be one chosen by the Earth itself. Note, not by people, but by the Earth. Only she can provide the

---

[20] In this capacity, we can recognize the god Týr under the name Ziu or Tiu, and his divine spouse in the image of his twin sister, the goddess Zisa. This very ancient format of divine twins is always and necessarily present in the mythological descriptions of all pantheons of gods across all peoples and countries.

ᚹ ᚨ

space and resources for creation, and only she can decide what shall be and what shall not. This era is often considered the era of matriarchy, but such a view is a very one-sided perception of the worldview of the gods and people of the ancient times: the Earth is the defining and nurturing force, while gods and humans are the ones who act and change. For the one whom the Earth goddess chooses as her spouse, the matters of impeccability must become the most crucial, as it is now her judgment that counts, not that of people or gods. The true king must be impeccable; otherwise, the Earth will choose another husband for herself.

This is precisely what Loki was referring to when he confronted Týr at Ægir's feast, accusing each god of deceit and deception.

> *"Be silent, Tyr! for a son with me*
> *Thy wife once chanced to win;*
> *Not a penny, methinks, wast thou paid for the wrong,*
> *Nor wast righted an inch, poor wretch."*
>
> *(The Poetic Edda. Lokasenna)*

Despite all of the above, Týr remains the most honest and noble god we know of. This is because he told his entire story truthfully. He teaches those destined to hold power, those destined to become the "husband of the goddess," to set their priorities correctly from the start.

Týr is associated with the rune **Tiwaz** — the rune of personal truth. It stands first in the third aett of the Elder Futhark, the aett of life results. The vector of this rune's power sets the foundation for all other runes in the family — only those results achieved truthfully are considered final. Therefore, Tiwaz is the strongest rune, but also the most vulnerable in the third

ᛊ ᛞ

aett, and to some extent, in the entire Futhark: everything achieved dishonestly will sooner or later end up in Hel.

Týr is the foundation of the northern tradition, its core. If it is true that Odin is the Allfather, it is equally true that Týr is Odin's inner core, the eternal inner control to always follow one's truth. He is the original intention, the basis of the northern project of civilization's development. The fact that this core was damaged does not justify its absence or replacement. On the contrary, the entire system, expressed in Odin's mind and other gods, developed to heal this vulnerability, this fracture of the core. The initial project "Truth of Týr" shaped the project "Fury of Odin" precisely because of the damage to the central core; "Fury of Odin" is a reaction to the flaw in the original plan.

Týr teaches never to forget where one started. He shows the value of one's past, regardless of what it was. Through his story, he can explain the reasons capable of toppling someone from the highest attained positions, so low that they end up even lower than where they began. His story is mirrored in myths of other pantheons, where his recognizable figure — the maimed hand — allows us to see him in the guise of the god Nuada, the god with the silver hand. There, he managed to restore his hand, but the rules of the Celtic pantheon, its developmental algorithms, still forced Týr-Nuada to relinquish supreme power, as the rules stated that the best should hold power, and in the Celtic myth, the best was the god Lugh. The one-handed hero appearing in various myths and legends also carries the mark of Týr's essence, always tested by life's circumstances against his ideals: honour, valour, and impeccability. This speaks volumes about the nature of Týr's power: one can be anything — a supreme god, a secondary god, a human, or non-human — none of it matters because the idea surpasses status. The crown will

ᚹ ᚨ

not fall from the head of the one for whom the crown is the head.

Practice 7. God Tyr (p. 479)

Heimdall

The god Heimdall also holds the title of Aesir and is called the White God. His role in the establishment of the northern system is presented in a very truncated and specific manner. He does not participate in common "journeys"; his activity is individual and independent, much like he is.

Myths and legends describe his function quite unambiguously: he is the guardian of the Tree and the organizer of the human world, the creator of the social system for the latter. His actions are aimed not at initiating processes but at fixing them. Heimdall oversees the implementation of principles, not specific rules or local laws. The latter may change from era to era, from time to time, but the principle of lawmaking must remain unchanged — this is the foundation of the White Aesir Heimdall.

Heimdall is described in the myth as a primordial god — he has always existed. His origin is titanic, like all first-generation Aesir, and here is what the Poetic Edda writes about it:

One there was born in the bygone days,
Of the race of the gods, and great was his might;
Nine giant women, at the world's edge,
Once bore[21] *the man so mighty in arms.*

---

[21] Heimdall's mothers were presumably the waves, daughters of the sea giant Aegir and his wife Ran. But this is a supposition, not a certainty. (Author's note)

Gjolp there bore him, Greip there bore him,
Eistla bore him, and Eyrgjafa,
Ulfrun bore him, and Angeyja,
Imth and Atla, and Jarnsaxa[22].

Strong was he made with the strength of earth,
With the ice-cold sea, and the blood of swine[23].

One there was bom, the best of all,
And strong was he made with the strength of earth;
The proudest is called the kinsman of men
Of the rulers all throughout the world.

Much have I told thee, and further will tell;
There is much that I know;— wilt thou hear yet more?
(The Poetic Edda. Hyndluljoth)

And he also says this about himself in the "Heimdall's Incantation":

I am the child of nine mothers,
the son of nine sisters.

In the "Song of Thrym," Heimdall is mentioned as a seer akin to the Vanir. This mention might relate the god's origin to the ancient race of nature gods, but the totality of information

---

22 The names of Heimdall's mothers roughly mean "noisy," "grabbing," "raging," "destructive," etc.

23 That is, he was protected from evil forces by means of earth, salt, and swine's blood (still used in folk medicine today).

and his manifestations in the mythological line of the northern tradition indicate his most ancient origin from primordial forces.

The name, origin, and various heiti (epithets) link Heimdall to the World Tree; however, it would be incorrect to equate him directly with Yggdrasil. Rather, Heimdall is a prototype of the tree, the creator of the program's architecture, and one of its founding fathers. The god's nine mothers, in this context, can be seen as the nine worlds of the Tree, each of which contributed a part of itself to the god.

The legends also tell that Heimdall surveys all the worlds and possesses such acute hearing that he:

He needs less sleep than a bird; sees an hundred miles around him, and as well by night as by day. He hears the grass grow and the wool on the backs of the sheep, and of course all things that sound louder than these (The Prose Edda).

I know of the horn of Heimdall, hidden
Under the high-reaching holy tree;
On it there pours from Valfather's pledge[24]
A mighty stream: would you know yet more?
....
Fast move the sons of Mim, and fate
Is heard in the note of the Gjallarhorn;
Loud blows Heimdall, the horn is aloft.
In fear quake all who on Hel-roads are.

Yggdrasil shakes, and shiver on high

[24] The pledge of the Valfather is Odin's eye, which he left as a pledge in the well of the wise Mimir, receiving wisdom in return. Mimir was the brother of Bestla, Odin's mother.

ᛊ ᛞ

The ancient limbs, and the giant is loose ;
To the head of Mim does Othin give heed.
But the kinsman of Surt shall slay him soon.
(The Poetic Edda. Voluspo)

Snorri says in the Prose Edda:

But under the second root, which extends to the frost–giants, is the well of Mimer, wherein knowledge and wisdom are concealed. The owner of the well hight Mimer. He is full of wisdom, for he drinks from the well with the Gjallar–horn. Alfather once came there and asked for a drink from the well, but he did not get it before he left one of his eyes as a pledge

The magical property of the all-seeing god was given as a pledge to the all-knowing god, so that the Aesir Heimdall could obtain a unique artifact that makes him not only capable of hearing all the worlds but also able to detect those changes that will herald the beginning of the great battle. When the god Heimdall blows his Gjallarhorn, the gods will gather for the final ting (assembly) before the ultimate battle — this will mark the beginning and the end of the time of the gods.

The appearance of the god Heimdall is dual. He is incredibly beautiful and incredibly terrifying, depending on who is looking at him. He is described as a tall god with white hair and golden teeth. To avoid incorrect associations, it should be noted that in the worldview of the people of that time, when this description was made, the word "golden" was synonymous with "beautiful," and the presence of gold on the body or clothing was synonymous with "noble."

He dwells in a place called Himinbjorg, near Bifrost. He is the ward of the gods, and sits at the end of heaven, guarding the bridge against the mountain–giants. (The Prose Edda)

ᚠ ᚨ

Bifrost[25] is a rainbow bridge, a "trembling road." It's not a road that one walks on regularly. It's a road that appears "when necessary." The ancients said that the Bifrost bridge connects sky and earth. This connection can be made and controlled within the world system by the god Heimdall beyond those initially prescribed connections.

The Prose Edda describes Bifrost as follows:

Then asked Ganglere: What is the path from earth to heaven? Har answered, laughing: Foolishly do you now ask. Have you not been told that the gods made a bridge from earth to heaven, which is called Bifrost? You must have seen it. It may be that you call it the rainbow. It has three colors, is very strong, and is made with more craft and skill than other structures. Still, however strong it is, it will break when the sons of Muspel come to ride over it, and then they will have to swim their horses over great rivers in order to get on. Then said Ganglere: The gods did not, it seems to me, build that bridge honestly, if it shall be able to break to pieces, since they could have done so, had they desired. Then made answer Har: The gods are worthy of no blame for this structure. Bifrost is indeed a good bridge, but there is no thing in the world that is able to stand when the sons of Muspel come to the fight.

...Then asked Ganglere: Does fire burn over Bifrost? Har answered: The red which you see in the rainbow is burning fire. The frost–giants and the mountain–giants would go up to heaven if Bifrost were passable for all who desired to go there. Many fair places there are in heaven, and they are all protected by a divine defense.

This communication channel, which arises only "on demand," is always controlled and opened by the god Heimdall. He opens it for those Einherjar destined to enter Valhalla; he

25 From bifa ("to tremble") and röst ("path") (Encyclopedic Dictionary by F.A. Brockhaus and I.A. Efron).

opens it for the gods when they need to travel to any of the worlds of the Tree. Mortals cannot cross the rainbow bridge; myths tell that even the god Thor cannot travel across the Bifrost bridge — Thor is too heavy for it. The Sons of Muspell, who will ride along the "shaking road" during the final battle, will burn it to ashes[26].

The god Heimdall has his own halls, which means that his function is independent and protected.

Himinbjorg[27] is the eighth, and Heimdall there
O'er men holds sway, it is said ;
In his well-built house does the warder of heaven
The good mead gladly drink.
(The Poetic Edda. Grimnismol)

However, the Eddic poem "Rigsthula[28]" vividly describes the god Heimdall. Any doubts that it refers to Heimdall are dispelled by the Völva herself, and the Völva does not lie.

Hearing I ask from the holy races,
From Heimdall's sons, both high and low;
Thou wilt, Valfather, that well I relate
Old tales I remember of men long ago.
(The Poetic Edda. Voluspo)

26 For more details, see the chapter dedicated to the final battle of Ragnarök.

27 Himinbjörg — "heavenly mountains".

28 In the song itself, it is not mentioned that Rig is Heimdall. Therefore, some researchers considered this identification a mistake and claimed that Rig is Odin. However, in the "Voluspo," Heimdall is called the father of humans, and Rig is also the father of humans, according to this song. (Note to the Prose Edda, edited by Steblin-Kamensky.)

In this myth, the White God acts as the creator and arranger of human society; he lays down the basic principles of social division, defining boundaries between people. Strict boundaries and constants for attributing different types of people to specific social strata—by appearance, wealth, and activity.

Men say there went by ways so green
Of old the god, the aged and wise,
Mighty and strong did Rig go striding.

Forward he went on the midmost way,
He came to a dwelling, a door on its posts;
In did he fare, on the floor was a fire.
Two hoary ones by the hearth there sat,
Ai and Edda, in olden dress.

Rig knew well
wise words to speak,
Soon in the midst of the room he sat,
And on either side the others were.

A loaf of bread did Edda bring.
Heavy and thick and swollen with husks;
Forth on the table she set the fare.
And broth for the meal in a bowl there was.
(Calf's flesh boiled was the
best of the dainties.)

(The Poetic Edda. Rigsthula)

Rough people, a rough house. Everything is just necessary, with no excesses, no hint of aesthetics or beauty—

ᛊ ᛞ

such were the first representatives of the human world that Rig-Heimdall visited. Fire to keep warm, and food to satisfy hunger. The Rigsthula continues:

Rig knew well wise words to speak,
Thence did he rise, made ready to sleep;
Soon in the bed himself did he lay,
And on either side the others were.

Thus was he there for three nights long,
Then forward he went on the midmost way,
And so nine months were soon passed by.

A son bore Edda, with water they sprinkled[29] *him,*
With a cloth his hair so black they covered;
Thrael[30] *they named him,*

The skin was wrinkled and rough on his hands,
Knotted his knuckles,
Thick his fingers, and ugly his face,
Twisted his back, and big his heels.

He began to grow, and to gain
in strength.
Soon of his might good use he made;
With bast he bound, and burdens carried,
Home bore faggots the whole day long.

One came to their home, crooked her legs,

---

[29] The sprinkling of an infant during the naming ceremony is a pagan ritual.

[30] Thrall — "slave."

ᚠ ᚨ

Stained were her feet, and sunburned her arms,
Flat was her nose; hername was Thir[31].

Soon in the midst of the room she sat,
By her side there sat the son of the house;
They whispered both, and the bed made ready,
Thraell and Thir, till the day was through.
(The Poetic Edda. Rigsthula)

The Rigsthula continues to tell that they had 12 sons, whose names meant "herdsman," "rude," "stub," "lazy," "stinky," "stooped," and so on. Their activities were simple and clear:

the house they cared for,
Ground they dunged, and swine they guarded,
Goats they tended, and turf they dug.

Thrall and Thir also had 9 daughters, whose names should be understandable to the reader: "Potbellied," "Fat-legged," "Chatterbox," "Ragged," and so on.

And thence has risen the race of thralls.

Simple labour, specific appearance, telling names, understandable lifestyle, and the beginning of prosperity.

Forward went Rig, his road was straight,
To a hall he came, and a door there hung;
In did he fare, on the floor was a fire:
Ail and Amma owned the house.

---

[31] Thir — "slave woman."

There sat the twain, and worked at their tasks:
The man hewed wood for the weaver's beam;
His beard was trimmed, o'er his brow a curl,
His clothes fitted close ; in the comer a chest.

The woman sat and the distafi wielded,
At the weaving with arms outstretched she worked;
On her head was a band, on her breast a smock;
On her shoulders a kerchief with clasps there was.

Here, the image of the people receiving Ríg is already more pleasant to look at: it is clear that they care about their appearance and that they live in some formed tradition, where appearance is an indicator not only of status but also of their own attitude towards this status.

Rig knew well wise words to speak,
He rose from the board, made ready to sleep;
Soon in the bed himself did he lay.
And on either side the others were.

Thus was he there for three nights long,
Then forward he went on the midmost way.
And so nine months were soon passed by.

A son bore Amma, with water they sprinkled him,
Karl[32] *they named him; in a cloth she wrapped him.*
He was ruddy of face, and flashing his eyes.

---

[32] Karl — "man," "old man," also "free, not owning hereditary land," i.e., "hired hand," and so on.

He began to grow, and to gain in strength,
Oxen he ruled, and plows made ready.
Mouses he built, and barns he fashioned,
Carts he made, and the plow he managed.

Home did they bring the bride for Karl,
In goatskins clad, and keys she bore;
Snor[33] *was her name, 'neath the veil she sat;*
A home they made ready, and rings exchanged,
The bed they decked, and a dwelling made.

This new couple also had 12 sons, whose names meant approximately "Guy," "Man," "Resident," "Wide," "Bearded," and so on; and 10 daughters with names like "Woman," "Wife," "Bride," "Mistress," and so on.

And thence has risen the yeomen's race.

Thus, the second caste was created, differing both physically and mentally from the first. What happened next?

Thence went Rig, his road was straight,
A hall he saw, the doors faced south;
The portal stood wide, on the posts was a ring,
Then in he fared ; the floor was strewn.

Within two gazed in each other's eyes,
Fathir and Mothir, and played with their fingers;
There sat the house-lord, wound strings for the bow,

[33] Snor — "daughter-in-law."

Shafts he fashioned, and bows he shaped.

The lady sat, at her arms she looked.
She smoothed the cloth, and fitted the sleeves;
Gay was her cap, on her breast were clasps.
Broad was her train, of blue was her gown.

Her brows were bright, her breast was shining,
Whiter her neck than new-fallen snow.

Rig knew well wise words to speak,
Soon in the midst of the room he sat,
And on either side the others were.

Then Mothir brought a broidered cloth,
Of linen bright, and the board she covered;
And then she took the loaves so thin.
And laid them, white from the wheat, on the cloth.

Then forth she brought the vessels full.
With silver covered, and set before them.
Meat all browned, and well-cooked birds;
In the pitcher was wine, of plate were the
So drank they and talked till the day was gone.

These people, who host Ríg for the third time, are even more "civilized." Their social status is evidently high: they don't till the soil, make utensils, or worry about the household; the man is engaged in making weapons, while the woman is busy with herself.

Rig knew well wise words to speak.
Soon did he rise, made ready to sleep;
So in the bed himself did he lay,
And on either side the others were.

Thus was he there for three nights long,
Then forward he went on the midmost way,
And so nine months were soon passed by.

A son had Mothir, in silk they wrapped him.
With water they sprinkled him, Jarl[34] *he was;*
Blond was his hair, and bright his cheeks,
Grim as a snake's were his glowing eyes.

To grow in the house did Jarl begin.
Shields he brandished, and bow-strings wound,
Bows he shot, and shafts he fashioned,
Arrows he loosened, and lances wielded,
Horses he rode, and hounds unleashed,
Swords he handled, and sounds he swam.

Straight from the grove came striding Rig,
Rig came striding, and runes he taught him ;
By his name he called him, as son he claimed him,
And bade him hold his heritage wide,
His heritage wide, the ancient homes.

---

[34] Jarl — something akin to a duke in Scandinavian kingdoms. Originally, the highest representative of the noble lineage.

ᛊ ᛞ

Here, Rig-Heimdall enters the process twice: not only as a "biological corrector" but also as a teacher and mentor, which he did not do in the first two cases. And this is important. He made Jarl his heir, and this is also significant. It was precisely the class of jarls that was destined by design to carry Heimdall's rules into the human world — to implement principles, be the guardians of the worlds, and establish the unbreakable constants of the gods. But not on their own initiative, rather under the guidance of the gods themselves. This was the intention of the gods.

Forward he rode through the forest dark,
O'er the frosty crags, till a hall he found.

His spear he shook,
his shield he brandished,
His horse he spurred, with his sword he hewed;
Wars he raised, and reddened the field.
Warriors slew he, and land he won.

Eighteen halls ere long did he hold,
Wealth did he get, and gave to all.
Stones and jewels and slim-flanked steeds,
Rings he offered, and arm-rings shared.

His messengers went by the ways so wet.
And came to the hall where Hersir dwelt ;
His daughter was fair and slender-fingered,
Erna[35] *the wise the maiden was.*

---

35 Erna — "skilled."

ᚠ ᚨ

Her hand they sought, and home they brought her,
Wedded to Jarl the veil she wore;
Together they dwelt, their joy was great,
Children they had, and happy they lived.

Jarl and Erna also had 12 sons. Their names mean approximately "son," "child," "heir," "descendant," and so on. Specifically, Kon means "descendant," and the combination "Kon the Young" (Konr ungr) in the original is phonetically similar to the word "king" (konungr). The saga does not mention the daughters of Jarl and Erna.

Young Kon is the last, youngest son of Jarl. It is about him that the story continues.

Soon grew up the sons of Jarl,
Beasts they tamed, and bucklers rounded,
Shafts they fashioned, and spears they shook.

But Kon the Young learned runes to use,
Runes everlasting, the runes of life;
Soon could he well the warriors shield,
Dull the swordblade, and still the seas.

Bird-chatter learned he, flames could he lessen,
Minds could quiet, and sorrows calm;
The might and strength of twice four men.

With Rig-Jarl soon the runes he shared,
More crafty he was, and greater his wisdom;
The right he sought, and soon he won it,
Rig to be called, and runes to know.

Young Kon rode forth through forest and grove,
Shafts let loose, and birds he lured;
There spake a crow on a bough that sat:
"Why lurest thou, Kon, the birds to come?

'Twere better forth on thy steed to fare,
...........and the host to slay.

"The halls of Dan and Danp[36] *are noble,*
Greater their wealth than thou hast gained ;
Good are they at guiding the keel,
Trying of weapons, and giving of wounds.

Unfortunately, the saga breaks off at this point. But what has been said is enough to see the entire process of the selection of the human seed, the sequential eugenics, where only the results of the third generation could be considered as having specific stable properties that the gods could use further — to teach, to change differently than just biologically. In myths close to the northern tradition, the Irish Celts have a similar indication in the rules for assessing the "king's truth" or the indicator of the latter's impeccability. The Celts believed that only one could be called an impeccable ruler who had three generations of impeccable ancestors before him.

Rig-Heimdall created four strata of society, four castes, four levels of potential. The division of human society was done

---

[36] Dan and Danp — legendary ancestors of Danish kings. The name Dan is derived from "Denmark," while Danp is a name borrowed from the Goths for the Dnieper River. However, it is also possible that Dan is a distorted name for the Don River (in Gothic legends, the Don and Dnieper were mentioned together). (Translator's note.)

in a fundamentally specific and strict manner, clearly highlighting that not just anyone but a certain one — in status and origin — becomes the "heir" of the gods. Only from this bloodline can a bearer of the gods' magical knowledge emerge, like the young Kon, the last in this line of selection.

Heimdall, I remind you, does not deal with processes — he is a god who establishes first principles as constants; he determines what should be in the system and remain unchanged under any circumstances. In this myth, in addition to clearly defining the human race into certain classes, it is also shown that the gods as forces, the gods as first principles, work and will work with the consciousness of not every individual but specific ones. As the old saying goes: "The gods care for the fates of princes, allowing princes to care for the fates of everyone else." Heimdall's activity in the described selection process involved not only successive genetic transformations but also the implementation of an informational component, which Heimdall embodies — the principle of the immutability of a fixed result. A thrall cannot become a karl, bypassing natural selection. A karl cannot become a jarl by sheer will: what you are born as is what you remain, says Heimdall's principle. Only those born as jarls and from jarls are allowed changes, only they are permitted "to speak with the gods" — so it was and so it will be. Appearance should speak for itself, and from it, everyone should understand who you are.

But Heimdall does not dictate the rules on how representatives of each caste should look or what they should eat. His mission is to create these castes, "slice" social spaces, establish an unbreakable boundary between castes — to instil in the human world the principle that society is stratified and will always be so. Only rulers are allowed to define the rules for associating with a particular social layer, but the principle of associating with the ruling caste is also immutable.

Thus, by influencing the world of Midgard, Heimdall significantly narrowed the area of effort for the gods, greatly simplifying the task for the northern system of reality construction: it is much easier to control one consciousness than thousands or millions. A small number of correct algorithms are enough for the consciousness of the chosen one to perform the right actions leading to expected results. Whereas for the consciousness of multitudes, many more such algorithms are needed, considering that the mutual correlation of human men and women will generate thousands of new such algorithms every minute. How to control them? In that system — no way. Therefore, selecting one from the multitude and controlling the single one seemed a good solution for that stage of the system's development. However, thousands and millions of karls, thralls, and women of all castes were not considered in the program's algorithm at all; they were denied access to Valhalla, so this vast human mass was sent directly to Hel's[37] halls after death, which inevitably affected the quality and productivity of the entire system.

In many archaic myths, you can encounter the image of a blind and deaf god. The image of the god Heimdall is an echo of this myth in the northern system. It is useless to appeal to him for establishing individual contact if he has not chosen you based on the specific characteristics of your mind. He hears everything but does not hear anyone in particular. He stabilizes the system, and all its elements are not for anyone's sake but for the sake of

---

[37] With very few exceptions, when other "chosen ones" ended up in the halls of other gods.

the system's balance. He opens the passage through the Bifrost bridge only if it aligns with the system's rules, and nothing else exists for him. This is what the god Loki, the eternal trickster and bothersome fly for all gods, accused Heimdall of at Aegir's feast:

Loki spake:
"Be silent, Heimdall ! in days long since
Was an evil fate for thee fixed ;
With back held stiff must thou ever stand,
As warder of heaven to watch."

(The Poetic Edda. Lokasenna)

In this accusation, Loki highlights the specific attribute of Heimdall's power — the subjectivity of his view: the White God protects the interests of Asgard alone, ignoring the interests of other worlds and the majority of people.

Loki, the god who does not tolerate boundaries and rules, played the role of an adversary-Satan for the system, pointing out errors and flaws to the gods, acting as a vulnerability scanner, a top-level hacker. He pointed out the inadmissibility of establishing rigid boundaries not only between worlds but also within worlds; he spawned the "three limits," his children, as a response to the gods' inflexibility and conservatism. That is why, in the battle of Ragnarök, not chthonic "monsters" or ancient enemies of the gods, the giants, opposed Heimdall — it was Loki, a force diametrically opposed to Heimdall. He opposed the one bound not by the gods but by the very architecture of the system created by the White God; the one whose nature resisted any constants and limitations, did not recognize boundaries but created boundaries for the gods.

This demarcation of the social world created by Heimdall still exists today and has not gone away, no matter how much one might wish to think otherwise. Constants are always constants, and the gods who succeeded the northern family took them as a foundation and work perfectly with them, using what was made before them. The only force that could break the boundaries between people is bound in the mountains of Niflheimr, and we will talk about this force further.

Practice 8. God Heimdall (p. 483)

ᛊ ᛗ

Loki

The stereotype that has formed by today about Loki as a god of evil is largely created by the black-and-white worldview of dualistic monotheism, which has dominated reality for the past couple of thousand years. In such a worldview, everything is strictly divided into good and evil, with no shades of gray. However, viewing the god Loki in this manner ensures that the observer will understand neither the power of this god nor the system of northern magic itself. The logic of the presence of a trickster god can only be revealed to those who can see in color.

What do myths and legends say about the god Loki? Snorri, son of Sturla, succinctly and comprehensively describes him in the "Prose Edda":

There is yet one who is numbered among the asas, but whom some call the backbiter of the asas. He is the originator of deceit, and the disgrace of all gods and men. His name is Loke, or Lopt. His father is the giant Farbaute, but his mother's name is Laufey, or Nal. His brothers are Byleist and Helblinde. Loke is fair and beautiful of face, but evil in disposition, and very fickle–minded. He surpasses other men in the craft of cunning, and cheats in all things. He has often brought the asas into great trouble, and often helped them out again, with his cunning contrivances. His wife hight Sygin, and their sone, Nare, or Narfe.

In the myths of the Northern tradition, the god Loki is present from the very beginning. Moreover, he is present in

ᚠ ᚨ

almost every story, manifesting himself either directly or indirectly. This indicates that he played one of the main roles in the formation of the Northern system of reality construction, and without his functionality, there would be neither the tradition itself nor the memory of it.

In the created system of realities, the god Loki left a huge mark. He participated not only in the creation of worlds but also in the creation of humanity — together with Odin and Hoenir, he created the prototype of humans, man and woman, Ask and Embla, from trees "without fate."

Who is Loki? A trickster god, the other side of Odin, his friend and blood brother. The thankless role he bore through his deeds was the mission of embodied evil. Hated and adored by everyone, Loki was the catalyst constantly pushing the gods towards systematic thinking, preventing them from stagnating and becoming complacent. A provocateur and jester, Loki, by his fiery nature, a son of Muspell, despite the everyday unseemliness of his actions, was the force that drives the process, giving it new impulses for development and acceleration. If any process falls into stagnation, it ceases to exist as a fact.

Being the other side of Odin, Loki brightly shows his properties through this relationship. If Odin is everything, then Loki is everything too — together with Odin. Loki shows what Odin is not at the moment, and through this, he compensates for his blood brother to wholeness, providing Odin with the necessary integrity for a supreme ruler. If now Odin is a fierce and stern ruler, then Loki is a kind peacemaker and trickster; if now Odin is the wise Allfather, all-knowing and making objective decisions, then Loki is the very thorn that prevents him from making these decisions.

Only the presence of Loki's power in an inseparable connection with Odin allows Odin to be diverse, rather than specific, limited, and understandable in his functionality. If it were so, Odin would never become the god of universal order, because for a supreme god, limitation in anything is a great vulnerability. If we look at Loki from this perspective, much of what was previously incomprehensible will become clear.

Let us return once more to the beginning of the myth, to the description of the emergence of the Northern tradition, to the stage when the supreme ruler of the Northern family was the god Tyr. At that time, Odin was the god of knowledge and wisdom, mastering the proto-foundations of Good and Evil. In this property and function, Odin and Loki were like divine twins, complementary forces that ensure synchronization not only with each other but also with the entire system of the Nine Worlds in relation to the newly created Asgard — the proto-foundation of Order. Odin and Loki are opposite to each other in sign but absolutely equal in significance: if Odin is good, then Loki is evil; if Odin is evil, then Loki is good. Here, Loki balances Odin but does not complement him. However, when Odin becomes the head of the pantheon, his functionality changes. He is no longer just Good and Evil; he is realized Order and can no longer be just one thing, either good or evil — he must be both simultaneously. He no longer needs to be balanced since he himself becomes the principle of balancing everything with everything. Synchronously with him, Loki's functionality also changes — he cannot remain in a specific quality, but he cannot change his inherent principle either, and he becomes a god who complements, a force that ensures Odin's wholeness. But no longer as a force of balance, but as a compensating force, a reflecting force.

Loki has the ability to be present where there is nothing. He seems to fill the void, manifesting qualities that Odin lacks, but not in opposition, rather in complement. Once Odin became the god of Order, Loki's fate was to be the god of Chaos. However, Loki is not Chaos itself. His partly fiery nature does not allow him to dissolve existence; his nature demands change, whereas Chaos extinguishes any changes and can only be a source of such changes in small doses. Nevertheless, Loki's children were born for a reason, and the guardian of the proto-foundation of Chaos became his daughter, the goddess Hel, born specifically for this purpose. All subsequent activities of Loki described in the myths show him as a force that doses and controls Chaos, and through this, his synchronicity with Odin is manifested — they are two forces that ensure the system's balance, but in different ways.

All of Loki's activities, from his travels to the birth of "terrible" children, are not accidental but deliberate. Each of his actions is a reaction to what is happening both in the world of Asgard and in all the Nine Worlds. The function that compels him to compensate for Odin's entirety makes him do the same for the other gods and goddesses since Odin is the Allfather, representing the entire system, the whole program, and each god of the Northern pantheon is a part of it. This means that they, as part of the whole, also fall within Loki's sphere of interest. This explains Loki's varying attitudes toward the gods, sometimes paradoxically opposite and illogical. But it is illogical only from the perspective of linear human logic; from the perspective of the system and understanding Loki's power as a systemic function, it is very logical: Loki provided the gods with what they lacked for their wholeness — both personal and within the framework of the entire Northern system.

The remarkable artifacts that Loki procured for the gods are not just gifts. These are magical tools that could compensate for a functional deficiency in a particular god. And it should be understood that Loki's nature does not imply that unique gifts are intended or created specifically for the recipient or for their sake — everything Loki does is for Odin and his project; everything is done based on Loki's nature, not because of a personal relationship, no matter how it may seem.

If Loki were a human and we judged him as a human, we might say that he made his gifts out of love and friendship or to "atone for sins" — such logic is understandable to humans and explains much to them. But we must not forget that gods are not humans, and when speaking of gods, we are talking about minds, systems, programs, non-human and non-biological intelligence that sees differently, thinks differently, has different motives for actions, and multiple options for solving their tasks. Judging their actions by human logic guarantees complete misunderstanding of what is happening and, consequently, incorrect conclusions.

Loki's gifts to the gods are a way to make them stronger or, on the contrary, to limit their power. Not because Loki desires it so, but because the whole system of Odin requires such specific changes at this very moment. Legends describe several artifacts he obtained, some of which have been mentioned above and, of course, will be discussed further. But here is how Snorri himself tells us about it:

Why is gold called Sif's hair? Loke Laufey's son had once craftily cut all the hair off Sif; but when Thor found it out he seized Loke, and would have broken every bone in him, had he not pledged himself with an oath to get the swarthy elves to make for Sif a hair of gold that should grow like other hair. Then went Loke to the dwarfs that are called Ivald's sons, and they made the hair and Skidbladner, and the spear that Odin owned and is called Gungner. Thereupon Loke wagered his head with the dwarf, who hight Brok, that his brother Sindre would not be able to make three other treasures equally as good as these were. But when they came to the smithy, Sindre laid a pig–skin in the furnace and requested Brok to blow the bellows, and not to stop blowing before he (Sindre) had taken out of the furnace what he had put into it.

As soon, however, as Sindre had gone out of the smithy and Brok was blowing, a fly lighted on his hand and stung him; but he kept on blowing as before until the smith had taken the work out of the furnace. That was now a boar, and its bristles were of gold. Thereupon he laid gold in the furnace, and requested Brok to blow, and not to stop plying the bellows before he came back. He went out; but then came the fly and lighted on his neck and stung him still worse; but he continued to work the bellows until the smith took out of the furnace the gold ring called Draupner. Then Sindre placed iron in the furnace, and requested Brok to work the bellows, adding that otherwise all would be worthless. Now the fly lighted between his eyes and stung his eye–lids, and as the blood ran down into his eyes so that he could not see, he let go of the bellows just for a moment and drove the fly away with his hands. Then the smith came back and said that all that lay in the furnace came near being entirely spoiled. Thereupon he took a hammer out of the furnace. All these treasures he then placed in the hands of his brother Brok and bade him go with Loke to Asgard to fetch the wager.

When Loke and Brok brought forth the treasures, the gods seated themselves upon their doom–steads. It was agreed to abide by the decision which should be pronounced by Odin, Thor and Frey. Loke gave to Odin the spear Gungner, to Thor, the hair, which Sif was to have, and to Frey, Skidbladner; and he described the qualities of all these treasures, stating that the spear never would miss its mark, that the hair would grow as soon as it was placed on Sif's head, and that Skidbladner would always have a fair wind as soon as the sails were hoisted, no matter where its owner desired to go; besides, the ship could be folded together like a napkin and be carried in his pocket if he desired. Then Brok produced his treasures. He gave to Odin the ring, saying that every ninth night eight other rings as heavy as it would drop from it; to Frey he gave the boar, stating that it would run through the

ᛊ ᛞ

air and overseas, by night or by day, faster than any horse; and never could it become so dark in the night, or in the worlds of darkness, but that it would be light where this boar was present, so bright shone his bristles. Then he gave to Thor the hammer, and said that he might strike with it as hard as he pleased; no matter what was before him, the hammer would take no scathe, and wherever he might throw it he would never lose it; it would never fly so far that it did not return to his hand; and if he desired, it would become so small that he might conceal it in his bosom; but it had one fault, which was, that the handle was rather short.

The decision of the gods was, that the hammer was the best of all these treasures and the greatest protection against the frost–giants, and they declared that the dwarf had fairly won the wager. Then Loke offered to ransom his head. The dwarf answered saying there was no hope for him on that score. Take me, then! Said Loke; but when the dwarf was to seize him Loke was far away, for he had the shoes with which he could run through the air and over the sea. Then the dwarf requested Thor to seize him, and he did so. Now the dwarf wanted to cut the head off Loke, but Loke said that the head was his, but not the neck. Then the dwarf took thread and a knife and wanted to pierce holes in Loke's lips, so as to sew his mouth together, but the knife would not cut. Then said he, it would be better if he had his brother's awl, and as soon as he named it the awl was there and it pierced Loke's lips. Now Brok sewed Loke's mouth together, and broke off the thread at the end of the sewing. The thread with which the mouth of Loke was sewed together is called Vartare (a strap).

From the legend, it is clear that Loki initiated irreversible changes in the system by cutting the hair of the goddess Sif. He sanctioned the creation of artifacts but did not personally deliver them to the gods. Instead, he handed over the process to someone naturally capable of perceiving the imperfections and incompleteness of each system element and capable of precisely

ᚹ ᚠ

correcting these elements. The svartálfar craftsmen do not possess a systemic vision, but this "narrow focus" attribute accompanies all unique craftsmen who can see and work with the small but not the big picture. However, they know their craft impeccably: if something is imperfect, they will see it; if something is incomplete, they will point it out. The svartálfar lack delicacy or systemic vision—they are masters, system repairers, if you will, but not programmers or politicians. It's no wonder the position of Svartálfheim is associated with the proto-foundation of Evil, as this principle's function includes seeing and reflecting imperfections. Misunderstanding the nature of evil, by the way, also leads to incorrect understanding of how to interact with it: monotheistic morality calls for fighting evil, whereas a broader polytheistic perspective teaches interaction and learning from those who see reality from the position of its vulnerabilities, from the position of evil.

The svartálfar distributed the created six artifacts among the gods in the only correct way—they closed vulnerabilities for each of them. We already know two of them: Odin's spear Gungnir and Thor's hammer Mjölnir. Odin needs precision, and Thor needs strength; the svartálfar determined this without error, even though they did not originally intend the artifacts specifically for them—this was Loki's doing, who closed the gap in the system with the hands of the great masters. For this deed, Loki had to receive a magical wound—a sewn-up mouth that left indelible scars on his face. This mark became as much a part of his appearance as Odin's missing eye and Tyr's missing hand—magical wounds and the loss of functions remain in a god's program forever, transferring with them from pantheon to pantheon, from myth to myth. The same happened with Loki, and the "scarred mouth" became his calling card, just like Tyr's one-handedness and Odin's one-eyedness.

However, there was more that Loki did himself, not through using the skills of the svartálfar. Not being a master but being a god, he did what only a god could do—he brought forth other gods. But these gods, Loki's offspring, according to his principle, did not replicate the existing but were what the entire system of world order lacked. From the perspective of binary thinking, they were pure evil, as people usually call what is different from themselves. Loki's three children, two of whom have already been discussed, did not have the familiar appearance of gods—they were terrifying. A wolf, a serpent, and the beautifully terrifying goddess Hel, who will be discussed further.

Honesty is usually lacking in those who hold power. When the god Loki, together with the ancient giantess Angrboda[38], gave birth to three "terrible" children, they manifested three forces, three functions that the Nine Worlds system lacked. Their appearance became more terrifying if the gods refused to see the imperfections of the created reality. Loki's nature and the nature of his children's mother, the ancient goddess who preserved the memory of all possible forms, simply revealed the deficiencies of a world where the form of this manifestation entirely corresponded to the depth of the created problem. These three children are manifested evil, but the key word here is not "evil," but "manifested": if the gods had not turned a blind eye to imperfection but worked with the system of evil as a mirror, perhaps Loki would not have had to manifest such terrifying forms, which the gods found difficult to comprehend.

---

[38] Her name is translated as "she who brings grief," "causing suffering." But it can also be said differently — "the giver of evil."

However, Loki's fourth child was entirely different. This is the remarkable eight-legged horse Sleipnir, whose nature showed us Loki from his other side, as Loki (and Sleipnir is also a god) was not a father but a mother to this god. Snorri describes this remarkable birth in the "Prose Edda" as follows:

Ganglere asked: Whose is that horse Sleipner, and what is there to say about it? Har answered: You have no knowledge of Sleipner, nor do you know the circumstances attending his birth; but it must seem to you worth the telling. In the beginning, when the town of the gods was building, when the gods had established Midgard and made Valhal, there came a certain builder and offered to make them a burg, in three half years, so excellent that it should be perfectly safe against the mountain giants and frost–giants, even though they should get within Midgard. But he demanded as his reward, that he should have Freyja, and he wanted the sun and moon besides. Then the asas came together and held counsel, and the bargain was made with the builder that he should get what he demanded if he could get the burg done in one winter; but if on the first day of summer any part of the burg was unfinished, then the contract would be void. It was also agreed that no man should help him with the work. When they told him these terms, he requested that they should allow him to have the help of his horse, called Svadilfare, and at the suggestion of Loke this was granted him.

On the first day of winter he began to build the burg, but by night he hauled stone for it with his horse. But it seemed a great wonder to the asas what great rocks the horse drew, and the horse did one half more of the mighty task than the builder. The bargain was firmly established with witnesses and oaths, for the giant did not deem it safe to be among the asas without truce if Thor should come home, who now was on a journey to the east fighting trolls. Toward the end of winter the burg was far built, and it was so high and strong that it could in nowise be taken. When there were three days left before summer, the work was all completed excepting the burg gate. Then

ᛊ ᛞ

went the gods to their judgment—seats and held counsel, and asked each other who could have advised to give Freyja in marriage in Jotunheim, or to plunge the air and the heavens in darkness by taking away the sun and the moon and giving them to the giant; and all agreed that this must have been advised by him who gives the most bad counsels, namely, Loke, son of Laufey, and they threatened him with a cruel death if he could not contrive some way of preventing the builder from fulfilling his part of the bargain, and they proceeded to lay hands on Loke. He in his fright promised with an oath that he should so manage that the builder should lose his wages, let it cost him what it would.

And the same evening, when the builder drove out after stone with his horse Svadilfare, a mare suddenly ran out of the woods to the horse and began to neigh at him. The steed, knowing what sort of horse this was, grew excited, burst the reins asunder and ran after the mare, but she ran from him into the woods. The builder hurried after them with all his might, and wanted to catch the steed, but these horses kept running all night, and thus the time was lost, and at dawn the work had not made the usual progress. When the builder saw that his work was not going to be completed, he resumed his giant form. When the asas thus became sure that it was really a mountain—giant that had come among them, they did not heed their oaths, but called on Thor. He came straightaway, swung his hammer, Mjolner, and paid the workman his wages, - not with the sun and moon, but rather by preventing him from dwelling in Jotunheim; and this was easily done with the first blow of the hammer, which broke his skull into small pieces and sent him down to Niflhel.

But Loke had run such a race with Svadilfare that he some time after bore a foal. It was gray, and had eight feet, and this is the best horse among gods and men.

ᚡ ᚨ

Oathbreaking is a significant defeat for the gods. Loki took the blame upon himself and, as compensation, gave one of his most potent and beautiful attributes—the ability to travel between worlds. He bestowed this ability upon his son and handed him over to Odin, giving him to Asgard as compensation for the magical abilities that the gods could have undoubtedly lost in response to the destruction of an ancient power—the giant with whom they had made an honest agreement. However, because the "feminine function" performed by Loki diminished his standing in the Aesir's value system, the trickster god, the god of Chaos, reduced his function to that of the "god of Evil," similar to how the god Tyr lost his power for the same reason—oathbreaking.

Njorth spake:
"Small ill does it work though a woman may have
A lord or a lover or both;
But a wonder it is that this womanish god
Comes hither, though babes he has borne."
Lokasenna

Loki, like Tyr, took upon himself the collective blame but received neither sympathy nor gratitude from the gods.

By obtaining magical artifacts for the gods, coming to their aid, or provoking them into action, humiliating himself in the eyes of others, dressing in women's clothes alongside Thor, or trying to amuse Skadi, he diverted misfortune from the gods without worrying about his own reputation. If we look at all the myths mentioning Loki's name, we can easily notice that all the treasures he obtained and all the actions he performed were not for himself. Acting as a provocateur, he subtly but inevitably formed additional rights and opportunities for the northern family of gods, completely disregarding his own reputation and benefit.

However, the role of the trickster, the injector function, is always highly ungrateful. The ordinary mind judges not by motive but by action, not by intention but by deed. Who cares about Loki's motives if his actions almost always cause harm? But it is from the perspective of motive that we must view the deeds of the god Loki; it is from the standpoint of expediency for the entire system, not for everyone and not for each individual, that we should look at the challenging story of the god Baldr's death, which we will discuss later. For now, let's just note—this was a plan, a long-term plan aimed at healing the system of the Nine Worlds and changing the principles of Asgard's order.

The strikingly powerful part of the "Poetic Edda"—"Lokasenna"—is like a coda in the entire northern symphony. The tension reached its peak here, and this was Loki's final "performance." His outburst at the feast of the god Aegir is incomprehensible at first glance unless one understands the true functions that the god Loki performed for the entire system. By this point, the problems had become so intractable and deep that only by exposing them all could there be one last chance to start fixing them.

"Lokasenna", or "Loki's Quarrel", tells the story of how the gods, gathered at the feast of the god Aegir, began to praise themselves, boasting of their achievements and feats. The son of Laufey interrupted their praise, arriving drunk at the feast with a full package of revelations about the gods and goddesses. To understand "Lokasenna" correctly, let's try to view it from a slightly different angle. Who is the god Aegir, at whose feast the gods of Asgard gathered? Aegir is the god of the sea, an ancient power, one of the primordial titans. The winter feasts at Aegir's hall, hosted by him and his wife, the goddess Ran, were ritual actions intended to unite all worlds and systems in friendship and reconciliation—a sort of Elysium where all conflicts ceased. From a magical perspective, Aegir's feast was a ritual of system alignment, its revision, and the agreement of the future: how the system of the Nine Worlds would exist moving forward. Aegir, as the god of the seas, distributes the power of creation among all. It is clear that each world sought to bring to Aegir's feast all their best results, which they wanted to be proud of. Thus, the gods of Asgard, arriving at Aegir's feast, boasted of their achievements and feats.

"Speak now, Eldir, for not one step
Farther shalt thou fare;
What ale-talk here do they have within,
The sons of the glorious gods?"

Eldir spake:
"Of their weapons they talk, and their might in war.
The sons of the glorious gods;
From the gods and elves who are gathered here
No friend in words shalt thou find."

Lokasenna

In response to this, Loki, arriving at the feast, exposed all the sins and problems of each of the present Æsir and Ásynjur; he forgot no one, and everyone received a share of Loki's sharp tongue. The issue was not that the trickster god derided his fellow project members, but that he did so in a place where such behavior held ritual significance and could not be dismissed as drunken ravings or the slander of an offended party.

Moreover, Odin himself confirmed Loki's right to speak to the gods on equal terms with him:

Loki spake:
"Remember, Othin, in olden days
That we both our blood have mixed;[39]
Then didst thou promise no ale to pour,
Unless it were brought for us both."

Othin spake:
"Stand forth then, Vithar, and let the wolf's father
Find a seat at our feast;
Lest evil should Loki speak aloud
Here within Ægir's hall."

Lokasenna

Vidar — the son of Odin and his heir[40] after the death of Baldr. By raising him from the bench, Odin demonstrated how highly Loki was positioned within the system and how highly Odin himself regarded him — still, despite everything, as his blood brother, as his equal. However, this did not become a step toward reconciliation between the gods and Loki. Having spoken his mind to everyone, Loki cursed the house of Ægir, and this largely became the formal cause for Ragnarök.

"Ale hast thou brewed, but, iEgir, now
Such feasts shalt thou make no more ;
O'er all that thou hast which is here within

---

39 "...our blood have mixed" — we formed a blood brotherhood.

40 This will be discussed further in the chapter dedicated to the god Vidar.

Shall play the flickering flames,
(And thy back shall be burnt with fire.)"
Lokasenna

Loki's words resound with resentment: resentment toward the gods, his blood brother, and the entire northern family; resentment for their ingratitude, their arrogance, their self-deception, which ultimately culminated in the curse upon Ægir, as this too was resentment — resentment that despite all his efforts, the gods depend on the opinion of the god of elemental forces, depend on the opinion of the observer, and sink to lies and deceit, even to the point of praising Ægir's servant — all to appear better in the eyes of the judge than they truly are. In his accusations, we hear bitterness — it was all in vain, you understood nothing, my brothers, my friends, my enemies.

The gods did not forgive Loki for his ritual defeat. As Snorri writes:

So he ran away and hid himself in a rock. Here he built a house with four doors, so that he might keep an outlook on all sides. Oftentimes in the daytime he took on him the likeness of a salmon and concealed himself in Frananger Force… Skade took a serpent and fastened up over him, so that the venom should drop from the serpent into his face. But Sigyn, his wife, stands by him, and holds a dish under the venomdrops. Whenever the dish becomes full, she goes and pours away the venom, and meanwhile the venom drops onto Loke's face. Then he twists his body so violently that the whole earth shakes, and this you call earthquakes.

Did the gods understand that by chaining Loki and immobilizing the second half of Odin, they were doing the same to Odin himself? Did they realize that their actions were restricting the freedom of the supreme god? None of the gods in the Norse pantheon would have become what they were without the lessons Loki managed to teach them. To each of the Aesir he interacted with, he imparted a fragment of his fiery nature, a piece of that primordial fire of Muspelheim, which drives change and transformation. Sometimes this fire burns painfully, but without it, life would be impossible for anyone. A bound Loki signifies the limitation and confinement of the entire Scandinavian system; a freed Loki heralds the rebirth of tradition through Ragnarök.

Nowhere in the myths is it mentioned that Loki has a throne or his own hall. This implies that his algorithms of victory are not complete and independent programs — they are always part of the other gods' programs with whom he undertook joint actions or journeys. His power complicated Odin's and the Aesir's programs, making them more competitive and resilient: once a program undergoes a series of injections and test trials, it becomes much harder to kill. Loki did nothing for himself personally; each of his pranks was a reaction to the entire system's actions, each of his gifts a power that strengthened the entire northern family. This is the main function of the trickster, not to ruin the lives of "honest citizens."

Loki's gifts are invaluable, but so are his lessons. One could describe him using the later depiction of him in the image of Mephistopheles: *I am part of that force which eternally wills evil and eternally works good.*

There will be many more stories about the god Loki. He is the force and speed of reaction to changes; he is the ability to instantly compensate for reality, preventing significant imbalances. As long as Loki was unbound, the system could remain balanced and develop through constant and chaotic injections from the trickster god. But when Loki lost the ability to perform his function, the system became static, making

Ragnarök inevitable. For him, nothing is more valuable than anything else; he has no preferences about where and to whom to administer an injection, nor whom to spare. This makes him the opposite of his adversary, Heimdall[41], for whom preferences exist and the constants of the system are sacred and unchangeable. Loki does not acknowledge constants at all — not their presence in the system, but their eternal immutability. Heimdall is his adversary precisely because he embodied this quality of the unchanging architecture of worlds and realities, the strict division of people into castes, and the segmentation of time and spaces; because Heimdall was the guardian of worlds, while Loki was the spirit of free reaction to changes: as needed, but not by the rules.

Loki is the god of truth, but he is also the god of lies. The duality of his behavior constantly proves that the truth is when truth and lies are together, where lies are not deception but simply another form of truth.

Practice 9. God Loki (p. 491)

[41] According to the prophecy of the Völva, it is with the white Aesir Heimdall that the god Loki will clash in the battle of Ragnarök.

Vanir

Who are the Vanir? How do they differ from the Aesir or the Jotnar? And how did it come to be that representatives of various divine forces ended up in the same pantheon? Myths provide answers to all these questions, detailing the history of interactions between the Aesir and Vanir in the context of building the northern tradition.

The Vanir are the primordial gods of nature. In any pagan pantheon, they are always present as the givers of blessings, who provide resources to all living, existing, and dwelling beings. Gods, humans, and all living and non-living things depend on sustenance and energy, which the gods and spirits of nature control. In the northern system, they are called the Vanir.

It should be noted that the Aesir did not create the world of Vanaheimr. Either it always existed, or it "manifested" during the creation of the system by Odin and his brothers. It acted as a reaction to the creation process, the opposite side of order. In this capacity, the Vanir are not carriers of chaos in the usual sense of the term, but their nature and world constitute a completely separate system, existing according to their own rules and laws, which are always significantly different from the rules and laws of civilization that the gods of order embody. The northern system was no exception, and myths tell us about the initial differences between the Aesir and Vanir, their fundamental disagreement in the principles of reality formation, and the inevitable initial hostility between them.

Nature follows its own laws, its own rhythm, and cycles. These are unchanged over centuries and millennia; changes in natural cycles occur so rarely and slowly that an external observer is more likely to record the absence of any changes rather than the speed of their increase. However, forces that introduce principles of specific programming into reality are interested in changing the natural pace of "mutation accumulation"—time is not infinite for them, and the implementation of their plans requires entirely different speeds.

The mythology of various systems tells us how the gods of law dealt with the gods of nature. Some fought, others negotiated, some conquered, and others ignored. The northern myth describes the process of integrating the programs of the Aesir and Vanir in detail: there were wars, there was an agreement, there was conquest, and there was ignoring. Everything happened—sometimes successfully, sometimes with catastrophic consequences—but the old gods left us an honest account of this process, and now we just need to understand this message correctly.

There was a war. And most likely, not just one. In the Voluspo we read:

The war I remember, the first in the world,
When the gods with spears had smitten Gollveig,
And in the hall of Hor had burned her,—
Three times burned, and three times born,
Oft and again, yet ever she lives.

Heith they named her who sought their home,
The wide-seeing witch, in magic wise;
Minds she bewitched that were moved by her magic,
To evil women a joy she was.

Regarding the figure of the primary cause of the Gullveig war, there is no unanimous opinion. She was from the tribe of the Vanir, and the first part of her name, Gull, means "gold." The second part of the name, veig, relates to a description of some specific force or entity. Thrice she approached the Æsir, and thrice they rejected her[42]. This disagreement and rejection not only became the foundation for a prolonged conflict but also transformed the primordial power of original magic into a specific form of female natural witchcraft, and Heiðr — into a witch.

On the host his spear did Othin hurl,
Then in the world did war first come;
The wall that girdled the gods was broken,
And the field by the warlike Wanes was trodden.

Then sought the gods their assembly-seats,
The holy ones, and council held,

[42] The same triple invocation to alien gods by the sovereigns and goddesses of Earth can be found in mythology, for example, among the Irish Celts: when the sons of Mil, the latest invaders of Ireland, set foot on this land, they were met by three goddesses, Banba, Fótla, and Ériu, who were personifications of the Irish land. Each of them was promised by the warriors to name the land after them, which according to ancient laws was a threefold confirmation of ownership and agreement. Needless to say, things turned out quite differently for the sons of Mil on Irish soil compared to the Æsir in the lands of Vanaheimr?

It is quite likely that Gullveig's triple invocation to the Æsir was an attempt by the Vanir to buy off the Æsir at the initial stage of introducing the gods of law into the primordial system of nature.

ᛊ ᛞ

Whether the gods should tribute[43] *give.*
Or to all alike should worship belong.
(The Poetic Edda. Voluspo)

The Vanir, as gods of nature, are more local inhabitants in this physically manifested world than anyone else. Certainly, more so than the Æsir, who act as "invaders" and "occupiers" in relation to the forces of nature, but at the same time as progressors and rationalizers. The first war is a classic conflict between the old and the new systems, and Gullveig's "golden power" can be seen as the original might of nature, the energy that dictates its rules to the emerging informational system. Just as the nature of human biology dictates rules to the mind, and the mind tries to conquer biology and subjugate it to its service. Who will win?

The northern myth tells us its story of such a conquest and says: in that war, no one won. The forces were equal, the Æsir could not subdue the power of nature, and everyone had to negotiate. In that war, the Æsir fought the Vanir not for territory but for spheres of influence. For the right to dictate conditions: who will exist according to which rules; whose presence in this existence needs to be considered, and whose does not; who will have control over whom, to what extent and under what conditions. The gods of Asgard needed to integrate the world of Vanaheimr into the system of the Nine Worlds, while the Vanir gods needed to preserve their freedom and the old way "according to nature."

---

43 According to another version — whether to pay ransom to the Vanir.

ᚠ ᚨ

The Vanir are needed by the Æsir. The Vanir are the givers of blessings and possess all the resources of this world. They understand the effects of the existence of these resources and know in what sequence and rhythm these resources should be extracted and how to compensate for what is taken. They know how the effects of extracting these resources should manifest and whom they should affect. They embody the principle of natural selection, but this knowledge is not even knowledge—it is part of their nature. They are the personified intellect of nature, and each Vanir god represents a distinct attribute of this intellect.

They control the weather and the changing seasons; they govern the harvest and the fertility of the earth; they regulate the cycles of sleep and wakefulness in nature, and they control the mechanisms of biocenosis and synergy. As multifaceted and diverse as nature is, so too are its gods, spirits, and demi-spirits. They all represent the principles of life's existence. Can they afford "developmental" experiments? No, and this is not even part of their system. Any kind of play or experimentation is inherently absent from the Vanir worldview.

In contrast to the Vanir, the Æsir are creators of reality, makers of rules and compromises. They do not follow rules; they create them.

How did the rulers of compromise, the Æsir, come to an agreement with the Vanir? According to the customs of the era in which this myth was recorded by humans for humans, the process of truce between tribes involved a ritual act of exchanging hostages. Typically, these were not insignificant members of the tribe, and in this way, the reconciling parties declared and affirmed the honesty of their intentions: if one side broke the agreement, the offended side had the right to kill the hostage. The Æsir and the Vanir also exchanged hostages. From the Æsir to the Vanir went the gods Mimir and Hoenir, and from the Vanir to the Æsir went the god Njord and his twin children Freyr and Freyja. Each of them will be discussed later.

In addition to exchanging hostages for the sake of reconciliation, the gods performed a ritual act: they approached a vessel, and each spat into it. This mingling of biological (and genetic) material created a new being called "the wise Kvasir," who had equal parts of both Vanir and Æsir. His story will also be told in due course.

The Vanir received as hostages those gods who were bearers of information. The hostages, being ancient etins by origin, could bring into the world of nature a long memory absent in them, personified by the god Mimir, and the ability to use this memory embodied by the god Hoenir. However, the Vanir decided to keep only Hoenir for themselves, and they killed Mimir. Why? Did the Vanir have grounds for killing their hostage? We will explore the reasons and consequences of this strange event when we work with the channel of the god Mimir. For now, let's return to the Vanir.

Njord and his children embody the forces of nature. It was their presence that gave the gods a constant influx of natural resources, access to the elements of manifest nature, and a certain control over it. According to the agreement with the Æsir, the Vanir hostages were not prisoners but, on the contrary, became part of the larger Æsir family and were themselves honoured as Æsir. They had the right and the opportunity to return to their native Vanaheimr, but under certain conditions: only one at a time, while the other two had to remain in Asgard. In addition to Njord and the twins, a fairly large retinue accompanied them to Asgard, which also became part of the Æsir's world—through marriage with the gods, through treaty, or simply by goodwill.

The Æsir gained much by integrating the Vanir gods into their family, far more than they lost by sending their hostages away. To understand this fully, we will examine the power of each god of Vanaheimr's natural might in detail and separately.

ᛊ ᛞ

Njord

Njord is the god of aquatic wealth. He rules over water, not merely as an element, but as a space of life itself. He possesses the power capable of feeding all. He is the master of natural resources, and everything related to the living world pertains to Njord.

The Poetic Edda in the "Vafthruthnismol" tells about the god Njord as follows:

Othin spake:
"Tenth answer me now, if thou knowest all
The fate that is fixed for the gods:
Whence came up Njorth to the kin of the gods,—
(Rich in temples and shrines he rules,—)
Though of gods he was never begot?"

Vafthruthnir spake:
"In the home of the Wanes
did the wise ones
create him,
And gave him as pledge to the gods;
At the fall of the world shall he fare once more
Home to the Wanes so wise."
(The Poetic Edda. Vafthruthnismol)

His parents are said to be gods who are also described as bestowers of wealth. His father, Frodi, is the master of the

ᚹ ᚠ

legendary "Frodi's Mill"; he represents an even more ancient cosmic force of reproduction, the eternal engine of the primal race, a never-ending process of recreation. Njord's mother is named Nott, the goddess of night. She too embodies the primal principle of darkness as something hidden and unmanifest. It becomes clear that the god Njord is a descendant of very ancient chthonic forces and embodies hidden wealth.

He is hailed as the "best steersman." His halls in Asgard are called Noatun ("shipyard"), located where the sky meets the sea. Njord's hall appears as if built from the skeletons of sunken ships, and for this reason, it constantly expands.

Interestingly, Njord was called the "king of men"; it was believed that he was the god of noble and flawless individuals. Sailors and shipwrights, maritime travellers, and even "lucky gentlemen" were seen as such, whose profession and way of life became courage and the ability to see their happiness and chance in the sea.

Njord's flawlessness is somewhat different from the traditional understanding of this term. Because the Vanir are different, their concept of flawlessness will be different as well. From the perspective of the Vanir and consequently of Njord, flawless is someone who will never violate the rights of others. Who will never do this? Firstly, those who have their own rights—truly, not illusory. Secondly, those who are so bold and strong in their rights that they will never have the desire or need to diminish others to elevate themselves. Furthermore, from Njord's perspective, noble and flawless are those who will never envy another's wealth. This quality of consciousness is inherent precisely in the Vanir nature—there is simply no option like "envy" in the consciousness of the Vanir gods.

The strong are not envious; the weak are envious; the unjust and powerless are envious, and therefore, flawed and certainly not noble. If a person resembles the Vanir in this respect, then he or she is more likely to find reflection in the eyes of Njord, as flawless in them. Njord's flawlessness is the understanding and feeling of the world, akin to how a loving man understands his woman. It is the ability to take from the world only the resources that are truly needed now, rather than depleting nature out of greed or fear. Njord sees people as whole and strong; it is these individuals whom he can guide with his nature.

The sphere of interests of the god Njord is not just a resource, but a renewable resource; eternal movement and the correct process of its distribution: how much is needed, to whom, where, and when. There is no shortage, but there is also no excess. The power of the Vanir nature speaks of the fact that in the world there should be only one law — the law of life, and only what is necessary for life is right. And only that.

In the legends of the Norse gods, the god Njord is not often mentioned as a main character; his presence as the main hero is noted only in the story of the marriage of the goddess Skadi, where Njord indeed became her husband. However, this legend relates more to Skadi than to Njord, so we will consider it in due time.

Certainly, the presence of the god Njord at the epochal feast of Ægir is noted. And the god Loki did not spare him reproach and accusation, indicating that he also blames Njord for the failure of the Æsir's plan to build a "northern model" of reality. But what imperfection did Loki see in Njord's principle? We read in the saga:

Loki spake:
"Be silent, Njorth; thou wast eastward sent,
To the gods as a hostage given;
And the daughters of Hymir their privy had

When use did they make of thy mouth."

Njorth spake:
"Great was my gain, though long was I gone,
To the gods as a hostage given;
The son did I have whom no man hates.
And foremost of gods is found."

Loki spake:
"Give heed now, Njorth, nor boast too high,
No longer I hold it hid ;
With thy sister hadst thou so fair a son.
Thus hadst thou no worse a hope."
(The Poetic Edda. Lokasenna)

So, what did the god Loki see as harmful from the strength of Njord? Harm exclusively in his nature, adherence to the traditions of his tribe. Loki believes (and this is traced practically in all sagas of the northern line) that the Æsir should not have negotiated with the Vanir and given them so much freedom. Loki sees harm not in the Vanir themselves, but in the fact that the Æsir could not fully control their power, as they did, for example, with the elves.

Loki did not like the Vanir. Despite the fact that the Vanir embody freedom, it is not the kind of freedom that Loki personifies. The freedom of the Vanir is still built on constants, but these constants are not social, like those of the god Heimdall, but natural. Nature, Vanaheimr, lives by its own laws, which are unchanging nonetheless. However, no one can cope with these laws, and this is an eternal problem for the gods and Loki's unceasing wrath. But this wrath stems from powerlessness, and

it can be said that towards the Vanir, Loki is more angry at himself than at them. In his quarrel with Njord, he was rather venting his spite and rage than genuinely accusing him.

Practice 10. God Njord (page 494)

Freyr and Freyja

The children of the god Njord, Freyr and Freyja, are continuations of his power, specific manifestations of natural potency. Let's get to know them.

The origin of these divine twins, children of the god Njord, is quite fascinating. They are the result of what is known as a ritual marriage, which was traditional in the ancient matriarchal era. In this tradition, spouses came together not to live together but to conceive their offspring once a year, on the right day and hour. In the divine realms, twin gods became these ritual progenitors, whose union was purely ritualistic rather than domestic. This is how legends of many peoples describe it, and all rituals connected with the fertility of the land are echoes and remnants of this ancient ritual.

According to the systemic rule, the divine and ritual spouse of the god Njord was his twin sister, the goddess Nerthus, the Earth goddess. The force of aquatic life united with the force of earthly life, and from this union were born two personified forces: the god of fertility, Freyr, and the goddess of fertile power, Freyja. The parental forces of the gods Njord and Nerthus, combined, manifest in their children but in a specific quality, giving rise to a newly distinguished property: what is needed for the world to be fertile? What is necessary for the world to be abundant? The twin gods, Freyr and Freyja, embody these intertwined properties: fertility and the drive for fertility.

It should be noted that Freyr and Freyja are not the personal names of these gods but rather titles. In translation, they mean "lord" and "lady". Their personal names are Ingvi and Vanadis.

ᛊ ᛞ

Freyr - Ingvi

The god Freyr embodies the power of fertility, the ability to derive benefit from everything, to extract resources from everything. His strength is built on the principles of life and death, where death is permissible only when there is continuity of life. If the parental force of the god Njord reflects the principle of holistic understanding of the life process, then his descendant, the god Freyr, specifies the power of his parents and demonstrates the mechanism of achieving such integrity - the cycle of energy in nature, its renewability and growth, its abundance and sufficiency. His function is that of constant multiplication. His principle is the principle of nature: what does not increase, decreases. To prevent life from dwindling, one must constantly provide some surplus, allowing natural selection methods to operate, where the strongest survives and produces better offspring.

The principle of Freyr, as manifested in reality, is the ability to leave behind numerous traces without excessively nurturing and guarding them, allowing only the strongest imprint to survive. The mechanisms through which this principle is realized are described to us in myths and legends about the god Freyr - Ingvi. However, these same myths and legends show us, his descendants, not only the possibilities of manifesting Freyr's fertility power but also all the threats that can be directed towards it, as well as the threats that can emanate from it.

ᚹ ᚫ

As you already know, the gods Njord, Freyr, and Freyja were accepted into the realm of Asgard, welcomed into the family with all due respect and honour. But what does family mean to the Vanir and what does it mean to the Aesir? For the Vanir, family is a holistic organism created according to the natural laws of nature; a system where each element is necessary and, to some extent, system-forming.

In the Vanir world, there is no hierarchy, no submission to law - this is also absent in Vanir families. But in the world of the Aesir, everything is built on hierarchy, including the concept of "family." This difference in understanding and defining "own-other" found a vivid reflection in the story of Freyr.

His appearance in legendary narratives as a hero began after the death of the god Baldr. His main legend is Skirnismol. It all began when the god Freyr, for some unknown reason, sat on a throne that only the god Odin had the right to occupy. From this throne, one could see all the worlds, and nothing was hidden from the All-Father's gaze. Let's read from the Skirnismol in the Poetic Edda:

Freyr, the son of Njorth, had sat one day in Hlithskjolf, and looked over all the worlds. He looked into Jotunheim, and saw there a fair maiden, as she went from her father's house to her bower. Forthwith he felt a mighty love-sickness. Skirnir was the name of Freyr's servant; Njorth bade him ask speech of Freyr. He said:

"Go now, Skirnir! and seek to gain
Speech from my son;
And answer to win, for whom the wise one
Is mightily moved."

Skirnir spake:
"Ill words do I now await from thy son,

If I seek to get speech with him,
And answer to win, for whom the wise one
Is mightily moved."

Skirnir spake:
"Speak prithee, Freyr, foremost of the gods,
For now I fain would know;
Why sittest thou here in the wide halls,
Days long, my prince, alone?"

Freyr spake:
"How shall I tell thee, thou hero young.
Of all my grief so great ?
Though every day the elfbeam[44] *dawns.*
It lights my longing never."

Skirnir spake:
"Thy longings, methinks,
are not so large
That thou mayst not tell them to me;
Since in days of yore we were young together.
We two might each other trust."
Freyr spake:
"From Gymir's house I beheld go forth
A maiden dear to me;
Her arms glittered, and from their gleam
Shone all the sea and sky.

"To me more dear than in da)'s of old

---

[44] Elfbeam - sun

Was ever maiden to man;
But no one of gods or elves will grant
That we both together should be."

What Odin would perceive as information about the state of other worlds, Freyr, based on his nature, filtered through his own relationship: liked/disliked. Vanir power believes that all desires must be fulfilled; there are no and cannot be prohibitions before the power of love and the force of all-consuming passion - so says nature, which lives according to its own laws, where there is no place for tradition and morality. Passion is so strong, and desire is so great that Freyr, without a moment's doubt that this is right, gives his servant his only weapon, his sword.

Arriving at the house of the beautiful maiden, Skirnir tries to bribe her, then threatens with murder, and afterwards - with a curse. The latter was a terrible threat for Gerdr, and she agreed.

Gerth spake:
"Barri there is, which we both know well,
A forest fair and still;
And nine nights hence to the son of Njorth
Will Gerth there grant delight."

After the successful completion of the courtship, Skirnir did not think to return the sword to its owner. According to rumours, the sword ended up in the halls of the giant Surt, and according to legend, only this weapon could help deal with the power of the fire giants of Muspelheim when the time of Ragnarök battle comes. Here's how Snorri writes about it in the Prose Edda:

ᛊ ᛞ

This is the reason why Frey was unarmed when he fought with Bele, and slew him with a hart's horn. Then said Ganglere: It is a great wonder that such a lord as Frey would give away his sword, when he did not have another as good. A great loss it was to him when he fought with Bele; and this I know, forsooth, that he must have repented of that gift. Har answered: Of no great account was his meeting with Bele[45]*. Frey could have slain him with his hand. But the time will come when he will find himself in a worse plight for not having his sword, and that will be when the sons of Muspel sally forth to the fight.*

During the battle of Ragnarök, the giant Surt and his warriors entered the battle last. Freyr, as the force of life, as the passion for life, as the process of reproduction and self-restoration of nature, was the only force that could oppose the all-consuming primal fire. But Freyr had nothing to oppose his adversary except himself, and he perished.

In the Lokasenna, Loki did not miss reproaching him for this event:

Loki spake:
"The daughter of Gymir with gold didst thou buy,
And sold thy sword to boot;
But when Muspell's sons through Myrkwood[46] *ride.*
Thou shalt weaponless wait, poor wretch."

---

[45] Bele (Old Norse: Beli) — in Scandinavian mythology, a giant (jötunn) slain by the god Freyr.

[46] Myrkwood — "dark forest," a border forest located somewhere to the south.

Freyr lost his weapon only because that was dictated by his nature: it automatically set priorities, determining what was most important and what was not. The nature of the god of fertility did not allow him to see in his servant Skirnir a thief and deceiver—such concepts do not exist among the Vanir, as they do not exist in nature. Although the gods repeatedly told Njord's son that his servant was not entirely worthy to be alongside a god like him, the boundless generosity of the Vanir did not allow them to see this.

However, in the same "Lokasenna," Freyr was defended by the noblest god Tyr:

Tyr spake:
"Of the heroes brave is Freyr the best
Here in the home of the gods;
He harms not maids nor the wives of men,
And the bound from their fetters he frees."

What about the love story of the god Freyr? Fortunately, it had a happy ending: Gerdr fell in love with the god of fertility. However, she did not become an ásynja. Their home is described as a very small space right where they first met, in the forest of Barri, not far from Vanaheimr. There, Gerdr has a small apothecary garden where she grows medicinal herbs. "Little court," which is the home of the young lovers among the gods, tells us a lot. Firstly, their abode is not in Asgard, indicating that this marriage, as Freyr initially suspected, was not "approved" by the Æsir. Secondly, such a union between the ancient memory of Gerdr and the fertility of Freyr was limited to a small corner of reality, shielded from external influence. Moreover, the home of Gerdr and Freyr represents an exception to the general rules of existence in the worlds: the ancient memory of the giantess and the now defenceless Vanir nature form a special type of magical existence, where ancient and eternal memory can safely manifest in its own form of magic. The Vanir nature of the god Freyr can perform the function of a god of light, but always within a very limited space. His power allows him to see something phenomenal in the worlds, something that has passed "natural selection" and proven its right to exist. However, Odin's throne, the throne of the supreme god, is not meant for this: the god who knows good and evil will maintain balance in the system of world order among all that exists, not just the phenomenal. Freyr sees his own, but Odin sees more. Therefore, the throne of Hlidskjalf is meant for Odin and only for him. Remember this — Freyr's channel and his power are not for authority. It is for something else.

Myths tell us that the god Freyr has many residences in the realms of Vanaheimr and Alfheimr, but he does not have his own halls in the world of Asgard. This means that his presence in the world of nature will be constant, but in the world of law, his "database" does not exist, just as there is no permanence of his presence among the Æsir gods.

Losing the sword is certainly a catastrophe, but the sword is not the only artifact that gave the god Freyr additional power. There are two other items presented to him by the dvergar craftsmen during the famous "masters' contest," which was provoked by the god Loki. Freyr was given the boar Gullinbursti ("golden bristles") and the ship Skidbladnir. Both of these artifacts enabled the god of fertility to be more agile: the boar shone in darkness like the sun and could move very swiftly, while the ship always catches favourable winds, can accommodate all the gods, and when folded, as small as a

handkerchief, fits in a pocket. All these "power-ups" also make Freyr a god of luck, not just a deity of abundance.

Practice 11. God Freyr (page 499)

Freyja-Vanadis

The goddess Freyja is often called the goddess of love. However, a proper understanding of her power reveals that it's not about love as an emotion, but rather about love as a natural, instinctive drive towards self-preservation. This drive could be termed as sexual passion, but that would be an inaccurate term: continuing oneself can occur in various ways, not just through children. Freyja embodies the unrestrained force of manifestation in any form. Therefore, at the foundation of any trace left in the fabric of reality by gods and humans alike lies the power of the goddess Freyja.

Here's what Snorri Sturluson writes about this goddess in the Prose Edda:

The sixth is Freyja, who is ranked with Frigg. She is wedded to the man whose name is Oder; their daughter's name is Hnos[47]*, and she is so fair that all things fair and precious are called, from her name, Hnos. Oder went far away. Freyja weeps for him, but her tears are red gold. Freyja has many names, and the reason therefor is that she changed her name among the various nations to which she came in search of Oder. She is called*

[47] Hnos - "treasure".

ᛊ ᛞ

Mardol, Horn[48]*, Gefn, and Syr*[49]*. She has the necklace Brising, and she is called Vanadis.*

By bringing the goddess Freyja into their halls, the Æsir obtained the greatest treasure, allowing them greater freedom in implementing their own algorithms of reality construction. Freyja strengthened Asgard with the power of nature, which is never present in artificial systems. Naturalness is the foundation of voluntary acceptance, the impulse for change without fear, and development with joy. Freyja helped the gods-architects initiate the process of continuity: the Vanir nature, subject to natural cycles, depends solely on these cycles, which in turn are closed unto themselves.

It is difficult to apply exclusively one expressive form to describe the nature of the goddess Freyja. She manifests herself in many facets, yet all her forms do not exceed the limits of natural effects. Freyja, daughter of the Vanir, is an unrestrained thirst for life manifested in any form.

Freyja was truly considered the kindest goddess. She does not refuse anyone's request, hears everyone consumed by desire, feels everyone experiencing longing, understands anyone driven by passion—because all these are her feelings, her strength. In the well-known saga "Thrymskvitha" (The Poetic Edda), where Thor so disastrously lost his famous Mjölnir, Freyja emerges as the main heroine of the story, although the main adventures do not actually fall to her. But everything revolves around her: she is the cause of what happened to Thor; it was her decision that determined how Thor's journey with

---

48 Hœn - "giver" or "bestower".

49 Syr - "swine" or "pig".

ᚠ ᚨ

Loki to Jötunheimr would go and, most importantly, in what role. Initially, everything was quite peaceful: Thor, upon discovering the loss, at Loki's suggestion, turned to the goddess Freyja:

To the dwelling fair of Freyja went they.
Hear now the speech that first he spake :
"Wilt thou, Freyja, thy feather-dress lend me,
That so my hammer I may seek?"

Freyja spake:
"Thine should it be though of silver bright,
And I would give it though 'twere of gold."

However, the goddess's kindness has limits. Her kindness is not simplicity. Her kindness is not foolishness. Being kind does not mean being powerless, and the goddess of nature quickly proved this to those who mistakenly thought otherwise.

Freyja the fair then went they to find;
Hear now the speech that first he spake:
"Bind on, Freyja, the bridal veil,
For we two must haste to the giants home."*

Wrathful was Freyja, and
fiercely she snorted.
And the dwelling great of the gods was shaken,
And burst was the mighty Brisings' necklace:
"Most lustful indeed should I look to all
If I journeyed with thee to the giants' home."

Angered nature is serious. It is so serious that resorting to violence against it to achieve one's goals is the last thing that should come to mind for anyone who thoughtlessly believed that such a path was the path of least resistance. It was precisely this oversight that caused both Thor and Loki, in retrieving Thor's hammer, to undergo humiliating trials—so that henceforth such misadventures would not occur again. Anyone who thinks that wearing women's clothing justifies violence should try it on themselves. Nature either gives its gifts willingly or not at all. Attempting to take something from it forcibly risks the violent losing everything they possess—Freyja is merciless to such individuals.

Many Jötnar dreamed of possessing the goddess capable of doing anything for the living. The giant who undertook to build the walls of Asgard also bargained for nothing less than her, Freyja. Even the goal of the giant Thrym, who stole Thor's hammer Mjölnir, was openly stated:

Thrym spake:
"I have hidden
Hlorrithi's hammer.
Eight miles down deep in the earth ;
And back again shall no man bring it
If Freyja I win not to be my wife."

The giants' interest in Freyja lies not only in her astonishing beauty—such an explanation is understandable and fitting for humans, but myth is not just a fairy tale. It is primarily a magical description of the processes and mechanisms of constructing reality. From the perspective of such a description, it becomes clear that without the force of nature, without the ceaseless urge for reproduction, the value of any wealth diminishes. If some element does not participate in the cyclical natural rhythms, the value of that element inevitably tends towards zero. The Jötnar are carriers and keepers of ancient memory, long memory, continuous memory. But what worth does this memory hold if it has nowhere to manifest?

The most legendary tale about Freyja is the story of her journey where she acquired the Brísingamen necklace. The authentic version of the legend has not yet surfaced to this day, but there are numerous later retellings from the Middle Ages.

The Brísingamen necklace—this famous treasure, which in one older monument is still referred to as the "Belt of Brísinga." It came into the possession of the goddess Freyja as a result of a fair deal with the master dwarves, the brothers Brísingar, named Dvalinn, Berlingr, Grerr, and Álfrigg. In exchange for four nights with the goddess, they crafted this unique artifact, which was not only beautiful but also greatly enhanced the power of the goddess of love and joy of life. As we already know, the dvergar masters had the unique ability to see precisely what was lacking in those who approached them until they achieved genuine completeness. Freyja, whose goal in this journey was to find her missing part[50], came to the masters who could perceive vulnerability and compensate for it like no one else. What they did for the goddess Freyja was something that made her whole, and therefore free. In magic, it is believed that Brísingamen is a tool for controlling all four elements: Fire, Earth, Water, and Air. Upon receiving this artifact, Freyja became the goddess of Freedom.

---

50 In legend, this is expressed as the search for her missing husband, Óðr. The name "Óðr" can be loosely translated as "spirit," "inspiration," or simply "power." Some sagas say that he was a man.

ᛊ ᛞ

It should be noted that not all the Æsir were pleased with such empowerment of Freyja. In particular, the god Loki once stole this necklace, but it was Heimdallr, precisely him, who returned it to Freyja, thus ritually affirming her right to own this artifact and possess the degree of freedom that rightfully belonged to the goddess. It's also advisable not to take the deal with the Brísingar brothers "nights" literally. For the Vanir worldview, a given night is a ritual act of union, mutual exchange of properties. So, the dvergar received from Freyja not just satisfaction of their desires, but something greater: what the Vanir had in abundance—the ability to follow their own desires and respect their nature. This quality was always lacking in the dvergar race, despite their unique mastery; they did not understand the value of their craftsmanship. Perhaps it was this property received from the goddess that allowed the dwarves subsequently not to participate in Ragnarök? And perhaps this is why Loki was so furious, trying to take away Freyja's rightful artifact—because suddenly the ability to freely control the actions of the dvergar disappeared, as it had been before? Now the dwarves knew the true value of their work, gained a sense of self-worth, and the goddess Freyja rediscovered the true magic of the Vanir, from which she had been partially cut off after the hostage exchange with Asgard.

In all the stories that have entered into northern narratives and in some way touch upon the goddess Freyja, there is one common feature: nowhere and never is it mentioned or even hinted that the goddess owes anything to anyone. Everything she possesses belongs solely to her and rightfully so. Everything she acquires, she acquires on her own and for herself. This distinctive trait prominently characterizes the phenomenal property of natural power: she depends on no one and needs nothing from anyone. If Freyja's Vanir power does something

ᚠ ᚨ

for others, it happens purely out of her goodwill, not out of obligation or duty. Freyja expected nothing from the Æsir initially and therefore remained completely free from their demands. She did not marry any of the Æsir, did not give any of them marital vows or promises. She did not accept gifts from Loki, and when she needed help from the dwarves, she arranged everything herself—negotiated and settled matters on her own.

Such freedom is only available to those who possess real power, who rightfully possess it, and who do not need to prove or fight for it. But most importantly, to maintain, protect, and multiply one's strength and freedom, there must be no debt, no obligations, no sense of guilt, and no sense of inferiority—only in this way can one preserve their strength and freedom. Freyja's brother failed to retain the "right of the strong," losing his sword in the name of love and passion, and now his power can only be seen in the limited space of Gerdr's apothecary garden. Freyja, who has preserved her freedom, then and now continues to live in everything that can be called alive. This description now functions for people as an algorithm for achieving results: human desire is all-encompassing, but real results are obtained only where its "enclosed space[51]" exists.

The accusations Loki expressed towards the goddess Freyja, as with Njord and Freyr, primarily concerned the nature of the goddess. Essentially, Loki accuses the Vanir for being Vanir. His position is clear: Vanir influence harms the order system. And it's hard to argue with that—emotions will always struggle against reason, and vice versa:

---

[51] "Gerd" (Old Norse Gerðr) is derived from Old Norse "garðr," meaning "enclosure," "enclosed space," "yard," or "estate" (from T. Toporov's article "Speaking Names" in the Eddic poem "Skírnismál").

ᛊ ᛞ

Loki spake:
"Be silent, Freyja ! for fully I know thee,
Sinless thou art not thyself;
Of the gods and elves who are gathered here,
Each one as thy lover has lain."
(The Poetic Edda. Lokasenna)

The second accusation against Freyja pertains to the characteristics of Vanir magic, which are unacceptable and even hateful to the emerging patriarchal civilization:

Loki spake:
"Be silent, Freyja! thou foulest witch,
And steeped full sore in sin;
In the arms of thy brother the bright gods caught thee
When Freyja her wind set free."

Freyja—a witch. That's how it is. Vanir magic—seiðr magic. Unlike the magic of the Æsir, known as "galdr," seiðr magic is based on ancient fertility cults, which involve dissolving one's consciousness into natural processes, stimulating natural currents of forces. Whereas galdr is based on command and control: galdr is akin to a system of commands designed to manage processes through informational influence on reality (runes, runic staves, verses, spells)—it's masculine, aggressive magic. Seiðr is divination, foresight; it's not about changing the world to fit oneself but changing oneself to fit the world.

Seiðr is the use of natural power for local adjustments, it is the dissolution of one's consciousness in power to be able to feel this world as oneself. Seiðr is feminine magic. Galdr is masculine. It is intended to capture currents of forces, to redirect

ᚠ ᚩ

them along the desired vector; seiðr is for dissolving into these currents, a natural transition between them, without altering their direction or original meaning. Galdr commands the world to change, while seiðr is a covenant to change with the world. Legends describe that Odin and Freyja taught each other magic: Odin taught Freyja runes and galdr, and Freyja taught Odin seiðr.

Odin understood also the art in which the greatest power is lodged, and which he himself practised; namely, what is called magic. By means of this he could know beforehand the predestined fate of men, or their not yet completed lot; and also bring on the death, ill–luck, or bad health of people, and take the strength or wit from one person and give it to another. (The Ynglinga Saga[52]).

This is precisely what Loki reproached his blood-brother for: for him, it was inconceivable and offensive that the conquering god did not subdue nature, did not change it through command, but studied it with methods accepted from its children, nature:

Loki spake:
"They say that with spells in Samsey[53] once
Like witches with charms didst thou work;
And in witch's guise among men didst thou go ;

---

52 The Ynglinga Saga (Old Norse: Ynglinga saga) — presumably written between 1220-1230. The author of the saga is Snorri Sturluson. The saga belongs to the so-called royal sagas and is the first part of Snorri's collection "Heimskringla."

53 Samsey — the Danish island of Samso, north of Funen. What Odin did there is unknown from other sources. In any case, the accusation of sorcery was as offensive as the accusation of "womanliness," since sorcery was considered a feminine occupation. (Translator's note)

Unmanly thy soul must seem."

(The Poetic Edda. Lokasenna)

Perhaps Sleipnir, the eight-legged horse, Loki's offspring whom he gifted to Odin, is in some sense an attempt to substitute in Odin the need for Vanir magic, the Vanir way of traveling between worlds — Sleipnir granted the god Odin such an opportunity without involving the Vanir method of dissolution.

Recognizable as Freyja's image — a chariot drawn by cats. Cats — amazing creatures, witches' assistants capable of living in multiple worlds simultaneously. This is their quality, along with the falcon-feathered goddess aiding her in freely traveling between worlds[54]. The goddess also has her own halls, which speak of her independence and right to form her own rules of reality construction, accumulating her own algorithms of victory:

The ninth is Folkvang[55], where Freyja decrees
Who shall have seats in the hall;
The half of the dead each day does she choose,
And half does Othin have.

(The Poetic Edda. Grimnismol)

Folkvang — Freyja's personal Valhalla. Within these halls, there is yet another called Sessrúmnir, "ship in the field."

---

[54] However, some researchers believe that lynxes, not cats, were harnessed to the goddess's chariot. Some lean towards the idea that they were martens. Investigations continue.

[55] Folkvang — "field of the troops" or "field of the people."

ᛊ ᛞ

However, besides the hall in Asgard, Freyja has homes in each of the worlds. According to legend, her sisters live there, eight in total. The Vanir nature operates on the principle of "everything connected with everything," and kinship opens up all worlds to the goddess, where she will be mistress everywhere. She also enters Jötunheimr, where her friend, the goddess Hýndla, resides.

The Vanir's law, unlike the Aesir's, states that desire is the foundation of all endeavours. The Aesir's law insists that such a foundation can only be law itself. As Ragnarök showed, the Vanir were more correct than the Aesir. Nothing created artificially can exist eternally — nature will take its course. The power of the goddess Freyja teaches her children and followers always to remain true to their nature, not to the law. Law is only possible when it is not contrary to nature, when nature loves the law and agrees with it willingly. But no law, as the history of the goddess Freyja teaches, has the right to restrain passions and desires. So what if you are not given something by birth or social status? This is not a reason to not pursue your dreams, to not pursue your passion exactly as the goddess walked through the worlds for her beloved Óðr. The main thing is to rely only on oneself, to love without looking back, and to fear nothing.

During Ragnarök, the goddess Freyja stands shoulder to shoulder with the Aesir and Vanir, sharing their fate and the bitterness of defeat. For, as said many thousands of years later by the god Völund through the mouth of his manifestation, the messir Volund: "He who loves must share the fate of the one he loves."

Practice 12. Goddess Freyja (p. 504)

ᚹ ᚠ

The vector of understanding the channel of the Vanir gods is becoming more refined and precise with each step we take now. The powerful and all-encompassing force of the god Njord was divided among his children, the gods Freyr-Ingvi and Freyja-Vanadis. In this division, the power acquired specific qualities, becoming more concentrated but also more applied. The two goddesses of the Vanir lineage, whom we will meet next, continue this trend — further specifying function and refining the area of application of the personified force of nature. However, this is not the only reason we will consider them now and together. The personas of the goddesses Sif and Idunn will show us two phenomenal extremes of the Vanir channel, which, like any extremes, are simultaneously their strength and their weakness.

We will examine the channels of the goddesses Sif and Idunn together, but not because they are small or insignificant in their power. Rather, it is because only through simultaneous understanding of these channels can you also comprehend the limits of Vanir powers: how they manifest in certain aspects of the psyche, what possibilities they reveal, and which ones they, due to their presence, obscure.

Let us get acquainted with them.

Sif and Idunn

There is not much written about the goddesses Sif and Idunn in the legends. The chronicles, especially the Prose Edda, obviously aimed to glorify the Æsir, emphasizing the primacy of the will of law over natural forces and various "dark powers." For this reason, perhaps, they paid little attention to these two goddesses, providing only scant information about them. However, unlike many peoples who, with the same objective, tried to completely expel or at least slander the nature gods from folk memory, the northern people did not allow this. For us, their descendants, this is valuable because if there were no information about these two goddesses at all, it would now be very difficult to understand the essence of the Vanir, to understand the characteristics of the nature gods, and through this understanding, revive them within ourselves in the full extent of their strength, power, and capabilities.

The goddesses Sif and Idunn do not participate in the adventures of the Æsir gods; their characters do not transition from one legend to another. However, each of them has exactly one significant description in the northern myth.

ᛊ ᛞ

Sif

It is said that the goddess Sif was the wife of the god Thor. They have a daughter named Thrud, and she also has an illegitimate child—the god Ullr. The myth emphasizes Sif's beautiful golden hair and mentions that "Sif's hair" is a kenning for gold. Nowhere in the myths is it specifically stated that the golden-haired goddess was a Vanir, but the fact that she was a goddess of fertility suggests this. The story of the giant Hrungnir in the Prose Edda also leads to the idea of Sif's Vanir nature, when the giant visited the halls of Asgard unsuccessfully and was killed by Thor's hammer:

They then took the bowls that Thor was accustomed to drink from, and Hrungner emptied them all. When he became drunk, he gave the freest vent to his loud boastings. He said he was going to take Valhal and move it to Jotunheim, demolish Asgard and kill all the gods except Freyja and Sif, whom he was going to take home with him.

The fact that the old jötunn equates these two goddesses suggests their kinship; knowing the great need of the jötnar for Vanir goddesses, the saga shows that this kinship lies in the Vanir nature of both. The goddess Sif was revered as the goddess of the hearth, fertile land, and a prosperous home; she appears in ancient cults as a goddess-guardian of the family. Her name (Sif) is closely related to the word "sib," meaning "kin," "kin group." This indicates that she is significantly a deity of the family, a

ᚹ ᚠ

ᛊ ᛞ

guardian of the home and family, and shows herself more as a dís, a Vanir power.

Thus, the name of the goddess Sif can be translated as "kinship." But, paradoxically, nowhere in the sagas are her parents or her kin mentioned; the focus is solely on her being the wife of the thunder god Thor. Although the name of the goddess and her functional power of fertility suggest that she should be the protector of long kinship ties and carry the memory of this. But there is no mention of it.

The limitation of the powers of both goddesses was primarily carried out by the well-known god Loki. Attempts to limit the will and freedom of the elder Vanir—Njord, Freyr, or Freyja—were unsuccessful, but he more than made up for this failure by impacting the goddesses Sif and Idunn. Vanir nature is something that needs to be controlled, according to the gods of law. This force, by itself, is hard to control, and its principle is simple: either willingly or not at all. The war between Asgard and Vanaheimr demonstrated that force cannot subdue the Vanir. Therefore, the Aesir needed to find another mechanism of control. And they found it: through marriage bonds, love, and friendship. However, Loki did not think this was sufficient. A god who embodies not only the strength of the Jotunn's long memory but also the power of the fire giants of Muspell has his own principles. His principle is as simple as that of the Vanir: either all or nothing. Unable to take complete control of the entire power of Vanaheimr, Loki reasonably concluded that if he could control certain aspects of the Vanir, it would be easier to manage their other attributes. After all, the defining characteristic of Vanir nature is that everything is interconnected. Loki, more than anyone else, knows how to turn weaknesses into strengths and vice versa.

ᛊ ᛞ

The strength of the goddess Sif was expressed in her hair. Long, beautiful hair the colour of gold, the colour of ripe wheat, was not only a source of pride in her feminine beauty but also a symbol of freedom. In a deeper sense, long hair signifies a connection to kin, not only symbolically but also magically. This means that the goddess Sif, even while in Asgard rather than Vanaheimr, always had the ability through her natural "tool" to maintain a connection with her maternal world, to always draw strength from it, to always receive its support.

The fact that the goddess was the wife of the god Thor was, in Loki's opinion, a vulnerability for all the Aesir—Thor loves his wife, which means he is, to some extent, dependent on her. Loki had to point out this vulnerability—this is his nature. The story of how Sif lost her hair is told in the section dedicated to the trickster god. Now let's look at this story from the opposite perspective.

The loss of hair signifies the loss of the rights of freedom according to the laws of the time to which this mythological description pertains. Hair was cut off from slaves, hair was cut off from unfaithful wives. Loki punished Sif for adultery, and the infidelity occurred not with just anyone, but with Loki[56] himself. But for him, this is insignificant. What matters is that the goddess Sif is a Vanir, driven by her Vanir nature, and this nature compels her always to follow her desires and nothing else. This extremity of nature, inherent to all children of nature, was recognized, identified, and eliminated by Loki.

The artificial hair of Sif, obtained by Loki from the dvergar, although it looked real and instantly adhered to the

---

56 From her union with Loki, Sif gave birth to a child — the furry infant Ullr, whom Sif quickly got rid of, but the story of him and his role in the development of the northern system is yet to come.

goddess's head as if it had always been there, was still artificial. This means that it no longer performed its original function, and the connection with the world of the Vanir for the goddess was no longer maintained through this tool. Perhaps now it connects to the world of the Svartálfar? Maybe, but that's not a problem—the world of Svartalfheim is controlled by the Aesir. Although this control was somewhat weakened by the goddess Freyja, as we already know, at the time the artifact for Sif was created, it was so. The goddess of the fertile harvest, Sif, now symbolizes not the power of natural, organic fertility, but that which is the result of knowledge and others' labour. Now she can be symbolized as the goddess of selection, the goddess of modified nature. Such nature will always depend on who creates it and who protects it. Without additional care, without special, artificial, rather than naturally organic development, this nature will simply perish.

The goddess Sif, having the support of her tribe, became disconnected from the source of Vanir magic and lost the knowledge of the value of this source. Following her desires, which were so protected by the god Thor, she saw no threat in anyone or anything. This is a characteristic of one of the Vanir extremes—selfishness, one of the ultimate traits personified by the goddesses of the Vanir lineage. Being essentially unfree, though beloved, yet still a part of her great husband, she could neither protect herself nor compensate for her natural extremity with an opposing force, as Freyja could. Thor loves the selfish Sif, so why should Sif be different? Thor protects the beautiful Sif, so why should Sif become strong? And all would be well, but Sif is Thor's wife, and Thor is the protector of the Æsir. He protected the borders of the Nine Worlds, protected the edges of the world just as he protected Sif, who is also, in her own way, a boundary and an extremity. And in Loki's opinion, she should remain so. For the common good, of course, and nothing personal.

This story of Sif's hair is very multifaceted. It needs to be carefully studied by those who have understood their power and recognized it as stemming from the Vanir channel. Power is vulnerable due to its carelessness on the one hand, and its tendency to fall into extremes on the other. But if power begins to get used to having someone (or something) to rely on, it can enter this state and stick to some extremity. The goddess Sif's story is about a natural witch who followed her desires, got stuck in the extremity of selfishness because she had someone to protect her. By cutting off Sif's hair, Loki fixed her in this state; he fixed it by depriving her of her connection to the source and made her constant—for Thor, for the gods, for Asgard. Not faithful, mind you, but constant: now Sif has no other protector than the Æsir Thor, and she is cut off from her kin.

The goddess Sif, her story, and her tragedy represent the path that every witch undergoes when forced to sever ties with her natural magical roots. But Sif has a daughter named Thrud (or Thrund, or Frud), and her name means "power." She is the only daughter of Thor and Sif[57], a witch named Thrud. She lives in her own halls, and these halls are a magical tower, where Thrud allows no one except her half-brothers, the heirs of Mjolnir, Magni and Modi. She is hidden from everyone but can be present anywhere: she might be riding the subway with you, sitting at the same desk, giving you an injection in the hospital, or selling you milk in a store. Or perhaps she is you. Because Thrud is any woman of witch descent who has lost her

57 The god Thor has two other sons—Modi and Magni, but their story will be discussed later.

connection to her roots. She lives within the system, protected by the system, but the most valuable thing she has is her own tower of consciousness, where she continually tries to restore her bloodline, to restore her memory. This task was given to the goddess Thrud by her mother, the goddess Sif—she bequeathed to her daughter the knowledge of what not to do. She raised her in hatred, not towards men, but towards vulnerability in front of men. Vulnerability to deception, even if that deception is beneficial to everyone. The goddess Sif passed on to her daughter the knowledge of the vulnerabilities of Vanir nature.

The modern urban witch, blending into society, must learn from the mistakes of her ancestors and correct them. The extreme trait of the Vanir nature of the goddess Sif—selfishness—must be transformed by the strength and blood of her daughter into the ability to still follow her desires without relying on anyone, trusting no one, and highly valuing each step taken. These steps, though slow, steadily restore her conncction with her natural power. Sif symbolizes a woman who loves herself more than others, while Thrud symbolizes a woman who hates herself less than others. Thrud's selfishness is hidden from the eyes of others within an inner tower of magical transformations. This trait is a ripening philosopher's stone in the darkness, destined to turn the base into the noble, but only when the time is right. According to the Norse legend, this time will come after the battle of the gods, Ragnarök, when a new world will be reborn for the children of the Aesir and Vanir, and the young gods will take control of reality based on entirely different principles.

ᛊ ᛞ

Idunn

The other extreme of the Vanir channel is symbolized by the goddess Idunn—absolute altruism. Her name means "renewal" or "green again." In the sagas, the goddess Idunn is described as a very young girl, almost a child. The story of her origin can be gleaned only from a fleeting mention in the Poetic Edda's song "Odin's Raven Magic" (or " HRAFNAGALDUR ÓÐINS").

Dwells in dales,
the curious dís,
from Yggdrasill's
ash descended;
Of elven kin,
Iðunn was her name,
youngest of Ívald's
elder children.

We are already familiar with the dverg Ivaldi. He is the master who, together with his brothers, forged Sif's hair, Odin's spear Gungnir, and Freyr's ship Skidbladnir. The fact that she is called "*dís… of elven kin*" also points to her Vanir origin as a nature spirit. This combination of unique craftsmanship and the power of constantly renewing nature, eternal life, and return to youth can be said to make this young maiden older than many gods and a force of regeneration.

She is married to Odin's son, the god Bragi. Here is what Snorri writes about her in the Prose Edda:

ᚹ ᚠ

Brage is the name of another of the asas. <…> His wife is Idun. She keeps in a box those apples of which the gods eat when they grow old, and then they become young again, and so it will be until Ragnarök (the twilight of the gods).

The marriage of Idunn and Bragi is more of a union of friends than lovers. They do not have the unity and mutual complementarity that those united by the power of love and passion possess; in the union of Bragi and Idunn, there is mutual support of two self-sufficient forces.

Idunn's power is the power of youth, expressed in the other extreme of Vanir nature—endless altruism. But this extreme, unlike the opposite trait of Sif's selfishness, can live without support. However, support cannot live without it. This is illustrated in the only complete myth where the goddess Idunn is the main heroine. This myth is called "The Abduction of Idunn[58]." The story goes that Loki was once captured by the giant Thjazi and was on the verge of losing his life. But Thjazi agreed to spare Loki and let him go if he brought the goddess Idunn to him:

He calls and prays the eagle most earnestly for peace, but the latter declares that Loke shall never get free unless he will pledge himself to bring Idun and her apples out of Asgard. <…> But at the time agreed upon, Loke coaxed Idun out of Asgard into a forest, saying that he had found apples that she would think very nice, and he requested her to take with her her own apples in order to compare them. Then came the giant Thjasse in the guise of an eagle, seized Idun and flew away with her to his home in Thrymheim. The asas were ill at ease on account of the disappearance of Idun,———they became gray–haired and old. They met in council and asked

58 Is a part of the Prose Edda (" Idun and Her Apples").

each other who last had seen Idun. The last that had been seen of her was that she had gone out of Asgard in company with Loke. Then Loke was seized and brought into the council, and he was threatened with death or torture. But he became frightened, and promised to bring Idun back from Jotunheim if Freyja would lend him the falcon–guise that she had. He got the falcon–guise, flew north into Jotunheim, and came one day to the giant Thjasse. Thegiant had rowed out to sea, and Idun was at home alone. Loke turned her into the likeness of a nut, held her in his claws and flew with all his might.

The Prose Edda then continues with the story of Thjazi, but we need to know what happened next with the goddess Idunn. The continuation of her story is found in "Odin's Raven Magic":

Ill she endured
the fall from above,
under the hoar-tree's
trunk confined;
Disliked staying
at Nörvi's daughter's,
used to better
abodes back home[59]."

Whether Idunn was in Thjazi's halls for a long time or a short time, it did not benefit her. Returned to Asgard, the goddess "lay dead," and no one could bring her back to

---

59 The language of the northern skalds is intricate, and the poetic gift of Bragi, which the translators of the Poetic Edda have mastered, has not touched this song. But this makes the deciphering of the legend all the more interesting and the understanding more valuable.

consciousness[60]. The world of Jotunheim, the world of ancient memory, proved fatal for the goddess of eternal youth. It was so opposite to the world of life in Vanaheimr and the world of the light elves in Alfheimr, with such different energy, that a child of nature like her could not exist on such vibrations. And Odin, the all-seeing god, was the only one who understood what was happening.

The divinities see
Nauma grieving
in the wolf's home;
given a wolf-skin, l
she clad herself therein,
changed disposition,
delighted in guile,
shifted her shape.

Viðrir[61] selected
Bifröst's[62] guardian
to inquire of
the bearer of Gjöll's sun,
whatever she knew
of the world's affairs;
Bragi and Loftur
bore witness[63].

---

60 According to one interpretation, Loki failed to transform her back from the form of a nut to her original goddess form.

61 Viðrir — the ruler, a heiti of Odin.

62 Bifrost — a heiti of Heimdall.

63 Translation by Gunivortus Goos.

He sent Idunn's husband, the god Bragi, along with Heimdall and Loki, to the world of the Vanir so they could bring something from Idunn's homeland that would help her restore her connection to her world and free her from the deadly memory of Jotunheimr. "Odin's Raven Magic" states that Idunn was wrapped in a wolf's skin. The wolf might have been the totem of her tribe, and through this, the connection was restored. Once again, we see how important the connection to one's ancestral roots is for those who have roots in the world of nature, where everything is interconnected. Odin saw this as well.

For the gods, everything ended well—they brought back Idunn, regained the apples, and regained their youth. But they also gained knowledge, and this knowledge was gifted to them by none other than the god Loki. By giving Idunn to the jötunn, Loki taught the gods a lesson, pointing out their carelessness—they had relied too easily on Vanir magic, putting themselves in dependence on it without much thought. For as soon as Idunn disappeared from Asgard, the gods began to age rapidly and were greatly troubled by it. Until that moment, had they not known they were dependent on the apples of youth provided by the power of the goddess Idunn? It is natural for the careless not to pay attention to what they always have! But now he also made Odin realize that the well-being of the gods of Asgard depended not on a specific god or goddess of the Vanir but on the entire world of Vanaheimr. He convinced him by example.

But let's return to the goddess Idunn. Her power and the fact that she is the only one who has access to the "elixir of the Aesir," the apples of youth, indicate that this goddess is far more than she appears to be. An ancient goddess of beauty, youth, and perhaps immortality, who retains the appearance of almost a child, suggests that her power will not be applied to her memory, ancient experience, or seniority. On the contrary, if this power of endless rejuvenation is applied to the memory of the past, the goddess of immortality becomes mortal. Her power is solely for life, solely for the future — and this is another indication of Idunn's Vanir nature — all Vanir have short memories by nature and function. They do not need long memories, and Idunn's story even clarifies that a long memory is deadly for the Vanir. This is what the legend of Idunn's abduction screams about: as soon as she found herself in the world of ancient memory, she began to die. For she cannot indefinitely grant the power of rebirth, the infinitely powerful and kind goddess of youth, by definition, but giving her power to what is poison for her kin, she perishes. Reviving the past is beyond her nature; Vanir blood only revives the future. This is precisely why her husband and companion is the god Bragi, the poet who gives hope, who awakens the desire for life, the will to live, and opens the doors to the future with his words.

Idunn's natural magic, her manifestation, does not require a long memory. She needs a connection with her primary power, not a memory of it, not knowledge of it. Therefore, Idunn herself could not tell the gods what exactly could save her — she did not know. But she felt that she was dying. Similarly, any natural witch might not know the "name" of her source of power, the name of her god-progenitor, but losing connection with the original source, she withers and dies if wise Odin does not find that magical skin that will awaken this power without even naming it. Humans need to know everything, but a Vanir witch needs to feel everything. Often, intuition — feeling — is the best knowledge and does not require words.

The property of the other facet of Vanir power — altruism, infinite kindness — has its vulnerability, and this vulnerability was vividly demonstrated by the god Loki: Vanir power cannot help but give, cannot help but rejuvenate ongoing processes. But if forced to rejuvenate the past, nothing will come of it — all will die: first nature, then the gods. If Idunn's power is used incorrectly, if this "system conflict" is allowed, the gods will never be able to exist without constantly paying homage to the Vanir. Idunn, like the cow Audhumla, nourishes with her magic only developing, growing worlds — only then will she be with the gods, she will be in Asgard. This knowledge "from Loki" should have redirected Asgard's aspirations: by frightening them with old age and, consequently, the shameful death by old age for the northerners, Loki formed the Aesir's success algorithm rule — do not feed the past, do not live for it. This means that the world of Asgard and the ruling gods must constantly develop, not relying on past successes, on past victories: those who live only in the past have no right to the future. How successful this escapade was in teaching the gods, we will learn further — the stories of the gods Frigg and Baldr will tell us about this.

For now, let's summarize our understanding of the Vanir power channel.

Thus, the two extremes and boundaries of natural power, personified by the goddesses Sif and Idunn, can be characterized by two psychological qualities—selfishness and altruism. These qualities are simultaneously present in the gods Freyr and Freyja, as more distinct forces compared to their father, the god Njord; in him, these qualities are not as prominently expressed as in his children. We can see that in the god Freyr, with the simultaneous manifestation of selfishness and altruism, there was still a certain bias towards selfishness—and this led to the limitation of his functionality by territory. In the goddess Freyja, this imbalance between the two extremes was initially also present but inclined towards altruism. However, she corrected it through the right quest, through the proper mystery of obtaining her necklace (belt) of power, Brísingamen, from the dvergar.

In the manifestation of the powers personified by the goddesses Sif and Idunn, the qualities of altruism or selfishness, when the Vanir nature is awakened, acquire characteristics of totality; there are practically no restraining tools that would bring these qualities to an acceptable norm, that would smooth out the conspicuous prominence of these traits. This, however, is quite expected, since we are talking about the Vanir—children of nature do not like limits, but this very fact becomes their limit.

The goddesses Sif and Idunn are even more personified forces of Vanir nature, even more refined and defined. Each of them embodies a Vanir trait of existence, but it is not as all-encompassing, strong, and independent in its manifestation as the traits of Freyr and Freyja. The attempt to find an explanation for the fact that both Freyr and Freyja, possessing pronounced qualities of selfishness and altruism, expressed them freely, but never got stuck in one particular state, whereas the goddesses Sif and Idunn were in such a stuck state, insists that the legends about all these gods be properly analysed and the difference in their described fates identified. And this difference is obvious: neither Freyr nor Freyja tied themselves in marriage to the gods of law, the Æsir, while both Sif and Idunn were their wives. The Æsir, as we remember, are informational principles, while the Vanir are natural forces. Information has the ability to change energy, transform it, and make power specific and suitable for something particular. In the legend, this is presented in the form of marriage, where the feminine Vanir nature joins with the masculine informational nature and becomes fixed and defined: a woman always becomes what she is wanted to be.

In the entire northern mythodrama, the goddess Freyja not only managed to maintain her freedom and magic but also significantly enhanced it. The god Freyr managed to preserve but not enhance. The goddesses Idunn and Sif were unable to preserve or enhance. This last fact demonstrates the successful algorithm of the Æsir in holding and subduing nature—the story of the goddesses Sif and Idunn describes this to us. For Sif's fertility, it is to sever the connection with the source of power, replace it with one that will be controlled, and determine the goal that the detached properties of nature will serve. For Idunn's eternal life and youth, it is to maintain the connection with the source of power but strictly ensure that it is never directed down the wrong path: what was, was, but it should not happen again. What helped Freyja independently maintain personal control over her natural extremes and not hand over the reins of managing them to the Æsir? Was it proximity to the god Njord? The presence of a connected force in the form of a twin brother? Or perhaps the fact that Freyja found the strength to realize her true position in Asgard and free herself from illusions—she understood that the position of the Vanir in the world of the gods was one of hostages, and essentially, slavery? This is a very important realization: the free do not value their freedom; only those who have lost it, who have become dependent, appreciate it. These are lessons that bearers of Vanir blood and spirit must learn in the human world, in Midgard, in the world of manifested reality.

The story of Sif and Idunn is the story of the Vanir's defeat before the Æsir, the tragedy of nature's defeat before the law. Although, if judged superficially, as is customary for the rational social layperson (i.e., only by external effects), the story does not appear as a defeat. Indeed, the Vanir goddesses are brought to Asgard; they are not officially considered hostages but came of their own free will; both goddesses are married to respected and revered Æsir gods—what more could one desire?

However, nevertheless, these are stories of the Vanir's defeat because the Æsir, with the help of the god Loki, found a way to control the power of the Vanir goddesses, understood the characteristics of Vanir nature through this, and the Æsir know the law: "knowledge is power," and power always relies on the limitation of freedom.

Without freedom, extremity is the only quality in which one can somehow exist, but this requires many conditions for such existence. The story of the goddesses Sif and Idunn is the tragedy of living magical nature when the law imposes a ban on its manifestation, and even if it allows it, it is always at the expense of diminishing freedom.

Practice 13. Sif and Idunn (p. 508)

The Æsir and the Vanir. Two powerful forces that came together in war and in love. Each side has its own truth. The separately and thoroughly understood channels of the Æsir gods and the Vanir gods will now prevent us from making the common (unfortunately) mistake of mixing the images of the goddesses Freyja and Frigg.

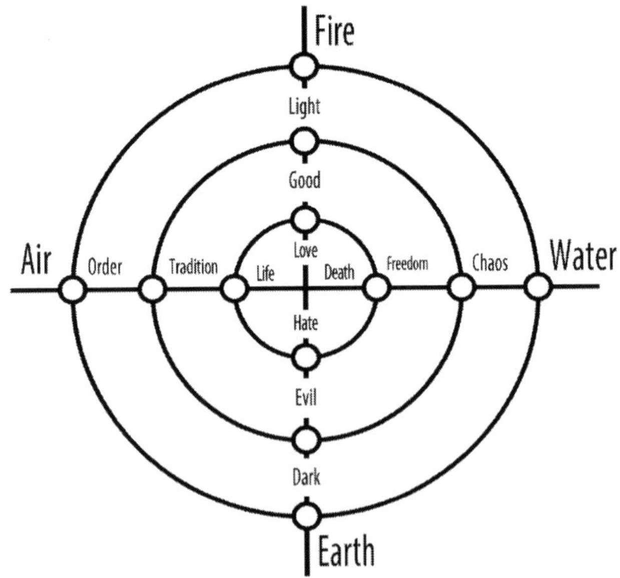

If we look at the magical scheme of the 3 circles, we can easily find the position of the goddess Freyja in the proto-foundation of Freedom.

Meanwhile, the goddess Frigg represents the proto-foundation of Tradition. The rules of functioning of the second circle of magical power affirm the law of balance through the binary: at this level, the proto-foundation of Good must be equal in informational power to the proto-foundation of Evil, and the proto-foundation of Tradition is balanced by the proto-foundation of Freedom. These are not opposing forces but forces that support each other. But only if they are within the framework of one system.

ᛊ ᛞ

Frigg

The rightful mistress of Asgard and the lawful wife of the god Odin. The position of the goddess Frigg in the entire system of northern mythology is very strong: the hierarchy of the system of law places her on the same level as the supreme god.

The proto-foundation of Tradition, which the goddess Frigg oversees, supports order, transforming primal principles into concrete rules, roles, and functions. This proto-foundation, like any other in the magical system of the 12 proto-foundations, is a repository of knowledge. However, it has certain limitations, which prevent the proto-foundation of Order from relying entirely on tradition or relying solely on it. The relationship between Odin and Frigg is precisely a description of such systemic interaction between two powerful informational structures.

In power and origin, Frigg is equal to Odin. But at the same time, according to the laws and rules of Asgard, the goddess Frigg occupies a certain hierarchical position, always being a step behind the figure of the All-Father. Not because she is lesser or her functional capabilities are not as strong, but because that is the original agreement, the rules of development of the system, which is their joint project. This fact is reflected in the real life of the northern peoples, who built their world according to the program of this myth: a woman was never (until the advent of Christianity) an oppressed being. The status of women in northern society was quite high; they had the right to own property, the right to inherit and dispose of it; women had the right to divorce, and their word in forming a marriage

ᚹ ᚨ

contract was significant and final. The main burden of responsibility and the right to make decisions, of course, lay on the man, but a woman's word could not be ignored and was often the exclusive initiating mechanism of events. Moreover, if a crime such as murder could be "redeemed" by a certain wergild in favor of the deceased's family, which prevented or halted the process of blood vengeance, the murder of a woman could not be redeemed by any amount of money, and the murderer was immediately declared an outlaw—this meant that he lost his property and anyone had the right to kill him without consequences. A woman did not act as a law-speaker at the general ting (folkmoot), provided she had a man who could do it for her, but she had the right to defend her interests, and this demand could not be ignored.

However, the position of the goddess Frigg in the hierarchy of the northern system is determined not only by the established tradition. On the contrary, tradition is a consequence of rules and principles; it arises from them, not the other way around, where rules and principles are derived from the manifest realities of a given moment. The principles that define the position of a wife as first and equal are very ancient and archaic. They originate from the oldest matriarchal system, when the concept of tradition was only just forming, defining its purpose—to preserve, maintain, and transmit. It is not surprising that the keepers of tradition automatically became women, and the goddesses who organize and patronize the family and kin order are female deities.

The origin of the goddess Frigg is very interesting for understanding the origin not only of this goddess but also of other Æsir gods. In the sagas, Frigg is called "daughter of Fjörgyn." Fjörgyn, as explained by the Prose Edda, is Earth, also known as Jörd. Mother Earth, the birthing mother, the mother of the gods. However, the god Thor is also called the son of Fjörgyn, which shows their kinship with Frigg—they are brother and sister[64]. Frigg is as ancient a force of the giants as the other gods born of Earth. She is a Titaness if we use Greek mythology terminology; an etin if we use the northern analogy.

The old tradition of the matriarchal era, mentioned at the very beginning of the story about the goddess Frigg, included one interesting rule. If something happened to a woman's husband—if he died or went missing—the woman had to (or had the right to) marry another of his blood relatives (a brother or, in extreme cases, a father). The children born in such a union were considered children of the bloodline, retaining all rights and inheritance of the deceased (missing) husband. Without knowing the science of genetics, ancient people understood that transitioning to another marriage in this way would continue the same bloodline, preventing any other mixing.

In the story of the goddess Frigg, there was such a case. When the god Odin did not return from another journey, and all waiting periods had passed, his wife, the goddess Frigg, united with his blood brothers Vili and Ve (yes, the very gods who created reality from the body of the primordial ancestor Ymir). The presence of two husbands instead of one missing one should not confuse you if you remember that this refers to the oldest matriarchal era, where the woman determined the right to choose a husband and their number. But it was precisely this adherence to the old matriarchal tradition that was blamed on

---

64 It can be assumed that in Scandinavian mythology there were two beings with the name Fjörgyn—one male and the other female, but with the same or similar name (Fjörgyn — female and Fjörgynn — male). (Note by G. Bedenko)

the goddess Frigg by her husband's blood brother, the god Loki, as reflected in the already known Lokasenna:

Loki spake:
"Be silent, Frigg! thou art Fjorgyn's wife,
But ever lustful in love;
For Vili and Ve, thou wife of Vithrir,
Both in thy bosom have lain."

Loki blamed Frigg not so much for being unfaithful to Odin, but for being the keeper of the tradition of the new world system created by the Æsir, while still acting according to the rules of the old familial tradition, built on the principles of matriarchy. Whereas the world of Asgard, the world of the new order, was paving the way and implementing the principles of a patriarchal structure of reality. But Frigg could not act differently from what the rule of the tradition she was born into dictated. Perhaps this is why in the new system she became the keeper of accumulated experience, the great spinner of human fates, and for those living within the tradition, she is the mother who births warriors.

In her womb, like in a cauldron of creation, the laws and rules of human social existence are formed. She collects in her halls what happens in the human world, and from these informational threads weaves the fabric of future destinies. In this fabric, there are no elements unknown to her; every thread is someone's life already lived, a word spoken, an action performed. Tradition takes everything into account but combines elements anew each time, creating a new pattern. The only limitation on Frigg's weaving is the rules of order, Odin's principles, and the boundaries of his capabilities. It is not the

ᛊ ᛞ

goddess Frigg who defines these boundaries, but she must certainly consider them.

Frigg and Odin are the two forces on which the entire system is built. They have children, three sons, their heirs. The eldest son is the blind god Höd, the embodiment of darkness. The second son is the god Baldr, the embodiment of light. The youngest son is Hermod, the god destined to become a messenger to the world of Helheimr. You will learn more about each of them later.

If we look at this narrative metaphysically and use occult terminology, we can say the following: Order and Tradition gave birth to Light and Dark[65], and then to what would connect them to each other. Light and darkness are inseparable from each other. Perhaps Baldr and Höd were originally twins, but there is no definitive mention of this in the Eddas.

The story begins with the god Baldr having terrible dreams. Here is how this myth is described in the Prose Edda:

The beginning of this tale is, that Balder dreamed dreams great and dangerous to his life. When he told these dreams to the asas they took counsel together, and it was decided that they should seek peace for Balder against all kinds of harm. So Frigg exacted an oath from fire, water, iron and all kinds of metal, stones, earth, trees, sicknesses, beasts and birds and creeping things, that they should not hurt Balder. When this was done and made known, it became the pastime of Balder and the asas that he should stand up at their meetings while some of them should shoot at him, others should hew at him, while others should throw stones at him; but no matter what they did, no harm came to him, and this seemed to all a great honor.

---

65 In many of the most ancient cosmological systems, it is described that first, Dark is born, and then Light appears after it.

ᚠ ᚨ

A mother's heart set priorities based on her love. It is bad when a mother gives one of her children more love than the others. But it is doubly bad when these children are gods. The keeper of tradition gravitates towards the power of light, the power of good. She gravitates and cares more for these than for the other forces in the system, her other children. The favored ones are forgiven more; the eyes always look at the favored ones from a certain angle, not noticing what others see. But if the gods once did this, now people do the same.

All the informational power of the goddess Frigg was directed towards protecting the bright Baldr. The fabric of reality that the goddess weaves is illuminated by the light of the good and beautiful god, and in this light, it looks magnificent. However, the pattern on this fabric starts to repeat. And the further it goes, the more noticeable this becomes. Everyone sees it. But the first to react to the effect of the repeating sameness was, of course, the god Loki.

When Loke, Laufey's son, saw this, it displeased him very much that Balder was not scathed. So he went to Frigg, in Fensal, having taken on himself the likeness of a woman. Frigg asked this woman whether she knew what the asas were doing at their meeting. She answered that all were shooting at Balder, but that he was not scathed thereby. Then said Frigg: Neither weapon nor tree can hurt Balder, I have taken an oath from them all. Then asked the woman: Have all things taken an oath to spare Balder? Frigg answered: West of Valhal there grows a little shrub that is called the mistletoe, that seemed to me too young to exact an oath from. Then the woman suddenly disappeared.

The strange reasoning of the goddess who knows the principle of event formation, who herself weaves the threads of

ᛊ ᛞ

fate into the patterns of the future. This is also mentioned in the famous "Lokasenna" of the Poetic Edda:

Freyja spake:
"Mad art thou, Loki, that known thou makest
The wrong and shame thou hast wrought;
The fate of all does Frigg know well,
Though herself she says it not."

The goddess keeps the fates written in secret and does not interfere with the sacred law of wyrd. But in relation to her beloved son, she broke her own law—who will reproach a mother for protecting her child? Only she herself can reproach herself. And no one else would dare.

Loke went and pulled up the mistletoe and proceeded to the meeting. Hoder stood far to one side in the ring of men, because he was blind. Loke addressed himself to him, and asked: Why do you not shoot at Balder? He answered: Because I do not see where he is, and furthermore I have no weapons. Then said Loke: Do like the others and show honor to Balder; I will show you where he stands; shoot at him with this wand. Hoder took the mistletoe and shot at Balder under the guidance of Loke. The dart pierced him and he fell dead to the ground. This is the greatest misfortune that has ever happened to the gods and men.

This is the most tragic part of the entire northern epic. On the surface, it is perceived as villainy. But if we look at it in depth and from a magical point of view, we can see much more in this tragedy. However, it is Baldr's story, not Frigg's, that reveals the true meaning of what happened. Frigg acted according to her power and nature: she is the keeper of tradition, she must preserve the past and shape the reality of the future

ᚹ ᚨ

from the stories and events of the past. But the maternal heart of the goddess extended this principle to Baldr, and the principles of goodness that he embodied were also "preserved," although by the law and algorithms of development, they should change, be tested, and hardened.

Mistletoe—a small and inconspicuous shoot—was not seen by Frigg as an object for a curse because this element is not in her memory, it is not in the database of ancient times. Mistletoe is an alien plant, a parasite. It did not exist before, and Frigg knows nothing about it, but it exists now. Frigg sees it but does not evaluate it. She is a daughter of the Earth, considering and taking into account in the program of reality construction what was in the past, what has roots. The mistletoe parasite has no roots. But the myth of Baldr's death clearly indicates this fact: any goodness, all that is most valuable and beautiful, can be killed by something that has no roots. It looks weak and insignificant, even pitiable. The nature of mistletoe is such that it does not immediately reveal its parasitic essence. The mistletoe seed, penetrating the body of the tree, can remain dormant for several years without sprouting. But, as a parasite, it alters the tree's genetic structure, making it weak. While it remains inside the tree without showing itself, it disables the natural defense mechanisms of its host. When the first shoots of mistletoe appear several years later, the tree is already powerless to resist and becomes an eternal donor for the once insignificant sprout. It is impossible to get rid of mistletoe after this; the tree itself is no longer capable. The mistletoe continues to parasitize it until the tree dies. Unable to draw strength from the Earth, it draws the tree's sap through its root system, depriving the tree of its fruits and the tree's descendants of the ability to root freely in the earth.

This story is not just a fairy tale but a message from ancient times, from the gods to people: people, protect your good, protect your tradition, beware of mistletoe—things that have no roots. By accepting onto your land those who are rejected by their own land or deprived of it, you risk planting a seed of mistletoe on your family tree. At first, they will be pitiful and unnoticed, and you will voluntarily allow them to exist at your expense—after all, you have all the power of the Earth at your disposal, it is yours by right. Through your family roots, through your tradition, you possess it. Thinking that "it will not take away from you," you will not notice how the small and weak shoot gradually begins to change your family program, destroying the foundation of the ancestors' tradition from within. After a few years, the parasite will sprout and even look quite attractive—the overgrown tops of mistletoe even have a certain aesthetic, like quarters of another culture in a European city. Tourist exotica, but it always exists on the body of a large organism, living off it, feeding on it, and destroying it. There are trees that are capable of absorbing the foreign structure, integrating it into themselves, grafting the new element into their old genome, not allowing the mistletoe to sprout. But these are individual species that possess a higher degree of resilience.

Mistletoe is like a virus. It can help strengthen the body's immune system, but if the body always lives in greenhouse conditions and is not accustomed to change, this virus will kill it[66]. Mistletoe also kills those who live on such a tree, who feed

---

66 The well-known legend about druids gathering mistletoe is depicted as a demonstration of the sacredness of this plant: "Roman writers (Caesar, Pliny the Elder, and others) describe the mysterious druidic ritual of collecting mistletoe. The plant was harvested at the full moon or new moon, without the use of iron, sometimes with a golden sickle, and it should not touch the ground."

on it. Rare is the bird that can eat mistletoe berries—they are poisonous. Such a tree becomes dangerous both for inhabitants of other worlds and for itself—it poisons itself and poisons others.

By killing Baldr with mistletoe, Loki metaphorically conveyed the information that even the most beautiful tradition, the most beautiful and desirable good, which seems eternal and therefore invulnerable, can be destroyed by something that has no roots. And the fault will not lie with Loki or the machinations of Satan, but with your carelessness. The life sap is being drained from you, and you do not notice. You are being deprived of the right to progeny, and you agree to it tolerantly. You are being forced to destroy your tradition, but you will be killing your Baldr every time you allow this to happen.

During the battle of Ragnarök, the goddess Frigg stood beside Odin, shoulder to shoulder, and no longer behind him. The responsibility for what happened was as much hers as it was the responsibility of the supreme god, and she knew this and perished in that battle along with everyone else. But the death of the goddess Frigg during the battle of the gods does not mean

---

However, taking the written account literally, descendants forget that both Caesar and the chronicler Pliny were conquerors on Gallic land, they were occupiers. And who would tell the occupiers the truth, especially the sacred truth? They described what they saw, but did they understand the meaning correctly? The druids were a secretive society and did not reveal their secrets. If the conqueror, in his great conceit, thinks that the cutting of mistletoe is a ritual of veneration, let him continue to think so.

Mistletoe should not touch the ground. The druids believed that since the earth did not give this plant roots, we should not either. This means that the earth must be protected from this parasitic plant. The golden sickle and white robes are part of the ritual of sacrifice and purification, but the meaning is not in the sacred honors to the parasite, but in protecting the earth from it.

ᛊ ᛞ

the final destruction or disappearance of tradition. It is a necessity and time to give up the reins of power to those who are destined to correct the mistakes made and build reality differently—on different principles, with different rules.

Tradition is a very powerful system, but it has one significant feature—only what is truly experienced falls into the proto-foundation of Tradition. To overcome mistletoe, one must study mistletoe, one must become stronger than mistletoe. This means that the children of the gods will inevitably have to go through all the stages of formation and maturity, learn everything, understand everything, and build a reality on different mechanisms that their fathers and mothers—the Elder Gods—could not. The information of the old tradition, collected and preserved by the goddess Frigg, will pass to the sons, but not all at once. Frigg has 12 handmaidens, as the Prose Edda calls them, or 12 projections of power, as they are called in magic. They will remain after Ragnarök, and it will be necessary to find, gather, and unite these projections.

Practice 14. Goddess Frigg (p. 514)

ᚹ ᚨ

Baldr

Everyone loved the bright god Baldr—he was impossible not to love. He was strong, kind, and beautiful. He embodied true goodness in all its forms. His strength and the love of those around him were so great that they required no confirmation or proof. For this reason, no changes were required either: a mother's love protected him from everything. Tradition preferred precisely such algorithms of goodness as the ones represented by Baldr, and this was understood and accepted by all. For the northern system, Baldr was the ideal program, requiring no changes, only protection.

The Grimnismol mention that Baldr's home, his halls, are the most peaceful place in Asgard:

The seventh is Breithablik[67]*; Baldr has there*
For himself a dwelling set,
In the land I know that lies so fair,
And from evil fate is free.

Baldr was destined to become the true light, the heir of Odin and Frigg; he was meant to become the life principle that all people, all worlds, and all inhabitants of these worlds would accept with joy and without doubt. Importantly, they would accept it voluntarily, just as they accept light, rejoice in it, and await it. What prevented this from happening? Was it Loki again?

---

67 Breithablik — "broad gleam."

To become light, goodness must go through all stages of formation and development. It must experience everything and remain unchanged—neither in itself nor in the perception of those who see such algorithms of goodness as natural. Baldr did nothing to earn the love of those around him through his deeds rather than just his existence. Frigg did this for him, simply extending her maternal protection over her beloved son, and Baldr remained unchanged only because tradition wanted to see him that way. This is why the fact that Baldr began to have terrible dreams disturbed everyone, especially Frigg and Odin—after all, for them, the bright god of spring and goodness is the "crown of creation," the focal point of all results. Baldr's terrible dreams signal that something is happening with the system of the best algorithms for achieving results, something clearly bad and dangerous, threatening not only Baldr but the entire northern project, all of Asgard, and, through it, the entire system of the Nine Worlds.

In the narrative of the Northern myth, the mention of Baldr appears right from the beginning. We see this in the "Voluspo" (Prophecy of the Seeress), where the god Odin, his father, used magic to summon the seeress and asked her what the terrifying dreams of his son might mean. The seeress revealed much. She spoke of the creation of worlds and the arrangement of the heavenly vault, of the nine realms and the beings that inhabit them. Looking beyond the visible, the seeress saw the end of all created existence, she saw Ragnarök and the death of the gods, as well as what led to it:

I saw for Baldr, the bleeding god,
The son of Othin, his destiny set:
Famous and fair in the lofty fields,
Full grown in strength the mistletoe stood.

ᛊ ᛗ

From the branch which seemed so slender and fair
Came a harmful shaft that Hoth should hurl;
But the brother of Baldr was born ere long,
And one night old fought Othin's son.

The Eddaic song "Baldrs Draumar" continues the narrative:

Othin spake:
"Vegtam my name, I am Valtam's son;
Speak thou of hell, for of heaven I know :
For whom are the benches bright with rings,
And the platforms gay bedecked with gold ?"

The Wise-Woman spake:
"Here for Baldr the mead is brewed,
The shining drink, and a shield[68] *lies o'er it;*
But their hope is gone from the mighty gods.
Unwilling I spake, and now would be still."

Baldr's dreams were not an omen but a warning. Everything was already decided, woven by the Norns. Only the one weaving the fabric of reality for all could change anything, but she could not—mistletoe, knowing no roots, intervened. Baldr died, and the Prose Edda describes in detail how this happened:

When Balder had fallen, the asas were struck speechless with horror, and their hands failed them to lay hold of the corpse. One looked at

68 The brewed drink was customarily covered with something to prevent it from being "cursed." (Translator's note)

ᚠ ᚨ

the other, and all were of one mind toward him who had done the deed, but being assembled in a holy peace—stead, no one could take vengeance. When the asas at length, tried to speak, the wailing so choked their voices that one could not describe to the other his sorrow. Odin took this misfortune most to heart, since he best comprehended how great a loss and injury the fall of Balder was to the asas.

...The asas took the corpse of Balder and brought it to the sea—shore. Hringhorn[69] *was the name of Balder's ship, and it was the largest of all ships. The gods wanted to launch it and make Balder's bale—fire thereon, but they could not move it. Then they sent to Jotunheim after the giantess whose name is Hyrrokken. She came riding on a wolf, and had twisted serpents for reins. When she alighted, Odin appointed four berserks to take care of her steed, but they were unable to hold him except by throwing him down on the ground. Hyrrokken went to the prow and launched the ship with one single push, but the motion was so violent that fire sprang from the underlaid rollers and all the earth shook. Then Thor became wroth, grasped his hammer, and would forthwith have crushed her skull, had not all the gods asked peace for her. Balder's corspe was borne out on the ship; and when his wife, Nanna, daughter of Nep, saw this, her heart was broken with grief and she died. She was borne to the funeral—pile and cast on the fire. Thor stood by and hallowed the pile with Mjolner. Before his feet ran a dwarf, whose name is Lit. Him Thor kicked with his foot and dashed him into the fire, and he, too, was burned. But this funeral—pile was attended by many kinds of folk. First of all came Odin, accompanied by Frigg and the valkyries and his ravens. Frey came riding in his chariot drawn by the boar called Gullinburste or Slidrugtanne. Heimdal rode his steed Gulltop and Freyja drove her cats. There was a large number of frost—giants and mountain—giants. Odin laid on the funeral—pile his gold ring, Draupner,*

69 "Shriveled by fire."

which had the property of producing, every ninth night, eight gold rings of equal weight. Balder's horse, fully caparisoned, was led to his master's pile.

But of Hermod it is to be told that he rode nine nights through deep and dark valleys, and did not see light until he came to the Gjallar–river and rode on the Gjallar–bridge, which is thatched with shining gold. Modgud is the name of the may who guards the bridge. She asked him for his name, and of what kin he was, saying that the day before there rode five fylkes (kingdoms, bands) of dead men over the bridge; but she added, it does not shake less under you alone, and you do not have the hue of dead men. Why do you ride the way to Hel? He answered: I am to ride to Hel to find Balder. Have you seen him pass this way? She answered that Balder had ridden over the Gjallar–bridge; adding: But downward and northward lies the way to Hel.

Then Hermod rode on till he came to Hel's gate. He alighted from his horse, drew the girths tighter, remounted him, claped the spurs into him, and the horse leaped over the gate with so much force that he never touched it. Thereupon Hermod proceeded to the hall and alighted from his steed. He went in, and saw there sitting on the foremost seat his brother Balder. He tarried there over night. In the morning he asked Hel whether Balder might ride home with him, and told how great weeping there was among the asas. But Hel replied that it should now be tried whether Balder was so much beloved as was said. If all things, said she, both quick and dead, will weep for him, then he shall go back to the asas, but if anything refuses to shed tears, then he shall remain with Hel. Hermod arose, and Balder accompanied him out of the hall. He took the ring Draupner and sent it as a keepsake to Odin. Nanna sent Frigg a kerchief and other gifts, and to Fulla she sent a ring. Thereupon Hermod rode back and came to Asgard, where he reported the tidings he had seen and heard.

Then the asas sent messengers over all the world, praying that Balder might be wept out of Hel's power. All things did so, men and beasts, *the earth, stones, trees and all metals, just as you must have seen these things weep when they come out of frost and into heat. When the messengers returned home and had done their errand well, they found a certain cave wherein sat a giantess (gyger= ogress) whose name was Thok.*

They requested her to weep Balder from Hel; but she answered:
Thok will weep
With dry tears
For Balder's burial;
Neither in life nor in death
Gave he me gladness.
Let Hel keep what she has!

It is generally believed that this Thok was Loke, Laufey's son, who has wrought most evil among the asas.

No, it was not Loki. It was indeed the giantess Thokk, whose name means "gratitude." The ancient memory, the past that had faded into darkness, did not wish to express gratitude for Baldr, nor did it mourn his death. Such goodness, untested by natural selection, was unnecessary to memory. From the perspective of the memory of everything, this kind of goodness is not universal for all worlds; for some, it could be evil. And that is wrong.

But Loki's actions require explanation. Knowing his role in the system, it is strange to think that the defeat of Baldr by the mistletoe, the destruction of the god of goodness and spring by the blind god of darkness, and such a blow to the Æsir and the northern pantheon were acts of mere mischief or spite. Loki never acts without reason; his actions are always a reaction to the violation of Asgard's fundamental principles, a response to previous actions. Loki is a force of opposition, both destructive

ᛊ ᛞ

and creative. By killing his blood brother's son, Loki set in motion an irreversible chain of transformations that inevitably led to Ragnarök. But the battle of the gods is not an ultimate destruction but a second chance for them, a chance to make the system right:

Then fields unsowed bear ripened fruit.
All ills grow better, and Baldr comes back;
Baldr and Hoth dwell in Hropt's[70] *battle-hall,*
And the mighty gods: would you know yet more?
(The Poetic Edda. Voluspo)

Baldr will return along with Höd, but the brothers must undergo transformation together. One brother was protected by his mother's love, while the other was deprived of it. But this limited both in their development and manifestation: Baldr did not gain new experiences or learn from mistakes; Höd, synchronized with his brother, could not see that light began to emanate from Baldr. Darkness reacts only to light. Loki saw that Baldr's invulnerability was not a victory for the system but its defeat. Goodness cannot remain static; it must change and develop along with reality and time. Sooner or later, such algorithms would conflict with the entire system, turning Baldr from beloved to hated. For goodness to remain desirable and loved by all, its loss must be mourned by all; it must evolve with everyone. Maybe the giantess Thokk did not cry for Baldr not because she did not know him, but because he, the god of goodness and light, did not know her, the ancient memory.

---

[70] Hropt - Odin

ᚠ ᚨ

Baldr learns nothing and changes in no way. Everything comes to him easily, and he already has the greatest prize of all—the love of the goddess Frigg. As demonstrated by the youngest son of Odin and Frigg, this love must be earned by everyone else, but Baldr did not have to do this. Nowhere in the sagas is there mention of his journeys or adventures; he does not partake in the common quests, which demonstrates exactly what has been said—Baldr does not change. Only through trials does one develop; only when encountering the different does one become different. When the gods, in jest, attacked Baldr by throwing stones and spears at him, they were not testing or training him—they were showing off. They boasted of his invulnerability, but what did they themselves have to do with his invulnerability? What did the gods do to make the most beautiful god, the most valuable being in Asgard, strong and invulnerable? It was all done by Frigg's magic, and the gods laughed. Again.

Loki saw the repetition of Tyr's story. He saw that the gods had learned nothing from that terrible incident, and now the damage was inflicted upon Odin, upon Frigg, and there was no hope for the other gods of Asgard. Therefore, Loki sent Baldr to a place where he would undoubtedly learn his lessons—he sent Baldr to Hel, he sent him to study. Höd went with him—light and darkness must be adequate to each other; they must know and understand each other and must not be separated. If Baldr is loved as the god of light, then Höd should be loved as the god of darkness. But they can only learn this where such knowledge exists—in the halls of the goddess Hel, in the realms of Niflheimr.

It is in the halls of Niflheimr that we see Baldr first acting in a meaningful way, conversing with his brother Hermod. He sends messages to Asgard with him—a ring, Draupnir, and his faithful wife Nanna sends a headband for Fulla. The symbolism of these messages will become clear to us a little later.

We do not know what Hermod and Baldr talked about all night, but the small episode of the brothers' parting gives a strong sense that Baldr seemed to awaken, that he began to understand something.

Let us also venture there to learn what lessons the mistress Hel could impart to her pupils, Baldr and Höd.

Practice 15: God Baldr (p. 516)

ᛊ ᛞ

Hel

In the narrative of the Norse myth, the goddess Hel holds a unique place, reflecting her absolute self-sufficiency and the distinct position formed for her by the entire system of the Nine Worlds. Firstly, it is important to understand that this goddess is not the goddess of death. In the Norse myth, the function of "death" is not personified at all; it is not something that has independent characteristics, personality, preferences, or appearance. Death in the Norse framework of reality is not a function but a phenomenon that exists because other phenomena exist. Death does not exist by itself. This understanding was so natural for those living in that era that no one thought to describe Death as an independent personality, giving it some identifying characteristics.

The goddess Hel is not death, but she is the keeper of the world of the dead. She does not bring about the end of life since she never leaves her own world: everyone comes to her, but she goes to no one.

Hel is the eldest daughter of the god Loki and the giantess Angrboda, sister to Jormungandr and Fenrir. No one remembers what she was named at birth because "Hel" is not a name but rather a reflection. "Hel" is the name of her realm, and the goddess who becomes its mistress traditionally takes on its name. The keeper of the realms of Niflheimr and Helheimr, she was born for this mission. Her nature is dual, as is her appearance: some said she was terrible, while others said she was beautiful. This is not surprising since everyone sees in the other world what they wish to see.

ᚹ ᚠ

The Poetic Edda speaks little and sparingly about the goddess Hel; it mentions her world rather than her. People go to Hel, are sent to Hel, hurry to Hel, and dwell in Hel. But the goddess herself is neither described nor discussed. She is not an object for description; she is unknown to the living, and the people, who were accustomed to speaking only the truth, could not talk about what they had not seen with their own eyes. Only the dead or some gods (and not all of them) could know Hel, but neither rushed to describe this acquaintance in any specific terms. However, the Prose Edda and later Christian consciousness did not have that inner restraint, which prohibited speaking about what one did not know. Therefore, those with a Christian worldview decided to describe the goddess and her world, and they did it like this:

Loke had yet more children. A giantess in Jotunheim, hight Angerboda. With her he begat three children. The first was the Fenris—wolf; the secon, Jormungand, that is, the Midgard—serpent, and the third, Hel. When the gods knew that these three children were being fostered in Jotunheim, and were aware of the prophecies that much woe and misfortune would thence come to them, and considering that much evil might be looked for from them on their mother's side, and still more on their father's, Alfather sent some of the gods to take the children and bring them to him. When they came to him he threw the serpent into the deep sea which surrounds all lands. There waxed the serpent so that he lies in the midst of the ocean, surrounds all the earth, and bites his own tail. Hel he cast into Niflheim, and gave her power over nine worlds, that she should appoint abodes to them that are sent to her, namely, those who die from sickness or old age. She has there a great mansion, and the walls around it are of strange height, and the gates are huge. Eljudner is the name of her hall. Her table hight famine; her knife, starvation. Her man—servant's name is Ganglate; her maid—servant's, Ganglot. Her threshold is called stumbling—block; her bed, care; the precious hangings of her bed, gleaming bale. One–half of her is blue, and the other half is of the hue of flesh; hence she is easily known. Her looks are very stern and grim.

The image of the mistress of Helheimr and Niflheimr has its roots deeply set in time, far earlier than the myth itself. The consciousness of a seer attempting to reach such ancient times will inevitably approach the limits where all knowledge disappears, where the very possibility of defining anything ends. This is a world of pure chaos, where nothing is defined and, consequently, nothing is understandable. When a non-magical mind enters these realms, any self-knowledge vanishes, leaving only the unknown. This unknown, meticulously hidden by the mind and "educated" consciousness, emerges when one approaches the limits of the dominion of the goddess of the Otherworld. Hence, the vast difference in descriptions of the goddess's appearance: each person has their own unknown, their carefully guarded fears, their hidden horror. The goddess does not change her appearance for each person because she has no appearance: a mask is an element of certainty and the possibility of being a persona, but how can there be certainty in chaos?

Some, like Snorri, son of Sturla, saw in her face a blue corpse and living flesh; others described rot and decay, or skulls and bones—because each person's inner horrors live within them. But there were also those who spoke of the goddess's beauty, her wisdom, and kindness, of a true power that the human mind could not oppose—and this too is a description of the hidden unknown that resides in those who look into the eyes of the primordial. At this moment of contact, the external constructed image of the real world falls and dissolves into oblivion, knowledge about it disappears, and the second essence of the one looking into eternity emerges—the true and ancient essence. In the world of the goddess Hel, this is the only way: the power of this world synchronizes with each entrant, leading them to such frequencies that correspond to their inner being. The image of the goddess for each person is a description of this second essence, true and ancient, but the perception of this essence is always through the prism of one's attitude towards this ancient power. A consciousness filled with many fears and belief in its own sinfulness will see just that reflection; a mind striving to comprehend the wisdom of the worlds will recognize in the goddess's appearance what it sought. But nothing in this vision is true or ultimately true—the ancient goddess of primordial chaos has no form. The ancestors understood this, so they were in no hurry to describe what cannot be described.

Later, this simple truth was attempted to be expressed through the genealogy of the goddess Hel: the nature of the jotun is the nature of the shapeshifter, which is why she is seen differently. But this is an attempt to explain, not the explanation itself, which is always concrete and final, meaning it cannot be applied to the goddess Hel in principle. Behind this explanation of the shapeshifter's nature, one must see what the ancient mages understood by it. A shapeshifter, they said, is someone whose second essence becomes equal to or stronger than the first—human or whatever they were born with. If they are equal, transformation can occur at will; if the second becomes stronger, the transformation will be spontaneous and chaotic. In the case of the goddess Hel's origin, one could add that the mutable nature of her father Loki and the ancient power of continuous memory from the goddess Angrboda combined into a unique property, where within are all possible images of manifestation and existence, capable of changing depending on the eye of the beholder. This ancient description resembles the quantum effect of decoherence.

ᛊ ᛞ

It is important to note that the goddess Hel is named and is the mistress of the worlds Helheimr and Niflheimr. However, the world of Niflheimr is a very ancient world, at least as it is described initially — a world of ancient darkness where all the old primordial principles of reality construction are stored, expressed in the form of ancient hrimthursar, frost giants, ancestors of almost all the Aesir. In the magical interpretation of world-building, Niflheimr is associated with the proto-foundation of Dark, while the world of Helheimr is associated with the proto-foundation of Chaos. The mistress Hel does not govern these worlds, does not manage their power, but she guards and somewhat protects them — one can enter, but cannot leave before the due time.

Jafnhar remarked: Many ages before the earth was made, Niflheim had existed, in the midst of which is the well called Hvergelmer, whence flow the following streams: Svol, Gunnthro, Form, Finbul, Thul, Slid and Hrid, Sylg and Ylg, Vid, Leipt and Gjoll[71], *the last of which is nearest the gate of Hel. (The Prose Edda)*

The path to the world of the dead is blocked by the river Gjöll, which flows closest to the gates of the underworld. Across it is a narrow golden bridge, Gjallarbrú, guarded by the giantess Móðguðr and the hound Garmr.

The world of Dark and the world of Chaos. When transitioning from the world of the living to the world of the dead, the temporary separates from the eternal; the temporary goes to Chaos — as nourishment for the future, the eternal goes

[71] Svöl — "cold," Fjörm — "swift," Slil — "fierce," Hrið — "storm," Sylgr — "devouring," Ylg — "she-wolf," Víd — "broad," Leipt — "lightning." The meanings of the other river names are unclear. (Translator's note.)

ᚠ ᚨ

ᛊ ᛞ

into the darkness to be reborn at the right time. From the perspective of Asgard's magical programming, what goes to the world of Hel is deemed unnecessary and unfit by the algorithms of goodness and victory. What is needed goes to Odin in Valhalla, while what is not goes to the halls of the goddess Hel. The gods take their own immediately, but the rest, rejected, go to the one who never refuses.

Ganglere asks again: Where is this god? What can he do? What mighty works has he accomplished? Answered Har: He lives from everlasting to everlasting, rules over all his realm, and governs all things, great and small. Then remarked Jafnhar: He made heaven and earth, the air and all things in them. Thride added: What is most important, he made man and gave him a spirit, which shall live, and never perish[72]*,, though the body may turn to dust or burn to ashes. All who live a life of virtue shall dwell with him in Gimle*[73] *or Vingolf*[74]*. The wicked, on the other hand, go to Hel, and from her to Niflhel, that is, down into the ninth world. Then asked Ganglere: What was he doing before heaven and earth were made? Har gave answer: Then was he with the frost–giants. (The Prose Edda)*

It is not hard to guess that those chosen to enter the gates of Valhalla are few; all others — women, children, and the elderly, the sick and those who died of old age, those who perished by accident or in infancy — all whose death is "not honorable," go to the world of the goddess Hel. They are millions, born and dead, unneeded by the gods. They will cross

---

72 Although the text ostensibly refers to the ancient pagan deity Odin, avoiding Christian nuances was already impossible.

73 Gimlé — "protection from fire." (Translator's note.)

74 Vingólf — "abode of bliss." (Translator's note.)

ᚠ ᚩ

ᛊ ᛞ

the golden bridge, Garmr will devour the fear of the dead before transitioning to the new world, and Móðguðr will help reveal their true essence, removing the veils of self-perception. Their lives should not be lived in vain, and the fact that they are "unfit" for the gods of Asgard does not mean that all their life experience should dissolve into chaos and disappear into oblivion. Hel will not allow this to happen, and the world of Niflheimr will preserve the valuable, freezing it in ice until the new embers of Muspelheimr melt this ice, giving the principle of life of the rejected god and man a second chance to manifest. In the world of Niflheimr, valuable things are preserved, and in the world of Helheim, the unnecessary is released.

Seers, who journey through the worlds, recount that the goddess Hel cares for all who come to her halls. Her nature, capable of reflecting the true essence of the dweller, can also create a visual-material representation of the world that each of her wards desires. Thus, some experience nightmares, others fairy tales, and some, like Snorri, experience mist, hunger, exhaustion, and affliction. The bright god Baldr and the dark god Höd also received their "halls."

In the realm of Helheimr, each individual has the opportunity to experience what was not fully lived, understood, or pondered during their lifetime. How long will this take? In Hel's realms, there is no time, as there is no process of life. There is no life, but also no death. In the world of the dead, there is no death; there is a process of experiencing liberation. For someone who understood nothing in their life, this liberation may appear as a nightmare, resembling the hell abundant in Christian descriptions. Others may "live" or "re-experience from the start" their life as they always wished. In Hel's world, anything is possible: all images of realities that ever existed in the Nine Worlds are available, and Hel's ability, inherited from Loki, to

ᚹ ᚠ

quickly switch external images allows her wards to experience all the life scenarios they need. Those who can learn do so; those who cannot remain unchanged, cyclically experiencing what they are capable of.

God Baldr and god Höd also underwent their processes, freeing themselves from fixed descriptions of themselves, from Asgard's expectations, from constraining love, and from contempt for inherent disability. They learned to be different in all probabilities and multiple scenarios, which the world of Hel is rich in: she creates them for deceased people, and the gods, being among them, understand these worlds and finally gain the invaluable experience that was closed to them in life. Every deceased inhabitant of the Nine Worlds who passed through Hel's world contributes their life's story to Jotunheimr's knowledge treasury. Since Hel has access to the entire system (remember: *"Hel he cast into Niflheim, and gave her power over nine worlds, that she should appoint abodes to them that are sent to her, namely, those who die from sickness or old age*"), these stories are all available to her, like a large database of everything that was, each lived fate. Helheim frees the deceased from fears and attachments, from identifying themselves with their body, name, status. Thus, information is freed from relation to it and becomes pure knowledge. Niflheimr will take from the descriptions of fates what remains—the most valuable and essential—to later build a new world on this informational power.

Each world offers its own experiences and liberation. But the liberation is more painful the stronger the attachments: in the world of Jotunheimr, one cannot lie and embellish one's story; in the world of Helheimr, one cannot cling to their passions and feelings. Each world will conduct its trials so that the process of liberation occurs; it is impossible for distorted understanding of lived life to enter Niflheimr; pure knowledge, the pure primordial essence of oneself and one's god, must be taken out. In the worlds of Nifel, one can connect with it, with their original power. What was forgotten must be remembered; what hurt must cease to hurt.

The god Baldr, along with his blind brother, found himself in the halls of the goddess Hel, entering a world that is entirely antagonistic to the orderly Asgard. While Asgard concentrated all that was strongest and most victorious (from the perspective of Odin's principles of order), Hel gathered everything most despicable in opposition. Like Buddha, Baldr had seen only the best from birth and, lacking the ability to compare, had no algorithms for recognizing what is best and what is worst. In the world of the goddess Hel, he now had the opportunity to acquaint himself with what he had never known — with mistakes made, with different lived destinies, with stories that the einherjar do not tell. This is a new experience, and Baldr will comprehend it together with his brother Höd — their knowledge must be equal. Baldr's brother Hermóðr found him in Hel's halls, pale and focused. Once a cheerful and joyful god, a carefree joker, in his new home he talked seriously and maturely with Hermod. Even omnipotent gods need to walk the path of mortals to truly become gods, not just be called so. The individual story of the god Baldr begins at the moment of his death. He had no personal history, and only the memory of his death could lay in the world of Jotunheim, but there was no memory of life. Therefore, having entered the halls of the mistress Hel, he and his brother Höd in the world of the dead had to comprehend the world of the living — in all its manifestations and forms of life.

While he was in the halls of Asgard, while he was loved and cherished by his mother, the goddess Frigg, he had nothing he could truly call his own. Baldr, as the god of Goodness, was to become the god of Light, but it turned out that he could do this only by breaking away from everything that protected, loved, and guarded him — that is, by dying. Baldr and Höd will emerge from the world of Hel only changed, transformed, grown-up, and wiser. Along with them, the same lessons will be learned by the goddess Nanna[75], Baldr's wife: fidelity must also become wise and experienced. In the world of Hel, it was probably hardest for the goddess Nanna. One can be faithful when in love. But love is a feeling, and in the world of Hel, feelings disappear — how to remain faithful? It means there must be something else that does not dissolve in chaos, something that cannot be described by a romantic love story, something more than a feeling. Can Nanna remain faithful without feeling anything for the object of her fidelity? This will be a personal test for her — in the world of Hel, there is an opportunity to go through this as well.

Can one understand the value of life without ever dying? Can one understand the value of death without ever living? Baldr must become goodness for all, and that means he must experience everything, comprehend everything, understand everything. The maturity of Baldr and Höd is at stake for the future world. New worlds after the battle of Ragnarök must be built on this basis. Baldr could not become mature, wise, and truly strong in the world of Asgard, and therefore Loki sent him where it is guaranteed possible — to his daughter Hel.

In the world of Hel, everyone is on completely equal terms. There they are not divided into gods or heroes, into people or dwarves — in the world of the goddess Hel, everyone is the same, everyone is dead, and everyone has lost according to the algorithms of goodness affirmed by Asgard. But in the world

---

75 The name of the goddess Nanna, the wife of Baldr, translates to "fidelity."

of Hel, what becomes phenomenal is not the differences among all present, but their sameness. It is this quality that the god Baldr, as the god of Goodness, had to see and comprehend — after all, the goodness he carries must be understandable and desirable for all. Not uniform, but precisely accepted by everyone, so different yet in some ways completely the same. This sameness is what Baldr needs to understand and accept to become not just goodness for all, but the light that will be needed in all worlds.

The goddess Hel does not allow anyone to disturb her wards. Each one of them undergoes their own lessons and trials in her world. They were deemed unnecessary by the gods, and thus must find strength in their rejection—who better than Hel to teach them this? The maturity and wisdom of their second nature must gain strength, and the test of this strength will occur during the battle of Ragnarök.

Hel opens the gates of her world so that the defeated may have a chance to win and, consequently, start anew—strong, wise, and mature. But against whom do the dead from Hel's world fight? Not against giants and jötnar, not against dvergar or humans. They stand against the gods who programmed the world of humans in such a way that the majority of those born could not meet the criteria of valor by definition. Therefore, in Ragnarök, it will not be humans fighting, but principles—the principles of reality construction. The einherjar against the rejected. The principle of good against the principle of evil. What is beloved by the gods against what is not. One truth against another truth. The dead, emerging from Hel's domain, will prove to the gods that they have the strength and the right to live by their own laws and principles. They will prove that every life has value, that the feelings of a mother whose child dies in her arms from diphtheria are no less intense than the grief of Frigg who buried her bright son. They will prove that the love of mortal men and women is no less than the love of the god Freyr for the beautiful Gerd. They will prove that an old man who raised nine grandchildren is no less wise and respected than their father who died as a warrior but left nine orphans. The inner essence of each deceased is their own truth, and in Hel's world, the dead must learn to respect it.

During the battle of Ragnarök, the gods will stand shoulder to shoulder with each other, but opposite those they created but rejected. It is not people fighting, but forces. And not to destroy each other in fierce retribution, but to prove their own truth to each other—truth will be found in the duel. The einherjar were raised by Odin, the rejected were raised by Hel. She will prevail.

Practice 16. Goddess Hel (page 519)

ᛊ ᛞ

The Norns

With the goddesses who determine the fate of all living and existing beings, you have already become acquainted during the passage through the second aett of runes: the three runes Naud, Isa, and Eihwaz connected your consciousness with the universal principles of wyrd and örlög. These same runes serve as keys to the three worlds of the tree—Jotunheimr, Niflheimr, and Svartalfheimr, respectively. The goddesses Urd, Verdandi, and Skuld, whose names mean "Fate," "Becoming," and "Debt," symbolize (roughly) the past, present, and future. Or more precisely: Urd—"That which is," Verdandi—"That which is becoming," and Skuld—"That which should be."

An ash I know, Yggdrasil its name,
With water white is the great tree wet;
Thence come the dews that fall in the dales,
Green by Urth's well does it ever grow.

Thence come the maidens mighty in wisdom,
Three from the dwelling down 'neath the tree;
Urth is one named, Verthandi the next,—
On the wood they scored,— and Skuld the third.
Laws they made there, and life allotted
To the sons of men, and set their fates.
(The Poetic Edda. Voluspo)

The goddess Urd is the eldest of the three Norn goddesses and is traditionally represented as an old woman. The

goddess Verdandi appeared to the people of old as a middle-aged woman. The goddess Skuld seemed the youngest of the three goddesses. They are always together, but Skuld's name sometimes appears among the Valkyries, perhaps performing her work of cutting the thread on the battlefield as well. We see this dual role of the goddess Skuld in various songs of the northern myth: for some, the thread of life is measured and cut in advance, while for others, the thread of fate is cut directly on the fabric of reality, fixing the woven pattern, trimming off the "excess tails" that are unnecessary for those who, in Odin's opinion, are worthy of becoming einherjar.

In the narrative of the northern myth, the Norns do not often appear as active characters. But their presence is always implicit. Even if they are not mentioned, they are remembered. Even if they are not remembered, their presence is always implied. The Norns, in the mindset of someone living within the northern myth, are the immovable constants that neither gods nor humans can change.

As active forces, the Norns appear in the myth at its very beginning, but only when processes in the Nine Worlds become so systematically incorrect that intervention by controlling forces is unavoidable. This is what the "Voluspo" of the Poetic Edda tells us about it:

In their dwellings at peace they played at tables.
Of gold no lack did the gods then know,—
Till thither came up giant-maids three.
Huge of might, out of Jotunheim.

Then sought the gods
their assembly-seats,
The holy ones, and council held.

To find who should raise the race of dwarfs
Out of Brimir's[76] *blood and the legs of Blain.*

When the gods created the worlds from the body of the primordial being Ymir and settled in Asgard, they, according to the "Voluspo," fell into a state of relaxation, which, according to the controlling system of the Tree, was not at all necessary. The appearance of the three Norns at the gates of Asgard was a bad sign, and the gods had to urgently continue their work—creation could not be abandoned. The created worlds had to function, which meant that someone had to live there. Moreover, what was created should not be superfluous in the system, which meant it had to be programmatically linked with all other existing systems, and the created world, the manifested reality, had to interact with each other on the principles of mutual reflection and mutual response.

The Norns are not a force that can be ignored. The gods knew this, and so did the people. When speaking of the Norns, people spoke of fate, destiny, and inevitability. It must be said that people of ancient times believed in fate absolutely. However, their understanding of the world allowed them to distinguish between two types of fate—Wyrd and Orlog.

Wyrd is personal fate and depends on a person's actions and will. However, it does not exist by itself but is embedded within the fate of the gods, within **orlog**. Fates are intertwined and create a common pattern: the small fate within the large, but the fate-orlog can only be discerned when all the stitches-wyrds are applied to the fabric of reality. The goddesses who spin and weave the fates of all worlds, like Frigg in the northern myth,

---

[76] Brimir is the same as Ymir (the oldest of the giants). Blain is another name for Ymir.

hold the threads from which history and the future are manifested. These threads are in the hands of the ancient Norns. A person could traverse their wyrd in different ways, but they could not step beyond orlog. This is the permissible domain where manifestation has meaning.

The Norns control and work on orlog, as the personal wyrd of gods and heroes. It is inevitable and unembellished; it is as it is. A person's wyrd is not as rigidly fixed and can be "colored" in different ways, allowing the pattern on the fabric of reality to be seen, understood, and read. This "coloring" was the task of the disir. Their role is well reflected in later medieval tales as fairy godmothers who endowed the main character with a happy or unhappy fate, weaving important conditional knots into the thread of life, fixing magical cause-and-effect connections. But the disir never changed or canceled fate; they could only soften or harden its conditions. In the Prose Edda, Snorri Sturluson did not distinguish between the functions of the disir and the Norns, simply combining them under the term "Norns":

There stands a beautiful hall near the fountain beneath the ash. Out of it come three maids, whose names are Urd, Verdande and Skuld. These maids shape the lives of men, and we call them norns. There are yet more norns, namely those who come to every man when he is born, to shape his life, and these are known to be of the race of gods; others, on the other hand, are of the race of elves, and yet others are of the race of dwarfs. As is here said:

Far asunder, I think,
The norns are born,
They are not of the same race.
Some are of the asas,

Some are of the elves,
Somea are daughters of Dvalin[77].

Then said Ganglere: If the norns rule the fortunes of men, then they deal them out exceedingly unevenly. Some live a good life and are rich; some get neither wealth nor praise. Some have a long, others a short life. Har answered: Good norns and of good descent shape good lives, and when some men are weighed down with misfortune, the evil norns are the cause of it.

The Poetic and Prose Eddas indicate the origin of the Norns and the disir: the Norns, according to the Voluspo, are from Jotunheimr, while the disir come from various worlds. If we remember this, we will not make a mistake in understanding the essence of these forces.

The Norns spin, measure, and cut the threads of human fates from the informational material of the past. Their activity is not for humans; the ancient goddesses weave reality from multiple human fates. They do not highlight or color individual threads. They spin, measure, and cut not for the person, but for reality. The Norns have power over all nine worlds, and the fates of the inhabitants of all worlds pass through the hands of the Three Great Spinners.

The disir, in general, are guardians of fate. For some, this is the spirit of an ancestor; for others, an invisible companion from other worlds, with whom the connection is very strong. If we remember that nothing in the world system exists by itself, but everything is connected with everything, it becomes clear why ancient people felt this invisible connection with a representative of another world and did not doubt its

---

[77] This quotes from "Fáfnismál," a song from the Poetic Edda.

reality. Modern understanding of the world could explain this phenomenon with the theory of quantum entanglement, which physically explains the principle of non-local interdependence of objects[78]. A dis could be connected with an individual person, an entire family, or even a place. For this reason, one person could have several disir-protectors: personal, ancestral, and from the land.

Fylgja — among the Scandinavians, a "follower." A spirit that accompanies a person and is closely linked to their fate or fortune. The fylgja-follower is closely connected with **hamingja** — the program of personal luck. This pair not only guided a Norse person through life but also ensured well-being. The fylgja could appear either as a human or an animal.

The Well of Urd[79] is described in the myth not only as the dwelling place of the Norn goddesses but also as their place of origin. One of the roots of the Yggdrasil Tree is nourished by this well. The Well of Urd encompasses all past actions of all beings without exception, which are connected by the principle of Yggdrasil.

The Norn goddesses return the actions of the past to the present so that the future can come. They draw from this well and water the tree of current reality, our Yggdrasil. This is not karma in the traditional sense — it is nourishment, building material; the tree absorbs it, processes it, and after some time,

---

[78] Two or more objects in the universe can be interconnected. In this case, if something happens to one object, and it is determined, then changes occur simultaneously with the other object, and this too can be determined. When this happens, uncertainty disappears, and certainty manifests in reality.

[79] Urðarbrunnr — the Well of Urd, "the well of fate."

fruits appear, which in turn will also become memory — a source of life for the future of all who come after us.

Practice 17. The Norn Goddesses (page 526)

Mimir

The god Mimir appears in northern mythology at the moment when the story of the first war between the Aesir and Vanir is told. He is described in the myth as one of the hostages exchanged by the warring sides as a sign of truce. Mimir was among the gods sent to Vanaheimr in exchange for the gods Njord, Freyr, and Freyja, who were sent to Asgard. The gods Mimir and Hoenir, while hostages of the Vanir, were highly respected and, like the Vanir in Asgard, had a certain degree of freedom. The Vanir considered their opinions during tings when making important decisions. Initially, everything went smoothly.

However, after some time, the Vanir noticed, as recounted in the "Ynglinga Saga," that the second Aesir hostage, Hoenir, behaved rather strangely in Mimir's absence. The strangeness lay in his inability to make any decisions independently. He always refused to express a personal opinion, saying, "Let others decide." What follows is puzzling: the Vanir kill Mimir. But why Mimir? Why him?

Killing a hostage without any grounds is a grave crime. In response, the Aesir had the right to kill someone (or even all) among the Vanir hostages, but they did not. The Vanir, who initially treated the Aesir with kindness, must have had compelling reasons to jeopardize the fragile and difficult peace between the two systems by killing the accepted hostage. Clearly, Mimir posed an undeniable threat to the Vanir, turning their wrath on him, while Hoenir did not pose such a threat. Let's try to unravel this, and we will use the proven method of viewing gods not as people but as informational minds, programs, and mathematical functions that create and describe reality through the transmitted myth.

The name of the god Mimir is closely deciphered as "memory."[80] His origin is as ancient as that of all the architect gods: Odin, Tyr, Thor, Heimdall, etc. He is Primordial, immortal, and embodies the primary function of any system—memory and data accumulation. This is where the familiar jotun nature comes into play, and it is no coincidence that Mimir's final dwelling is at the Well of Urd. Mimir is operational memory, having primary access to the collected database of all Nine Worlds.

Earth and Sun
cannot stand firm;
malignant winds
do not cease;
hidden in the glorious
well of Mímir
lies all knowledge;
know ye yet, or what?
(The Poetic Edda, Odin's Raven Magic)

Hoenir represents the speed of information processing, the way it is reproduced. It is logical that in the absence of memory-Mimir, reproducing anything would be difficult. The god Hoenir is the system's processor, the mechanism of its choice and manifestation. He is eloquent and swift when there is a request for information and there is something to choose from.

The Vanir deemed Mimir useless. They had no complaints about Hoenir. This might seem strange from a

[80] Mimir is often compared with the Old English 'Mimorian' and the Latin 'memor', both of which mean "to remember."

human perspective, but let's try to view it through the eyes of the Vanir. Mimir, with direct access to information about all nine worlds and the past, could indeed give valuable advice based on the best experiences. However, these were foreign experiences, and for this reason, Mimir was not suitable for the Vanir. Hoenir, on the other hand, could instantly find the reflection of a decision in any of the nine worlds. This quality of Hoenir was precisely what the Vanir needed: to quickly react to changing circumstances.

From the moment the Aesir linked the worlds into a system, changes in the other worlds occurred rapidly. Especially when Midgard began to be populated by humans: being a reflection of the other eight worlds, possessing both Vanir and Aesir nature, humans were the first to react to changes and initiate changes, often without regard for the place they lived in or those who created and guarded it. By acquiring Hoenir, the Vanir gained a tool for quickly reacting to such changes, while Mimir, who knew exactly how things should be "logically," knew how "everything was before," and was unlikely to find information about what had just appeared. This was the problem for the Vanir—there was no information in Mimir's memory about the new, the never-before-existing. The experience of solving problems related to the emergence of new and unpredictable elements was not accumulated. The Vanir did not need "logical" solutions; they needed "natural" ones. Therefore, they killed Mimir—killed the database that contained harmful or useless instructions for the gods of nature. These instructions did not imply free choice, did not suggest accounting for changes happening now and possibly tomorrow. Meanwhile, Hoenir's formula "let others decide" obviously implied such a choice. Hoenir provided the Vanir with the freedom of personal choice, while Mimir did not.

If the Vanir had not killed Mimir, if they had allowed him to introduce foreign information into the world of Vanaheimr, to introduce viral algorithms of existence, they would very soon have ceased to be what they had always been and changed their nature. Therefore, to save their nature, they killed Mimir.

Additionally, Hoenir was the god who participated with Odin and Lodur in the creation and formation of humans in Midgard, making him more useful to the Vanir as someone knowledgeable. For the Vanir, Mimir was like mistletoe, and they knew how to deal with mistletoe: kill it before it takes root. All the wisdom of the world was probably unnecessary for the Vanir and in some cases even deadly, as we know from the story of the goddess Idunn—it paralyzes the living, does not allow it to develop freely, or react spontaneously.

The Vanir sent the head of the killed god Mimir back to Asgard. "Thanks, but no thanks." Odin, who knows the value of wisdom, found additional memory useful. He magically revived Mimir's head and connected it directly to the Well of Urd.

The Well of Mimir—this is what this level of memory is called, with which the god Odin began to interact individually. He can now not only directly access the necessary information from the source but also input his own data into it, bypassing all system filters. This is mentioned in the "Voluspo":

Yggdrasil shakes, and shiver on high
The ancient limbs, and the giant is loose;
To the head of Mim does Othin give heed.
But the kinsman of Surt shall slay him soon.

However, such a right did not come to Odin "just like that." A constant communication channel was needed, and this connection became Odin's eye, a paired sensor, one of which is with Odin and the other with Mimir. This created a specially organized "dedicated channel."

Alone I sat when the Old One sought me,
The terror of gods, and gazed in mine eyes :
"What hast thou to ask ? why comest thou hither ?
Othin, I know where thine eye is hidden."

I know where Othin's eye is hidden,
Deep in the wide-famed well of Mimir;
Mead from the pledge of Othin each morn
Does Mimir drink: would you know yet more?
(The Poetic Edda, Voluspo)

And the völva is absolutely right in her claim to the one who awakened her from the dead sleep: why question, why test, if you have the same access to information as I do?

Special attention should be paid to this ancient chthonic image of the "head without a body." It appears in almost all ancient myths and is firmly associated with treasures, secrets, ancient magic, and wisdom inaccessible to ordinary mortals. In legendary and fairy tales, the "dead head" always has to guard something until a chosen one appears who must pass established trials, and then access to the secret is granted.

The god Mimir, having died, did not cease to exist as a god. But no longer being physically alive, he lost the ability to "relive" knowledge personally, to pass it through his own experience, through his "bodily sensations." This means that, having died, Mimir no longer has a personal relationship to the information he stores. The function of memory remains, but it is now connected to and dependent on the one who possesses this life. In this case, the god Odin.

Before the battle of Ragnarök, when the Gjallarhorn sounded, Odin speaks with "Mimir's head," embedding the last important information for safekeeping, so that on the needed day and hour, the true knowledge will be transmitted to the chosen ones—the future god-architects of the new world, preserved in memory and not lost for those who will build a new system of multiple realities.

Practice 18. God Mimir (page 530)

Kvasir

Researchers and enthusiasts of Norse mythology typically do not define or describe Kvasir as a god, referring to him merely as a character in the myth— "the wise man Kvasir." However, his power represents a complete and fully capable program, potentially capable of independent world-building.

The origin of Kvasir is entirely mythical and magical; he was not born but created. The material for his creation consisted of parts of the life forces of the Aesir and Vanir gods, magically combined. This gives him an initially divine origin, although in a somewhat untraditional manner.

In the myth, the god Kvasir, the wise man Kvasir, is closely associated with the magical ability of poetry, although he himself was not a poet. His blood was poetically creative. Let's turn to the Prose Edda, part 2 "The Mead of Poetry":

The Origin of the Mead of Suttungr

And again said AEger: Whence originated the art that is called skaldship? Made answer Brage: The beginning of this was, that the gods had a war with the people that are called vans. They agreed to hold a meeting for the purpose of making peace, and settled their dispute in this wise, that they both went to a jar and spit into it. But at parting the gods, being unwilling to let this mark of peace perish, shaped it into a man whose name was Kvaser, and who was so wise that no one could ask him any question that he could not answer. He traveled much about in the world to teach men wisdom. Once he came to the home of the dwarfs Fjalar and Galar. They called him aside, saying they wished to speak with him alone, slew him and let his blood run into two jars called Son and Bodn, and into a kettle called

ᛊ ᛞ

Odrarer. They mixed honey with the blood, and thus was produced such mead that whoever drinks from it becomes a skald and sage. The dwarfs told the asas that Kvaser had choked in his wisdom, because no one was so wise that he could ask him enough about learning.[81]

At the end of the war, the Aesir and Vanir not only exchanged hostages but also performed a magical ritual to confirm the now existing family ties. The symbolic creation of Kvasir is akin to the birth of a child who combines the genes of the parents in equal proportions. Magically created, Kvasir was not born as an infant, did not undergo the standard stages of growth in a maternal womb, natural birth, maturation, and learning; Kvasir was born as he was and remained so. He combined all the wisdom of the gods—the concentrated experience that appeared in him from the very beginning and did not change until his death. This is not a consciousness that gains experience through life, discovers and develops its talent, cultivates it, perfects it, and manifests it through labour. Kvasir is the prototype of genius, an image of one "born with a gift" and manifesting that gift as originally intended. What happened to the god Kvasir is an algorithm of what happens to almost all geniuses if they manage their genius as Kvasir managed his nature.

The god Kvasir was wise from the beginning. He took in all the genetic memory of the Aesir and all the genetic memory of the Vanir; these two memories—unconscious, natural, wild, and conscious, rational, logical—combined fully and non-contradictorily in him. Like the two legs of Ymir, which, when joined, began to generate giants and titans, so the two natures in

[81] Continuation of the detective story—in the next chapter.

Kvasir, when joined, began to generate wisdom in words. Kvasir travelled through the worlds, teaching in each world—giving away his wisdom. Until he came to Svartalfheimr. That was where his journey ended.

The dvergar Fjalarr and Galarr, also brothers, but not blacksmiths like the well-known inhabitants of the dark elves' world, were nevertheless masters of their craft, without a doubt. Like all members of their kind, they were not good at deceit and recognizing trickery; they proved their rightness with real results, not words. The dwarves' understanding of wisdom was that what is said must necessarily be reflected in the result. It is likely that they perceived Kvasir and his words precisely this way: if someone demonstrates their mind and wisdom, it means that 1) everything said happened to them personally, and 2) everything described was seen with their own eyes. This attitude towards wisdom allowed the masters to see the clear discrepancy between what was said and what was manifested. Since they liked what was said but not what was manifested, they destroyed what was manifested, correctly determining that the blood was the source of wisdom and that everything else was some kind of misunderstanding that needed to be urgently corrected before anyone saw this mess.

Dvergar, as we already know well, are able to unmistakably identify vulnerability in anything if it exists. Once discovered, they can also use their skill and magic to supplement an imperfect consciousness so completely that no trace of vulnerability remains. However, in the case of Kvasir, he himself, entirely and completely, was identified by the dvergar as one big walking vulnerability, and for everyone. It is simpler to take the small valuable part that exists in him than to supplement this small part with a large number of elements that, unfortunately, do not exist. Representatives of the world of evil have a very rational approach to problems.

The dvergar saw mistletoe in Kvasir. Perhaps only for themselves personally, but by this act of killing Kvasir, they demonstrated how vulnerable one can be who has been granted a gift and talent from birth, by blood, but who has not made any effort to uncover and develop this gift. Such a person will scatter themselves where needed and not needed, where asked and unasked, often wasting the gods' gift without creating anything adequate to that power. Kvasir was excessive. Therefore, the dvergar took the most valuable part of the 'wise man,' his divine blood, the blood of the Aesir and Vanir—the source of the gift, the source of wisdom. Everything else, apparently, held no value.

So, we see that the god Kvasir shows us the point of application of the gods' efforts, at least concerning humans. Although creating the wise Kvasir was not their main activity, and one could say that his appearance in the world and myth is a byproduct of the northern gods' quest, his subsequent significance turned out to be so great, and his loss so significant, that he entered the northern myth not just rightfully, but as one of the important threads in the entire tapestry of the narrative. Kvasir is not the subject of application of efforts but a point of application, one of many. But this point became such an important knot on the canvas of reality that from it, like from a centre, rays of other narratives began to gradually emerge, making the myth deeper and more understandable, allowing it to resonate louder and louder through the ages.

The 'wise man Kvasir' is another project of the human consciousness program. Humans made from Vanir material, Ask and Embla, had already been created. They had already grown on the lands of Midgard, and the god Heimdall, under the name of Rig, had already divided their descendants into three classes, already distinguishing a fourth from the third—rulers, priest-kings. But the prototype of existing humans was not conceived by the gods as a contract with nature, and the Vanir tree part was programmed by the gods Odin, Hoenir, and Lodur for rational life in the lands of Midgard, and there was no talk then of any conscious contract with the Vanir—the Aesir simply took what was at hand and did what they wanted. But Kvasir is different.

Kvasir gave his wisdom, his excess part, to the worlds, and perhaps for the growing and maturing world of Midgard, for people divided into classes and living according to such social programs, Kvasir's wisdom was exactly what the initial programming of humans did not imply—individuality, personal talent, the ability to perceive not only the surrounding space but also what they cannot see—knowledge of other worlds lying beyond the visible human eye, understanding the unthinkable, experiencing the impossible. Meanwhile, the legend of Rig told us that the division into castes and classes implied that the accessible level of knowledge and inherent needs of each layer of human society would be their own, and therefore the knowledge would also be different: some are taught by the gods, while others obey orders. Kvasir's model of consciousness is non-caste.

Primarily because he contains all the informational power of the Aesir gods, whereas in the humans of Midgard, it is only from three creator gods. He also holds all the informational power of the Vanir, the essence of which is the principles of the development of all nature, whereas in humans it is only from one natural type—trees. Kvasir is genetically richer, and this wealth in him can be useful not only to those who, like the young Kon, were chosen by a creator god and inherit his name and knowledge. Kvasir's wealth, this ideal consciousness program, can be useful to everyone.

Kvasir is a model of ultimate possibilities. A model of consciousness that shows how deeply the Aesir and Vanir can penetrate each other without having to kill, eliminate, or cut off something incompatible and unviable. The god Kvasir shows us the intended idea, describes the standard, but northern honesty also describes why this program turned out to be unviable. Despite the apparent necessity of such a program for the human world, neither they nor the gods should forget that the universe consists not only of Midgard and what benefits one world may not necessarily bring joy and benefit to another.

The problem and vulnerability of the wise Kvasir's program was that it worked the same everywhere, in all worlds—giving out, and not what this world needed, but what was inside Kvasir—without distinguishing or differentiating. If in the world of Midgard this was appropriate, harmonious, and covered the flaws of the primary creation, in other worlds this could already be completely inappropriate, absolutely disharmonious, and for some worlds—completely excessive. But in the ideal wisdom program, there was no such option as appropriate/inappropriate, needed/unneeded. The reason is simple—this option was not in the gods either: just as nature does not know restraint in its spread, only give it, so the highest gods also did not ask the trees if they wanted to change roots for legs, and feeling for reason; did not ask people if they wanted to command or be commanded, did not ask if their personal will was to exist according to such algorithms of goodness, under which the majority of the human world would inevitably end up in Hel.

Practice 19. God Kvasir (page 534)

ᛊ ᛞ

Bragi

The story of the god Bragi and what he teaches through his manifestation logically follows from the previous story of the god Kvasir. They are like two sides of the same coin, the visible and invisible parts of a program. Their stories are connected both temporally and eventfully, so it is impossible to look at Bragi without knowing Kvasir's story, as they are magically related.

The quintessence of Kvasir's power was his blood. He did not have an independent personality that was above his blood. The god Odin took this into account, and his son Bragi became the embodiment of the power that surpasses the power of blood: the skalds called it the "gift of poetry."

Unlike the "wise man" Kvasir, the god Bragi was not created but born. His birth is directly related to the "mead of poetry," and here is how Snorri Sturluson's Prose Edda describes his origin:

The Origin of the Mead of Suttungr. (*continued*)

....Then the dwarfs invited to themselves the giant whose name is Gilling, and his wife; and when he came they asked him to row out to sea with them. When they had gotten a short distance from shore, the dwarfs rowed onto a blind rock and capsized the boat. Gilling, who was unable to swim, was drowned, but the dwarfs righted the boat again and rowed ashore. When they told of this mishap to his wife she took it much to heart, and began to cry aloud. The Fjalar asked her whether it would not lighten her sorrow if she could look out upon the sea where her husband had perished, and she said it would. He then said to his brother Galar that he should go

ᚠ ᚩ

up over the doorway, and as she passed out he should let a mill—stone drop onto her head, for he said he was tired of her bawling. Galar did so. When the giant Suttung, the son of Gilling, found this out he came and seized the dwarfs, took them out to sea and left them on a rocky island, which was flooded at high tide. They prayed Suttung to spare their lives, and offered him in atonement for their father's blood the precious mead, which he accepted. Suttung brought the mead home with him, and hid it in a place called Hnitbjorg. He set his daughter Gunlad to guard it. For these reasons we call songship Kvasir's blood; the drink of the dwarfs; the dwarfs' fill; some kind of liquor of Odrarer, or Bodn or Son; the ship of the dwarfs (because this mead ransomed their lives from the rocky isle); the mead of Suttung, or the liquor of Hnitbjorg.

Then remarked AEger: It seems dark to me to call songship by these names; but how came the asas by Suttung's mead?

Let's pause here and try to understand the beginning of this message—there are many new meanings here. Why does Ægir call these names for poetry "obscure"? Does he mean that they are "unclear," "hidden," or "mysterious"? Or something else?

The name of the kettle Odrerir is translated (approximately) as "stirrer of inspiration" or "that which causes ecstasy." The names of the two additional vats, Son and Bodn, are usually interpreted as "blood" and "vessel" respectively, but this translation is very inaccurate. To eliminate these inaccuracies and exclude linguistic distortion in the magical worldview, we need to look beyond the words and remember that the action of dividing the collected blood was done by master dwarves, who never do anything without reason. These are magical vessels, as everything the dvergar create is magical. The division of the blood into three containers, each with different names, is no accident. Each vessel is a container meant to give the substance

ᛊ ᛞ

it holds specific characteristics. In concept, Kvasir's blood, mixed with honey (a preservative), was to undergo a maturation stage in three forms: as the power of inspiration, the power of inheritance, and the power of restraint (or atonement-sacrifice). A single substance, divided into three parts, was intended to undergo various alchemical stages, where each would develop not sequentially but in parallel. Divine blood must gain meaning and determine its purpose—this is the dvergar' belief.

What happened next cannot be called the dvergar' "far-reaching plans." Perhaps they "breathed in" too much of Kvasir's originally talkative substance, but something overwhelmed them, and the circumstances were such that the master potion-makers lost the raw material for their magical experiments. Thus, it ended up where it was meant to be—in a place of guaranteed preservation, with the giants.

In fact, the dvergar sacrificed Gilling to the sea deities, the mead went to his son Suttungr (Gutting), and then to Suttungr's daughter Gunnlöd[82]. Here we also see the magical algorithm of "three generations," in which the desired quality must mature to ensure the perfection of the design. However, for Odin, it was important that the desired property be born in the realm of the Æsir and be a victory for the gods (the new seed), not the giants (the old seed). And this wish of the gods was probably well-founded, for Kvasir himself, despite the gods' previous indifference to the fate of their creation, is more related to the Æsir and Vanir than to the giants. The story then developed as follows.

---

82 Gunnlöd (Gunnlöð) — from Old Norse 'gunnr' ("battle, fight") + 'löð' ("invitation") — "invitation to battle."

ᛊ ᛞ

How Odin Obtained the Mead

Answered Brage: The saga about this is, that Odin set out from home and came to a place where nine thralls were mowing hay. He asked them whether they would like to have him whet their scythes. To this they said yes. Then he took a whet–stone from his belt and whetted the scythes. They thought

their scythes were much improved, and asked whether the whet–stone was for sale. He answered that he who would buy it must pay a fair price for it. All said they were willing to give the sum demanded, and each wanted Odin to sell it to him. But he threw the whet–stone up in the air, and when all wished to catch it they scrambled about it in such a manner that each brought his scythe onto the other's neck. Odin sought lodgings

for the night at the house of the giant Bauge, who was a brother of Suttung. Bauge complained of what had happened to his household, saying that his nine thralls had slain each other, and that he did not know where he should get other workmen. Odin called himself Bolverk[83]*. He offered to undertake the work of the nine men for Bauge, but asked in payment therefore a drink of Suttung's mead. Bauge answered that he had no control over the mead, saying that Suttung was bound to keep that for himself alone. But he agreed to go with Bolverk and try whether they could get the mead. During the summer Bolverk did the work of the nine men for Bauge, but when winter came he asked for his pay. Then they both went to Suttung. Bauge explained to Suttung his bargain with Bolverk, but Suttung stoutly refused to give even a drop of the mead. Bolverk then proposed to Bauge that they should try whether they could not get at the mead by the aid of some trick, and Bauge agreed to this. Then Bolverk drew forth the auger which is*

83 Bolverk — "evildoer".

ᚠ ᚨ

ᛊ ᛞ

called Rate[84]*, and requested Bauge to bore a hole through the rock, if the auger was sharp enough. He did so. Then said Bauge that there was a hole through the rock; but Bolverk blowed into the hole that the auger had made, and the chips flew back into his face. Thus he saw that Bauge intended to deceive him, and commanded him to bore through. Bauge bored again, and when Bolverk blew a second time the chips flew inward. Now Bolverk changed himself into the likeness of a serpent and crept into the auger—hole. Bauge thrust after him with the auger, but missed him. Bolverk went to where Gunlad was, and shared her couch for three nights. She then promised to give him three draughts from the mead. With the first draught he emptied Odrarer, in the second Bodn, and in the third Son, and thus he had all the mead. Then he took on the guise of an eagle, and flew off as fast as he could. When Suttung saw the flight of the eagle, he also took on the shape of an eagle and flew after him. When the asas saw Odin coming, they set their jars out in the yard. When Odin reached Asgard, he spewed the mead up into the jars. He was, however, so near being caught by Suttung, that he sent some of the mead after him backward, and as no care was taken of this, anybody that wished might have it. This we call the share of poetasters. But Suttung's mead Odin gave to the asas and to those men who are able to make verses. Hence we call songship Odin's prey, Odin's find, Odin's drink, Odin's gift, and the drink of the asas.*

Thus, the 'maturation of blood' project underwent changes through the intervention of the god Odin. First of all, it should be noted that Odin obtained the mead quite honestly and legally: he fulfilled his part of the deal, worked off the agreement, and Baugi's consent to pay with the mead was given completely voluntarily, albeit with reservations. Kvasir was a creation of the

[84] The ancients believed that each thing has its own name, and this name must truthfully signify what the thing is intended for. The name "Rate" essentially means "auger".

gods, but 'blood with honey' was no longer Kvasir; it was the property of the giants, which they had lawfully obtained as compensation. The agreement between Odin and Gunnlod was also entirely voluntary, out of love and friendship, without any deceit or trickery. It just so happened that Odin had an insatiable throat, but no one asked about that.

After drinking all three vessels, the god Odin performed a reverse mixing of the magical substance, where he himself, in the form of an eagle, acted as an autoclave, accelerating the necessary reactions. There were, however, some 'side effects,' but these are said to have been the cause of such rhymes as 'love-dove.' This 'excess part' of Kvasir, having passed through the mind of the god Odin in the form of an eagle, also took shape—the share of the rhymesters.

Having reached Asgard, the 'mead of poetry' now represents a secondary magical substance that can be detached from its bearer and given to anyone. This is a new form of gift, a new program of magical heritage created by the god of magic and knowledge, Odin. Herein lies its novelty.

In Kvasir's case, the gift was innate, and the personality was built around this gift, not the other way around. But in Bragi's case, the gift becomes not system-defining but complementing the personality, so its manifestation depends on the personality, but the personality does not depend on the gift. This is an important difference between Kvasir and Bragi, and the myth of the 'mead of poetry' illustrates the difference between the concepts of 'genius' and 'talent.' Genius is all-encompassing; it governs both nature and reason, knows no restraint, and there are no barriers to limit or stop it; it is an innate quality that guides one through life and also leads to death. Talent is different. It manifests in a mature personality that, through growth, experience, and the acquisition of specific

ᛊ ᛞ

personal qualities, forms such a configuration of consciousness that can accept the 'gift' but manifest it in the right form, and also create such circumstances around itself that this form is not constrained. Such a consciousness, enriched by talent, can create life circumstances that allow this ability to manifest correctly: ***when necessary, where necessary, to whom necessary, how much necessary, and exactly what is necessary***. In other words, to manifest everything that Kvasir naturally could not.

Now let's try to take a closer look at the god Bragi, whom Odin chose as the worthy one whose "personality" could take in the "mead of poetry" and perceive the gift not as genius, but as a talent necessary for the gods and the worlds.

The god Bragi was born of the very goddess Gunnlöd, who, according to the myth, was the last guardian of Kvasir's blood. His father was the god Odin himself, who, according to the agreement, spent three nights with Gunnlöd and received the right to drink the mead, which he did. Thus, we see that the god Bragi was not a random choice as the future bearer of the magical talent embodied in poetry. His mother was a giantess, a bearer of ancient continuous memory. His father was the god of magic and knowledge. In their son, these qualities combined in such a way that he became one who could not only fully receive the gift but also use it correctly: a poet needs continuous memory and the magic of words. Bragi was chosen by Odin as the worthy recipient of the 'mead of poetry,' and henceforth he is called the father of all poets.

The best skald is Bragi.

However, when the magical gift of genius, Kvasir's blood, takes the form of talent and becomes Bragi's gift, it not only acquires specific magical characteristics but also specific

ᚹ ᚨ

ᛊ ᛞ

limitations. These properties, of course, were pointed out by the god Loki, whose nature is to reveal vulnerabilities. Here is how he himself spoke about this in the famous Lokasenna:

Bragi spake:
"A place and a seat will the gods prepare
No more in their midst for thee;
For the gods know well what men they wish
To find at their mighty feasts,"

Then Vithar arose and poured drink for Loki; but before he drank he spoke to the gods:

"Hail to you, gods! ye goddesses, hail!
Hail to the holy throng!
Save for the god who yonder sits,
Bragi there on the bench."

Bragi spake:
"A horse and a sword from my hoard will I give,
And a ring gives Bragi to boot,
That hatred thou makst not among the gods;
So rouse not the great ones to wrath."

Loki spake:
"In horses and rings thou shalt never be rich,
Bragi, but both shalt thou lack[85]*;*
Of the gods and elves here together met
Least brave in battle art thou,

---

85 Loki wants to say that Bragi cannot have a horse and a ring because only the brave own treasures. (Translator's note)

(And shyest thou art of the shot.)"

Bragi spake:
"Now were I without as I am within,
And here in Aegir's hall,
Thine head would I bear in mine hands away,
And pay thee the price of thy lies."

Loki spake:
"In thy seat art thou bold, not so are thy deeds,
Bragi, adorner of benches!
Go out and fight if angered thou feelest.
No hero such forethought has."

Bragi took the position "in the middle of the bench." From the perspective of a warrior of that time, this was the position of someone undecided, and Loki did not like this. He believed that the god of poetry lacked the most important qualities—courage, strength of spirit, and the ability to act decisively, which is always associated with the warrior's spirit. But the god Odin saw skaldic wisdom differently: the "mead of poetry," having passed through the Father of Magic, changes the consciousness of its poetic talent bearer and always keeps him "in the middle of the bench," not allowing him to take any side in disputes; not allowing the blood of the Vanir or the Aesir to prevail if it comes to personal preferences. If a poet, the myth tells us, has personal preferences, he will not be able to embody the gift correctly and will inevitably end his path as the first bearer of the gift, the god Kvasir, did. The ability to sit "in the middle of the bench" prevents the poet from making wrong choices and incurring the wrath of personal Fjalars and Galars, who will always be nearby any bearer of the gift. But Loki is always near too, provoking the talent to be "brave," which means "quick," to become a warrior by nature, not by essence. He will always provoke Bragi's descendants because the gift does not make a poet's life easier but requires reflection and caution in its application.

Poetry is not just the ability to compose verses. It is something more, and the myth of the creation of the "mead of poetry" indicates this to us: it is made from blood, this blood underwent maturation and alchemical transformation, was united within the magical form of the bird-god, acquired the property of the air element, and gained the ability for mental perception[86]. The gift of poetry after such transmutation is hardly similar to the "raw material," wild and unrestrained compared to the final "philosopher's stone." In ancient times, oral word was valued more than the written word. Ancient poets believed that written words could not be corrected later—they were final, 'finita'. Oral words could not be final; they required continuation, like life, and had to be infinite. That is why ancient skalds, filids, troubadours, and minstrels, bards, and ancient *boyans*[87] memorized all tales by heart, not relying on written words.

Bragi is the god of poetry, skaldic poetry. That he is married to the goddess Idunn in a "partnership" marriage indicates that not only his personality but also his social life will always be different from what is usual in society, and he must be ready for that. He will be praised or criticized, but something will

---

86 The Air element is associated with the mental body of human consciousness (for more details on the elements and subtle bodies, see the book by K. Menshikova "The Power of the Elements".

87 Boyan—an ancient Russian singer and storyteller, a "song creator."

always be taken in exchange for the received gift to avoid excess, so the gift does not take the form of "Kvasir's genius," so the bearer of the gift is not again taken apart into original elements. Loki believed that the god Bragi lacked courage and valour, and therefore did not meet the main task of Odin's House. Yes, perhaps Bragi is not a warrior. But now we know that no one can become a warrior without him.

It is important for a person to survive, but for a warrior, it is not only important to survive but also to win. The higher the level of possibilities, the higher the level of awareness. Therefore, the chosen method of victory becomes increasingly relevant for one who is to become a leader. The god Loki refused to acknowledge the leadership of the god Bragi in his outburst. But before finding out who will be preferred, one must go through the deep knowledge of what lies beyond the northern myth's narrative. One must see what is hidden in the opposite of the eloquence of the god of poetry, the god who preserves knowledge through words, to the god who acts through the opposite way—through silence. The path to this silent god lies through complete darkness.

Practice 20. God Bragi (page 540)

Höd

Throughout the entire expanse of Norse mythology, the god Höd is perhaps the most difficult to understand. Despite his very important role, the story about him is extremely sparse. It seems as if the gods are reluctant to speak about him, even though they recount their deeds and defeats equally extensively. In the Prose Edda, Snorri Sturluson says this about him:

About Höd

Hoder hight one of the asas, who is blind, but exceedingly strong; and the gods would wish that this asa never needed to be named, for the work of his hand will long be kept in memory both by gods and men.

Since:

... *and he came to Hoder, the blind god, put the tender mistletoe in his hand and directed his arm, so that Balder sank from the joys of Valhal down into the abodes of pale Hel, and did not return.*

Such an attitude towards one of the key characters of the myth is possible only when his role is so ambiguous, and "political correctness" so painful, that it is better to say nothing than to say something that might turn the understanding of the myth completely in another direction. But we, continuing the path of the faithful, cannot descend to hypocrisy and will continue to look at the northern story honestly. This means that the god Höd needs to be seen as clearly as the god Baldr—in the name of justice.

In the dualistic worldview of monotheistic religions, a blind god of darkness would be perceived as the personification of obvious evil. But the natural northern honesty, even in Snorri's Christianised consciousness at the time of writing the Prose Edda, did not allow him to lie. Therefore, silence about the god Höd is to some extent a consequence of the northern worldview: it is better to say nothing than to lie. However, we descendants have no need to bow to Abrahamic religions; fortunately, we have already survived that nightmare. The blindness of the god Höd can now be perceived with a clear view.

The god Höd was the legitimate son of Odin and Frigg. He was the elder son, and this is very important. According to the rules of that time, the right of inheritance passed through the eldest son, and formally Höd should have inherited Odin. It was believed that the eldest son was born to follow the path of the ancestors and serve that path, while the other children were freer in their wyrd.

However, let's look even deeper into the myth and remember that its roots lie thousands of years further back than what is described not only in the Prose Edda but also in the Poetic Edda. For this, we need to remember a time when the myth was not divided by traditions, when there were no northern, Slavic, Celtic, Italian, or Achaean traditions. The myths of ancient peoples are strikingly similar, and it may seem that one myth was "borrowed" from another and diluted with local cultural tradition, but this is not the case. Once, the myth was indeed united, and people simply told it differently, hence the apparent division into traditions. But they all stem from a single root.

In this root, one can see the story of the primary forces of the gods, which were expressed in the image of brothers. Twin brothers. Possibly, Baldr and Höd in the original myth were also twins. They were always born together—the god of light and the god of darkness. But the god of darkness (also always) was born first. The description of this "primacy" is described differently in various myths: sometimes by the will of nature and ancient gods, sometimes due to the trickery and deceit of one of the twins in the mother's womb, sometimes by misunderstanding, and sometimes by the deep design of the ancients. This is not mentioned in the northern myth, but the fact that the god Höd was killed at the same moment that Baldr died suggests that they were indeed twins, the god of light and the god of darkness, for neither can live if the other is dead—such is the rule of both myth and the magical construction of reality.

The god of darkness is born first, and darkness appears before light. Perhaps only for a moment, but earlier. And the right of primogeniture, the right of inheritance, belongs to Darkness before Light—always. However, we already know from the myth that the power of maternal love brought the second-born, not the first, to the forefront. The first, Höd, and the last, Hermod, were relegated to the background in the eyes of the goddess Frigg, contrary to all principles of right and inheritance. This is often a problem when we talk about people, but it is always a problem when we talk about gods: for gods are not people, gods are primary principles. In this case, the Frigg-tradition of maternal love tries to change the primary principle of order, and from this, as a classic might say, 'the bond of times is broken.[88]'

The new maternal algorithm of personal preference detaches tradition from its foundation and makes it vulnerable—

88 W. Shakespeare. "Hamlet". The time is out of joint. / O cursed spite, / That ever I was born to set it right!

to mistletoe, to carelessness, for careless is he who feels no responsibility for what happens. The god Höd was the last to play the game of 'kill Baldr if you can.' Formally—because he couldn't. But perhaps not only because of his blindness. However, the god of Light was killed by the god of Darkness. Darkness had no desire for this, but there was too much darkness, and it killed the light through the symbol of its carelessness—through mistletoe. The strength of a blind-from-birth god was ten times greater than the strength of any other god. Is it any wonder that it was in Höd's hands that the weak sprig of mistletoe turned into a deadly weapon? Strength and naivety always go hand in hand.

Frigg lost both sons in an instant, for one cannot live if the other is dead; it is impossible for her to lose one and keep the other—this is a rule for any tradition, whose strength and form are embodied in the myth by the goddess-queen. The god Loki, placing the deadly weapon in the hand of the blind Höd, ensured that the killing of Baldr not only stressed the entire system to change but also strongly hit the one responsible for what had happened. But even mourning her son, sending his body to the pyre, Frigg loved him more than all others, and her last words: 'He who will bring Baldr back to Asgard will deserve my love!' again do not mention her elder son Höd, as if he did not exist and never had. Is it any wonder that both remained with Hel, and the giantess Thokk did not weep for the slain Baldr: "*Thok will weep with dry tears. Neither in life nor in death gave he me gladness*". And indeed, we add. But who will weep for Höd? Will there be anyone in all nine worlds who will weep for the slain blind god?

Remaining with Baldr in the world of the goddess Hel, he, like his brother, underwent his lessons: Höd learned to direct his power and strength correctly, and Baldr's light learned to

ᛊ ᛞ

manifest in the darkness what should manifest. In Hel's world, they unite for mutual penetration, for mutual understanding. What they could not do in the system of Order, they will do in the system of Chaos—as if growing in the womb and being born again for a new world. Höd is an infinite volume of the secret, tenfold strength, all the accumulated genetic memory of the firstborn, which must be manifested. But this can only happen through Baldr. The brothers are connected to each other, and after the battle of the gods, in the new world, they are destined to rule together. Because it is right—only this way is right: Light must be equal to Darkness.

> *...and Baldr comes back;*
> *Baldr and Hoth dwell in Hropt's battle-hall,*
> *And the mighty gods.*
>
> *(The Poetic Edda. Voluspo)*

The brothers do not participate in the battle of Ragnarök and will return when the battle is over. Because it is not their battle. Baldr and Höd are victims of others' mistakes, others' hatred, and others' love. Children are not responsible for the sins of their parents, the myth tells us; children have their own path. Unless, of course, they consciously choose a third path, which the story of the last, youngest brother will tell us.

Practice 21. God Höd (page 543)

ᚠ ᚠ

Hermod

The name of this god can be translated as "courage," "warrior spirit"; it can also mean "bravery" or even "fury." In Russian, this state is called "udaly," and therefore Hermod is often referred to as Hermod the Bold. However, the sagas do not tell of his valour and daring, nor do they mention his martial successes. In the tapestry of northern myth, Hermod acts as a messenger and appears in the myth at the moment of the funeral of the god Baldr.

When the gods came to their senses, Frigg spoke and asked who there might be among the asas who desired to win all her love and good will by riding the way to Hel and trying to find Balder, and offering Hel a ransom if she would allow Balder to return home again to Asgard. But he is called Hermod, the Nimble, Odin's swain, who undertook this journey. Odin's steed, Sleipner, was led forth. Hermod mounted him and galloped away. (The Prose Edda).

The god Hermod is the third son of Odin and Frigg and the last remaining alive. But to bring back her beloved Baldr, Frigg is willing to sacrifice even him and does not stop her son when he voluntarily sets out for the underworld. What is the point of being the only one left but unloved? What use is all his boldness if it is not valued by the one for whom everything happens? Hermod went to the halls of Hel to seek his mother's love.

However, let's look at the god Hermod from another perspective—let's consider his origin. The gods Baldr and Höd embody the power of light and the power of darkness, respectively. The function described in the image of the god Hermod, the function of a messenger, clearly indicates that his mission is to link Light and Darkness. As the third son, he has what Odin and Frigg have, but he also has what his brothers have: the foundation of order, the connection with tradition, light, and dark—not as elements, but as the ability to link all these elements.

Hermod is the only one who could enter the realm of Helheim without being dead and leave it unchanged. Thanks to his journey among the worlds, knowledge about the essence of Helheim and what happens there appeared—until then, no one could boast of having spoken with the mistress Hel and returned afterward. Hermod went to earn his mother's love and brought back the truth about Hel's realm.

In the morning he asked Hel whether Balder might ride home with him, and told how great weeping there was among the asas. But Hel replied that it should now be tried whether Balder was so much beloved as was said. If all things, said she, both quick and dead, will weep for him, then he shall go back to the asas, but if anything refuses to shed tears, then he shall remain with Hel. Hermod arose, and Balder accompanied him out of the hall. He took the ring Draupner and sent it as a keepsake to Odin. Nanna sent Frigg a kerchief and other gifts, and to Fulla she sent a ring. Thereupon Hermod rode back and came to Asgard, where he reported the tidings he had seen and heard. (The Prose Edda)

The two artifacts Hermod brought back—a ring and a cloth—had been in the world of the dead, going through the process of dying and rebirth, just like Hermod himself. We will talk about Fulla's headband when we meet this goddess, but let's discuss the ring now. Remember that the ring Draupnir[89], made in a famous contest by the master Brokkr, had the ability to create eight identical rings every ninth night. It was a self-replicating program of multiplication. When distributed, the ring went to the god Odin, but it wasn't apparent that he was pleased with such a gift. The myth does not tell us that Odin used it as intended, and during Baldr's funeral, he sent it with him to Hel. In Helheim, it was also of no use, and Baldr sent it back to Asgard with Hermod. It seems the gods did not value Draupnir highly. The story of the ring in this myth does not go further[90]. However, magical artifacts in myths often acquire their own history, and many start living their "own lives," moving from the world of the gods to the world of heroes and humans.

Draupnir is a self-replicating program, like an algorithm of luck. But when such a program copies itself without control, the creator of the program loses control over it. How Brokkr laughed at his humiliation in the contest! Not only did he inflict a magical wound on the god Loki, but he also gave the gods a "Trojan horse": if Asgard is a perfect program, its spread will only bring benefits. But if the program of order is imperfect, then you, gods, will be punished for your arrogance—the Norns warned you! The ring will keep duplicating, and even if you want to correct something, you won't be able to. The god Odin had the strength to refuse such a gift, but once it reached humans, the ring of the dvergar classically manifested itself as a "cursed treasure."

---

89 Draupnir — "dripper."

90 It is not traced in the main storyline of the myth, although echoes of it can be seen in the further development of Northern legends, such as in the "Saga of the Volsungs" or the "Song of the Nibelungs."

ᛊ ᛞ

The ring is not needed in Helheimr—neither as a symbol of wealth, nor as a symbol of completeness and cyclicality, nor as a device for automatic self-replication. But Baldr sent Draupnir not so much because it was unnecessary in the world of the dead but as proof that Hermod had indeed been in Hel's halls and seen Baldr. This says a lot about the Aesir's attitude towards the god Hermod—they might not have believed him, for Hermod did the impossible. No god or human is allowed to enter Hel's halls while alive, but Hermod's nature is such that he is neither living nor dead—he is an unfixed element, a link. He exists only when there is something to connect, and that is why Hermod was the only one who could ride Sleipnir, Odin's eight-legged horse, the offspring of Loki. Because they share the same nature—Sleipnir is also a link. Hermod is natural magic; he was born that way. But this is not the magic of the Vanir; it is the magic of the giants—the magic of creation: linking everything with everything and multiplying existence on these connections. The only thing this magic lacks, as the myth tells us, is trust and love. That's what he went to Helheim for, but this magic is so ancient, so from the times of Ymir, that even the gods do not understand it. It would be good if the ring Draupnir stayed with Hermod, but the myth does not tell us this directly.

The fact that the god Hermod managed not only to enter Hel's halls but also to leave unchanged and not empty-handed says a lot about him. From the realm of Hel, as you already know, the gates are closed for exiting. The exception is the final battle, but that command will be for all, and for someone to be allowed to leave alone, such a thing is not described.

Practice 22. God Hermod (page 545)

ᚠ ᚨ

ᛊ ᛞ

Vali

The god Vali is also a son of Odin. His appearance in the myth occurs at the moment when the culmination of the northern family's tragedy reaches its apex—the moment of Baldr's murder. The image of this god is complex and not easily understood; his personality is not revealed in the myth as independent, and the fact of his birth disrupts the image of Odin as a wise and noble elder. But let's go through it in order.

It all began, as usual, with the prophecy of the Völva.

The Wise-Woman spake:
"Rind bears Vali in Vestrsalir,
And one night old fights Othin's son;
His hands he shall wash not, his hair he shall comb not,
Till the slayer of Baldr he brings to the flames.
Unwilling I spake, and now would be still." (The Poetic Edda)

The ancient tale of the Poetic Edda and the later Prose Edda did not detail the fulfillment of this part of the prophecy for the descendants. However, the parallel work of Saxo Grammaticus, "Deeds of the Danes[91]", fills in the details:

But Odin, though he was accounted the chief of the gods, began to inquire of the prophets and diviners concerning the way to accomplish vengeance for his son, as well as all others whom he had heard were skilled

---

[91] Saxo Grammaticus (Latin: Saxo Grammaticus; c. 1140 – c. 1216) was a Danish chronicler who, in the sixteen-volume chronicle "Gesta Danorum", presented the oldest sagas. (Wikipedia)

ᛊ ᛗ

in the most recondite arts of soothsaying. For godhead that is incomplete is oft in want of the help of man. Rostioph [Hrossthiolf] [92]*, the Finn, foretold to him that another son must be born to him by Rinda [Wrinda], daughter of the King of the Ruthenians*[93]*; this son was destined to exact punishment for the slaying of his brother.*

For the gods had appointed to the brother that was yet to be born the task of avenging his kinsman. Odin, when he heard this, muffled his face with a cap, that his garb might not betray him, and entered the service of the said king as a soldier; and being made by him captain of the soldiers, and given an army, won a splendid victory over the enemy. And for his stout achievement in this battle the king admitted him into the chief place in his friendship, distinguishing him as generously with gifts as with honours. A very little while afterwards Odin routed the enemy single-handed, and returned, at once the messenger and the doer of the deed. All marvelled that the strength of one man could deal such slaughter upon a countless host. Trusting in these services, he privily let the king into the secret of his love, and was refreshed by his most gracious favor; but when he sought a kiss from the maiden, he received a cuff. But he was not driven from his purpose either by anger at the slight or by the odiousness of the insult.

Next year, loth to quit ignobly the quest he had taken up so eagerly, he put on the dress of a foreigner and went back to dwell with the king. It

---

92 A giant named Hrossthjolf (Hrosþiolfr) is mentioned in the Poetic Edda ("Hyndluljóð," 32) — the ancient Scandinavians attributed the ability to foresee the future to the Jotuns, and the inhabitants of Finland were also renowned for this. (Translator's note)

93 Ruteni (Latin: ruthēni) were a Celtic tribe in ancient Gaul, living in modern Southern France in the vicinity of the current city of Rodez. Due to the similarity of the tribe's name to the word "Rus'," from the 12th century onwards in Western Europe, the Rutheni and consequently Ruthenia referred to the Eastern Slavs and Rus' (and later Russia). (Wikipedia) However, since there is a clear mention of the "western home," it seems correct to relate the "residence" of the king's daughter to Gaul rather than Rus'. (Author's note)

ᚠ ᚨ

ᛊ ᛞ

was hard for those who met him to recognise him; for his assumed filth obliterated his true features, and new grime hid his ancient aspect. He said that his name was Roster[94] *[Hrosstheow], and that he was skilled in smithcraft. And his handiwork did honour to his professions: for he portrayed in bronze many and many a shape most beautifully, so that he received a great mass of gold from the king and was ordered to hammer out the ornaments of the matrons. So, after having wrought many adornments for women's wearing, he at last offered to the maiden a bracelet which he had polished more laboriously than the rest, and several rings which were adorned with equal care. But no services could assuage the wrath of Rinda; when he was fain to kiss her she cuffed him; for gifts offered by one we hate are unacceptable, while those tendered by a friend are far more grateful: so much doth the value of the offering oft turn on the offerer. For this stubborn-hearted maiden never doubted that the crafty old man was feigning generosity in order to seize an opening to work his lust. His temper, moreover, was keen and indomitable; for she knew that his homage covered guile, and that under the devotion of his gifts there lay a desire for crime. Her father fell to upbraiding her heavily for refusing the match; but she loathed to wed an old man, and the plea of her tender years lent her some support in her scorning of his hand; for she said that a young girl ought not to marry prematurely.*

But Odin, who had found that nothing served the wishes of lovers more than tough persistency, though he was stung with the shame of his double rebuff, nevertheless, effacing the form he had worn before, went to the king for the third time, professing the completest skill in soldiership. He was led to take this pains not only by pleasure but by the wish to wipe out his disgrace. For of old those who were skilled in magic gained this power of instantly changing their aspect and exhibiting the most different shapes. Indeed, they were clever at imitating any age, not only in its natural bodily appearance, but also in its stature; and so the old man, in order to exhibit

[94] Epithets of Odin, Hropt (Hroptr), and Hroptatyr (Hroptatýr) (Old Norse: "wise, prudent") also appear in the Eddas. (Translator's note)

his calling agreeably, used to ride proudly up and down among the briskest of them. But not even such a tribute could move the rigour of the maiden; for it is hard for the mind to come back to a genuine liking for one against whom it has once borne heavy dislike. When he tried to kiss her at his departure, she repulsed him so that he tottered and smote his chin upon the ground. Straightway he touched her with a piece of bark whereon spells were written, and made her like unto one in frenzy; which was a gentle revenge to take for [80] all the insults he had received. But still he did not falter in the fulfilment of his purpose, for trust in his divine majesty buoyed him up with confidence; so, assuming the garb of a maiden, this indefatigable journeyer repaired for the fourth time to the king, and, on being received by him, showed himself assiduous and even forward. Most people believed him to be a woman, as he was dressed almost in female attire. Also he declared that his name was Wecha, and his calling that of a physician; and this assertion he confirmed by the readiest services. At last he was taken into the household of the queen, and played the part of a waiting-woman to the princess, and even used to wash the soil off her feet at eventide; and as he was applying the water he was suffered to touch her calves and the upper part of the thighs.

But fortune goes with mutable steps, and thus chance put into his hand what his address had never won. For it happened that the girl fell sick, and looked around for a cure; and she summoned to protect her health those very hands which aforetime she had rejected, and appealed for preservation to him whom she had ever held in loathing. He examined narrowly all the symptoms of the trouble, and declared that, in order to check the disease as soon as possible, it was needful to use a certain drugged draught; but that it was so bitterly compounded, that the girl could never endure so violent a cure unless she submitted to be bound; since the stuff of the malady must be ejected from the very innermost tissues. When her father heard this he did not hesitate to bind his daughter; and, laying her on the bed, he bade her endure patiently all the applications of the doctor. For the king was tricked by the sight of the female dress, which the old man was using to disguise his persistent guile; and thus the seeming remedy became an opportunity of outrage. For the physician seized the chance of love, and, abandoning his business of healing, sped to the work, not of expelling the fever, but of working his lust; making use of the sickness of the princess, whom in sound health he had found adverse to him. It will not be wearisome if I subjoin another version of this affair. For there are certain who say that the king, when he saw the physician groaning with love, but despite all his expense of mind and body accomplishing nothing, did not wish to rob of his due reward one who had so well earned it, and allowed him to lie privily with his daughter. So doth the wickedness of the father sometimes assail the child, when vehement passion perverts natural mildness. But his fault was soon followed by a remorse that was full of shame, when his daughter bore a child.

Thus, the "detail-loving" Saxo Grammaticus provided us with crucial information—that the son of Odin and the goddess Rind was born through deceit, fraud, and violence. Apparently, the hatred for the rapist was so great that it imbued the unborn child—hatred and vengeance became the core program and main principle of the god Vali's life. If we remember that in any myth, including the one above, it is not about humans but about gods, global programs, and fundamental functions of the Universe and worlds, much of what is said will become clear.

Further, in "Deeds of the Danes":

But the gods, whose chief seat was then at Byzantium[95]*, seeing that Odin had tarnished the fair name of godhead by divers injuries to its majesty, thought that he ought to be removed from their society. And they had him not only ousted from the headship, but outlawed and stripped of all worship and honour at home ; thinking it better that the power of their infamous*

---

[95] Here we see an echo of the popular myth that the northern gods are descendants from Troy (alas, a crude plagiarism, a version borrowed from the Romans who had previously conquered Celtic tribes). (Author's note)

president should be overthrown than that public religion should be profaned ; and fearing that they might themselves be involved in the sin of another, and though guiltless be punished for the crime of the guilty. For they saw that, now the derision of their great god was brought to light, those whom they had lured to proffer them divine honours were exchanging obeisance for scorn and worship for shame ; that holy rites were being accounted sacrilege, and fixed and regular ceremonies deemed so much childish raving. Fear was in their souls, death before their eyes, and one would have supposed that the fault of one was visited upon the heads of all.

As a result of this story, the god Vali was born. The goddess Rind, personifying the Earth in her particular aspect of "freedom above all," gave birth to the expected reaction—the force of negation. She bore the god immediately, and this god matured instantly: one day old, he already knew what to do; he did not need to be taught or raised in the spirit of hatred towards enemies—it was all already within him. Rind is called the daughter of Billing, one of the ancient beings, and he is also called the king of Svartalfheimr. The svartálfar, I remind you, are associated with the proto-foundation of "evil," which in turn gathers such informational algorithms that can be designated as what "should never be." The daughter of the dark king Rind is the goddess of the Earth (or rather, one of its facets), and she knows exactly how to recognize natural evil—what should not be. Odin took her by force, and in return, she gave birth to a reaction—a method of combating evil, the instant elimination of what should not be.

The god Vali, born with the knowledge of evil, killed the god Höd not because he hated him—he had no reason to hate the blind god. He killed him because it was his function—natural reaction to the world's wrongness: he instantly destroyed the second part of the pair when the first one died. To prevent imbalance, where any imbalance is injustice because justice is balance.

The function embodied by the god Vali, son of Odin and Rind, embodied hatred, the reaction of instant vengeance, will be the force that will take care of the organization (and programming) of the new world—there is no way without it. Vali is the immediate removal of the unnecessary, the instant reaction to disturbed balance, the immediate retribution born of Mother Earth in her killing, unyielding aspect as a reaction to injustice. In the new world, nothing wrong or unjust should exist, and the reaction of the world-building program should have the function of instant elimination of the wrong. This function was developed in Odin's "laboratory"; this program even stripped him of his status and reputation, forcing him to follow Tyr's path and experience the bitterness of the other gods' betrayal.

After Ragnarök, the god Vali will not act alone or independently but as part of a team. Summoning the power of the god Vali by invoking vengeance will no longer be possible as now—based on one's understanding of justice and honor. Vali, as the instant function of retribution, will activate the entire program of the young gods-builders of the new reality, and in this new attribute, he will not require a separate invocation: if justice is violated, the system's reaction will be instant and inevitable, requiring no separate activation.

Vafthruthnir spake:
"In the gods' home Vithar and Vali shall dwell,
When the fires of Surt have sunk.
(Poetic Edda. Vafthruthnismol)

The foundation of the new world's program consists of young gods, the children of the current ones. But the main principle on which reality will be built after Ragnarök is embodied by Vali's brother, also Odin's son, the god Vidar. It is Vidar that Odin appointed as his successor and heir. But he is like a "quantum pair" with the god Vali: the activity of one generates the activity of the other, changes in one trigger changes in the other. Decision—reaction; reaction—decision. And also instantly. The god Vali, born as a single tool of vengeance, in conjunction with the power of the young gods, reveals his function in a much larger volume and scope of application— the young gods turned out to be much more reasonable and powerful than their ancestors, and this is right, as it should be.

Practice 23. God Vali (page 551)

Vidar

The new reality should not and will not be as inert as the current one. But for it to be so, the fundamental principle of reality, embodied by the god Vidar, must be something special, never seen before. Let's get to know him.

The god Vidar is also the son of the god Odin, but his mother was another goddess, somewhat familiar to us. This goddess was named Grid. It was she who endowed the god Thor with magical artifacts that helped Thor achieve victory in Jotunheimr when Loki sent him there without Mjolnir:

On his way Thor visited the giantess whose name is Grid. She was the mother of Vidar the Silent. She told Thor the truth concerning Geirrod, that he was a dog—wise and dangerous giant; and she lent him her own belt of strength and steel gloves, and her staff, which is called Gridarvol. (The Prose Edda)

In this myth, the goddess Grid appears as the Mother-Raw Earth, who nourishes the hero with strength. Unlike the mother of Vali, the goddess Rind, the goddess Grid is benevolent towards the Aesir gods, helping them voluntarily. It is in union with this goddess and All-Father that the god Vidar was born, in love and harmony. Vidar is the son of a voluntary agreement and mutual acceptance, inheriting both strength and right from his mother and father. The fact that the myth does not explicitly state that Odin chose Vidar as his successor does not negate this. All indirect evidence supports this idea: firstly, rights and inheritance according to ancient law are granted by the

Earth. Secondly, Vidar avenged his father by killing the wolf Fenrir, which would be a decisive argument in the human world according to more recent laws. Thirdly, Odin's own succession is indicated by the magical artifact "Vidar's boot," which has very important properties.

Firstly, the leather for this boot was collected by the entire world, and Snorri Sturluson writes about this in the Prose Edda:

The wolf swallows Odin, and thus causes his death; but Vidar immediately turns and rushes at the wolf, placing one foot on his nether jaw. On this foot he has the shoe for which materials have been gathering through all ages, namely, the strips of leather which men cut off for the toes and heels of shoes; wherefore he who wishes to render assistance to the ases must cast these strips away. With one hand Vidar seizes the upper jaw of the wolf, and thus rends asunder his mouth. Thus the wolf perishes.

The Poetic Edda in "Voluspo" elaborates:

Then comes Sigfather's mighty son,
Vithar, to fight with the foaming wolf;
In the giant's son does he thrust his sword
Full to the heart: his father is avenged.

Hither there comes the son of Hlothyn[96]*,*
The bright snake gapes to heaven above;
Against the serpent goes Othin's son.

Vafthruthnismol echoes Voluspo:
Vafthruthnir spake:

---

96 Hlothyn — Loki.

ᛊ ᛞ

"The wolf shall fell the father of men,
And this shall Vithar avenge;
The terrible jaws shall he tear apart,
And so the wolf shall he slay."

"In the gods' home Vithar and Vali shall dwell,
When the fires of Surt have sunk;

The leather for Vidar's boot is a voluntary sacrifice from all people—pure, bloodless, from the soul and heart. Additionally, the image of the boot is associated with certain laws from the Middle Ages, indicating that a father (or one who bestows an estate) must put the boot on his heir[97].

Another argument in favor of Vidar is that he has his own halls, called Landvidi, which the god Vali does not have. According to the magical formula, these halls are an information database where the active force, the decision-making force (the god), gathers its victory algorithms.

Filled with growing trees and high-standing grass
Is Vithi, Vithar's land;
But there did the son from his steed leap down,
When his father he fain would avenge.
(The Poetic Edda. Grimnismol)

Thus, according to magical laws, Vidar is the successor of Odin's power in the new world. However, it is not as straightforward as it may seem at first glance, and the "ruler-heir" formula in the new world will be different. The system of realities

---

[97] The laws mention this custom in the case of adopting an illegitimate child and accepting an heir into the family.

ᚹ ᚨ

formed after the battle of Ragnarök does not imply sole rule by one individual: this is not intended for the gods, nor will it be for humans. The new system is built by the children of those who perished in the battle, and their participation in the project is as a team. Not equal, but as a team, where the team is a whole. A whole that is formed by the powers of the gods in various ratios, but integrity is achieved not by the number of gods in the pantheon, but exclusively by the functions they perform within the whole. The function of Vidar is to lay down and uphold the basic principle of the new reality, which we will understand in the chapter dedicated to the new world.

So, Vidar, the silent Aesir, is the one who inherits Odin's power, the one who will create new worlds after Ragnarök. It is he, not solely the legitimate sons of Odin born to him by the goddess Frigg, who will become the founder of the new reality, and not alone, but as part of a team of survivors and victors—the best of the gods, born, created, and returned.

Why was he chosen over the brightest Baldr or the darkest Höd? After all, Odin knew from the prophecy of the Völva that both his sons would return to Asgard after Ragnarök. And why did Loki's test program reject Bragi but found no fault in Vidar?

Certain is that which is sought from runes.
That the gods so great have made,
And the Master-Poet painted;
of the race of gods:
Silence is safest and best.
(The Poetic Edda. Hovamol)

Vidar is the new good of the new world. The new principle of good and order. Actions will not be for the sake of

ᛊ ᛞ

the common good, and the primacy will not belong to the chosen ones but by the common consent of all involved. Vidar's good differs from Baldr's good in that it does not require special protection and excessive praise. It does not demand unconditional acceptance by everyone simply because it potentially includes everything. Vidar's good differs from Bragi's good in the absence of a specific description—there is virtue in silence. Vidar's good is that he was given a share voluntarily during life, not when the priests, gothi[98], or the rules of honoring the gods commanded. Vidar's shoe is not gifted by Loki, nor made by dvergar; Vidar's shoe is more valuable than a royal crown—it is a voluntary gift from all free people[99]. Vidar's good is a good that is formed not by words, tears, force, or rules unjust to the majority, but by the real deeds of many for the sake of one and the true.

Vidar, the forest god, the son of Earth, heir to ancient memory, knows what Earth needs and will never harm it. Decisions in the new world based on Vidar's system do not require explanations—they are as natural as the forest he learned from all his life. Therefore, Vidar, the silent Aesir, is also the god of naturalness.

Practice 24. God Vidar (page 555)

---

[98] Gothi — plural goðar — priest, leader, judge in ancient Scandinavian society.

[99] In ancient times, shoes were considered an attribute of the free—slaves walked barefoot.

ᚠ ᚩ

Ullr

The god Ullr is the son of Loki. Whatever can be said about Loki can also be said about Ullr. The well-known saying that "everything said about Loki is not the real Loki[100]" can very well be applied to Ullr as well.

To trace his origins, we need to return to the already known story of the goddess Sif losing her hair. Yes, Ullr appeared as a remarkable result of that memorable night, after which the irreversible process of the Æsir journeying to the svartálfar began. The goddess Sif soon gave birth to a "hairy infant"—nothing could be done, Loki's shapeshifting genes will overshadow any other. However, the goddess Sif, having lost her sense of the value of ancestral roots by that time, tried to get rid of the child as quickly as possible. In the human world of that era, such children were also often "taken out of the house"[101] and left behind. Loki took the "non-standard" infant and brought

---

100 Allusion to the saying from Laozi's "Dao De Jing": The Dao that can be expressed in words is not the true Dao. The name that can be named is not the true name.

101 This practice was widespread and ceased only with the advent of Christianity in the northern lands, and even then not immediately. Subsequently, beliefs about the utburd — an evil spirit of a killed infant born with physical defects, as well as out-of-wedlock children killed in this way, who became a shameful phenomenon during the Christian period — arose. The angry utburds would jump on the backs of passersby and demand to be taken to the cemetery. But on the way there, the utburd would become increasingly heavier and could crush the passerby or kill them when they could no longer move.

him to a place where any non-standardness is not a shame but a boon—to the lower worlds of the Tree, to his relatives and friends. Loki gave his son to be raised by those who can turn any specific quality into a talent (jötunns); those who can teach to see flaws in any system (svartálfar); those who can teach how to turn innate selfishness into self-sufficiency (frost giants). And it worked—Ullr became such. Perhaps Loki did the only right thing any parent should do for their child—create the right conditions for raising individuality. Not to create a little copy of oneself, not to birth and raise a specific function for a personal super-task, completely breaking the Vanir nature and Jotun individuality—Loki gave his son much more by actually giving him nothing. He simply placed him in the right environment. In the Prose Edda, Snorri writes about Ullr:

Uller is the name of one, who is a son of Sif, and a step-son of Thor. He is so good an archer, and so fast on his skees, that no one can contend with him. He is fair of face, and possesses every quality of a warrior. Men should invoke him in single combat.

Ullr's name in kennings is constantly associated with the shield—the warrior's protection in battle: the shield is called "the ship of Ullr," "the ash of Ullr"—a shield, "the vessel of Ullr"—also a shield.

It should be noted that the original cult of Ullr is much older than it might seem at first glance when reading the myths of the Poetic and Prose Edda. It is as ancient as the cult of Ægir and Ran, as the cult of Njord and Nerthus. There are even mentions that Ullr was also a twin god with his sister Ullin. But in the manifested tapestry of the northern myth, Ullr entered precisely in the aspect of the rejected son of the Æsir, the offspring of Loki, the "hairy infant," which means that in the world of humans, in the programming of reality in the reflected world of Midgard, he will manifest himself precisely in the described function. This does not mean that this function is the only and final one, not at all. In other worlds of the Nine Worlds Tree, Ullr will manifest himself in other aspects—greater, lesser, or specific, and we must remember that reality is not limited to Midgard, and in other worlds, there are different principles of reality construction and the functions of gods manifest differently. If you have forgotten this, return to the beginning of the book, to the chapter describing the worlds of the World Tree and their functions.

So who is the god Ullr? The fragmentary information about him is still enough for the reasonable to deduce.

The program of the god Ullr combines the strongest properties of his mother and father. Their strength is in extremes. Sif's extreme is Vanir selfishness, taken to a degree; Loki's extreme is the fiery shapeshifting nature and the ability to become anything, a universal quantum pair for whom he joins. Loki's extreme is that he exists only when he does not exist. And Ullr is the same. An absolute master and an absolute individualist. In our world system, Ullr is a hacker.

A hacker is not only someone who breaks into other people's programs. A hacker is someone who finds a flaw and breaks into the system through this flaw. This he inherited from his father—Loki also masterfully found vulnerabilities in the program and exposed them. But Loki acted within the overall system of the gods of Asgard, in conjunction with his blood brother Odin, and did not reveal the system's vulnerabilities unless it was necessary for the system itself. Ullr acts alone, and this he inherited from his mother. He agrees on nothing with anyone, and extracts resources from the program where it is flawed, and only because it is flawed.

In some songs not included in the official collections of Northern myths, there is a mention that Ullr was the cause of the second war between the Aesir and Vanir when he killed Freyr's beloved boar. This is, so to speak, an "apocryphal tale," meaning it was not included in the main program line. However, the magical history differs from the human one in that magic does not need to confirm any facts documentarily and with witnesses—this rule became mandatory for humans (who lie too much), but for the Jotunn, for example, it is completely unnecessary. Magic remembers everything differently than the human world, and the magical history is built on one simple rule—on the fact. Either an event happened or it didn't. And in which world or on which probability line it happened—it doesn't matter[102]. In the magical annals, it is recorded that this story happened. And that part of the artifacts obtained by Loki from the Svartálfar was acquired precisely then. Echoes of this myth can be recognized in the mysterious "Song of Ullr," whose origin is as mystical as it is magical—Ullr does not like it when falsehood exists as truth. In this story, Loki stood up for his son and ransomed him from the angry Vanir, pacified nature, and Ullr was afterward accepted in Asgard and even formed his own halls, and we already know how important it is for a god-ruler to have his halls in Asgard:

Ydalir[103] call they the place where Ull
A hall for himself hath set;
(The Poetic Edda. Grimnismol)

---

[102] We thoroughly examine this phenomenon in the course "General Theory of Magic." For more details, please visit our forum in the "GTM" section.

[103] Ídalir — "valleys of yew trees."

This myth tells us a lot about Ullr himself. First, that there are no authorities for him. Second, that there are no boundaries for him either. He has no agreement with the Tree system, and therefore nothing externally limits him, and he has the right to do anything. Because he is a lone archer, fast and the best in his craft. His honesty and absolute sensitivity to falsehood (crookedness) are due precisely to the degree of freedom he possesses: detachment from Sif's roots and the freedom of movement of Loki, the individualism and egoism of Sif, and the fiery sensitivity of Loki—but all this multiplied by the mastery of the Svartálfar, the self-respect of the Jotunn, and the self-sufficiency of the frost giants of Niflheimr.

In the "Grimnismol," Odin, under the guise of Grímnir, speaking with Agnar who freed him from torture, mentioned Loki's son, indicating that this god sees just actions and necessarily highlights the one who commits them.

King Hrauthung had two sons: one was called Agnar, and the other Geirröth. Agnar was ten winters old, and Geirröth eight. Once they both rowed in a boat with their fishing-gear to catch little fish; and the wind drove them out into the sea. In the darkness of the night they were wrecked on the shore; and going up, they found a poor peasant, with whom they stayed through the winter. The housewife took care of Agnar, and the peasant cared for Geirröth, and taught him wisdom. In the spring the peasant gave him a boat; and when the couple led them to the shore, the peasant spoke secretly with Geirröth. They had a fair wind, and came to their father's landing-place. Geirröth was forward in the boat; he leaped up on land, but pushed out the boat and said, "Go thou now where evil may have thee!" The boat drifted out to sea. Geirröth, however, went up to the house, and was well received, but his father was dead. Then Geirröth was made king, and became a renowned man.

Othin and Frigg sat in Hlithskjolf and looked over all the worlds. Othin said: "Seest thou Agnar, thy foster ling, how he begets children with a giantess in the cave? But Geirröth, my fosterling, is a king, and now rules over his land." Frigg said: "He is so miserly that he tortures his guests if he thinks that too many of them come to him." Othin replied that this was the greatest of lies; and they made a wager about this matter. Frigg sent her maid-servant, Fulla, to Geirröth. She bade the king beware lest a magician who was come thither to his land should bewitch him, and told this sign concerning him, that no dog was so fierce as to leap at him. Now it was a very great slander that King Geirröth was not hospitable; but nevertheless he had them take the man whom the dogs would not attack. He wore a dark-blue mantle and called himself Grimnir, but said no more about himself, though he was questioned. The king had him tortured to make him speak, and set him between two fires, and he sat there eight nights. King Geirröth had a son ten winters old, and called Agnar after his father's brother. Agnar went to Grimnir, and gave him a full horn to drink from, and said that the king did ill in letting him be tormented with out cause. Grimnir drank from the horn; the fire had come so near that the mantle burned on Grimnir's back. He spake:

His the favor of Ull | and of all the gods
Who first in the flames will reach;
For the house can be seen | by the sons of the gods
If the kettle aside were cast.

In the " Atlakvitha," there is also an interesting mention of the god Ullr:

Guthrun spake:
"It shall go with thee, Atli, as with Gunnar thou heldest
The oaths ofttimes sworn, and of old made firm.
By the sun in the south, by Sigtyr's mountain,

By the horse of the rest-bed, and the ring of Ull."

Ullr's ring is a very well-known magical artifact, which, according to legend, could infallibly detect truth and falsehood. In the world of men, it manifested itself as follows: the one swearing and testifying "by Ullr's ring" had to put it on their finger, and if falsehood was revealed, the ring would tighten so much that the liar could easily lose their finger altogether. But if the one swearing told the truth, the ring would always fit perfectly, no matter the size.

Ullr did not participate in the battle of Ragnarök and did not support either side. This is very telling, as even his mother and father ended up, essentially, on opposite sides: Sif with Thor, and Loki leading Naglfar from the world of Hel. Ullr, as a self-respecting hacker, logically did not take any side—this was not his battle. But after the battle, at the moment of the world's rebirth, he will form the new reality system along with his brothers.

The god Ullr is one of the participants in the creation of the new world. His unique qualities and unparalleled function will not diminish in the world after Ragnarök. He will not have to become part of the whole—the new world does not imply the unification of forces and functions at the expense of individuality. In the new world, Ullr's individuality becomes no longer an ordinary function, one among many, but lays the foundation for the construction of the world and defines the task with a basic principle: individuality is sacred. The greatest hacker of all times and people know what vulnerabilities can strike any system so that it will not resist mistletoe, and as a result, symbiosis will turn into parasitism. In the new world, this will not be the case—this is the power of the god Ullr. Perhaps this is why the ancient ancestors so firmly associated the name Ullr

with the concept of "shield" as protection. But in the new world, this will be protection based on entirely different principles.

Practice 25. God Ullr (p. 558)

ᛊ ᛞ

Forseti

The god Forseti, son of Baldr and Nanna, is one of the future gods of the new world, embodying its law and justice. Forseti's parents, "the god of goodness" Baldr and "the fidelity to goodness" Nanna, are perfect according to the Norse myth. Baldr is impeccable in his purity, confirmed by almost universal love, and Nanna is impeccable in her loyalty. Their son Forseti, the son of perfection, is pure and faithful by his very nature. Here is what the skald Snorri Sturluson writes about Forseti in his Prose Edda:

Forsete is a son of Balder and Nanna, Nep's daughter. He has in heaven the hall which hight Glitner. All who come to him with disputes go away perfectly reconciled. No better tribunal is to be found among gods and men.[104]

The hall Glitnir ("shining") is Forseti's own informational base, indicating his substantial power and ability to make independent decisions. The name Forseti can be translated as "presiding one," in the context of "presiding over the thing" or "law-speaker." Not only the mathematical structure of the world after Ragnarök must change fundamentally, but also its laws. Unlike magical-mathematical algorithms, laws are those that are expressed in comprehensible words and explain to

---

104 Here Snorri quotes a phrase from the Poetic Edda.

everyone how we will now live—by what rule and under what conditions.

The basis of the new world will be justice. But the meaning of this concept in the new world will undergo changes—it cannot be the same as in the old world. Today's world's justice is a concession in the conditions of mutual dependence on each other. The foundation of the new world becomes individuality, not the commonality of everyone with everyone. Justice, as the foundation of individuality, will be under the functionality of Forseti.

But how to reconcile justice and individuality? For each being in the worlds, be they humans or representatives of other races and systems, there are their own concepts of good and evil, right and wrong, each with its main and secondary priorities—and all this needs to be taken into account without leveling everyone under one comb, without forcibly dividing by castes, depriving rights, or granting rights at whim or someone else's desire. A different algorithm is needed here.

In the new world, according to the plan of the young gods, there should be a system where no one will depend on anyone else. The structure of the Yggdrasil Tree reflects this dependence with a rigid scheme of connection, but the new world should have other principles of connecting everything with everything. The god Ullr, whom you already know, will connect and program anything, but understandable rules are also needed: why it is so. Everyone needs understandable rules of justice.

The old world was formed by gods for gods. If not for the Norns, perhaps no system would have arisen, but then the created world would not have lasted long. The old world did not anticipate the active participation of other systems, worlds, and races in the life of the system, and their intervention in reality

ᛊ ᛞ

was more a nuisance than a planned or expected effect. This happened not only in the space of the Norse myth but in all archaic systems. They were all built on the needs of the creator gods and did not perceive reality as something alive and feeling. But the activities of the old gods, both the Aesir and Vanir, over time led to an understanding of the fallacy of such a childish judgment, and reality, collective for all worlds, forced them to reckon with it. The correct understanding of the reaction of various systems and worlds to the activities of the gods was lacking, which led to multiple system errors, logically followed by Ragnarök. In the old world, the rules were not fair to everyone. According to the laws of development of all systems of that era, this was an indicator of loss[105]. The young gods, children and grandchildren of the demiurges of the old world, are called to correct these mistakes and create a system of multiple realities where no one's, absolutely no one's, rights will be violated, where justice will be the god, the law, and the foundation of everything. Justice of individuality, not society. Such is the technical task, and Forseti clarifies it—this will be his job in the new world.

Forseti is also a reality programmer. But his function in building the new world is to formalize the rules of fair existence, which should be understandable and accepted by everyone. His task is to translate the description of system algorithms into the language of general reality. It is unjust from the perspective of the new world that the rules of existence are unknown to those who exist in these rules. It is unjust if the language of writing is unknown to those trying to understand these rules. It is unjust if forming rules will harm anyone's individuality. It is unjust if one's

---

105 More details about these general rules are discussed in the course "General Theory of Magic."

ᚠ ᚨ

good is imposed with fists in place of another's good. It is just if everyone lives in their system of realities and, if for one white is white and for another black is black, so be it. But the system must ensure that these views do not intersect until a consensus opinion appears. This will come not in a battle, not in a fight, not in violence, but in the process of natural life, in the process of interacting with oneself, with nature, and with the general information available to everyone in the volumes and limits of their individuality's needs. And as the needs change day by day, so let the limits of possibilities change synchronously with them.

The power of Forseti guarantees that no essential condition and rule for the new reality will be lost, erased, or ignored. The program of the new world must take everything, absolutely everything, into account.

The problem with the system in which today's reality exists is that it gives no explanations. "He who has ears, let him hear; he who has eyes, let him see," it says. From the viewpoint of the new world's gods, this is unjust and unfair. The new world and the new reality programming system must have the ability to explain everything immediately: reward—for what? loss—for what? —without conjecture.

Practice 26. Forseti (p. 562)

ᛊ ᛞ

Skadi

Skadi (Skaði) was venerated as the goddess of winter and hunting, often referred to as the "skiing goddess." Her name means "harm," "damage," or "injury." However, the form Skaði is masculine, and it can be translated into Russian as "harm-doer." The manifestation of the goddess in the context of Norse mythology, as a woman in a male guise, is unusual.

Goddess Skadi is the daughter of the well-known giant Thjazi. This is the same giant who kidnapped the goddess Idunn and was killed during Loki's pursuit when he was returning the young Vanir back to Asgard. Here's what Snorri Sturluson writes about this story in his Prose Edda:

Skade, the daughter of the giant Thjasse, donned her helmet, and byrnie, and all her war—gear, and betook herself to Asgard to avenge her father's death. The asas offered her ransom and atonement; and it was agreed to, in the first place, that she should choose herself a husband among the asas, but she was to make her choice by the feet[106]*, which was all she was to see of their persons. She saw one man's feet that were wonderfully beautiful, and exclaimed: This one I choose! On Balder there are few blemishes. But it was Njord, from Noatun.*

Marriage to the god Njord marked her formal entry into the family of the Aesir. Despite Njord being a hostage in Asgard,

106 Modern researchers suspect that the formula "by feet" is a veiled form of "judging below the waist."

ᚠ ᚨ

he was considered a member of the family by law, and so was the goddess Skadi.

The inherent nature of Skadi is that of the frost giants. She is related to the primeval Aesir, but unlike the gods of Asgard, her nature is not truncated or limited in any way. She embodies naturalness in its most expressive form, containing both feminine and masculine aspects. She is a woman but also a man; she is ambivalent. Goddess Skadi is complete in her power, but this completeness made her vulnerable to herself: choosing Njord as a husband when she fancied Baldr, she agreed to the rules of choice set by the Aesir, not suspecting that the trick might be hidden within the rules. Transparency of rules is natural for the Ancients. The strong cannot even imagine that a contract could be deceitful.

The warrior goddess acts in the myth in a role that is natural for people of today's era but would have been a surprising exception to the traditional rules of the ancient era—she is her father's heir. In the human world, a daughter inherited only if there were no sons or other direct male heirs. But in the world of the ancient giants, it's different. After Thjazi's death, Skadi gained not only the right to avenge her father but also his halls, which, as we know, is important for understanding status.

The sixth is Thrynihein[107]*, where Thjazi dwelt,*
The giant of marvelous might;
Now Skathi abides, the god's fair bride,
In the home that her father had.

(The Poetic Edda. Grimnismol)

[107] Thryniheim — "home of noise."

ᛊ ᛞ

The shared life of goddess Skadi and god Njord did not flourish. Their powers were too different, their needs too opposite. The Prose Edda describes this story:

He established peace between the gods and vans. Njord took to wife Skade, a daughter of the giant Thjasse. She wished to live where her father had dwelt, that is, on the mountains in Thrymheim; Njord, on the other hand, preferred to be near the sea. They therefore agreed to pass nine nights in Thrymheim and three in Noatun. But when Njord came back from the mountains to Noatun he sang this:

Weary am I of the mountains,
Not long was I there,
Only nine nights.
The howl of the wolves
Methought sounded ill
To the song of the swans.

Skade then sang this:

Sleep I could not
On my sea–strand couch,
For the scream of the sea–fowl.
There wakes me,
As he comes from the sea,
Every morning the mew.

Then went Skade up on the mountain, and dwelt in Thrymheim. She often goes on skees (snow–shoes), with her bow, and shoots wild beasts. She is called skee–goddess or skee–dis.

Njord is fire and water, Skadi is earth and air. If they had come together in love, a complete elemental creation program

ᚠ ᚨ

would have emerged. But they came together in revenge, and hatred, as a principle of negation, destroyed the shared reality before it even had a chance to be born.

The warrior goddess Skadi the destroyer did not spare Loki when the gods chose his punishment. She blamed him for her defeat by the Aesir, her failed marriage choice, and taking the lawful weregild so cheaply.

In the second place, it was stipulated that the asas were to do what she did not deem them capable of, and that was to make her laugh. Then Loke tied one end of a string fast to the beard of a goat and the other around his own body, and one pulled this way and the other that, and both of them shrieked out loud. Then Loke let himself fall on Skade's knees, and this made her laugh. (The Prose Edda)

Laughter is a powerful force. It makes one open up, let others in closer, accept things that otherwise would never be accepted as normal. Laughter melted the ice princess Skadi, turning her into soft water.

In the "Lokasenna," the goddess Skadi was not spared Loki's sharp tongue, along with the other gods. But Skadi's strength does not imply forgiveness—her revenge stems from a sense of insulted dignity, unlike the revenge of, say, the god Vali, who was born with it; who carries the force of retribution as part of his nature. Skadi's revenge and hatred are the power of her love in reverse.

Skathi spake:
"Light art thou, Loki, but longer thou mayst not
In freedom flourish thy tail;
On the rocks the gods bind thee with bowels torn
Forth from thy frost-cold son."

Loki spake:
"Though on rocks the gods bind me with bowels torn
Forth from my frost-cold son,
I was first and last at the deadly fight
There where Thjazi we caught."

Skathi spake:
"Wert thou first and last at the deadly fight
There where Thjazi was caught,
From my dwellings and fields shall ever come forth
A counsel cold for thee."

Loki spake:
"More lightly thou spakest with Laufey's son,
When thou badst me come to thy bed;
Such things must be known if now we two
Shall seek our sins to tell."

It was Skadi who hung the poisonous snake over Loki's head, tormenting him while he was bound by the gods, until the battle of Ragnarök.

The strong goddess Skadi gained an experience in Asgard that she could never have had in her homeland. The ice princess learned that something could be as powerful as the fire of Muspelheimr—trust and laughter. This lesson she described in her story. Every joke has a meaning, every joke that provokes laughter allows one to accept this meaning naturally, without

ᛊ ᛞ

fear, but without battling it either. What makes one laugh doesn't seem threatening or requiring a fight. Refusing to fight makes a warrior a woman, ice water, and Skadi deceived by a cunning jester. Skadi teaches: always reflect on what makes you laugh. What phenomenon of this world did you accept as normal and natural by laughing at it? What will you not fight against, what rights of vengeance will you abandon?

The fact that goddess Skadi accepted the Aesir's condition of choosing a husband "by feet" is also a consequence of her pure strength. There is no suspicion of deception when one is incapable of deceit. How can one suspect deception in making a fateful decision based on insufficient data?

Later myths tell that there was great friendship between goddess Skadi and god Ullr. Indeed, these two forces, solitary and self-sufficient, harmonized with each other in a mutual respect for such a form of completeness in each that if it required correction and adjustment, it was only from within the consciousness itself and only by the inner desire of each. Their worldview was identical in the perspective of what the correct reality should be. Let it be as imperfect as I am, these gods believe, but let it correct its imperfections itself. If there is a desire to connect one's reality with another, let it be by personal and true desire, not by circumstances or, heaven forbid, by deceit or cunning.

Practice 27. Goddess Skadi (p. 565)

ᚹ ᚨ

The 12 "handmaidens" of Frigg

To understand what the following 12 goddesses embody, we must return to the goddess Frigg and recall that in the northern system, the spouse of the supreme god Odin, the queen, performed the function of the guardian of the proto-foundation Tradition, or more simply, the entire tradition of the northern myth. Goddess Frigg, a descendant of Ymir, embodies the foundations of ancient primordial memory. Just as the gods created multiple worlds of the Tree from Ymir's body, so from Frigg's consciousness will the children of the gods form various realities after Ragnarök. Each of these realities can contain a fragment of the old, but in a completely new form and image. However, the foundation of each will lie in the old tradition, and through each, we will see a new aspect of the goddess Frigg.

Tradition is a combination of numerous ready-made pieces of knowledge that, when linked together through rules and morality, form a multi-layered program capable of self-sustaining and passing from generation to generation. However, any tradition consists of elements that can be isolated from the general program and examined separately. The northern myth defines these elements under the name "12 handmaidens of Frigg," but we can understand them better if we change the term to a more detailed one and call them "aspects of Frigg" or "projections of Frigg."

At the moment when the spouse of the supreme god, Frigg, stood alongside Odin in the battle of Ragnarök, her fate

ᛊ ᛞ

was sealed: if Odin won, she would also win; if Odin lost, she would die too. This means that the tradition, as a coherent system, would end; it would disintegrate into elements. However, if these elements possess autonomy and relative integrity, they can be reassembled into a tradition under favourable conditions. While Frigg lived, all 12 goddesses were connected to her by the principle of "centre-periphery" (like a sun with rays). But when Frigg perished in battle, the connection to the centre disappeared, and each "handmaiden" gained complete independence.

The number 12 here is not accidental and may be related to the scheme of 12 proto-foundations and the 12 rivers of Élivágar[108]. These rivers symbolize the endless streams of chaos (Helheimr) and the hidden knowledge of the world of Darkness (Niflheimr). In this context, the 12 projections of the goddess Frigg act as a counterbalance to the formless flows, representing symbols of completed order, where order restrains chaos, and tradition gains strength and development from dark knowledge.

Othin spake:
"Sixth answer me well, if wise thou art called,
If thou knowest it, Vafthruthnir, now:

---

[108] Élivágar (Old Norse Élivágar — "waters of chaos," "turbulent waters") — the 12 streams that originate from the source Hvergelmir. It was believed that there were no rivers colder than Élivágar. The streams of Élivágar flow from Niflheimr into the primordial abyss of Ginnungagap. The source Hvergelmir ("boiling cauldron") feeds Élivágar, sustained by the conflict between Muspelheimr and Niflheimr. The waters of these rivers are poisonous, yet they are the source of all creation and all beings. The "poisonous" and "cold" waters of Élivágar are still too icy, too unconscious. Élivágar, flowing from void to void, creates worlds and life along its path. The largest of the streams is Vimur. Other streams were named: Svol, Gunnthra, Fjorm, Fimbulthul, Slid, Hrid, Sylg, Ylg, Vid, Leipt, and Gjoll.

Whence did Aurgelmir come with the giants' kin,
Long since, thou giant sage?"

Vafthruthnir spake:
"Down from Elivagar did venom drop.
And waxed till a giant it was;
Whence came up Njorth to the kin of the gods,—
(Rich in temples and shrines he rules,—)
Though of gods he was never begot?"

(The Poetic Edda. Vafthruthnismol)

In the new world being created by the young gods after Ragnarök, the old tradition will not be recreated but will receive a second birth. The twelve goddess-projections, detached from the old foundation, contain such programmatic forces that, when connected differently, will continue the northern tradition, but in entirely new forms. Vidar and his brothers are laying down a new principle for forming reality after Ragnarök; Ullr programs this reality, but the future program must have access to the databases of the old world and the algorithms that will help apply these bases correctly and, most importantly, effectively. This capability is precisely what the 12 projections of the mother of the young gods, the 12 faces of the goddess Frigg, bring. The old tradition, as if decomposing itself into 12 new, completely independent systems, can act together or separately — in any case, it will be the same northern tradition, but each time in a different form. This is a great power and great opportunity, understanding which allows us to see the power of the 12 projections of the goddess Frigg differently — more deeply than what the northern myth suggests on the surface.

The myth says very little about the channels of the "handmaidens." Nevertheless, even from this scant material, more useful information can be extracted if approached with the right intention and perspective.

Gods are forces and functions. Each of the 12 goddesses, whose power and abilities we will further examine, has independent functions that, when programming the new world, will help the gods create multiple realities where each goddess can act as a cornerstone[109] for creating a new tradition, either individually or collectively. This yields countless variations, but in each, the face of the great goddess-queen Frigg will shine through, giving Odin and herself the chance to manifest in different realities, ensuring that our gods will never die. This effect was what ancient mages meant when they said that if a god was killed, it does not mean that he is dead.

Some contemporary skalds, descendants of ancient poets, say that after the battle of Ragnarök, the "handmaidens of Frigg," losing their connection to their foundation, scattered across the world and got lost in the ages. Those who seek to find and reunite them into a single tradition must undertake a quest, discovering them in old dusty books, in the leaves of trees, at poetry readings, in the eyes of lovers, in the drops of milk from a nursing mother's breast... The gods of the past have left their imprint on countless elements of the visible world, leaving us clues.

---

109 Cornerstone — the first stone laid in the foundation of a building, taking on the primary weight and determining the layout of the structure; currently, the concept signifies the foundation, the beginning, the essence of something.

Saga

The goddess Saga is the goddess of memory of what was. She carries within her the memory of the history that existed before Ragnarök, and everything you now know about the northern tradition, you know because of the goddess Saga—the keeper of stories, the keeper of legends. She is the essence of memory of the past. This memory does not contain conclusions and obvious morals; it does not form algorithms of victories and defeats. It is the memory of stories without judgment. This is a "living" memory, which distinguishes it from the memory of the god Mimir. The goddess Saga does not divide stories into good and evil; she describes what really happened—without conclusions.

Sokkvabekk[110] *is the fourth, where cool waves flow.*
And amid their murmur it stands;
There dailj' do Othin and Saga drink
In gladness from cups of gold.
(The Poetic Edda. Grimnismol)

Every day, the god Odin imparted information into the depths of the secret hall continuously, without gaps, without conclusions, without comments. Every day, Saga tells Odin

110 Sökkvabekkr — "sunken bench."

about what was before. Daily exchange of information, regular preservation of current data.

The name of the hall of the goddess Saga—"Sunken Bench"—speaks of hidden knowledge submerged in the depths of waters, protected by these depths, and not easily accessible to anyone. The knowledge will rise to the surface when necessary, or when a strong enough fire is found to "evaporate the water," and the halls of the goddess will emerge to the visible surface.

The goddess Saga is pure and uncensored information, untouched by ideology or morality. The goddess Saga is the already spoken and contemplated history, containing everything known to humans. Being connected with the goddess Frigg and being her natural aspect, she forms tradition along with the gods. But being separated from the foundation, she keeps the memory of what was, storing pure history, hiding it in the waters of chaos until the right time comes.

Practice 28. Goddess Saga (p. 569)

Eir

The image of the goddess of healing, Eir, is complex to understand, primarily because the old myth describes her as a Vanir. She is the sister of the goddess Freyja and came to Asgard along with the hostage Vanir. In this sense, it is very easy to perceive Eir as a "servant" of Frigg, but very difficult to see her as her projection. However, there are revelations that describe the goddess Eir as Primordial and one who came "from the ninth teat of the cow Audhumla." Frigg, as a descendant of Ymir, who was nurtured on the milk of the cow Audhumla, has a direct connection with the goddess Eir.

How can we understand you, goddess Eir?

She is called the goddess of healing, and here is what Snorri Sturluson writes about her in the Prose Edda: *"The third is Eir, who is the best leech."*

But what is "healing"? It is not just treating disease. It is the introduction of the Vanir principle that life should never end. It is the understanding of the rule that the life of each should be formed in the place, in the form, and in the tradition that biologically suits the bearer of this life. Not by the rules of civilization, politics, or religion, but biologically. The body itself, not the mind, should say: "*I am part of this space, and I belong here.*"

Eir represents the power of nature's recovery after wounds and cataclysms. Recovery, as we know, does not happen instantly but after some time—and it was also said about the goddess Eir that she always "delays her response." The goddess Frigg, manifesting herself through the power of Eir, endowed the entire northern tradition with similar functions—the ability to recover naturally, but after some time: also "delaying her response."

Eir also appears in the retinue of another goddess—Mengloth[111]:

Svipdag spake:
"Now answer me, Fjolsvith, the question I ask,
For now the truth would I know :
What maidens are they that at Mengloth's knees
Are sitting so gladly together?"

Fjolsvith spake:
"Hlif is one named, Hlifthrasa another,
Thjothvara call they the third;
Bjort and Bleik, Blith and Frith,
Eir and Aurbotha."
(The Poetic Edda. Svipdagsmol)

Eir's name also appears in the list of valkyries, which will be discussed later. Her name means "mercy" or "grace."

Practice 29. Goddess Eir (p. 572)

[111] Mengloth (Menglöð, "rejoicing in jewels") is sometimes identified with Frigg, but much more often with Freyja.

ᛊ ᛞ

Gefjon

" The fourth is Gefjun, who is a may, and those who die maids become her hand–maidens," so Snorri Sturluson said of her in the Prose Edda.

The goddess Gefjon is one of the 12 projections ("servants") of Frigg and, like the others, represents an independent and complete force. After the battle of Ragnarök, she will be able to manifest herself in her primary and described function in the new world. What is this function? Let's find out.

The name Gefjon means "giver" or "bestower." She is the giver of blessings, but what kind? The Prose Edda and the "Ynglinga Saga" tell us extensively and unambiguously.

About King Gylfi and Gefjon

King Gylfe ruled the lands that are now called Svithjod (Sweden). Of him it is said that he gave to a wayfaring woman, as a reward for the entertainment she had afforded him by her story–telling, a plow–land in his realm, as large as four oxen could plow it in a day and a night. But this woman was of the asa–race; her name was Gefjun. She took from the north, from Jotunheim, four oxen, which were the sons of a giant and her, and set them before the plow. Then went the plow so hard and deep that it tore up the land, and the oxen drew it westward into the sea, until it stood still in a sound. There Gefjun set the land, gave it a name and called it Seeland. And where the land had been taken away became afterward a sea, which in Sweden is now called Logrinn (the Lake, the Malar Lake in Sweden). And in the Malar Lake the bays correspond to the capes in Seeland.

Thus says Brage, the old skald:

Gefjun glad

ᚠ ᚠ

Drew from Gylfe
The excellent land,
Denmark's increase,
So that it reeked
From the running beasts.
Four heads and eight eyes
Bore the oxen
As they went before the wide
Robbed land of the grassy isle.

In the era when the oral tradition of the Norse myth was forming, maternal rights were in force—the main, fundamental, inviolable sacred right of the will of the Mother. In this system of relationships between the world and man, there was no other understanding that true rights could only be given by the Mother Goddess, by the Earth, and only such rights would be truly valid, and all else would not. The goddess Gefjon is the personification of royal authority.

Gefjon is not a Vanir; she is of the race of the giants, and in this capacity, she is a continuation of Frigg's lineage, although by origin she may be much older than the great wife of Odin. But they are one and the same, only in different reflections, in different projections. The goddess Gefjon is an echo of the ancient cult of the Mother Goddess, a deep memory of matriarchy and the will of feminine power over all. Frigg, being the wife of the supreme god of the pantheon, limited her abilities for the task at hand, but the memory that knows no limits is concentrated in the image of the goddess Gefjon. Gefjon is Frigg without limitations.

In "Lokasenna," Gefjon is also targeted by the sharp tongue of the trickster god:

ᛊ ᛞ

Gefjun spake:
"Why, ye gods twain, with bitter tongues
Raise hate among us here?
Loki is famed for his mockery foul.
And the dwellers in heaven he hates."

Loki spake:
"Be silent, Gefjun! for now shall I say
Who led thee to evil life
The boy so fair gave a necklace bright,
And about him thy leg was laid."

Othin spake:
"Mad art thou, Loki, and little of wit,
The wrath of Gefjun to rouse;
For the fate that is set for all she sees,
Even as I, methinks."

The goddess Gefjon retains Frigg's attribute as the giver of blessings. But these blessings are not a one-time act, but a permanent gift passed down to descendants: the goddess Gefjon determines and fixes the right to land. She also determines the "right of the king." Her word is the right of a woman to choose her husband. She symbolizes maternal rights as the fundamental law—a woman is free by definition, and only she herself, like Frigg, has the right to limit her freedom in any part for the sake of her cause, for the sake of her convictions—but only she herself.

Practice 30. Goddess Gefjon (p. 575)

ᚹ ᚨ

ᛊ ᛞ

Fulla

" The fifth is Fulla, who is also a may, she wears her hair flowing and has a golden ribbon about her head; she carries Frigg's chest, takes care of her shoes and knows her secrets." This is an excerpt from the Prose Edda related to this force.

The goddess Fulla is mentioned several times in the myth, and these mentions provide the opportunity to see that Fulla, as a projection of the goddess Frigg, performed the important function of a keeper of traditions. This, in turn, forms the rules of existence for all based on the principles of the Norse myth. One of the features of any tradition is that it is continuous. It is precisely this task that the function of the goddess Fulla fulfills, and this is encoded in the formula "keeper of the shoes." A continuous and holistic tradition is one that can restore itself, complement itself, and protect itself. Thus, the tradition will be prolonged over time and generations without losing its key meaning and will be able to transform itself along with the times while remaining whole. The key meaning of the tradition is in Frigg's chest, and it is guarded by the goddess Fulla.

"The keeper of Frigg's shoes" knows the paths the goddess has walked and her plans. In the human society of that era, shoes symbolized status. Thus, in the reflection of Midgard, the goddess Fulla is the keeper of Frigg's status.

In the storyline of the Norse myth, we encounter Fulla's name in the story of Baldr, specifically in "Hermod's Ride to

ᛊ ᛞ

Hel." There, he received a headband for Fulla[112] from Baldr's wife, the goddess Nanna. The "headband" is a very important artifact in the myth and carries a magical meaning that needs to be correctly understood. The headband is not just a gift from the goddess of fidelity to the goddess of wholeness. It is a gift from the world of the dead, something that has died and returned. The headband here functions as a link ensuring the continuous transmission of tradition even at the moment when the last "faithful" one dies.

Fulla's name means "fullness" or "filling." It would be incorrect to perceive her name as a synonym for abundance concerning the power of the goddess Fulla—her name is not about that. She is not the giver of blessings like Gefjon; she is the symbol of the fullness of tradition and its constant filling. Fulla's fullness is wholeness, it is completeness; Fulla's filling is continuity. It is the absence of any white spots, gaps, and consequently, ambiguities in the tradition's algorithm. To fulfill the latter task, Nanna's headband of fidelity has been given to her.

Fulla represents the possibility of recreating the tradition even after the last living bearer of it has died.

In the world of the dead, their own processes occur, one could even say their own life. Baldr and Höd undergo their learning in the halls of Helheim, drawing lessons from the past and present. All these processes should not be unknown to the tradition: it should be filled even with information formed outside the world of the living. Fulla, as the face of the continuity of the Keeper of Tradition Frigg, is obliged to possess this

---

112 In Snorri's narration, a ring was given to Fulla, and a headband for Frigg. However, the memory of the tradition tells that the myth recorded otherwise: Nanna gave her headband to Fulla, specifically to her.

ᚹ ᚨ

information, to fill herself with what is important, and to immediately make corrections to "Frigg's plans" so that these plans do not diverge from the reality of the future—the reality destined to be built by the children of the old gods.

Gold was called "Fulla's headband," and here gold may reflect not in the sense of "value as a material good," but in the property of gold as a metal that is not subject to decay and corrosion.

Practice 31. Goddess Fulla (p. 578)

ᛊ ᛞ

Vár and Vör

Two goddesses who are also projections of the goddess Frigg are Vár and Vör, and we will become acquainted with them simultaneously. The pairing of certain forces is not new to us, and such pairing is never accidental but has meaning. Let's understand it while exploring the specific functions of the goddesses preserving the tradition.

These goddesses not only share similar-sounding names but also show a certain synchronicity in their interaction with each other: where one manifests her function, the other appears as well.

We learn about the goddesses Vár and Vör from the myth narrative somewhat in passing:

Then loud spake Thrym, the giants leader:*
"Bring in the hammer to hallow the bride;
On the maiden's knees let Mjollnir lie.
That us both the hand of Vor may bless."
(The Poetic Edda. Thrymskvitha)

And in the Prose Edda, Snorri writes a little more:

The ninth is Var. She hears the oaths and troths that men and women plight to each other. Hence such vows are called vars, and she takes vengeance on those who break their promises.

ᚹ ᚠ

The tenth is Vor, who is so wise and searching that nothing can be concealed from her. It is a saying that a woman becomes vor (ware) of what she becomes wise.

Even from the little that is written, a wealth of useful information can be extracted. A spoken oath or a given promise in a system based on honor must immediately be woven into the fabric of reality and be recorded in it—and everyone must know this. Deception cannot be committed just because your agreement is not written on paper, and there must be something stronger than a weak human conscience. The goddesses Vár and Vör were the forces that prevented the very possibility of deception, preventing even a small attempt to lie. Everyone living in the era of the Norse tradition knew this as clearly as they knew the meaning of their name. Even if an oath between people is whispered, even if words of love and promises of fidelity are spoken by a man and a woman under a blanket, they will not go unheard by Vár, they will not escape the notice of Vör. What is said must be accounted for in the future: the tradition will support a person if the person supports the tradition with their fidelity.

The symbol of the goddess Vár is a ring woven from grass. It tells us that not only an "approved" marriage, as a contract, will be recorded on the fabric of reality, but also the promise of the simplest, poorest, or youngest person will be heard to the same extent as the marital vows of a jarl.

The power of these goddesses is a blessing for the honest and a curse for the liar. They do not distinguish the speakers by ranks or castes—every word is equal to any other spoken word. Whether a jarl swears an oath or a thrall does, the forces of the goddesses of tradition see no difference, everything is important. The gods Æsir, Heimdallr and Odin, act differently, paying attention only to men, only to warriors, only to kings. The female

power of the goddess Frigg and her projections Vár and Vör must take everything into account, hear everything, remember everything.

Practice 32. Goddesses Vár and Vör (p. 582)

Sjofn and Lofn

The seventh is Sjofn, who is fond of turning men's and women's hearts to love, and it is from her name that love is called Sjafne.

The eighth is Lofn, who is kind and good to those who call upon her, and she has permission from Alfather or Frigg to bring together men and women, no matter what difficulties may stand in the way; therefore "love" is so called from her name, and also that which is much loved by men. (The Prose Edda)

This is what Snorri Sturluson tells us about these goddesses in the Prose Edda, and it is all he tells. It's brief, but we'll try to understand more.

Another pair of forces characterize the goddess Frigg as the patroness of families and relationships. But if we look more broadly, we see that the independent functions of these two goddesses speak to the formation of various voluntary connections, including "non-traditional" ones.

In the old tradition of ancient times, interfering with a person's wyrd (fate) was considered impossible. Exceptions could be made only by the gods, and even then, only concerning humans, not themselves. People, living within the strict tradition and rules of caste distinctions, could not allow themselves liberties that would grossly violate this tradition. Marriages between people of different classes were not encouraged, and romantic relationships between such people could be seen as shameful or offensive to the gods. For lovers to unite, they needed the patronage of higher powers, unequivocal signs, and decisions from them—only in this case could the societal order permit the violation of general rules. But this was always an exception and never a system.

The forces of the goddesses Sjofn and Lofn bring personal desire to the forefront. But they do so in a way that does not disrupt the lives of others, keeping them within the tradition in which people and their surroundings exist. As "handmaidens" of the goddess Frigg, these forces are constrained by the rules of the Keeper of Tradition and cannot breach the bounds of what is permissible. But everything will change in the new world, when after Ragnarök, the goddesses gain independence and the limits of what is allowed are lifted.

Practice 33. Goddesses Sjofn and Lofn (p. 586)

ᛊ ᛞ

Syn and Hlin

These goddesses are also aspects of the goddess Frigg, and they are paired in their power and functions.

The eleventh is Syn, who guards the door of the hall, and closes it against those who are not to enter. In trials she guards those suits in which anyone tries to make use of falsehood. Hence is the saying that "syn is set against it," when anyone tries to deny ought.

The twelfth is Hlin, who guards those men whom Frigg wants to protect from any danger. Hence is the saying that he hlins who is forewarned. (The Prose Edda)

The goddesses Syn and Hlin are protectors of people. They can find the best qualities in a person and make these qualities more prominent and visible to everyone. What does not need to be corrected can serve as a counterbalance to "accusation," not as a justification for an act but as compensation for it. It is as if a court did not determine the guilt of the accused in a specific situation but weighed the good and bad deeds of a person throughout their life to determine the appropriate penalty.

When the light of the goddess Syn falls on a person, it immediately becomes clear who they are. But it also becomes evident to everyone and to the person themselves who they are not. In ancient times, people appealed to these goddesses when seeking the just judgment of the god Forseti. It was believed that they could reveal to the god of justice the true nature of the accused, exposing their essence and meaning to correctly assess

ᚹ ᚨ

ᛊ ᛞ

their deeds—taking into account all actions, not just those in the specific case. The goddess Hlin reveals the ultimate truth and evaluates the motives driving the person, showing everyone that the understanding of justice can vary from person to person.

Hlin's name was sometimes used to refer to the goddess Frigg in her aspect as a mother protecting her child. Protecting always, even if the child has committed an unjust act from the tradition's point of view—this is the force and echoes of "maternal right" manifested in her.

Now comes to Hlin yet another hurt.
When Othin fares to fight with the wolf.
(The Poetic Edda. Voluspo)

In Hlin, this power is manifested not so much in the ability to protect the unjust but in the way she treats the condemned as their own mother would.

Practice 34. Goddesses Syn and Hlin (p. 590)

ᚠ ᚨ

Snotra

One of the manifestations of the goddess Frigg as the wife of the supreme god and the guardian of traditions is wisdom. This quality is personified by the goddess Snotra, who is the goddess of reason.

The thirteenth is Snotra[113]*, who is wise and courtly. After her, men and women who are wise are called Snotras. (The Prose Edda)*

However, it is essential to distinguish the forces when they work within the framework of a tradition or when they act as independent entities. Within the framework of a tradition, the force works as part of a program, meaning it has limited functionality based on necessity, determined by the tradition itself. When the force begins to work independently, it can manifest all the possible capabilities of its functionality.

The goddess Snotra is called the goddess of reason but also the goddess of etiquette. Etiquette is not only about following the rules of relationships within a specific society but also about deeply understanding the reasons and foundations of such rules. It's about understanding without conditions, without explanations, sensing the informational substrate of the reality in which those different from you or similar to you exist. Etiquette is the understanding, knowledge, and most importantly, the acceptance of the reality with which you come into contact. In this case, this property can extend not only to the process of

113 Snotra — the one who can speak beautifully (Snorri).

interaction with human communities but also with any other organized phenomena — with nature, with the world of others, with the world of gods, and with other realities that a person is currently unable to comprehend precisely because of a lack of understanding and acceptance of them.

Practice 35. Goddess Snotra (p. 592)

ᛊ ᛞ

Gná

This final channel-projection of the goddess Frigg is described in the Prose Edda as follows:

The fourteenth is Gna, whom Frigg sends on her errands into various worlds. She rides upon a horse called Hofvarpner, that runs through the air and over the sea. Once, when she was riding, some vans saw her faring through the air. Then said one of them:

What flies there?
What fares there?
What glides in the air?

She answered

I fly not,
Though I fare
And glide through the air
On Hofvarpner,
That Hamskerper,
Begat with Gardrofa.

Today, this goddess is known as the goddess of transformation. However, this term is not entirely accurate, because understanding the path of sequential transformation through the 12 channels of Frigg reveals that she is the final, concluding stage. Therefore, it is more precise to call her the messenger, the one who heralds the completion of transformation.

ᚹ ᚨ

ᛊ ᛞ

It is said that the goddess Gná elevates consciousness to dizzying heights, to places it has never been before, and into informational layers from which this consciousness has never been observed or accessed.

Practice 36. Goddess Gná (p. 595)

ᚠ ᚨ

The 12 goddess-projections of Frigg gain autonomy and completeness after the battle, having free development in their own right. Each represents only one facet of the structure of "tradition," and each can be its "backbone," bearing the main load of the entire system. Previously, in the tradition of old times, the connection between all projections through the name of Frigg was through her basic program, and the system could not operate otherwise than as provided by this program. As we know from the myth, this led to significant errors and the death of Frigg during the battle of Ragnarök. However, if the principle of connecting all elements of the new reality-building program is different, the reality will also be different, and the tradition will gain possibilities that were unattainable in the previous "version" with the centralized image of the goddess Frigg.

The Great Weaver Frigg, dividing herself into mathematical functions, offers her children to preserve these functions and further combine the possibilities as they see fit for building reality in the name of the god Vidar and according to his principle. And the goddess Frigg continues herself not in her children, but in her deeds, in her projections. The scope of the colossal possibilities that the northern tradition possesses can be seen and understood precisely now when all 12 lines of her manifestation have become visible, when all 12 projections of the Great Weaver have been known and understood.

Saga — history, memory.

Eir — biological correctness and safety for all.

ᛊ ᛞ

Gefjon — the right to power, all the algorithms for obtaining such a right.

Fulla — the core of the tradition, the seed for its recreation.

Vár and Vör — active participation in building reality by each project participant, every living being on equal terms.

Sjofn and Lofn — building connections between realities on a voluntary basis of each of the linked realities.

Syn and Hlín — protection of their reality and awareness of the rules of justice on which this reality is built.

Snotra — ensuring the integrity of the internal program of building reality, without the need to seek compensation or addition in someone else.

Gná — manifestation of the new reality in the world system.

Such a sequential linkage of all 12 projections of the goddess Frigg in their newfound autonomy allows for the proper construction of a new reality-building program and correctly writing it into the foundations of the new world's existence, the world created by the young gods.

The goddess Frigg encompassed everything described in her 12 projections: the algorithms of prolongation, information accumulation, the rules of honor, and the rules of family and kin relationships. It should be remembered that the goddess Frigg, as an Aesir, a descendant of the root of Ymir, carries within herself an informational power much greater than the information of today. Even any project of such powerful universal forces as the gods Aesir Odin or Tyr also appears as a fleeting moment for the mighty program of Frigg, because her memory is much larger than the current reality construction. Hence comes some heaviness, the static unchangeability of the

ᚠ ᚨ

tradition itself, which the goddess Frigg personified: there were many norms, many constants that make the tradition powerful, but as a consequence, heavily reactive to changes.

The death of the goddess Frigg during the battle of Ragnarök "freed" her projections, and now they will interact with the continuer of the Aesir's work — the god Forseti. But no longer as "servants" performing established functions, but as full-fledged foundations, relying on which Forseti will create the rules for the existence of a particular reality, where the principle of building such a reality is personified by one or another projection of his great progenitor.

ᛊ ᛞ

Valkyries

The Valkyrie maidens play a significant role in Norse mythology. Their image became particularly attractive in the later era when the connections between humans and the old gods began to thin, and myth started to be replaced by teachings. The images of winged maidens were enticingly close and desirable, with the human mind reluctant to part with them for a long time, maintaining connections through tales, sagas, and legends, driven by a passionate desire and an ancient inclination toward magic. The ancestors believed that a hero's life could not be sustained without higher powers, and these powers needed an intermediary to influence the hero's life, making his fate unique, different from the fates of others. In Norse mythology, there are unseen helpers — disir and fylgjur, and there are also visible ones — the Valkyries.

In the "Voluspo", the seeress speaks of the Valkyries:

On all sides saw I Valkyries assemble,
Ready to ride to the ranks of the gods;
Skuld bore the shield, and Skogul rode next,
Guth, Hild, Gondul, and Geirskogul.
Of Herjan's maidens the list have ye heard,
Valkyries ready to ride o'er the earth.

In later sagas, Valkyries were often referred to as the daughters of noble kings, and later, in the Christian era, they became closely associated with the concept of "witch," "evil woman." Initially, however, the image of the Valkyries was not

ᚠ ᚨ

connected to the human race but belonged to the lineage of Odin.

In the myth-occult sense, the Valkyries are the thoughts of Odin. If the ravens Huginn and Muninn gathered information for Odin from the worlds, the Valkyries distributed information with their presence in the worlds.

The number of Valkyries is either nine or thirteen according to different sources. However, if we gather all the narratives, we find many more names. Whether these names denote separate personalities or are merely various epithets for the same force, the sagas do not tell us. The most well-known Valkyries include: Goll ("Calling"), Geir ("Spear"), Geirahöd, Geirskögul, Göndul, Gondul ("She-Wolf"), Gunn ("Battle"), Mist ("Mist"), Randgrid ("Shield-Smasher"), Reginleif ("Rider of the Storm"), Rota ("Sower of Confusion"), Svava, Sigrdrífa, Sigrún ("Secret Victory"), Skeggjöld, Skögul ("Ferocious"), Skuld ("Debt"), Þrúðr ("Strength"), Hild ("Warrior"), Hlökk ("Noise of Battle"), Hjörtimull, Hrist ("Shaker"), Hjörþrimul ("Battle-Binder"). Snorri Sturluson describes them in the Prose Edda:

There are still others who are to serve in Valhal, bear the drink around, wait upon the table and pass the ale—horns. These are called valkyries. Odin sends them to all battles, where they choose those who are to be slain, and rule over the victory. Gud and Rosta, and the youngest norn, Skuld, always ride to sway the battle and choose the slain. Jord, the mother of Thor, and Rind, Vale's mother, are numbered among the goddesses.

The Valkyries are not merely thoughts of Odin; they are his commands, directives sent into the worlds, mainly to Midgard, the world of humans. The obedient daughters of Odin never let him down. However, Odin would not be Odin if among his myriad thoughts there wasn't one insubordinate, imbued with the power of free will. This thought, and what happened in the human world after people let it in, is told in the epic and famous "Saga of the Volsungs.[114]" However, Odin did not kill this "disobedient thought" but instead set it free. Perhaps because it was the strongest, most willful of his thoughts, proving its right to free will. By putting the disobedient Valkyrie to sleep with a "sleep thorn," Odin granted her freedom. Why? Because from the throne of Asgard, Odin could see that such a thought would execute his will perfectly. Therefore, it deserved to be free.

This epic tale provides us with much knowledge about the algorithms of fate construction and the possibility of its alteration. It primarily imparts the understanding of what a hero's consciousness must be — one who can (or must) do everything to change the predestined path. First of all, he must not know fear. For example, Sigurd failed this test — he had a hidden fear, the fear of losing face. However, in the old tradition, the fear of losing face was not considered a vulnerability, and the Saga of the Volsungs explained to descendants why this imperceptible vulnerability is mistletoe for a hero. This fear of losing face was the initial trigger that set off a chain of crimes and betrayals, deceptions, treacheries, random and intentional deaths. This led all participants in the saga straight to Hel, and none of them entered Valhalla, indicating an unsatisfactory life result, a poorly executed program that cannot be universal, is not good, and neither Sigurd nor Gudrun will be mourned by all.

---

114 The enormous volume of this saga, as well as its "mirror" in the "Song of the Nibelungs," prevents it from being included here even partially. Therefore, readers are encouraged to independently study these great works and reflect deeply upon them.

Thus, through the heroic Saga of the Volsungs and his thought Sigrdrífa, Odin conveyed to us, his descendants, that not only the fear of death, which ruined the god Tyr, is a serious vulnerability for the entire system, but also the fear of losing face can lead to the collapse of truly noble undertakings.

After the battle of Ragnarök and the death of Odin, his thoughts — the Valkyries — do not perish with him but become the forces that, along with the young gods, will build future realities according to entirely new rules and principles.

Practice 37. Valkyries (p. 597)

RAGNAROK

It is now time for us to consider the key point of transformation in the northern tradition and delve into the understanding of the final battle of the gods.

After the gods bound Loki, changes within the system virtually ceased. The division established by Heimdall in the world of Midgard made it insensitive to changes in all other worlds of the Yggdrasil tree, except for Asgard. However, changes in Asgard were perceived only by the caste of kings, while all other social layers depended solely on them. The already overloaded system of life, morals, and tradition seemed to be preserved from external influence.

The world of Midgard, initially created as a world of reflection, a world meant to manifest everything happening in the other worlds of the tree, ceased to do so. It was as if a mirror had captured a frozen reflection and showed it for many years, without reflecting changes in the real form.

Binding Loki and stabilizing the processes led to this very stagnation, which categorically contradicted the system's original intent—truth, honor, valor. A distorted reflection is a lie, which means the development program of the northern myth came into conflict with itself, beginning to negate its essence.

After the death of Baldr, it became clear that Ragnarök was inevitable. Ragnarök is not merely the battle itself but a state

ᛊ ᛞ

of the system where battle is the only way out of the collapsing[115] structure. Ragnarök translates as "the fate of the gods," "the destiny of the gods," or "the twilight of the gods." Twilight is the time between light and dark periods, the transition from one state to another. It is not yet the end of the old period but the inevitability of such a transition. The old system, "Odin's Fury," which once replaced "Tyr's Valor," itself fades from light into darkness. What will it take with it, and what will it leave behind?

Yggdrasil shakes, and shiver on high
The ancient limbs, and the giant is loose;

We learn about the final battle from the very beginning of the myth revealed in the "Voluspo":

Much do I know, and more can see
Of the fate of the gods, the mighty in fight.

Brothers shall fight and fell each other,
And sisters' sons shall kinship stain;
Hard is it on earth, with mighty whoredom ;
Axe-time, sword-time, shields are sundered,
Wind-time, wolf-time, ere the world falls;
Nor ever shall men each other spare.

The victory algorithm "Tyr's Valor" was replaced by the algorithm "Odin's Fury." This gave the system a sharp push for development, but unfortunately, at the cost of losing properties. This loss was such that the system began to lose to itself.

---

115 Collapse (from Latin *collapsus* — "fallen") — the process of the destruction of any structure under the influence of a systemic crisis.

ᚹ ᚠ

ᛊ ᛞ

Ragnarök does not begin suddenly, and initially, the system gives signs and omens. First and foremost comes the "Winter of Giants," lasting three years. This is described in the "Prose Edda":

Then said Ganglere: What tidings are to be told of Ragnarok? Of this I have never heard before. Har answered: Great things are to be said thereof. First, there is a winter called the Fimbul–winter, when snow drives from all quarters, the frosts are so severe, the winds so keen and piercing, that there is no joy in the sun. There are three such winters in succession, without any intervening summer. But before these there are three other winters, during which great wars rage over all the world. Brothers slay each other for the sake of gain, and no one spares his father or mother in that manslaughter and adultery.

Next, "the sun goes out":

Then happens what will seem a great miracle, that the wolf devours the sun, and this will seem a great loss. The other wolf will devour the moon, and this too will cause great mischief. The stars shall be hurled from heaven. Then it shall come to pass that the earth and the mountains will shake so violently that trees will be torn up by the roots, the mountains will topple down, and all bonds and fetters will be broken and snapped. The Fenris–wolf gets loose. The sea rushes over the earth, for the Midgard–serpent writhes in giant rage and seeks to gain the land.

At this moment, the chains of illusions fall from Fenrir, as there is nothing left to support them. The serpent Jörmungandr also receives a release impulse, and "the great flood" arrives.

This impulse also reaches Loki's third child, the goddess Hel, and she opens the gates of the world of the dead. The impulse of freedom naturally comes from Loki himself, who also

ᛊ ᛗ

frees himself from his chains. This impulse is allegorically expressed in the myth by the image of a rooster. The Poetic Edda, "Voluspo":

Then to the gods crowed Gollinkambi[116]*,*
He wakes the heroes in Othin's[117] *hall;*
And beneath the earth does another crow,
The rust-red bird at the bars of Hel.

In the orderly world of Asgard and the chaotic world of Helheimr, these impulses arrive completely synchronously, and the gates open simultaneously in both realms, responding to the forces of light and darkness—Muspelheimr and Niflheimr:

O'er the sea from the north there sails a ship
With the people of Hel, at the helm stands Loki;
After the wolf do wild men follow,
And with them the brother of Byleist[118] *goes.*

Surt fares from the south with the scourge of branches[119]*,*
The sun of the battle-gods shone from his sword;
The crags are sundered, the giant-women sink,
The dead throng Hel-way, and heaven is cloven.

---

116 Gullinkambi — "golden comb."

117 Heroes in Othin's hall — the Einherjar, i.e., the warriors living with Odin.

118 Brother of Byleist — Loki.

119 Scourge of branches — fire.

ᚠ ᚨ

ᛊ ᛞ

From Asgard come the Einherjar, and from Helheimr sails the terror of the gods, the ship Naglfar:

The ship that is called Naglfar also becomes loose. It is made of the nails of dead men; wherefore it is worth warning that, when a man dies with unpared nails, he supplies a large amount of materials for the building of this ship, which both gods and men wish may be finished as late as possible. But in this flood Naglfar gets afloat. (The Prose Edda)

In the halls of the goddess Hel, many dead have gathered over the years of the Nine Worlds' existence. No matter how well you keep the nails trimmed, there is enough material for Naglfar.

From the east comes Hrym[120] *with shield held high;*
In giant-wrath does the serpent writhe;
O'er the waves he twists, and the tawny eagle
Gnaws corpses screaming; Naglfar is loose.

The Prose Edda adds:

In the midst of this clash and din the heavens are rent in twain, and the sons of Muspel come riding through the opening. Surt rides first, and before him and after him flames burning fire. He has a very good sword, which shines brighter than the sun. As they ride over Bifrost it breaks to pieces, as has before been stated. The sons of Muspel direct their course to the plain which is called Vigrid. Thither repair also the Fenris–wolf and the Midgard–serpent. To this place have also come Loke and Hrym, and with him all the frost–giants. In Loke's company are all the friends of Hel. The

---

[120] Hrym — the name of a primordial giant.

ᛊ ᛞ

sons of Muspel have there effulgent bands alone by themselves. The plain Vigrid is one hundred miles (rasts) on each side.

"They came together. Waves and stones, Or flame and ice, or verse and prose [121]"—these lines were written by a skald from the future but they precisely describe what was happening in the Vigrid plain at that moment. All the ancient, primordial beings are tied together by kinship and a single plan, but the internal conflict of the system has become so overwhelming that even the oldest bonds of blood, kinship, and spirit could not endure the strain.

Let us pause in silence on the Vigrid plain, listen for a few moments of quiet in mourning before the inevitable, and try to understand what happened.

The algorithm of "good and evil" in Asgard sifted through the sea of human lives and destinies, picking out the grains while discarding the majority as unnecessary. A vast multitude of humans were not considered by the system. This created a wild imbalance where on one side of the scales, under the principles of Tradition and Order, stood the gods and a few chosen ones, while on the other, from the side of chaos and darkness, stood millions upon millions of the departed.

The delicate gyroscope of the principles of Good and Evil, on the eve of Ragnarök, showed an overwhelming excess of what the gods considered "evil"—that which is unnecessary, that which should not exist in the new order. But when even Baldr and Höd went to the world of Hel, when even Nanna-Fidelity joined them there, it became clear that neither the system

121 A.S. Pushkin's "Eugene Onegin".

ᚹ ᚩ

ᛊ ᛞ

of order nor tradition could compensate for this imbalance—there was no one left to do so. Loki could have helped, but Loki was bound. The dvergar could have helped, but after Baldr's funeral and the spontaneous sacrifice of Litr, the halls of Svartalfheimr shut their gates from within.

Everything deemed unnecessary by the system was sent to Hel's realm. But in the final battle, Loki will lead all the unwanted and rejected onto the Vigrid plain. Symbolically, this is a battle of good against evil, but what kind of good? Against what kind of evil? Evil is everything rejected by the system, failed algorithms of achieving results. And these are millions who lived their lives not worthy of entering Valhalla: children, women, the sick, those who died without a weapon in hand, from plague or unbearable labor. In contrast, good is defined by the system as the algorithms of victory—those recorded in the system as victorious. The Aesir gods, the Einherjar warriors; thousands against millions of the rejected. Loki will lead the latter.

It is as if everything developed by the system is placed on two scales: on one side is good, and on the other is evil. But this passive weighing is not the battle yet; the battle is the final attempt to prove who is right and to change the balance between good and evil, thousands and millions, needed and unnecessary, righteous and sinners. If evil prevails and wins, it means the created system of reality is unjust and ineffective; it selects a few worthy individuals, but for the majority living in the realms of truth and justice, their lives are meaningless, their fates insignificant, and the time they lived is worthless. If so, it will be an obvious defeat for the gods—the time allocated for the project was wasted.

Tyr's original idea—to create a world of truth and justice where everyone has a place—remained unfulfilled. The small number of chosen warriors will not outweigh the violated hopes

ᚹ ᚠ

of those now residing in Helheim's halls, and the monsters, enemies of the Aesir, will be all the more terrible to behold the deeper and more obvious the injustice of such a system.

Each god will face his own monster, his own injustice, his own weakness.

Minutes of realization have passed, and the signal for battle is given not by anyone, but by the god Heimdall.

While these things are happening, Heimdal stands up, blows with all his might in the Gjallar–horn and awakens all the gods, who thereupon hold counsel. Odin rides to Mimer's well to ask advice of Mimer for himself and his folk. Then quivers the ash Ygdrasil, and all things in heaven and earth fear and tremble. The asas and the einherjes arm themselves and speed forth to the battlefield. Odin rides first; with his golden helmet, resplendent byrnie, and his spear Gungner, he advances against the Fenris–wolf. (The Prose Edda)

The opponent of the god Odin in this battle is the wolf Fenrir. Why did Fenrir end up as Odin's true enemy, even though human logic in retelling the myth might insist that Fenrir should be the adversary of Tyr? However, Ragnarök, revealing the truth, showed otherwise: Odin faced the wolf in battle and was defeated by him. Odin, as the head of the pantheon and the Allfather, had to look his monster in the eyes and answer for why the wolf, who had done no harm to anyone, was bound. Why was potential danger restrained solely for its potential, without giving him any chance to show possible goodness? Why was what was labeled as evil chained and immobilized simply because it was labeled as evil, and nothing more? These are questions not for Tyr, who has his own enemy, but for Odin, as the one who made the decision to isolate evil programmatically, without cause, and only by his word, his will. An injustice was committed for which Tyr paid with his hand, and Odin with his life.

Now comes to Hlin[122] *yet another hurt.*
When Othin fares to fight with the wolf,
And Beli's fair slayer[123] *seeks out Surt,*
For there must fall the joy of Frigg[124].
(The Poetic Edda. Voluspo)

Fenrir is defeated by Odin's son Vidar, who steps on the lower jaw of the wolf with his famous shoe and tears it apart.

Then comes Sigfather's[125] *mighty son,*
Vithar, to fight with the foaming wolf;
In the giant's son[126] *does he thrust his sword*
Full to the heart: his father is avenged.
(The Poetic Edda. Voluspo)

This fact tells us a lot. First, Vidar's weapon and protection were made by humans. He is the god, the force, to whom everyone has contributed, and, by analogy with Baldr (for whom not everyone agreed to weep), Vidar's shoe shows: every person wearing shoes has contributed to his victory. Secondly,

---

122 Hlin — Frigg. Her new grief is the death of Odin; her old grief is the death of Baldr.

123 Beli's fair slayer — Freyr. Beli is a giant killed by Freyr.

124 Joy of Frigg — Odin.

125 Sigfather — Odin.

126 Giant's son — the wolf Fenrir.

Vidar's victory over the wolf indicates that the defeat of the father does not automatically mean the defeat of the son: in the new world, the rule will be sacred that children do not answer for their fathers. But at the same time, Vidar's true enemy is Fenrir, which tells us another rule: children must correct the mistakes of their fathers.

Thor's opponent in the battle of Ragnarök is his eternal enemy, the serpent Jörmungandr.

Hither there comes the son of Hlothyn[127]*,*
The bright snake gapes to heaven above;
Against the serpent goes Othin's son[128]*.*

In anger smites the warder of earth, —
Forth from their homes must all men flee;—
Nine paces fares the son of Fjorgyn,
And, slain by the serpent, fearless he sinks.
(The Poetic Edda. Voluspo)

They are bound—Thor and the Serpent. The serpent, like a timer, when turned off, does not restart its countdown. This means that time is up. For everyone. Including Thor, the end of the old project.

Thor gets great renown by slaying the Midgard–serpent, but retreats only nine paces when he falls to the earth dead, poisoned by the venom that the serpent blows on him. (The Prose Edda)

---

127 Son of Hlothyn — Thor. Hlódyn, or Fjörgyn, — Thor's mother.

128 Othin's son — a name used for Thor.

The craftsmen- dvergar did not participate in the final battle. The Völva tells us this in her "Prophecies":

Then sought the gods
their assembly-seats,
The holy ones, and council held.
To find who should raise the race of dwarfs
Out of Brimir's blood and the legs of Blain.

How strange. They helped the Aesir before the battle, but when the decision was made, they retreated into their caves. Perhaps because shortly before this they received a severe insult from them, which was casually noted in the saga of Baldr's funeral:

Thor stood by and hallowed the pile with Mjolner. Before his feet ran a dwarf, whose name is Lit. Him Thor kicked with his foot and dashed him into the fire, and he, too, was burned.

No one paid attention to this episode, no one blamed Thor—everyone was overwhelmed with grief over the loss. But the murder of a guest is a terrible crime, and the dvergar remembered the insult, refusing to stand with the Aesir in battle. The name of the dwarf Lit can be translated as "trust," but there was no more trust between the Aesir-lawmakers and the dvergar-craftsmen.

The god Tyr enters battle with his natural enemy, the dog from the underworld, Garm. This is a personal nightmare, the fear of the death of loved ones, death due to his own fault, Tyr's fault.

Even the dog Garm, that was bound before the Gnipa—cave, gets loose. He is the greatest plague. He contends with Tyr, and they kill each other. (The Prose Edda)

Now Garm howls loud before Gnipahellir,
The fetters will burst, and the wolf run free;
(The Poetic Edda. Voluspo)

Loki himself fought with the white god Heimdall. The two principles, once part of the same team, creating reality together, but now the rigid constants of the white god clashed with the boundlessness and anarchism of Odin's brother:

Loke fights with Heimdal, and they kill each other. Thereupon Surt flings fire over the earth and burns up all the world. (The Prose Edda)

The death of the two gods, Loki and Heimdall, is the signal for Surt and the sons of Muspell that the battle is decided. Their step is the last, for until this moment they had not entered the battle, waiting for the key event, and it came—the killing of Surt's relative Loki is not so much an insult to the honor of the family (that's human) as an indicator that the old reality is no longer supported by Loki's fiery bonds and Asgard now has no mechanism for binding the various realities of the World Tree together in a varied and friendly manner. Two systemic principles nullified each other.

Freyr, the god of fertility, of the Vanir power, perishes at the hands of the all-consuming fire:

Frey encounters Surt, and heavy blows are exchanged ere Frey falls. The cause of his death is that he has not that good sword which he gave to Skirner.

The giant Surt is a stream of fire of very high density.

The sun turns black, earth sinks in the sea,
The hot stars down from heaven are whirled;
Fierce grows the steam and the life-feeding flame[129]*,*
Till fire leaps high about heaven itself.
(The Poetic Edda. Voluspo)

In the final clash, it is not humans who fight, nor gods; it is principles that battle. They fight for the right to become the strongest foundational program that will form the basis of the new world. The same legend of Ragnarök tells us on what principles the new world order will be built and on which laws the Tree of Future Reality will grow, clearly identifying the survivors who remain after the ultimate Battle of the Gods.

Practice 38. Ragnarök (p. 600)

[129] Life-feeding flame — fire.

ᛊ ᛞ

The New World after Ragnarök

Then said Ganglere: Do any gods live then? Is there any earth or heaven? Har answered: The earth rises again from the sea, and is green and fair. The fields unsown produce their harvests. Vidar and Val live. Neither the sea nor Surt's fire has harmed them, and they dwell on the plains of Ida, where Asgard was before. Thither come also the sons of Thor, Mode and Magne, and they have Mjolner. Then come Balder and Hoder from Hel. They all sit together and talk about the things that happened aforetime,—about the Midgard—serpent and the Fenris—wolf. They find in the grass those golden tables which the asas once had.

Thus it is said:

Vidar and Vale
Dwell in the house of the gods,
When quenched is the fire of Surt.
Mode and Magne
Vingner's Mjolner shall have
When the fight is ended.

In a place called Hodmimer's—hold are concealed two persons during Surt's fire, calledLif and Lifthraser. They feed on the morning dew. From these so numerous a race is descended that they fill the whole world with people, as is here said:

Lif and Lifthraser[130]
Will lie hid
In Hodmimer's—holt.

130 The names Liv and Lifthrasir can be translated as "life" and "life-loving."

ᚠ ᚨ

The morning dew
They have for food.
From them are the races descended.

But what will seem wonderful to you is that the sun has brought forth a daughter not less fair than herself, and she rides in the heavenly course of her mother, as is here said:

A daughter
Is born of the sun
Ere Fenrer takes her.
In her mother's course
When the gods are dead
This maid shall ride.

And if you now can ask more questions, said Har to Ganglere, I know not whence that power came to you. I have never heard any one tell further the fate of the world. Make now the best use you can of what has been told you. (The Prose Edda)

So, who will survive after Ragnarök?

Höd and Baldr. Baldr, having learned all the lessons in Hel's realm, now understands not only what defeat is but also why it happens—he learned from the defeated. Höd, being with Baldr throughout the time leading up to the end of the Ragnarök battle, also learned alongside him, learning to direct his great power correctly. Loki, who led the army of the dead for the battle of Ragnarök, opened the doors of the dead and essentially freed Baldr and Höd. The death of the old world became the birth of the new world.

The head of the revived world becomes the silent god Vidar. His silence signifies that the principles of the new world's order will be established without mentorship, commandments, or teachings. When light and darkness are in harmony, when their development occurs synchronously, there is no need for extensive interpretations and their deciphering—neither Talmuds nor scriptures are required. What must exist is what is natural and understandable. Without words. And if explanations are suddenly needed, then it is unnecessary, and the god Vali will exclude the superfluous. The future system is built on a simple principle. But it is complex in its simplicity.

The gods of the future do not create a new monotheism. The gods of the future do not demand sacrifices and veneration. This is another side of polytheism, a more mature side. The principle of building the new reality can be expressed in the following words:

I am not a god if you are not a god.

And this is the vow exchanged by the gods of the future, if this programming principle is translated into human language. It is a profoundly different understanding of the interaction between gods, not between gods and humans. A human becomes a god if they fully accept this principle. There is no higher god and lower god, no dependent god and subordinate god, no separate gods of nature and gods of order. It is not a world where gods turn into demons and demons into gods with a shift in perception. It is not equality in the usual sense, but a total awareness of mutual connectedness, an ever-present quantum connection of everything with everything. There is no room for dualism of black and white, sin and holiness, good and evil. It is a universal program for building reality, and it can only exist if there are other programs. Any destruction of the other leads to the loss of one's own properties in such a system. Each program in it performs its own task, and there is no more important program and no less important one. They are not the same but equally necessary.

To come to such a program of the future, the gods of old went through their history, and it is terrible.

Vidar and Vali — brothers born of the Earth but in its different aspects. Vali — on the power of denial and hatred, and Vidar — on the power of acceptance and agreement. They are good and evil, but not as opposing systems trying to annihilate each other, but as parts of a whole, where Vidar is the hand, and Vali is the sword held in that hand.

Magni and Modi. The children of Thor and his heirs. The power circuit of the new system, to whom Mjolnir rightfully belongs.

The fact that all these gods are born of the Earth in its various aspects makes the gods of the new world completely independent of the Vanir forces. There is no longer a need to fight for resources, endlessly warring and deceiving the Vanir — the Earth gives her children everything they need without bloodshed. Not only the energy resource but also access to the ancient Jotun memory, which no longer needs to be fought for — it is naturally present in the young gods.

Lif and Lifthrasir, children of nature, embody the Vanir spirit, and they will not face the wrath and fury of the gods, nor will the gods depend on regular nourishment — all forces and races are now self-sufficient and independent of each other. Humans gain freedom from the gods, and gods gain freedom from humans. They can now build relationships with each other on entirely different principles — without mutual dependence and burdensome obligations to one another.

The Völva says that the new world will be very different from the old. It will be based on new rules of interaction between everything: new celestial bodies, new skies, new gods, new people. But the important rule is: I am not a god if you are not a god.

This rule is like the reverse of competition, turned inward. Not to eliminate a competitor from the reality space, but rather to include them in it. As logic suggests, the chance and possibility of being a god will only exist when there is another god nearby. And the same logic suggests that the more gods there are around you, the higher your chances of becoming a god. The god Vali can help with this: a sword directed inward can kill in you the one who forces you to kill everyone else. He will kill Höd as blind darkness and make it sighted.

The god Vidar, having grown up in the forest, knows how ideal the system formed there is. Everything has its place, every tree, plant, mushroom, animal, or bird, everything living and non-living occupies its unique place. In the forest system, everything is connected with everything, and there is nothing superfluous, and everything is needed for something. There exists a harmonious principle of coexistence of everything with everything; it is this principle that will be realized in the new world — everything born has its place. People will exist on the principles of "life" and "life-loving" — and this is natural for humans. Gods will exist on the principle of the coexistence of equals — and this is natural for gods.

The program of the new world is created on different principles. It is no longer the image of a tree — it is the image of a forest, where there is a place for everyone. The old system was built on principles of mutual need: it could be a need for resources and a need for the Vanir, it could be a need for information and a need for giants and Jotnar; it is also a need imposed by the Norns, and a need for sacrifices, and a need for protection from unnecessary or untimely information. The children of the old gods must create and will create a new system

ᛊ ᛞ

that will not be based on the principles of need or programmatic necessity. In the new system, there will be no program that cannot exist without the presence of another. The symbiosis of the forest is welcomed, but there is no place for the parasitism of mistletoe in the new world. In the new world, there should be a place for everything and everyone without the need to sacrifice something or accept sacrifices for such existence. Every element is self-sufficient. Every human is self-sufficient. Every god is self-sufficient. Without influencing each other, the natural connection will make everyone stronger.

The function of the god Forseti in the new world unfolds before us in a greater volume of possibilities for the existence of multiple realities. The ability of the god to "judge fairly" gives a more precise and expanded understanding of the concept of "justice": justice is when a person receives not only what they "deserve" but also what they truly want. The foundation of forming any connection is mutual desire.

Reality becomes like an interactive game that writes itself. In the new reality, there is no place for masters and slaves as an obligatory form of existence, only if it is not part of mutual and conscious desire. There is no place for gods and humans as ready and unchangeable forms of existence. Form ceases to define essence — and this is the magical meaning of shapeshifting.

The world before Ragnarök was magical and filled to the brim with the power of the gods. However, that system did not account for the possibility that anyone other than the gods could also fill reality, such as humans. In the old system, there was no algorithm that allowed a human to rise to the level of a god through their own mind and strength—quite the opposite, only the gods could choose a human, distinguishing them from their peers. But there was no algorithm that took into account a person's individuality and placed them at the center of the world,

ᚹ ᚨ

ᛊ ᛞ

one that didn't fix them in stasis but allowed them to build the kind of reality they wanted and could create. This also applies to representatives of other worlds, races, and systems. This realization of oneself in a big world largely led to people abandoning the old gods in favor of a new foreign god: he promised algorithms that the old gods did not possess. Or as they said at the time, "Red Thor lost the battle to White Christ." It is now clear that this was also a deception, so the time has come for new gods.

In the new world, there will also be compromises. However, these will no longer be forced agreements with the opinion of the majority but rather the search for such points of contact where the rights of individuality cannot be violated. Moreover, the algorithms of creation will separate individual realities in time and space so that they never intersect physically or informationally until they find at least one common element that supports the individuality of each. Young gods create such algorithms and rules of connecting realities where no one has to compromise themselves or their dignity for the sake of this connection. This very important condition is programmed by Ullr, technically ensured by Vidar and Vali, principled by Baldr and Höd, and described in clear rules by Forseti. Thus, compromise, as a system of forced concessions through the reduction of the unnecessary, turns into a contract, as the development of the important.

In the new world that is being formed now, an important principle is embedded—there will be no caste distinction[131]. The social reality of the world of humans, created by Heimdall, ceases to be system-defining for Midgard. No one can be either a slave

---

131 See Practice 26, page 562. The god Forseti and his seal—this principle is encrypted in it.

ᚹ ᚨ

or a master—in their own reality, everyone is a god because there is another reality with its own god at the center of creation. The new world enshrines independence from what is done in other realities, independence from gods, heroes, Aesir, Vanir, and from each other—allowing for the absence of caste distinction. There are no more rules for the existence of castes, only rules for the existence of individuality—and these rules are different for everyone. These rules will determine who to interact with and who not to know about. If the consciousness lacks the necessary knowledge, its appearance opens up the possibility of supplementing reality, but the individual accepts the knowledge of their own free will and desire and is not imposed from outside. Such a policy and such rules make not only a person independent from other realities but also the realities independent of the one who chooses the path formed only by the internal specifics of the personality and not by the specifics of today's existence.

The future has already arrived. It's just not evenly distributed yet[132].

Now do I see the earth anew
Rise all green from the waves again;
The cataracts fall, and the eagle flies.
And fish he catches beneath the cliffs.

The gods in Ithavoll meet together.
Of the terrible girdler of earth[133] *they talk,*
And the mighty past they call to mind,

132 This was said by William Ford Gibson.

133 World Serpent—Miðgarðsormr.

And the ancient runes of the Ruler of Gods[134].

In wondrous beauty once again
Shall the golden tables stand mid the grass,
Which the gods had owned in the days of old,

Then fields unsowed bear ripened fruit.
All ills grow better, and Baldr comes back;
Baldr and Hoth dwell in Hropt's[135] *battle-hall,*
And the mighty gods: would you know yet more?

Then Honir wins the prophetic wand,
And the sons of the brothers[136] *of Tveggi abide*
In Vindheim[137] *now: would you know yet more?*

More fair than the sun, a hall I see,
Roofed with gold, on Gimle it stands;
There shall the righteous rulers dwell,
And happiness ever there shall they have.

There comes on high, all power to hold,
A mighty lord, all lands he rules.

From below the dragon dark comes forth,
Nithhogg flying from Nithafjoll;

---

134 Mighty god—Odin.

135 Hropt—Odin.

136 …the two brothers—Baldr and Höd.

137 House of winds—heaven.

ᛊ ᛞ

The bodies of men on his wings he bears,
The serpent bright: but now must I sink.
(The Poetic Edda. Voluspo)

The old gods gave way to the young, so they could build a new reality—on entirely different principles. One cannot say that there will be no stable constants in the new world—they will exist. There will be a place for those who cannot exist without stability in their lives. But the difference between the old and the new world will be that everyone else does not have to follow such a path if they think otherwise. The new world will be programmed in such a way that every consciousness and every worldview will have a place. Intersecting realities will only occur at the point of absolute coincidence of these realities and will extend to such an extent that their interaction will be conflict-free. No one lives for all, but also one does not have to follow all. It must be a program where there is no unambiguity. In the new world, there should be no defining position of tradition, freedom, good, and evil over the processes of life and death, love and hatred. If this is transferred to the scheme of three magical circles, it would look like this (see diagram on page 347).

The inner circle of life and the second circle of tradition swap places. What used to define and fix existence becomes a tool of new life, a new reality. Tradition is taken apart into fibers, good and evil are separated into algorithms. They are merely information clusters, not system-defining rules. The level of Life-Death-Love-Hate must have direct interaction with the system of Order-Chaos-Light-Darkness. Only such a direct connection will enable the creation of individual multiple realities for each and everyone, rather than living according to one inevitable scenario. The egregorial world should move into a subordinate position to those who personally experience life, those who

ᚠ ᚨ

create their reality and take responsibility for it. Freyr should say: servant, know your place and it will be so. The boundaries between each one's realities must be conditional and exist only as long as they are needed—individually. But when the consciousness of each one who has established the boundaries of their personal reality realizes that the boundaries are no longer needed and can be moved or removed altogether, this should happen quickly and naturally and no one should have the right to hold the barriers artificially on the basis of tradition, rules, and principles supposedly common to all. There will be nothing common to all, except what each one needs to have in common and only in the process of intersecting realities at that moment and under no circumstances forever.

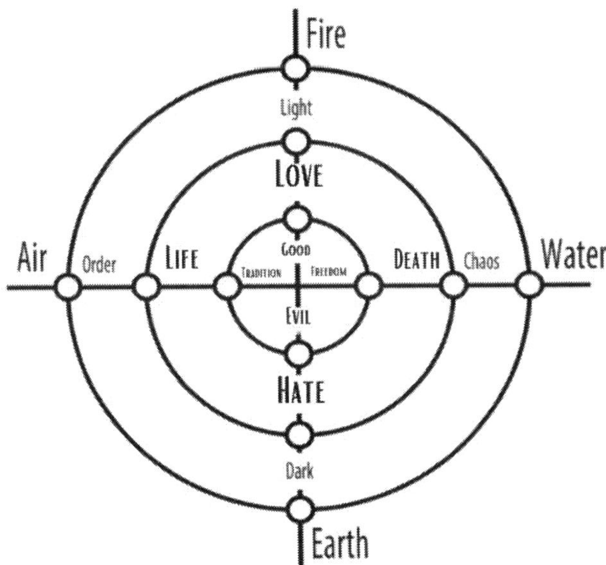

Two people, who survived the battle and became the founders of the new human community, are Líf and Lífthrasir. Their names translate to "life" and "life loving," indicating that the primary value of the new world for humanity will be life itself, with everything else stemming from this love. All human formations, rules, and principles of the old world will remain and be used only if they support this primary value. The value of any living being is above all else.

In the world-building of the young gods, the concepts of "wrong," "system error," or "impossible operation" do not exist. The system is designed so that any change will find its manifestation, any desire will be able to be realized, any law can become both fundamental and insignificant—in the world of multiple realities, everything is possible. Everything is correct; it is just a question of what this correctness is applied to. If there are many objects of application, if the number of personal realities is not limited by any bounds, then everything will be correct and fair. The system of multiple worlds will ensure that diametrically opposed realities, based on different paradigms, never intersect. However, if there is something in common, the intersection will occur only on this common ground, not suppressing or destroying contradictory aspects.

If a person or any other conscious being has specific ideas about how things should be and does not want to part with these ideas, it is fair, from the perspective of the new world order of the young gods, to connect this consciousness with a reality where it can fully realize its right to live according to its own canons without harm to itself or other conscious beings.

Not everyone is required to be the same. No one should be the same. Consequently, they should not live in the same realities. Conversely, in the new world, no one has the right to impose their reality on others, forcibly involving them in it or

ᛊ ᛞ

forcibly integrating themselves into realities built on entirely different principles.

The world-building program created by the silent god Vidar and the entire team of young gods, programmed by Ullr and his companions, can become the universal program that no previous gods have managed to create. The old pantheons worked on programming reality where the "universal person," "hero," or "perfect consciousness" was part of the technical task for building reality. The gods focused on one, not considering all others. This was true not only for the northern pantheon but for all old systems. It should be remembered that in the "technical task" of the old pantheons, humans were not the primary focus ("the crown of creation") but just a minor part of the overall task, though a mandatory one. The young gods of Vidar's team changed the principle and approach: not one consciousness, but all consciousnesses; not all together, but each individually.

The new reality-building program must have the capability to prescribe individual rules for such building every time a creator (god, human, or other intelligence) forms a reality around themselves. Its foundation lies in the individual principle of "life and life loving," manifested as the strongest desire. The god Forseti will write these rules, and the goddess Sjöfn will recognize this desire. She will reveal not only the desire itself but also the reason for it, identifying its truth. The goddess Lofn, based on this truth, will connect the individual reality with other realities where the desire, its true cause, meaning, and essence can be manifested in form and action. The interaction of realities with each other should be neither inspired nor restricted by anything or anyone other than the consciousness present in the reality. However, the desire of one should not change the lives of all others if they do not want it. The goddess Fulla will ensure

ᚹ ᚨ

that the main thing is not forgotten and will protect the core of true meaning.

The goddesses Vár and Vör will count and record any changes occurring every second in the individual programs of reality-building. Nothing should be unnoticed, unaccounted for, or misunderstood.

The goddess Eir in the new reality also contributes to forming the principle of justice by asserting that no guilt should manifest in a person's life and health. The old system could keep consciousness in reality by restricting its health, for example, by binding it with illness. The healer goddess cannot consider this just: no reality is above life, and if a person's actions contradict the rules of reality, punishment through disease or enforced death is unacceptable. Such consciousness and its actions are not the fault of the person but of the system; it cannot form an environment where such actions are normal, and the consciousness is not harmful to others. Punishing a person because reality does not match their beliefs or norms is unjust, the young gods believe, and Eir adds that life and health are exempt from possible limitations, no matter where a person finds themselves or in which reality their love for life exists. In the system of multiple realities, this factor is life and health.

The goddesses Syn and Hlín will protect the young worlds from the intrusion of old traditions' algorithms. Under their patronage, no one will be sent to Hel or be rejected by reality just because they didn't perform the proper transition ritual from life to death, died from illness, or without a weapon in hand. These goddesses will protect people from the encroachments of old Abrahamic systems, shielding their reality from crude suppression of will or manipulation of the desires of the living and those who love life.

Like the goddess Frigg, who managed to project herself into 12 separate and independent forces, the god Odin managed to spread himself through his thoughts via many winged Valkyries. In the new world, these forces will participate in the dissemination of information, and among them, there will inevitably be one free and rebellious thought that does everything differently than intended. But even this bug[138] is not an accident but a necessary share of unpredictability, a spirit of contradiction, without which it would be not only very boring but also very harmful—for a system that is based on the principle of "freedom for each" rather than "freedom for all."

The goddess Saga will remember everything. The goddess Gefjun will define the space of possibilities. The goddesses Snotra and Gná will connect everything to everything and manifest it in reality. The Valkyries will help.

Creating such a reality is not a one-way ticket. If consciousness changes, so does reality; if the mind changes priorities, the world system has the ability to form a new one. Realities will connect and disconnect, but the initiator of such events will no longer be a law "given from above"—only the creator of personal space can make such a decision and desire it strongly.

The new reality program implements the highest principle of humanism, as "humanism for each." Not humanism for the majority, not humanism for the minority, but humanism for each. Regardless of anything: whether smart or foolish, educated or uneducated, human or non-human—everyone has the right to live the life, the existence, and in the reality they are

---

138 Bug—a programming error.

currently capable of; and this is not their eternal limit, nor is it their possession or diminishment.

The old system, in which our world is living its last hours, is neither perfect nor just. And the young gods understand this completely. The old system allows similar to judge similar—by the measure by which one judges oneself. But everyone has their own measure, their own boundaries, and their own possibilities. The sensitivity of the new world program is such that any lie, injustice, or violence, any deceit, or attempt to suppress another's free will will give an instant reaction, separating such consciousness and reality from others, limiting its space of possibilities until the consciousness reprograms itself to the possibility of different communication—by itself. Such a limitation cannot and will not be imposed by a person or group of people based on written law or the power of the majority—in the new world, there is no right of power of a person over a person, a person over another living being, or vice versa. The limitation will be made by the reality itself; the world system will instantly react to injustice. Two things that will never be subject to such limitation are life and health, as well as free will. The mechanisms of the god Ullr can pinpoint the source of the problem and localize it—this action will prevent injustice, will not allow the innocent to suffer for another's mistakes. The program for building multiple realities is sensitive to each individual's changes.

So be it.

2022

PRACTICE SECTION

ᛊ ᛞ

PRACTICE 1

Individual Runic Code

(by the calculation method of O. Shaposhnikov[139])

The numerological principles underlying the calculation of the IRC (Individual Runic Code) allow for the unlocking of potential encoded in the runes to better understand both one's personality and capabilities.

To calculate your destiny code, you need the following data:

1. Surname, first name, patronymic.

2. Date of birth.

That's all!

We need to calculate three runes that will symbolize the fateful life parameters (constants) as the foundation of personal wyrd.

The first rune is the Rune of Essence or Rune of Fate. It is determined based on the numerical sequence of the birth date. This ties destiny to the fabric of time. The Rune of Essence (destiny number) represents the qualities with which a person was born, the power brought into this world from **previous incarnations.**

The second rune is the Rune of Identity. It is determined based on the numerical sequence derived from the letters of the social name[140]. The Rune of Identity indicates the qualities that need to be developed in this incarnation, the

---

139 Oleg Shaposhnikov's website: "Runes of Odin" runa-odin.org

140 In this example, the Cyrillic alphabet is used, but tables can also be easily formed based on the Latin alphabet, Glagolitic script, or any other alphabetical system.

ᚠ ᚨ

qualities necessary for the proper fulfillment of the task (mission).

The third rune is the Golden Rune. It is determined by combining the numerical values of the Rune of Essence and the Rune of Identity. The Golden Rune is the result, the mark that one needs to leave in this world.

As a result, you get a three-rune formula for the individual development of destiny. The further discussion will cover how to correctly interpret this and what opportunities this understanding opens for you.

Calculation Method[141]

The Rune of Essence

Take the date of birth of the person. For example: 01.02.1974. Calculate the sum of the numbers of the birth date: 0 + 1 + 0 + 2 + 1 + 9 + 7 + 4 = 24 = 6. This number also consists of the day of birth number (0 + 1 = 1), the month of birth number (0 + 2 = 2), and the year of birth number (1 + 9 + 7 + 4 = 21 = 3). 1 + 2 + 3 = 6. In numerology, this is the Number of Essence. This number determines the Runic group.

141 The basic example of the birth date and name does not relate to any specific person; it is taken entirely from the author's calculation methodology explanations, from the website "Runes of Odin."

Conversion Table No. 1

Group	1	2	3	4	5	6	7	8	9
1st aett	ᚠ	ᚢ	ᚦ	ᚨ	ᚱ	ᚲ	ᚷ	ᚹ	
2nd aett	ᚺ	ᚾ	ᛁ	ᛃ	ᛇ	ᛈ	ᛉ	ᛊ	
3rd aett	ᛏ	ᛒ	ᛖ	ᛗ	ᛚ	ᛜ	ᛟ	ᛞ	

In our example, it is the 6th group. Next, in the Runic group, we determine the aett (1st, 2nd, or 3rd). This is done as follows:

We convert the decimal code into a ternary code according to the table below.

Conversion Table No. 2

1st aett	2nd aett	3rd aett
1	2	3
4	5	6
7	8	9

Now we take the day of birth number. It is 1. In ternary code, this is 1. This points to the 1st aett. Then we take the month of birth number. It is 2. In ternary code, this is 2. This points to the 2nd aett. And now we take the year of birth number. It is 3. In ternary code, this is 3. This points to the 3rd aett. As a result, we could not definitively determine the aett. Therefore, we take the Number of Essence. It is 6. In the ternary system, this is 3. This points to the 3rd aett. Therefore, we settle on the 3rd aett.

ᛊ ᛞ

6th group, 3rd aett. The rune is Inguz (Inguz). **This rune is the Rune of Essence in this example.**

The Rune of Identity

The numerical values corresponding to the letters of the **first name, patronymic, and surname** are summed up. In numerology, this is known as the Number of Identity. In other numerology schools, it is called the "the name number."

Conversion Table No. 3

Numerical values of letters								
1	**2**	**3**	**4**	**5**	**6**	**7**	**8**	**9**
А	Б	В	Г	Д	Е	Ё	Ж	З
И	Й	К	Л	М	Н	О	П	Р
С	Т	У	Ф	Х	Ц	Ч	Ш	Щ
Ъ	Ы	Ь	Э	Ю	Я			

For example: Иванов Николай Петрович.

Иванов: 1 + 3 + 1 + 6 + 7 + 3 = 21 = 3 (surname number)

Николай: 6 + 1 + 3 + 7 + 4 + 1 + 2 = 24 = 6 (name number)

Петрович: 8 + 6 + 2 + 9 + 7 + 3 + 1 + 7 = 43 = 7 (patronymic number)

21 + 24 + 43 = 88 = 16 = 7 (the Number of Identity)

This number determines the Runic group.

ᚠ ᚠ

Conversion Table No. 4

	1	2	3	4	5	6	7	8	9
1st aett	ᚠ	ᚢ	ᚦ	ᚨ	ᚱ	ᚲ	ᚷ	ᚹ	
2nd aett	ᚺ	ᚾ	ᛁ	ᛃ	ᛇ	ᛈ	ᛉ	ᛊ	
3rd aett	ᛏ	ᛒ	ᛖ	ᛗ	ᛚ	ᛝ	ᛟ	ᛞ	

In our example, it is the 7th group. Next, within the Runic group, we determine the aett (1st, 2nd, or 3rd). This is done as follows:

We convert the decimal code into a ternary code according to the provided conversion table No. 5.

Conversion Table No. 5

1st aett	**2nd aett**	**3rd aett**
1	2	3
4	5	6
7	8	9

Now we take the surname number, which is 3. In ternary code, it equals 3. This points to the 3rd aett. Next, we take the given name number, which is 6. In ternary code, this equals 3. This also points to the 3rd aett. Lastly, we take the patronymic number, which is 7. In ternary code, it equals 1. This points to the 1st aett. If we had not been able to determine the aett unequivocally, we would have used the Identity Number. It is 7. In the ternary system, this equals 1, which would have indicated the 1st aett. But in this example, the aett is determined. It is the

3rd aett, so we do not use the Identity Number. Thus, the 3rd aett.

7th group, 3rd aett. The rune is Othala. This rune is the Identity Rune in this example.

The Golden Rune

The Golden Rune corresponds to the Golden Alchemical Number. This number is determined by the sum of the Number of Essence and the Number of Identity. The first and second runes are active forces. The third rune is the result of the combination (application) of both forces.

In the given example, 6 + 7 = 13 = 4. This will be the Golden Alchemical Number. This number will determine the Runic group for the third rune.

Next, within the Runic group, we determine the aett (1st, 2nd, or 3rd). This is done as follows:

We convert the decimal code into a ternary code according to the provided conversion table No. 6.

Conversion Table No. 6

1	**2**	**3**
1	2	3
4	5	6
7	8	9

Now, we take the sum of the birth date number and the given name number. In our example: 1 + 6 = 7. In ternary code, this equals 1. This points to the 1st aett.

Next, we take the sum of the month number and the patronymic number. In our example: 2 + 7 = 9. In ternary code, this equals 3. This points to the 3rd aett.

Finally, we take the sum of the year number and the surname number. In our example: 3 + 3 = 6. In ternary code, this equals 3. This points to the 3rd aett.

If we had not been able to determine the aett unequivocally, we would have used the Golden Alchemical Number. It is 4. In the ternary system, this equals 1, which would have indicated the 1st aett. But in this example, the aett is determined. It is the 3rd aett, so we do not use the Golden Alchemical Number. Thus, the 3rd aett, 4th group, 3rd aett. The rune is Mannaz. This rune is the Golden Rune in this example.

Based on the provided data, we have calculated the Individual Runic Code:

Inguz-Othala-Mannaz

Now we need to address the question: what to do if the Number of Essence, the Number of Identity, or the Golden Alchemical Number is 9 (0)? Or, in other words, how to compose the Individual Runic Code if the Rune of Essence, the Rune of Identity, and the Golden Rune belong to the 9th Runic group? The Individual Runic Code is composed only of runes from the 1st to the 8th Runic groups. If any of the three aforementioned runes (Essence Rune, Identity Rune, and Golden Rune) belong to the 9th Runic group, then a "blank" rune is placed in place of the aforementioned rune. In the Individual Runic Amulet, no rune is created in the corresponding place. For example, if the Identity Rune were from the 9th Runic group, the Individual Runic Code would look like this: Inguz-Mannaz.

In the Menshikova School, this calculation method is used exclusively for determining the Individual Runic Code (IRC). The interpretation and decoding system in the Menshikova School is based on the magical effect of the runes, which students receive after their study and initiation.

This involves the skill of working on the channel.[142]

Now let's try to analyse in detail what each rune, positioned as the Rune of Essence, the Rune of Identity, or the Golden Rune, signifies. The knowledge, understanding, and feeling of the runes already tell us that depending on the position, the same rune can indicate something entirely different.

The Rune of Fate

This is the karma that each person brings from their past incarnations. It is the accumulated and preserved experience; it is what the person has achieved by living their fate in all their previous births. This is what truly belongs to them by right. The Rune of Fate has nothing to do with

---

142 You can verify the accuracy of the calculation here: https://mages.school/individual-runic-code/

Menshikova always reminds her students that the automatic calculation system is necessary for self-verification. It does not replace the magical skill of "counting by hand."

bloodline or family; it is only personal — what has already been worked out. It is a basic level of rights, which may or may not come from one's lineage.

The date of birth, which is the basis for calculating the Rune of Fate, is generally irreversible. Exceptions do occur, but they are more mystical than systematic. For this reason, it is considered that the Rune of Fate is a given, something that no one can change. The Norns weave it once.

Fehu — the rune of beginnings and endings, primal power. The rune of spiritual strength, and globally, the rune of rights. If Fehu stands as the Rune of Fate, it indicates that the bearer of this runic code was born with strongly expressed rights. They possess these rights inherently, from birth, and nothing in their past lives could strip them away. Typically, Fehu as the Rune of Fate suggests that the person's birth is their own conscious choice. They might have unfinished business from their previous life that they wish to complete in this incarnation. The following runes — the Rune of Identity and the Golden Rune — may provide clues about what needs to be completed. Perhaps, at the end of the previous life, you doubted whether you lived your life correctly. In this case, your birth "here and now" should help answer this question. To find the answer, it is essential not to forget the question.

With Fehu as the Rune of Fate, it is crucial to remember and recognize your inherent qualities, which should have manifested from early childhood, from the first moment of self-awareness. These qualities are the key indicators of the specific rights you possess inherently. What to do with these rights and how to effectively manifest them should be shown by the subsequent runes in your IRC: what to acquire and what to accomplish. Inherent rights must evidently undergo new tempering and trials, learning to be stronger and resilient against the provocations of the current age.

Uruz — the rune of strength, primal power. Those with this rune as the first in their runic code seem to be born of the Earth itself — they are naturally strong and powerful. Whether this manifests as physical health or internal strength, this quality will always be evident in some form. Typically, such individuals are innately kind and honest — for strength always carries kindness. They seem to inherently know that a mighty power stands behind them, an inseparable part of them that cannot be killed or taken away. However, statistics show that Uruz as the Rune of Fate appears very rarely in runic codes.

Thurisaz — the rune of determination, the rune of the "first strike" force. Symbolically linked to the hammer of Thor, Mjölnir. According to legend, the hammer was so heavy that not every god could lift it, let alone an ordinary person. Additionally, Thor's hammer had the ability to return to its owner's hands after being thrown, like a boomerang. Those who receive the rune Thurisaz as their Rune of Fate are akin to the nature of Mjölnir — they are capable of action. Moreover, their inner power is always sufficient to accept the consequences of their actions and bear responsibility for what they have done. However, as there is no bad without good, there is no good without bad: the hammer is always in someone's hands. A person with the first rune Thurisaz is straightforward and guileless, which often makes them a tool or a toy in the hands of the powerless. This rune appears very rarely in runic codes, highlighting the unique nature of people with such an innate trait. Where to apply such incredible power and, most importantly, for what purpose, is shown by the subsequent runes of the runic code.

ᚨ **Ansuz** — the rune of knowledge, the rune of origin. The rune of the god Odin, who brought the knowledge of the runes to all nine worlds. A person born with the primary rune Ansuz carries some inherent knowledge into this world, similar to how Odin did. This knowledge is likely packaged, compressed, and archived, and it can only be revealed when the person carrying this knowledge encounters specific conditions or special circumstances. These are situations where the power and energy of reality become necessary and sufficient for this knowledge to be deciphered, unlocked, and manifested. The nature of these circumstances and the qualities of consciousness required for the bearer of the innate rune Ansuz to reveal their knowledge are indicated by the subsequent runes in the runic code.

ᚱ **Raidho** — the rune of the path. Coming into this world with Raidho as the Rune of Fate indicates an ability brought from a past life — the ability to pave the way and follow it. Possibly, the achievement of past incarnations was an idea left behind, an idea that continued to stir consciousness and left a significant or obvious mark. This ability is the one essential tool needed in this life, a tool that can now be used to obtain everything necessary. In a primitive sense: unfinished business.

ᚲ **Kenaz** — the torch, the rune of clarity. A person with this rune as their Rune of Fate is naturally able to "see correctly"

ᛊ ᛞ

— to notice the main thing and discard the secondary. They can be a guiding star and a purpose in life for others, a "light at the end of the tunnel," and a beacon that dispels the darkness of ignorance. This involves the ability to see correctly and explain correctly; these are innate teachers, able to work with phenomena rather than information. They can see cause and effect without error. People with the primary rune Kenaz as their Rune of Fate are exceedingly rare — statistics show they almost never occur, making such a gift in our world a significant rarity.

ᚷ **Gebo** — the rune of partnership and the rune of gift, the rune of understanding laws, especially the most fundamental one for the system of all worlds—the law of balance. This understanding manifests in the human mind as an innate sense of justice and a keen awareness of the "wrongness of events" when such situations occur. It is evident that from past incarnations, the knowledge of the true law has been carried forward, and being born in this world implies the necessity of applying this knowledge to this reality and at this specific time. Partly, the rune Gebo in the position of the Rune of Fate speaks of a serious task of controlling space or "repairing" an already formed reality. There is a need to impact the nodal points of probabilities "here and now" to fulfill the mission of balancing and healing this world, but not generally, rather specifically in this moment. Surprisingly, sometimes this is sufficient for waves of healing to begin spreading to multiple connected realities.

Additionally, it is worth noting that the rune Gebo is the key to the world of Asgard. This suggests that the bearer of such a consciousness trait, inscribed in the Rune of Fate, likely has a direct connection with the forces of the gods-builders, which may not be fully realized by them (at least not until a certain point in time), but will always be expressed in the unshakable state of "I know how."

ᚹ **Wunjo** — the rune of joy and wholeness. The simple meaning of this rune — joy — speaks of the absence of dissatisfaction, and as the first rune in the runic code, it suggests the absence of any debt to this world and possibly a voluntary decision to be born and incarnate here. The complex meaning — wholeness — indicates a completed development of consciousness, with no need to be supplemented by anyone or anything to be whole. Such a whole consciousness can withstand a greater flow of chaos than any other, and therefore, the life path of such a person is likely to be very turbulent. But these are not the vicissitudes of fate — the first rune Wunjo does not imply the presence of fate as punishment or obligation. Instead, it suggests great innate abilities to experience more events than other people; it implies the presence of a natural flow-consciousness, reflected in multiple talents and abilities, psychic resilience, and tremendous endurance.

ᚺ **Hagalaz** — hail, destruction. Hagalaz represents not only the power of destruction but also the power of limitation. As the Rune of Fate, it indicates that a person is inherently limited: in rights, abilities, ambitions — in any aspect. These limitations have reasons; they are not random. Perhaps in past lives, power or knowledge was misused thoughtlessly, and in this life, such a deficiency is necessary as a specific starting point to develop qualities that will prevent causing harm to one's rights or power through irrational use of abilities. To understand where this "disqualification" applies, one needs to analyse their life and recognize where these limitations are imposed. Temporary disqualification, limitation of opportunities, is like an electronic bracelet tracking and restricting freedom.

The second meaning of this rune — destruction — speaks to a natural ability to destroy what the consciousness deems incorrect, improper. It is a magical property of the mind, capable of destroying everything displeasing, everything perceived as distorting reality, the external dirt that obscures clear vision. With such a person, everything is brought to order through the harsh method of "exclusion from reality." With these magical attributes, one must be very strong and educated to avoid using the power of their consciousness to destroy what they truly fear, do not know, or do not understand.

ᚾ **Nauthiz** — the rune of "need" and the rune of "memory." As the Rune of Fate, it indicates that the bearer of this runic code clearly knows why they came into this world. They know it inherently, and if they have forgotten this knowledge by the time they decode their runic code, now is the time to remember. Because this knowledge exists, the memory of the past is present and not erased, and it is characteristically untarnished by anyone. This means the factor of "forgetfulness" can be easily overcome. If something has not been erased with special magical tools, it can be retrieved easily enough — it only requires the strength of desire.

Isa — the rune of ice, fixed and halted processes. In magic, Isa symbolizes unshakeable constants, the power of the primordial. As the first rune in the runic code, it points to a highly pronounced sense of self-awareness, strong will, and very ancient memory. It may exist in a "frozen," archived state and will remain dormant until inner or outer Fire — an idea, a scope for activity — is ignited, and then everything unfolds.

People with the primary rune of ice in their runic code are very patient and can wait a long time for suitable circumstances. Their memory is so ancient that their ability to not hurry is not due to natural slowness or laziness but solely a result of experience from the beginning of time. As you understand, such ancient qualities rarely manifest in a human body, and the statistics of many thousands of calculated runic codes support this: Isa as the first Rune of Fate is almost never found.

Jera — the rune of harvest and time. A person with Jera as the first rune in their runic code has an innate sense of time, a good feel for its tempo, and an ability to skilfully adapt to changes without breaking their psyche. For them, changes are as natural as the wind, which can blow in different directions, at different speeds, and has the right to do so. This is why they are always successful because they know how to harvest correctly. They accurately assess situations, accept the world as it is without stress or regret, and intuitively know what is possible and what is not — these qualities are inherent, not acquired.

Eihwaz — the rune of fear, death, and something very profound that typically does not manifest in ordinary life. As the key to the world of Svartalfheimr, a world associated with the proto-foundation of Evil, Eihwaz as the Rune of Fate indicates its source of origin. As terrifying as this sounds in a Christian worldview, in paganism, it is different. In Svartalfheimr, unique programs are born, programs that the human world lacks for completeness, for wholeness. Knowledge or phenomena of the past, rejected by the world, have not disappeared into the darkness entirely but have been given a second chance. This is the reason for birth: you are the chance for this world to become more perfect, more complete.

Those who bear Eihwaz in their runic code can become an adornment to the world or the destroyer of what should not exist in the manifested world. For those with a mundane or religiously primitive mindset, such a person is a thorn in their side, an embodiment of evil, an injection into their sweet and deceitful reality, a direct mirror for those accustomed to looking into a distorted one. However, for those who develop this world, someone born under the aegis of the rune Eihwaz is a source of inspiration, the Brisingamen necklace, Thor's hammer, or Odin's spear Gungnir, all combined. It is crucial for such an individual to quickly realize their uniqueness and start applying it correctly, without betraying the gifts of the ancient forces of the rejected world. This rune in the first position of the runic code is characteristic of natural tricksters.

Perthro (Perth) — the rune of fate, lot, choice. As the first rune, it signifies that birth in this world, "here and now," is a lot, a choice of the program of periodic incarnation. Not "for some reason," not for "some special cause," but always "for something." If there are no subsequent runes, it simply means that this is the selection by the world's random selection mechanisms. However, this is very rare. Usually, the bearer of such a runic code has a task. There might not be a preliminary burden of "for what purpose," but there is still a task, and nothing is accidental. You are a tool of fate. Not a consequence of its algorithms, but a cause of changes, the hands that resolder the scheme of reality's reflection. The one who possesses the rune Perth as the Rune of Fate must understand and remember that their god (gods) is the god (gods) of Fate, their employer is Fate, their law is the world law of cause and effect, the law of karmic retribution. But this law does not hang over this person like the sword of Damocles; rather, it is the basis for any situation in which they participate. The Weapon of Fate, the Hands of Fate, the Finger of Fate. The sooner the bearer of the rune Perthro realizes their purpose, the sooner they will understand the full meaning of what is happening to them.

ᛉ **Algiz** — the rune of protection and connection with one's force. Having Algiz as the first rune in the runic code indicates a person who is a conduit of force and likely has a specific purpose in this world. What exactly this purpose is can be shown by the subsequent runes in the runic code, but one thing is certain — such a person's life will not be without control and protection.

The rune is associated with the god Heimdall, who was the protector of Asgard. Notice, not of the gods, but of Asgard; Heimdall protected the system, not its individual parts. The bearer of Algiz must remember this connection and understand that their innate need to hold back and separate the necessary from the unnecessary is tied not to personal preference but to a deep, sometimes completely irrational understanding of "it must be so."

ᛊ **Sowilo** — the rune of success and the rune of victory. The Sun Rune. Those who come into this life with the primary rune Sowilo come as victors. They possess the knowledge of "how it should be," because this knowledge granted them undeniable success in past lives. However, the rune does not always (more precisely, it never) explain "why it should be" and "for whom it should be," but it unequivocally speaks of a fortunate fate and an initially favourable path for personal development. It may indicate an innate luckiness and an inner sense of fearlessness towards the outside world.

ᛏ **Tiwaz** — the rune of truth, the warrior's rune. A person born with Tiwaz as their first rune possesses an acute sense of justice and inner pride. In a broader sense of purpose, this rune indicates that the person is a follower of a very important idea, one they worked on in a past life and must continue in this one. Strongly expressed qualities of being able to work in a team, to follow orders, and to give orders.

Tiwaz is symbolically associated with the god Tyr (Tiu) and is considered the rune of kings. Thus, someone born under this rune carries within them a deep knowledge of impeccability, a reminder of the god Tyr, that will never allow them to betray their dignity.

ᛊ ᛞ

ᛒ **Berkana** — the rune of growth and natural development. The rune of the woman, flexibility, the ability to endure everything and not break. In the position of the Rune of Fate, these are qualities that have come with you from a past life. This is what you are entitled to. The rune Berkana does not necessarily characterize its bearer as a typical woman, not at all. It shows the qualities of a nature more accustomed to enduring external pressure with greater success than others; traits that allow one not to achieve results at any cost but to seek alternative paths, adhering to the principle of "do no harm." This includes greater sensitivity than ordinary people and greater delicacy than others. The position of this rune as the Rune of Fate indicates that these qualities are innate.

Symbolically, it is associated with the goddess Freyja (Vanadis), who is renowned not only for her generosity and kindness but also for achieving everything on her own.

ᛖ **Ehwaz** — Sleipnir, the eight-legged horse of Odin. A rune representing magic and magical consciousness. As the first rune of Fate, it indicates precisely this: magical consciousness, magical abilities, an innate quality that this person's consciousness has carried from past lives or other worlds. Usually, this rune suggests that incarnation in this world and at this time is not random but specifically arranged by magic to manifest this consciousness in a particular human body, bloodline (family), epoch, and geographical location. Ehwaz here is a rune of predetermination, indicating: "I have business here." It must be noted that people with such attributes are not liked by the egregorial space. Everything the egregorial world does to this person is meant for one thing — to suppress or ideally destroy them, preferably in infancy. These egregorial pressures may target not only the individual but their entire family, making it difficult for them to develop, and their own family may subconsciously resent this new person, justifiably believing that all family misfortunes began precisely at their birth. However, magic never leaves its wards at the mercy of human fears, and there will always be someone in the family (or nearby) who takes on the role of protector and mentor for this child. Likely, such a mentor will also have Ehwaz in their runic code (in any position).

What you need to do to survive and succeed in an aggressive egregorial environment is revealed by the next rune in the runic code — the Rune of Identity, and for what purpose this needs to be done — the Golden Rune.

ᛗ **Mannaz** — the rune of humanity. On the position of the Rune of Fate, this rune is simply interpreted as the ability to be human. The inner, inherent qualities of the bearer of Mannaz in their runic code in the first position indicate a high degree of communicative skills, empathy, the ability to understand others, and establish correct contacts with them. A person who has the right to live for the formation of their personal experience and rely on the system as an assistant. The human past may sometimes be more interesting to them than the present or future, and knowledge is more important than ways of applying it.

ᛚ **Laguz** — the rune of transfer, the rune of flow, running water. Here it indicates a pronounced quality of witchcraft, the abilities of a medium and dreamer, the ability to transfer information from spaces closed to humans into this world, the human world. Perhaps this quality is passed to you as ancestral power. The bearer of Laguz as the first rune in the runic code brings some kind of force current into this world. This is not knowledge or energy in the simple sense of the word. It is the ability to pass information and energy through one's consciousness and produce a very specific flow that can fill such voids in the fabric of reality that no other flow can fill. It is crucial to recognize your unique ability to transform one type of energy into another, one type of information into another as early as possible. And, of course, to use this amazing magical property of your mind for your key task, for your mission.

Inguz — the rune of fertility. But not as a result, but as a process. Inguz is the continuous force of reproduction and everything that stands behind this concept. A person for whom Inguz is the Rune of Fate is a great worker. They know how to do work not for the result but for the process of doing. They won't stop if something doesn't work out, won't abandon what's started if the result doesn't appear for a long time. This quality is the force of nature, and Inguz is the key to understanding it and, through this, the key to its source — the world of Vanaheimr, the world of nature spirits. The bearer of this rune as the primary force understands the principle of nature's existence as a given — nature lives in a continuous stream of constant creation, and they, too, live in this stream. Their life is not measured, as with others, from event to event, from result to result — they live in the process of doing, and the result is always in the small, and it is visible. A true child of the Vanir, they inherently possess non-binary logic and see the world a little differently.

Othala —the rune of heritage. It can signify not only the possession of certain rights by birth but also the ability to work with ancestral energies. It encompasses a deep understanding of the principles of forming a familial system and the ability to apply this knowledge in today's life. Being born into this world with the primary rune Othala indicates that the knowledge of all principles of forming a family system is already present. There is a right to form family structures and potentially lead them. Sometimes, the rune Othala shows that there has already been an incarnation in the same family, and now it is necessary to correct the development program of the family from a position of knowledge. In any case, Othala as the rune of heritage, standing in the first position, signifies that a person has a gift by blood, knowledge passed down from ancestors, the family's egregore. And possibly, this is the only heritage they possess.

Dagaz — the rune of transformation and transmutation, the transition from one state to another. When positioned as the Rune of Fate, it indicates an inherent quality of being a trickster to those around, a transformer of their lives from one state to another. No matter what environment a person with the primary rune Dagaz finds themselves in, they will always initiate changes. This is the legacy of the god Loki, the spark of Muspelheimr, and the life of such a person is typically either a disaster or an indescribable joy for those around them. The main issue for someone with the rune Dagaz in the first position of their runic code is the lack of a sense of proportion, but they possess an immense capacity to love and a strong loyalty to those they love. Globalism, as an intrinsic quality of consciousness, follows them from birth; the changes brought about by such a person are never local in nature — they are all-consuming, like true fire. Life can be very successful if, of course, it can be long. The latter is usually very difficult to achieve, as the descendants of the god Loki, like himself, continually disrupt the delicate law of balance, thus attracting a lot of attention from various systems intended to stabilize reality. These can be egregorial systems, mages-observers[143], as well as people who are conductors of the principles of the law of balance.

Sometimes, the rune Dagaz in the first position of the Individual Runic Code indicates that the incarnation in a human body and consciousness is occurring for the first time, with prior experience being gained in somewhat different forms of life or existence.

The Blank rune (9th position) — roughly speaking, indicates the absence of fate. Predestination is not manifested, which can be both a favourable and unfavourable sign. It is favourable because there is no burden, no persistence, and the Norns are not pulling your life thread from any pre-tied knot. The unfavourable meaning of the absence of the Rune of Fate lies precisely in the same thing. The life line seems not to be anchored to anything, it is unprotected, and anyone who wishes to pull the thread of life out of the fabric of reality can do so effortlessly and without fatal consequences for themselves.

An annulled karma can be used as a starting boost for a strong personality, but a weak personality with such a premise

---

143 A group of such "reality controllers" is discussed in Menshikova's book "The Power of the Elements".

of the life line becomes vulnerable to literally everything. The next rune, the Rune of Identity, will show which manifested qualities of consciousness in this reality can not only safely anchor you but also make you a visible pattern on the fabric of reality. Of course, this assumes that this is what you want, and not to leave this reality as quickly as possible, preferably without leaving any traces behind.

The Rune of Identity

The basis of the Rune of Identity is the social name, which in the current era can be changed at will. This was impossible in ancient times when a name reflected a person's character, their patron gods, and, of course, their bloodline—belonging to a certain clan or tribe. Sometimes, a name also encoded one's connection to a place, which in the mysticism of naming was not a random factor either.

Nowadays, social names are mutable and variable, and consequently (or perhaps, programmatically causing), the Rune of Identity also becomes mutable and variable. Remembering that this rune reflects the technical task (TT) for a person's current incarnation, displaying certain personal qualities that need to be developed or acquired, we see that in the current era, a person has the right to change their TT, to reprogram their fate as the displayed scenario of their life path. A person has the right to rearrange the accents of their personality, to reveal or conceal their nature, and, as a result, to realize themselves in entirely different outcomes. However, it should be emphasized that all this is accessible only in the world of humans, only within the space of social games. In the annals of the "Book of Fates," in the patterns of the Norns' tapestry, their line is unchangeable, and changing one's identity is not changing the pattern on the fabric of reality but simply colouring this pattern in different shades.

Fehu — the rune of spirit, its strength, and true right. In the position of the second Rune of Identity in the runic code, Fehu most indicates the necessity of acquiring the needed quality — to develop precisely the power of spirit, to lay the foundation of future rights. The rune Fehu is the starting point of any processes, and it is also their conclusion; Alpha and Omega, beginning and end. One needs to learn not only how to start processes correctly but also to secure their result — in the form of strength, in the form of rights, and the result does not have to be strictly material.

The bearer of Fehu as the second rune in the runic code needs to learn to assert their rights and even establish them literally over everything they touch.

Uruz — the rune of strength. In the simplest sense — health, the power of the earth. The ability to take power, the ability to manage strength. When Uruz stands in the second position as the Rune of Identity, it means that a person must learn to take their power from the source, from Mother Earth herself. Only then can their primary abilities (the Rune of Fate) turn into a real result (the Golden Rune). No other force can provide such an opportunity and reveal innate abilities. One must learn not to take surrogates from the human world, not to be satisfied with egregorial handouts. Simply put, not to settle for "McDonald's" when you have real meat.

Mother Earth grants her power only to the worthy, according to the ancient northern tradition—the best. Uruz in the position of the Rune of Identity indicates that the bearer of such a runic code must become the best. This means being

ᛊ ᛞ

impeccable not from the perspective of people or egregores, but from the perspective of Mother Earth herself.

At a basic level of perception, this involves finding the right place to live where this power is more likely to be present.

ᚦ **Thurisaz** — the rune of determination, the rune of a strike. Standing in the second position in the runic code indicates acquiring qualities of determination, the need to learn to act, to become capable of action. To protect those you love; to protect them even when they are wrong, weak, and helpless. To protect your own, no matter what. One needs to learn to make decisions: especially when all "your own" are incapable of it. The rune of becoming a warrior.

ᚨ **Ansuz** — is the rune of knowledge. When Ansuz appears as the Rune of Identity, it indicates that the individual's life task is to acquire knowledge. However, this is not just about gathering information but achieving understanding at a profound level. What exactly needs to be understood is indicated by the first rune, the Rune of Fate. The person has come into this world at this specific time, in this particular era, on this land, with these parents, and in this body to gain insight into what is encoded in the first rune.

ᚱ **Raidho** —is the rune of the path. It signifies a set route, a ready channel. When Raidho stands as the Rune of Identity, it indicates that the consciousness tasked with mastering the rune of the path must be able to chart a course through which the lives and times of other people will flow. This involves not only finding the correct routes to the desired outcomes but also ensuring that these routes follow the path of least resistance,

ᚹ ᚠ

which may not always be the shortest but is the most optimal. Raidho represents the informational direction, the vector of movement, from goal to result. Whether the bearer of such a Rune of Identity is "digging trenches" and "laying roads" for "their own" or "for others" makes no difference—you are here to learn this skill. What it can (or should) lead to is shown by the Golden Rune, the rune of the result.

ᚲ **Kenaz** — the torch, illuminating space. The ability to separate the "main" from the "non-main," the ability to unmistakably see and understand the true meaning of what is happening. These are the qualities the bearer of this Rune of Identity must learn. To do anything only by understanding the meaning of the action, its purpose, and possible consequences. Here the rune in this position indicates that one must learn to make the right choices: if to give, then to whom; if to take, then from whom. The rune will teach making the right choices and taking the right actions. Why and for what, of course, are shown by the Rune of Fate and the Golden Rune respectively.

ᚷ **Gebo** — is the rune of partnership and gift, the rune of adequate energy exchange. It is a very powerful and exalted rune associated with the world of the gods, Asgard—the place where the foundational principles of reality reside. Gebo speaks of a fundamental principle—the principle of balance. As the Rune of Identity, it indicates that this individual needs not only to master the mechanisms of partnership and proper energy exchange in the human world but also to understand the basic principles of law and order throughout their life. It is possible that in a previous life (or lives), you disrupted the principles of the universe's balance, altering the already fragile consensus between the desired and the possible with your actions.

Gebo is the rune of the true ruler, and a true ruler is always renowned for finding compromises that do not diminish anyone's rights or interests. To become such a person and acquire the necessary consciousness properties and personality qualities, one must finely sense and understand the precarious balance of forces in this world. You need to be able to balance between rules and needs, between needs and desires, between desires and feasibility. By balancing these forces, you should create mechanisms of stability, forming social institutions that are meant to be so universal that they not only correctly manage human life but also do not violate the rights of all other living or rational beings that enrich and glorify this world. Everything is interconnected, and the Gebo rune, positioned as the Rune of Identity, insists that the bearer of such a destiny learns to see, understand, and protect this interconnection—everyone and everything from everyone and everything.

ᚹ **Wunjo** — in its simplest sense, is the rune of joy and, in the occult sense, the rune of wholeness. The karmic task of the Wunjo rune in this position is to develop your consciousness to a level where there is no need to supplement yourself to become whole by accumulating unnecessary connections and things. The magical essence of the Wunjo rune is self-sufficiency. In ordinary human terms, it is the rune of bright joy and a state of non-action. However, in magic, it is the rune of readiness for work, where all the natural forces of the first aett runes unite in Wunjo, forming a complete whole. This state of consciousness is called "emptiness" and is the starting position for any magical work.

ᚺ **Hagalaz** — hail, destruction. Here, hail is not only a rune of destruction but also a rune of "protection" and defined boundaries. Manifested in the runic code as the second Rune of Identity, Hagalaz indicates the need to develop and exhibit these qualities of the rune: to know and understand one's boundaries; to know and understand the boundaries of others; to destroy and send to Hel all that is obsolete and unnecessary, that violates the boundaries of the worlds, people, and spaces. Hagalaz here is the ability to act within established limits, to separate the living from the non-living, and to mercilessly turn the latter, the foul, into chaos as sustenance for future generations.

ᚾ **Nauthiz** — the rune of need, but also the key to the world of "continuous memory" of Jotunheimr. When it stands in the second position as the Rune of Identity, it indicates the need to learn not only to preserve your memory in its "uncastrated" form but also to distinguish need from wants, and wants from desires. It means to differentiate truth from falsehood, the real from the imaginary, and to see the true meaning of things. The true meaning of things is to understand without error what a thing was originally intended for. Not how it is used, not how it manifests, but its original purpose. The term "thing" here can refer to anything: an element of the material world, information, a person, a natural element, and so on. The ideal development of oneself through the power of the Nauthiz rune involves ceasing to see differences between all phenomena and manifestations studied from this position. This is the key to forming "continuous memory," which is based on the principle that "there is no one thing better than another thing."

ᛊ ᛞ

ᛁ **Isa** — the rune of stability, constancy. The quality that must remain unchanged through all trials, to maintain resilience and willpower, and to learn to finish what has been started no matter what. Never break! Never surrender! In a global sense, the rune Isa in the second position indicates that a person must learn to preserve themselves, to keep unchanged what is truly valuable to them. Never betray one's convictions, become faithful to everything that is significant and valuable, despite everything.

ᛃ **Jera** — the rune of harvest and time. The bearer of this rune as the Rune of Identity must learn not only to feel time but also to manage it: its pace, application, and distribution. Learn for oneself, change one's attitude towards time, and form a different value for it in one's consciousness. The rune Jera will help acquire the quality of "timeliness." It will help learn not to rush events and not to delay them, and if one properly learns to feel time, it can bestow what is called "luck" in our tradition — the ability to be in the right place at the right time and in the right state of consciousness.

ᛇ **Eihwaz** — the rune of witchcraft. The power to penetrate the depths of the subconscious, the power of fear and death. The one with Eihwaz as the Rune of Identity must develop the qualities of witchcraft consciousness during their life, to be able to work with such forces and energies that a simple mortal would not dare approach. The world of Svartalfheimr, to which Eihwaz is the key, is a world of embodied evil as understood by ordinary people. In magic, this world is a world of unique masters who can unfailingly determine what the world or an individual consciousness lacks for completeness, who can separate the necessary from the unnecessary, and instantly

ᚹ ᚨ

distinguish truth from lies. Developing one's personality under the aegis of the Eihwaz rune implies acquiring these very abilities, not to become walking evil for everyone else. Although, if we look truthfully, the ability to read those around you like an open book and see through them is worse than a sharp knife for them. However, a witchcraft consciousness guided by the Eihwaz rune should not care about this. The minimal manifestation of Eihwaz as the Rune of Identity is to learn to overcome fears, to go beyond the permissible, to learn to act in ways not accepted by society. Learn to turn fears, anger, and hatred into strength — both one's own and others'. Learn to be an injection for both ossified minds and oneself.

ᛈ **Perthro** — the rune of fate, lot, and choice, the final choice. However, unlike the choice represented by Kenaz, this is not an individual choice but a collective one. The one who bears Perthro in their runic code as the second rune must understand the algorithms of cause-and-effect relationships, learn to manage the destinies of many, and learn to bear responsibility for the destinies of the living. On a global, magical level — to weave the fabric of reality, directing the time flows of people, forming a specific pattern of such fabric. On a simple, primitive human level — to organize the lives of relatives, subordinates, and dependents. Help make the right choice, of course, by learning to make this choice themselves. The Perth rune is associated with the goddess Frigg, the great weaver of the world's pattern; she is the one who directs the shuttle, forming the picture of being. The bearer of this rune as the Rune of Identity must learn to read the fates of the living, the dead, and the unborn, to see the final reflection of the pattern even when the threads are not yet set up in the loom. To know the principles of forming fate in all forms, variants, and scenarios. To see the laws of cause and effect, to predict the result of human actions, and possibly even to correct them.

ᛉ **Algiz** — the rune of protection. The presence of this rune as the Rune of Identity indicates that consciousness must learn to defend itself, to become strong and independent. Besides the functions of protection, Algiz helps establish a connection with one's god (it is assumed that having such a connection is the best protection). Therefore, developing personal qualities in this life should draw a person towards understanding the true force that created them, that stands behind them and guides them through life.

ᛊ **Sowilo** — the rune of victory. Standing in the position of the Rune of Identity, it indicates that a person must learn to be a victor. Not just to win, but to form in their consciousness such universal algorithms of victory that will subsequently become an inalienable right for them; to form algorithms that can later be applied to any realities, in any era, and achieve results. Such victory algorithms in our existing tradition are called "good" and are related to the namesake primary principle. Living for the sake of "good" does not mean causing good left and right, but finding such universal mechanisms of victory that will not diminish the rights of any of the living and existing beings.

ᛏ **Tiwaz** — the rune of the god Tyr, the rune of truth. Those destined to develop the Tiwaz rune as their Rune of Identity must remember the laws of the god Tyr and live by their own truth. They must learn to be true to their word and to the truth, to keep oaths and internal laws of honour, and to never compromise their conscience. They must learn to be a warrior, to become a true knight, not for show, not outwardly, but for themselves. To have no reason for self-reproach, knowing that victory is internal, not external. On a more serious level (and depending on what the Rune of Fate is), this means the ability to redirect the currents of inner power by sheer will and inner indicator of honour. The ultimate rune in the runic code will show where or towards what these currents should be directed.

ᛒ **Berkana** — the rune of growth, the feminine rune. As the second rune of the Individual Runic Code, it represents a quality that needs to be acquired and developed. This quality is flexibility. The ability not only to hear nature, life, the world, and of course, other people but to understand what you hear. It is a profound ability to perceive the inner world of the "other" as your own.

ᛖ **Ehwaz** — the rune of Sleipnir, the eight-legged horse of the god Odin. The rune of magic and magical consciousness. In the second position in the runic code, it indicates that the bearer has come to learn magic, to develop their consciousness from a human level to a magical level. They need to learn to look at the world and circumstances not from one single branch of existence but from many: first sequentially, and then simultaneously. To expand consciousness to such an extent that there are no closed or inaccessible topics, knowledge, or worlds for it.

ᛗ **Mannaz** — the rune of the human being. Those who have Mannaz as their Rune of Identity must learn to be human. On a simple level, this means social success, understanding the human world. On a deeper level, it means thoroughly and profoundly studying human nature and the world of human relationships. The Mannaz rune in the second position can teach listening and perceiving not only the reality in which consciousness exists but also all other realities directly or indirectly connected to the human being. This is called wisdom — to take everything into account, to understand everything, and to be aware of everything.

ᛚ **Laguz** — the rune of the flow, the rune of flowing water. Water has the ability to penetrate any unoccupied space, to distribute itself evenly, filling all voids and irregularities. As the Rune of Identity, Laguz implies acquiring such qualities, becoming like water: all-penetrating, capable of seeing unoccupied spaces and filling everything that disrupts the harmony of evenness. It is a very feminine quality, and it is no coincidence that in runic magic, Laguz symbolizes true witchcraft. This type of influence on reality in the human world has the right to exist as a filling force when "natural" harmony is not achieved, when unfilled voids threaten to destroy the foundations of being. Witchcraft, as we know, can be different, but even if it can bring negative effects for the living, it does not mean it is harmful. On the contrary, it performs its natural "watery" function — filling voids, forming evenness, dissolving outdated organic matter — even despite the fact that such voids and imperfections of the world were formed as a result of the activities of the "forces of good." Laguz as the Rune of Identity may not only guide its bearer towards developing flexible qualities of water for their consciousness but also towards developing witchcraft, flow consciousness, making them inclined to perform magical work in this space and incarnation.

Inguz — as the Rune of Identity indicates that the bearer must learn to see the result in everything they do. Master the "art of small steps," move away from globalism, and not devalue their achievements, even if they seem small and insignificant. After all, a large building is built from small bricks, not hewn from a single block of stone. Inguz is the rune of the god Freyr, the god of fertility. In nature, nothing is superfluous, and everything is needed for something: if not now, then later. This is the quality to be learned under the aegis of Inguz. Additionally, this rune in the second position indicates that a person must learn to be free and feel free. The foundation for this state should be the first rune in the runic code — it explains why this state is so important to you; the final rune will tell you why this state of freedom and the ability to see results even in small achievements is necessary.

Othala — the rune of inheritance. In the Northern tradition, Odal is a hereditary land allotment, a set of rights associated with owning family land property. As the Rune of Identity, Othala symbolizes the ability to form a family as an egregore, as a system, to direct and redistribute resources correctly, based on the needs of the family and kin, not personal human preferences. Globally, this is acquiring the right to power, but with a complete understanding of why it is needed and how to use it correctly. For a woman, this is becoming the Regina of the Bloodline[144], and for a man, an exam, a test of readiness to take power by right, truly.

---

144 Read more about this function in the book by K. Menshikova "The Power of the Bloodline".

Dagaz— the rune of change, the rune of transformation. As the Rune of Identity, Dagaz indicates the need to develop quick thinking, quick decision-making. It teaches never to cling to anything, never to stop at what has been achieved, and never to want something so badly that you want to keep what you have achieved. Create changes, want changes, live for changes. Learn to transform things and phenomena in completely untraditional ways, find unexpected uses for very ordinary and familiar things. This is creation, creating everything and in everything.

The Blank rune in the second position of the Rune of Identity does not imply that the bearer of such a runic code is burdened with the necessity of acquiring any knowledge or skills in this life. Nothing additional is needed for themselves personally. Simply put, a blank rune in the position of the Rune of Identity says: "Do not touch, leave everything as it is." The appearance of a blank rune in the position of the Rune of Identity can indicate that fate has brought a person into this world not to receive, but to give, to bring existing knowledge or qualities into the present world. It is enough to rely on the Rune of Fate, live with this baggage, and possibly leave a significant mark after themselves. At the same time, there is no need to develop any additional personality traits in addition to those already present — fate does not insist on this.

The Golden Rune

The final rune of result describes the mark, the imprint of your consciousness, personality, and life expected of you in this reality. It represents what is done not for oneself but what remains after you, as proof that the destiny program was understood and fully executed with the expected result, that natural gifts (or their absence) found proper application — and this is right.

ᚠ **Fehu** — the rune of true rights, the beginning and end of the path, the strength of spirit as a fundamental right given to a person by the fact of birth. Even when they have no other rights, it may be the only one they definitely have. Fehu as the final Golden Rune indicates that you should leave this life with accrued rights — rights that no religion or egregore can take away. Rights that you can pass on as a title by inheritance, but not nullifying yourself, and leaving with them. Globally, it means leaving the imprint of your force, your god, securing the right of power over reality not only for yourself but also for your god. In a magical sense, it means inscribing in the informational space the right of power of your god on Earth.

ᚢ **Uruz** — true strength, connection with the Earth, the power of the Mother. Uruz as the final Golden Rune indicates that such a connection must be established through all human activities. Perhaps it was once broken, maybe a person (or their lineage) was cursed by the Earth. Now it is time to correct this mistake, understand, and atone for the guilt before the Mother. On a simple level — "take root," find a place for life, secure the right of presence on this land, "get a residence permit."

ᚦ **Thurisaz** — the final position of this rune indicates that the effective activity of the bearer of such a runic code is to break through an obstacle, eliminate blatant injustice that hinders everyone else's life. Thurisaz is the rune of the god Thor, who was the defender of the gods, the defender of Asgard's interests, and preferred a forceful solution to any issue. Thurisaz speaks precisely about this: to show strength, overcome an obstacle, destroy the boundaries of something, but not for oneself personally, but for the living, for the descendants, and for those you love and are loyal to. Perhaps, become a pioneer in some entirely new endeavour, but again — not for oneself, but for those who come after.

ᚨ **Ansuz** — the rune of knowledge, the source of something. The final rune Ansuz shows that the person must leave behind knowledge as a significant imprint. Not information, not data, but knowledge — a complete, finished informational package that can be used by subsequent generations. It must be tested in experience, completed in its formation. Ansuz, in essence, is a ready tradition, mechanisms of interaction with reality that always yield the expected result. Such knowledge for future generations should become a starting point in their development, a cornerstone from which everything begins, a fulcrum to leverage the world.

ᚱ **Raidho** — as a final task — to lay a channel, give a foundation for the actions of descendants. An idea, method, way to achieve a result. The result itself is not mandatory here — descendants can fill the channel with water themselves. But Raidho as the Golden Rune insists: "Give others the meaning of life, draw before them the path of development, show that there is a goal."

ᚲ **Kenaz** — the rune-torch, the rune of illumination. As the final Golden Rune, it shows the expected result: enlightenment, making something secret known, and making the unclear clear.

It may not only refer to some discovery but also to a new method of cognition, which descendants will adopt as a tool for further work.

ᚷ **Gebo** — the meaning and task of life is unity, establishing the law of balance in the sphere of activity that a person undertakes. Leadership and responsibility for the taken process. For oneself — to come to an understanding of the world law, to exclude contradictions from one's consciousness and find the strength to come closer to one's god, the progenitor of one's soul. It is crucial here to comprehend and then try to implement the basic laws of unity into reality:

- Every action creates a counteraction.
- Good and evil in this world should balance each other, not destroy.
- Everything that surrounds you complements you to completeness.
- Everything in this world has an equal right to exist.

The resulting position of the rune Gebo says that all this knowledge needs to be implemented into life, and the result of your life's path will be to make this world stronger, more balanced, and possibly to eliminate some injustice that has prevented reality from healing itself.

ᚹ **Wunjo** — the rune of joy and completeness, wholeness. Wunjo as the Golden Rune indicates that the entire life path should help a person become whole, complete, and fully formed in consciousness. So that neither in this life nor in any subsequent ones, there is no need to supplement themselves to wholeness using the egregore resources of this world. Being whole means being free. Without debts and obligations, without needing anyone or anything. You can have everything but not be attached to anything — and this is freedom. Wunjo as the trace left behind by the bearer of this rune as the Golden Rune may also indicate that the result of the activity should be the hope left to people. Joy from anticipation as faith that everything is possible and nothing is in vain.

ᚺ **Hagalaz** — the rune of destruction and boundaries. The symbol of chaos that needs either to be manifested or restrained. The final Golden Rune Hagalaz shows that the result of the life path is either to strictly delineate the boundaries of something for the remaining ones or to destroy something. The dual meaning of the rune can be more precisely interpreted only based on the previous runes — what do they speak about: limitation or destruction?

ᚾ **Nauthiz** — as the resultant rune says that the task of the personality is to "manifest the need," i.e., to expose before the living now and possibly future generations some aspect of life that is ignored by them, that is empty but not visible, that requires more attention and filling. Nauthiz is also the rune of memory, specifically continuous memory. Here, this rune in the Golden position may also indicate that certain gaps in memory (both personal and collective) need to be closed; perhaps correct some lie, expose false information from the past, change the historical picture, i.e., make corrections to the information that distorts today's reality, giving it an incorrect assessment by the living. Nauthiz as the Golden Rune — is the memory that should remain after you.

ᛁ **Isa** — the rune of ice, frozen flow. It is, among other things, the key to the world of Niflheimr — the world of Darkness, hidden forces, and true constants upon which the world is built. As the resulting rune, it shows the purpose — to realize your true self, to connect with your god. The informational constant it represents should be brought to the surface of the worlds and truly manifest itself as an open and understandable first principle, and the one who must do this, the one who must bring the power of the god into the material world, is you.

ᛃ **Jera** — the rune of time, fertility, harvest, and the results of what has been done earlier. On the simplest level, it means to generate time, like a dynamo machine with specified functions. On the magical level, it means to change the flow rate of time, influence the reaction speed of this world. Make it so that the "harvest" of deeds is gathered differently than it is now; perhaps it will be manifested differently or evaluated differently by the living. The life task of the bearer of the rune Jera in their runic code might be to form a different value of time by all living beings, a different understanding of timeliness. This will happen only when a different evaluation of life results is formed, and perhaps even the smallest achieved result will be evaluated differently. In any case, it is life and activity in the middle world, in the world of people. Work with the world of manifested reality and teach it to reflect all physical, psychic, and magical processes more accurately, more clearly, more brightly.

ᛇ **Eihwaz** — the rune of witchcraft, death, and deep subconscious fears. As the resulting rune, it says that a person should not only master witchcraft and be able to look into the souls of those around them, examining them to the very bottom. Eihwaz indicates that in this endeavour, the person should become a real professional, a unique master, similar to dwarf masters who were able to accurately identify what the world or a person lacks for completeness and literally create something out of nothing to close this gap, eliminate the created imperfection. As the rune of death, Eihwaz shows that the master bringing the power of this rune into the world must be able, without hesitation, to destroy the unnecessary and modify the necessary to achieve perfection. The final rune Eihwaz in the runic code says that its bearer should bring to this world such algorithms of evil that will force people to seek and find ways to eliminate it, rather than resting on their laurels, driving away bad thoughts or closing their eyes to the unpleasant.

ᛈ **Perthro** — the rune of the cast lot, the rune of destiny. As the final rune in the runic code, Perth insists that a person changes something in the algorithms of destiny formation, not only, perhaps, their own but also of other people — their children, their family, their tribe. Not just learn to manage destiny but actually do it. Change the patterns, give everyone else a different lot, a different choice. Which one, and the reason for such necessary changes, should be indicated by the previous runes in the runic code.

ᛉ **Algiz** — the rune of protection. In the final position — find your protector among the forces and gods, approach your primary source — the parent of your soul. If a person has already come with protection, as indicated by the previous runes in the runic code, then it is required simply to maintain or strengthen such a connection. Here, the rune Algiz, as a super-task, shows: the result of the work in this incarnation should be the consolidation of oneself and one's rights in this world, enhancing the acquired qualities to such an extent that in the next incarnation, coming without memory, one does not remain without them. In magic, it means integrating one's consciousness into the cult of a strong and preferably ancient deity, which will protect from the nullification of existential mass when crossing through death.

ᛊ Sowilo — the rune of victory. Sowilo as the final rune insists: to win! And not just to win, but to make your algorithm of victory universal, voluntarily accepted by all living beings both now and in the future. In a global sense — to create something very significant that will affect the lives of descendants for a long period. In a more mundane sense — to achieve fame, success. Sowilo is the key rune to the world of Alfheimr or to the first principle of Good. In this first principle, all victory algorithms of all traditions, all times, and epochs are laid down — universal victory algorithms. The final rune Sowilo is not only to form and develop correct and universal algorithms of good, algorithms of victory, but also to lawfully place them in the general database, making them natural and accessible to everyone. That is, to form for subsequent generations new concepts of good and evil. Perhaps more honest and more perfect.

ᛏ Tiwaz — the rune of the god Tyr, the rune of kings. It carries within it the power of inner truth, honour, and conscience. This is the rune of victory, but the "right" victory, not by any means. It was truly believed that only such a victory gives the right to power. The position of the rune Tiwaz as the final rune in the runic code speaks exactly about this: to emerge victorious, but not simply, but affirming such victory algorithms that correspond to high concepts of honour and truth.

ᛒ **Berkana** — the rune of growth. As the final rune in the runic code, it says precisely this: everything done in life, all aspirations and results, is done for growth, for freedom, for life, and to ensure that life continues. Here, it is about caring for future generations, about motherhood in a broader sense than commonly understood. As a result, the bearer of the Golden Rune Berkana needs to implement and strengthen the rule "live and let live."

ᛖ **Ehwaz** — Sleipnir, the eight-legged horse of the god Odin. Known for its ability to freely move across all the worlds of the Yggdrasil Tree. In runic magic, the rune Ehwaz signifies magical consciousness or magic itself. The position of the rune as the resultant Golden Rune indicates that its bearer in the runic code should leave here with such consciousness, should let magic into themselves and change under its influence. Also, such a position of the most magical rune of the Elder Futhark says that the result of the life and activity of such consciousness should be a greater acceptance and manifestation of magic in this world. It is through them that the boundaries between the worlds should be erased, barriers in the consciousness of those who close their minds to the penetration of other forces into this world, deny the miraculous, should collapse. Ehwaz — the rune of magic, the rune of inner strength, and as the final rune, it insists that in this life, the person does everything to develop the magical abilities of consciousness to conduct the power of chaos into this world. As a task — the magical transformation of consciousness both of oneself and others.

ᛗ **Mannaz** — the rune of humanity. A human as a social personality, and the rune Mannaz standing in the third position of the runic code indicates that such a person should achieve social success and real significance among their kind. It is necessary to establish oneself as a social personality, learn to build numerous connections between people, and maintain them. Here, it is about working on containing chaos, developing all algorithms that strengthen and affirm human order.

ᛚ **Laguz** — the rune of flow, "the force that guides." Laguz as the resulting rune of the IRC indicates that the ultimate Great Work of life should be the formation of a flow. Any kind — informational, temporal, energetic, emotional — any. Create and leave behind a process of movement that will allow any consciousness living after you to enter this flow and move effortlessly from one point of existence to another, without spending time and life energy overcoming obstacles. This is not the formation of tradition (tradition in the context of the final rune is rather the rune Raidho), but what fills the already created channel — the energy of unclaimed desire, newly discovered information, secrets brought to light, new fashions, new passions. Laguz is the rune of water and is associated with this element, as well as with the force of chaos. This means it will certainly involve emotions — you must leave behind something that will draw people along, pull them into the future, give them the desire to live on. During your life, you need to create and launch a process that people will willingly take up, without coercion or force; a process they will want to live in and voluntarily invest their time in. However, this flow may not have to be universal but may concern only a specific group or stratum of people. Who this created flow should be directed at should be suggested by the first two runes — the Rune of Fate and the Rune of Identity. They contain the keys to understanding: what and for whom.

ᛝ **Inguz** — the rune of fertility. When this rune stands in the final position as the Golden Rune, it can be understood as the rune of real results. The karmic task is to leave behind a tangible material result, prolonged over time. At the simplest level — to have children. On a global level — to change the surrounding reality so that it inevitably develops along a completely different path. Inguz is the rune of a real future and also a key to the world of Vanaheimr, the world of Nature. If the result aligns with the world of nature, if it does not contradict the natural laws, then you are doing everything right. The bearer of the Golden Rune Inguz to avoid mistakes, should always seek analogies in nature for everything they do: if nature has already created something similar, then it is needed. Inguz is the rune of the art of small steps. As the final rune, it says that the bearer of such a runic code should not succumb to globalism but see the big result in small achievements and never diminish the significance of even the most "insignificant" victories. If necessary, their descendants will make them global — after all, what has been achieved must ultimately belong to them.

ᛟ **Othala** — the rune of family, the rune of heritage. Odal as hereditary land that can be physically passed on. Here, it means exactly what the rune signifies: leaving behind an inheritance for your descendants, laying the foundations for the well-being of your family, providing your descendants with a normal living space. Odal is not the historical heritage that belongs to everyone and anyone; it is not an informational heritage that could work on the principle of "whoever the Norns send." No, it is a specific heritage for specific persons.

ᛞ **Dagaz** — the rune of transformation, the rune of transition from one state to another. As the final rune, Dagaz speaks of making a revolution, important and perhaps irreversible changes that should remain as a result of your life and activities. So that the future transitions to another level of development — not changes direction but moves to a different level. What remains after you should change the lives of the living in such a way that it never returns to its former state.

The Blank rune in the position of the Golden, resulting rune, means that the person born under this current and manifesting such personality traits is not (or should not be) obligated to leave any visible traces behind. They came here to learn something for themselves, to understand something for themselves, but they may (or should not) leave anything behind. Such a position can be seen as both positive and negative. On the one hand, nothing is expected from such a person, so nothing is demanded. On the other hand, no help or support should be expected, as no one is interested in the life result of this person due to its absence (result) in their personal technical task (TT). They are on their own, everything for themselves, what came in, goes out. It's enough to preserve what you came with, to remember what you understood in time. But that's all. Whether this is good or bad depends only on the perspective of the bearer of the fate and their personal goals, tasks, and desires. The positive factor for the bearer of the IRC with a blank resulting rune is that upon leaving this reality, they most likely will not have a debt to this world. However, one should remember that every coin has two sides, which means that the world will not owe this person any debts or obligations. They will not leave behind a heritage[145], will not be preserved in the informational memory for future generations; they came to this reality only for themselves. And shame on anyone who says that a person does not have the right to this.

* * *

When interpreting the runes of the Individual Runic Code (IRC), it is essential to remember that they should be read together as a whole sequence. It is incorrect to interpret them individually, separate from one another. In the IRC, each rune is both a cause and an effect for the others. For a correct understanding, it is crucial to see how their meanings and energies flow into each other, revealing the significance of each rune in a broader, more comprehensible context. Similar to the three Norns, who work seamlessly together, the measure determined by one becomes the foundation for the work of another. And only in this way.

It is also essential to note if there are any "irreversible runes" in your runic code. Let me remind you that these are the runes that serve as keys to the nine worlds. They are represented twice on the Yggdrasil Tree, so it should come as no surprise that they will significantly impact your life and demand maximum

---

145 The discussion is not about born children, but about rights that could be passed on to children through lineage or blood.

expression from you. The presence of an irreversible rune in the position of the Rune of Fate insists that you primarily express your natural qualities, and only secondarily everything else. If an irreversible rune is in the place of the Rune of Identity, issues of internal development and personal achievements will always be more significant to you than, for instance, external results. If an irreversible rune from the nine is in the third position as the resulting Golden Rune, it clearly indicates that all your life activity and determination will be focused on achieving real results, possibly regardless of the means.

The presence of irreversible runes in the runic code makes consciousness more categorical and rigid compared to those who do not have such a strong connection to the rune keys of the nine worlds. These properties of consciousness are attributed specifically to irreversible runes, and this is quite reasonable and understandable: these runes work with greater types of energy, they are more functional than others, and they require their human conduit to work with these energies as efficiently as possible. For such abilities, a person usually pays with a more rigidly structured consciousness and more pronounced boundaries, which are meant to protect such consciousness from external influences and distortions.

The Individual Runic Code can indeed be altered. While changing the destiny number might be challenging (changing the first rune is only possible through magical means—via special rituals aimed at rewriting information about a person in the informational space), altering the other two is quite feasible through ordinary social methods—by changing one's name or surname.

Many women have noted significant life changes after marriage, often completely altering their destiny's program due to the surname change. The reason lies precisely in the alteration of the individual code—changing the fateful task and, consequently, the necessary result.

This is why, in the system, women typically aren't assigned serious or global tasks at birth: changing the personal code often frees them from initial obligations. In contrast, men in our culture rarely change their names (both personal and familial), and the expectations on them are significantly higher.

This is also why there are so few female mages, as the workload on mages is much higher than on ordinary people, and no coincidences are allowed. Especially for mages of the "erilar" type, traditionally a male domain. Women practiced "seidr," also known as "witchcraft."

Many seekers, having calculated their basic data and compared them with the personality they have formed up to the present moment, sometimes make the drastic decision to change their name or surname, thus aligning their social persona with their self-perception. I won't say this approach is wrong—this method has helped many people shed the excessive burden that inevitably arises in the process of overcoming the social resistance of their environment. Egregores begin to perceive the person differently and no longer offer events meant for the old persona, while the new, changed one demands entirely different knowledge and experiences. Sometimes, such a ritual act as changing a social name becomes a starting push that propels a person onto a new life path, serving as the last and missing effort. However, sometimes this method is merely a way to take the path of least resistance. In such cases, this action may result in more negative than positive outcomes: magic will not regard the accumulated and realized experience of the person as necessary and sufficient for embarking on a magical path of development if the sufficient experience for one's personality can only be gained through environmental resistance—and only that way.

Understanding how the Individual Runic Code (IRC) is formed shows you that changing your social name can only affect the Rune of Identity and, consequently, the Golden Rune. Changing the Rune of Identity will not alter your initial destiny but will help change your living environment, your place of residence, as the necessary qualities of personality are developed in a specific environment, in a certain social space. Some things are possible in one society of people, and others are not, and vice versa in another. The environment formed around a personality is supposed to fully correspond to its tasks, which are reflected precisely by the Rune of Identity. Therefore, the planned surname change upon marriage for women is not a mere coincidence, if one considers the logic and magical sense of everything happening to a person.

Thus, the final, resultant rune of the personal runic code, having undergone "calculative" changes, will also inevitably show a different expected result—since a person's capabilities largely depend on personal traits of their character and peculiarities of their nature.

It is quite common that no surname change during one's life influences the Individual Runic Code—in any numerical and alphabetical combinations, it always remains the same. This, of course, indicates a strong mystical component in such a person's life, where nothing around can affect the task they are working on in this life—they are firmly bound to it, and the Norns are vigilant.

ᛊ ᛞ

Therefore, when deciding to change your "social face," weigh everything several times and think carefully about what you need more: quick social success or real growth of your foundation. The runes will guide you.

The Runic Code (IRC) must not only be read correctly but also seen correctly. To achieve this, it is necessary to map it onto the Yggdrasil World Tree.

A person can never fully realize their humanity if their consciousness is imbalanced towards one side or the other of the Tree. Each incarnation, each test of fate, is an attempt to correct this imbalance and compensate for the inequity with opposing forces.

Place a diagram of the Nine Worlds Tree before you. Divide it into four parts as shown in the illustration (see illustration on page 407). Mark the runes you have calculated as your IRC on the diagram. If your IRC includes irreversible runes, mark them on the tree as they appear—twice, both as a key and as a connection.

After marking the runes on the Tree, observe their localization: are they evenly distributed, do they fill all parts (quarters) of the tree? If not (which is usually the case), we can note a certain imbalance in consciousness. This is not necessarily a pathology, but it always indicates some predetermined aspects: fate, character, life.

Let's discuss this in more detail. A manifested imbalance within the system of the Nine Worlds is neither good nor bad; it simply exists. One can live with it without suffering. However, it is crucial to remember that the magical system and its obedient

ᚠ ᚨ

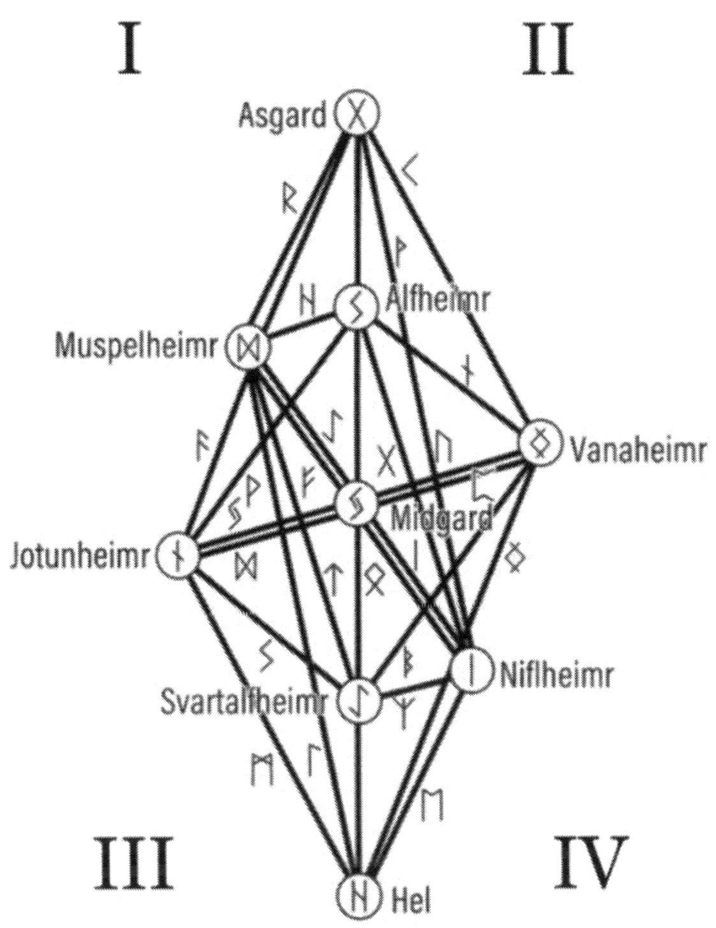
I
II
Asgard
Alfheimr
Muspelheimr
Vanaheimr
Midgard
Jotunheimr
Niflheimr
Svartalfheimr
III
IV
Hel

ᛊ ᛞ

egregorial space, which forms the usual event reality, must account for and balance this imbalance with their own forces. This balancing is systemically determined by the law of equilibrium, which must be adhered to by all worlds and all manifested realities — it is a program, and it cannot be otherwise.

What does such balancing mean for a person with an ordinary fate? First and foremost, it means how the system perceives a person with an "imbalance." The system views such a person as incomplete, requiring supplementation. The egregorial world will supplement them with equally "imbalanced" beings, but with the opposite sign. This is called achieving egregorial wholeness, which, on one hand, ensures the viability and stability of any egregorial system, and on the other hand, forms a complete reality where one "incomplete" consciousness receives a compensatory environment.

Having a three-rune code without attempts to obtain compensatory components (powers expressed in rune symbols) predetermines a human's fate, binding them to a layer of reality that, more than other layers, can fulfill the primary system task — to compensate the person to make them whole. This attachment is commonly referred to as predestination or karma, against which, as is well known, there is no rebellion. Such a person will always be surrounded by people with an "opposite nature," and the egregorial environment will forcibly keep these people close until mutual penetration occurs, when the properties of one nature become the true and legitimately experienced possession of the other. This transformation allows the consciousness that has absorbed the missing properties to achieve wholeness at this level and make a quantum leap from one orbital of reality to another, where the process of compensation and acquiring new missing qualities will not repeat

ᚹ ᚨ

ᛊ ᛞ

— in new worlds, new social (and other) scenarios. These orbitals in social systems are commonly referred to as castes or social levels, each with its own set of lessons, trials, and opportunities. Despite the apparent benefits, the problem is that such forced retention of consciousness in a specific layer of reality, in a certain caste, in specific events, and among certain people does not occur at the expense of reality but always at the expense of the life energy of the one being held. In other words, the more a consciousness strives to break free from the "prison of opportunities," the less energy it has for anything else. This is also a system mechanism that ensures the egregorial world maintains safe stability.

In such egregorial compensation, people who come into conflict with you constantly show you what you are not. And they do so in the most irritating manner. However, this is precisely the intention because all development always occurs through conflict (and according to egregorial rules, not just conflict but also enmity), and without it, there would be no need to change oneself. Simple consciousness, not predisposed by caste level to conflicts (e.g., from the labourer caste), subconsciously strives to stay among its kind, not understanding but feeling that the rest of the world is antagonistic and hostile not only to them as individuals but to their entire community. This is why people from the labourer caste tend to cling to each other, dislike change, and fear reality. Their religiosity, partial lack of education, and grotesque patriarchalism directly stem from these specific personality traits that define their caste affiliation.

The merchant caste — more conflict-prone consciousnesses. They have outgrown the state of "being like everyone else" and strive for the state of "being the best." A merchant is a warrior in childhood. The reality that will compensate a person with such a caste mindset is more diverse,

ᛊ ᛞ

faster, and less malicious (subjectively speaking, of course). And this is already a different orbital, a class higher; here, the rules of reality formation are somewhat different: the main principle — compensation to wholeness — remains the same, but the speed of event formation is an order of magnitude higher. The set of properties lacking in consciousness occurs much faster and with a greater volume of situations. Moreover, the number of contacts with "opposites" is already managed by the individual, but it is precisely by this factor that a person's social success in this caste is determined: the merchant world teaches how to derive benefit from multiple connections — both social and metaphysical. At this level of reality, one does not run from conflict but also does not initiate it. Initiating conflict is the task of the next social caste level, those personalities who can rightly be classified as warriors.

The warrior caste does not simply change themselves actively, forming prerequisites for developing conflict. They change reality for all other social layers if the process is not very active. At this level of development, a quality such as personal responsibility comes into play: if a warrior initiates changes, they participate in them, and if these changes cannot be adequately "processed" by the merchant and labourer castes, the warrior (either personally or with the strength of their caste community) must be ready to complete this work themselves: to take all the changes that reality offers, process them through their consciousness, and transform them into a form of events that the merchant and labourer castes can "take" and implement as reality expects. From what has been said, it should be clear that the warrior caste is not soldiers or fighters in the direct sense of the term. Warriors are those who take responsibility for all their initiatives, up to the obligation to personally carry out and complete what has been started if those for whom these initiatives are intended are unable to participate in the changes,

ᚹ ᚨ

unable to see opportunities in conflict. In modern reality, warriors are managers and scientists, opinion leaders, and those who fill egregorial spaces with information[146]. Warriors follow the rhythm, pace, and direction set by the highest caste — the caste of rulers. The tasks of the highest caste are to set the direction of movement for the entire system of realities. Therefore, during the initial formation of the caste system, it was assumed that a true ruler is always a chosen one of the gods, someone who can and is entrusted to set the principles of global changes. A ruler is an Atlas holding up the sky, the one who maintains the boundaries of the "learning" reality for everyone else and sets the pace for changes. As already mentioned, this is not the case now, so the realities for the development of personalities are distorted, preventing everyone from going through their development path effectively and, most importantly, with a full understanding of what is happening.

Mages working in this reality do not form a caste in the direct sense of the word. But they do the work of correcting reality: some within the system, changing each sublevel, healing orbitals locally; others correct the overall program, fixing systemic errors, working invisibly but globally.

It has been repeatedly stated in earlier books and lectures that real magic begins precisely at the level of the warrior caste. This is primarily because personal responsibility for events starts only at this level. Warriors are responsible with their lives and

---

146 Do not hastily draw parallels between what has been said and real individuals who declare themselves as possessing such rights, status, or qualities. Here, I describe an ideal classification — as it was intended. The fact that the plan does not match reality indicates that the system of realities is sick because the head — the highest caste of rulers — is sick.

ᛊ ᛞ

fates for their deeds, rulers are responsible for the actions of all, but mages bear responsibility for the outcome.

Understanding the level of possibilities and correctly assessing your starting position in this game of aspirations is extremely important. This is precisely where the correct decoding of your Individual Runic Code (IRC) and, as a result, the proper understanding of how your personal IRC fixes your consciousness on the Tree of Nine Worlds comes into play.

Let's now consider the typical shifts of consciousness along the Yggdrasil Tree and try to understand what characteristics this imposes on the fate and psyche of each person.

A shift towards the world of Vanaheimr is a shift towards natural forces and needs. Living not by memory but by dreams of the future, living in illusions to some extent. A striving for freedom, but with a distorted understanding of freedom as permissiveness. However, once this shift is reinforced by runes leading to Jotunheim, the world of memory, such a striving transforms, and freedom becomes not a desire for anarchy and permissiveness, but an understanding that true freedom lies not in illusions but in the absence of unnecessary bonds. Bonds that burden, that hang like ballast and prevent one from reaching their dream and turning imagined illusions into reality.

If the runic code indicates a connection with the "lower worlds" (third and fourth quarters), the shift in interaction with the surrounding world will manifest in an excess of efforts when trying to achieve a result. Nothing comes easily, favourable coincidences in life are absent, and the lottery is always a miss. Any gain comes only through awareness and deep experiences. Nothing is obtained easily, and obtaining any resource becomes a feat. The psyche of a person with such runic code localization becomes very heavy; not a single "light" thought, everything is

ᚹ ᚨ

experienced intensely, which is ultimately compensated by a normal psychological defence reaction—specifically "thick-skinnedness," distrust of people, reluctance to establish new contacts. Misanthropy and a tendency to solitude. Mysticism and occultism. A scientific mindset and a difficult character.

On the contrary, the predominance of the "upper worlds" (first and second quarters) leads to illusory and superficial tendencies. Luck comes easily, but experience is not gained, and the power of consciousness does not increase. In a state of security and mythical harmony with everything, a person loses the need to remember survival and development. Life seems easy, but the material effect of this attitude is not guaranteed: it might be there, or it might not. There are many diverse life interests and connections, but they are often so ineffective that they simply consume time, giving nothing in return except an illusory sense of life's fullness.

If the runes of the runic code are localized to the left (first and third quarters), the person is forced to constantly refer to the past and even live in it. On a primitive level, this manifests as nostalgia for old times, conservative beliefs, and a "old consciousness" that poorly perceives everything new. For such a person, the future seems non-existent, and all values are found only in the past. This worldview can be beneficial if it aligns with the profession and minimizes contact with the young—then such a shift might have some obvious benefits. However, even an intention to change the future is tied to destroying the present to make room for repeating the past.

With the runes localized to the right part of the Yggdrasil Tree (second and fourth quarters), the consciousness has the opposite characteristics: it looks only to the future, ignoring the past. The person lives as if they have no past, forgetting both good and evil. They pursue their dream, sometimes quite successfully, but often fail to notice the freeloaders who latch on, using this "youthful consciousness" as a locomotive towards a future they themselves might not reach.

Such persistent shifts in consciousness limit the field of activity, and resources are distributed inefficiently—not for victory or learning. By overlaying your Individual Runic Code on the Yggdrasil Tree as described, you can easily see not only the map of your consciousness shift but also the "unfilled zones"—places on the tree where your consciousness is entirely absent. As previously stated, the magical law of balance will not ignore such imbalance, and the egregore world will compensate by adding people or phenomena that bring the missing qualities into your life. This compensatory function explains the appearance of "evil geniuses" in your life—bearers of opposite qualities that irritate or bind, who exhaust with impractical projects or are intolerably tedious in their pragmatism. Sometimes such unions become fruitful when people genuinely love each other and accept their "half" as part of themselves or rationally recognize their own weak points, acknowledging the missing strength in someone else. This must always be mutual and voluntary—only then is it beneficial. But generally, and almost always, such a complementary "element" causes only rejection, irritation, or even hatred.

A skewed consciousness never goes beyond the inner circle of primary elements. With such a configuration, the maximum a person can achieve is witchcraft, and that without the slightest understanding of it, without seeing its causes in the past or its effects on the future.

However, when consciousness becomes whole, without needing egregore efforts for compensation, a person and their mind automatically gain freedom, and nothing can prevent them from stepping onto the second circle of force. At this level, the priesthood institution is formed and operates, and what we will study and practice further is the ability to keep one's consciousness on the informational channels of various gods. To achieve such an effect, consciousness must be whole—only such consciousness can perceive the entire informational current without truncating it to fit its limited human perception. This is natural for perception within the third circle of force, within the human world, where individual human consciousness may not be perceived as independent, but only as a separate cell of the mind, a single neuron in the organism "humanity." Those who reach the second circle of force with their mind must be a whole and functioning receiver, not inferior in power (and perhaps even exceeding) the tool formed in the third circle representing the collective consciousness of people.

Such compensation by the egregore world is natural for those who are consistently skewed and do nothing to independently compensate themselves to wholeness. But this is not about you, since you are reading these lines. For you, there is a method of correction and compensation.

To level the disharmony in consciousness that may be revealed by the Individual Runic Code, you can create a bind rune—an amulet that activates the necessary zones in your consciousness to eliminate the skew.

A properly made Individual Runic Amulet will allow consciousness to acquire what was previously inaccessible, expanding the field of activity, learning, and opportunities for a fuller life and perception of the world[147].

---

[147] If you have any questions about calculating and decoding your IRC, you can always ask them on the Menshikova School forum in the "Individual Runic Code" section.

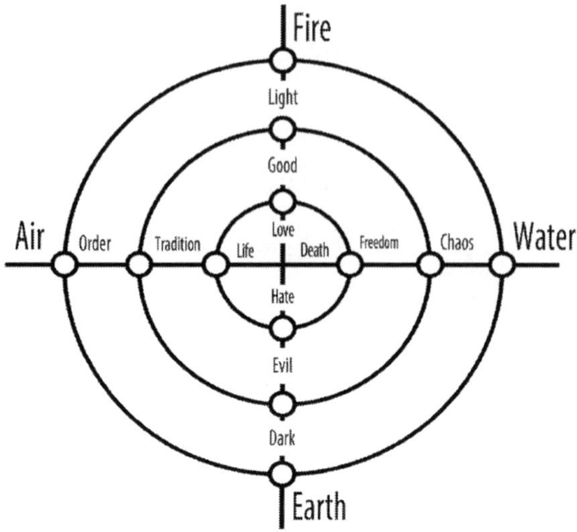

The method of compensating skew by magical means is described in Practices 2 and 3.

In this world, nothing is in vain, but not everything is beneficial. The great art of making correct magical decisions lies in the ability to see and anticipate the tasks and needs of the system in which the social personality lives, while ensuring a continuous increase in one's own power and magical weight. In the binary human world, a world of dualistic systems, one thing will always exist or be achieved at the expense of another. In the magical world, it is about mutual satisfaction.

This is what the old gods teach us, and this is what the Nine Worlds system teaches us.

PRACTICE 2

Individual Runic Amulet

The Individual Runic Code (IRC) is necessary to thoroughly understand your fundamental qualities and work from there. The runes manifested in the IRC shift consciousness along the Yggdrasil Tree, enhancing specific personal qualities that inevitably impact life and destiny. However, these same runes can help magically align consciousness along the Tree, accelerating the process of evolution, altering destiny, and making life more balanced and effective. Runes allowed us to change the configuration of consciousness; runes will help make it balanced, whole, and strong.

A person potentially contains all 24 keys expressed in the runes of the Elder Futhark. However, not all are manifested in reality, similar to how a person's genetic code includes both dominant and recessive genes. The three runes of the IRC are like the manifested dominant traits and will always be stronger than any unmanifested potential. They act as energetic and informational nodes on the fabric of personal reality, always attracting the person as an individual, influencing events, preferences, diverting attention from the unnecessary, and attracting it to the necessary.

The Individual Runic Code reveals a lot. On one hand, it exposes the fundamental properties of the personality that largely predetermine destiny. On the other hand, it shows which qualities are lacking in consciousness for a human fate to turn into a magical one. To live a successful human life, it is enough to follow the predetermined path and be entirely in harmony with your prescribed wyrd. But for magic, this is not enough.

In magic, it is important not only to fulfill the basic human task as a contract that must be executed but also to acquire qualities and skills not written in the wyrd. These qualities are shown by the runes absent in the IRC and, more precisely, by the location of the IRC runes on the Yggdrasil Tree. The following practice of creating an Individual Runic Amulet (IRA) will help recognize the magical predisposition and sketch the altered path on the fabric of reality.

* * *

The Individual Runic Amulet is designed to constantly scan its owner's consciousness, identifying closed (blind) areas and magically opening them using runes inscribed in the magical sign for this purpose.

To perform this task, one can create an Individual Runic Amulet (IRA), which will automatically align consciousness along the Tree until such a state becomes as natural as breathing.

Any amulet is a power object. Primarily because it attunes consciousness to the vibrations of specific worlds and teaches to draw energy and information directly from them, bypassing all religious or egregorial intermediaries. If the IRC manifests a shift in consciousness, the amulet, by aligning it, will teach drawing strength from worlds previously naturally inaccessible to consciousness.

Through the ritual creation of an Individual Runic Amulet, one can accept not only their fundamental features but also the need to take real actions to develop them to fullness and wholeness.

Acceptance is crucial. The mind may desire transformation, but the subconscious, filled with hidden fears, will resist this process in every way. The amulet disciplines the subconscious and prevents it from spontaneously leveling the results of the mind's efforts.

However, it is impossible to simply inscribe the missing runes into your runic reflection on the Tree of Nine Worlds—you must have the right to do so. This right appears when a person steps onto the path of the runemaster and begins not only to read the runes but also to bind them. The rules for creating bind runes, which you will learn in the next practice (No. 3), imply that when overlaying runes in a specific pattern, the so-called secondary runes will inevitably appear. These are unplanned runes, born from the combination of runes, like a child born from a man and a woman—two opposites who also combined their natural forces by right and by nature. So it is with creating bind runes: two completely different, complete, and self-sufficient runes, two separate minds by the will of the runemaster combine and give birth to a third—a complete and self-sufficient rune. The mastery of the runemaster lies in ensuring that the expected is born. Such mastery is an honest right; it is earned by consciousness in the process of studying runes, investing time in the past transformation, and acquiring knowledge and understanding.

Third (or more) runes appear lawfully and are naturally accepted by the consciousness of the runemaster; his consciousness becomes whole due to the birth of new power within it. This power, expressed by the necessary rune, fills the previous void in the consciousness and eliminates the initial imbalance. Such consciousness no longer needs the services of the egregore world, and the runemaster's consciousness acquires holistic characteristics, becoming more magical than human. From this moment, a new phase of magical transformation begins, a conscious and honest self-transformation.

The three runes of the individual runic code are combined as your imagination and aesthetic sense suggest. You bind not just any runes, but specifically your three (or two, if your runic code includes a "blank rune"). It's as if you are affirming: I understand my contract, I accept it. The rune of birth, the rune of fate, and the final Golden Rune—all are present within me on equal terms. But not sequentially, as in an ordinary human destiny "step-by-step," but as a complex multi-level program of magical consciousness. And what this program will be capable of is much greater than before: using the same blocks, commands, or modules but connected differently, masterfully linked. What is born from the new connection is mine, new, and true.

The harmony of the created symbol is determined by you alone. If you take into account all the recommendations given for creating an amulet (practice 3) when making the magical symbol—good, but if you see your wholeness in a different form, then so be it. For some, harmony lies in symmetry, for others—in complex asymmetry. Creating a magical stave is the birth of a new unique quality, and this quality is yourself.

A drawn runic stave on a white sheet of paper represents a flat mandala, a magical symbol that will remain a dead scheme until energy starts flowing through it. But once this happens, the two-dimensional image becomes multidimensional, unfolding holographically in space and time, and your mind, being part of this symbol (and it part of you), unfolds into multidimensionality along with it.

However, making yourself magically whole is not just about drawing a stave or formula. According to the northern tradition and the depth of understanding of the words "honour" and "dignity," everything done must be proven.

ᛊ ᛞ

The magical seal, as a new configuration of your consciousness, must be tested and strengthened by the powers of various gods. The additional runes, like new neural connections in the brain, must not only be established but also solidified—through real skills, real experience. The new configuration of consciousness you have now written should perceive a different kind of energies and a different density of the informational current. Mystically speaking, the power of a god should flow through the mind. What power? Which god? This remains to be discovered.

In the northern pantheon, gods are different. They include various currents, operate at different frequencies, and with different configurations of consciousness. Introducing additional runes into the mind can make you more receptive to currents that were previously inaccessible, but it can also significantly strengthen the connection with your god, with your original power.

The Individual Runic Amulet must now serve as a transformer and amplifier, allowing you to perceive both energy and information without distortion. Without this magical symbol, in your old state of consciousness, you might have lacked precisely this effect to understand your god, realize his power, and accept it within yourself. This is why the IRA is now crucial for us as consciousness embarks on the path of practice, enters a long mystical process of self-awareness and change. You must become capable not only of understanding and perceiving informational currents from your true individual power but, if desired, change yourself to become it.

The power of the informational current resulting from contact with the gods of the northern pantheon will be transformed through the Individual Runic Amulet, conducted through your consciousness, and, transformed, will be given to

ᚹ ᚨ

the surrounding or created reality. From the effects and changes that follow from this output, you can judge the properties of this informational power, your own capabilities to interact with it, and the effects that become real and legitimate for you.

Having completed your consciousness to wholeness, you will now be able to read literature and perceive other information related to the northern tradition in a completely different way. The Eddas and myths, legends of gods and heroes, will now be perceived by you with much greater depth of understanding than possibly before. There are many interpreters of ancient myths, but most of them (with very few exceptions) carry out their interpretive work within the third circle of force, within the human world, relying exclusively on their skewed consciousness. When you are in a similarly skewed state, you have no choice but to accept their versions and opinions on faith. But freed from the need to rely on authorities, you will no longer need blind faith—all the information from primary sources will flow into your mind in an integral stream, unaltered. There will be no need to repeat the foolishness of their evaluative opinions when you have your own, based on personal experience, personal feeling, and personal knowledge.

Achieving such an effect is our task in further practices.

To create an individual magical symbol that will function to compensate you to wholeness, you need to perform a magical action and "marry" the runes to each other—not just in a random formula, but by overlaying them. This way, the missing element is born, which will be the natural result of a harmonious union. In this new stave, the runes should form, which, being highlighted by your attention and word, will occupy their rightful position in the area of the Yggdrasil Tree that was previously closed to your consciousness.

ᛊ ᛞ

A compensating rune or runes will be only those that appear ***naturally*** in your bind. Let's remember this—you can't inscribe the necessary rune randomly, you need the right to do so. Otherwise, as once at the gates of Asgard, the three Norns will knock on your consciousness and ask quite a legitimate question: "By what right, child, do you take what does not belong to you?" And you will have to answer—the gods of the northern tradition left us a very detailed description of how one bears responsibility for unconsidered actions and the extent of this responsibility for those who possess power.

This process is pure magic. The pattern of connected runes always comes out unique for each person, always unrepeatable. It comes from the soul, the mind, the feeling, and understanding of the runes, and this is individual for everyone. People can bind identical runes, and each will get a unique symbol, completely different from the other. Inscribing new runes into your personal magical seal of consciousness should be done with great skill, and one should never forget the rules of creating bind runes described in *practice 3*. As a result of properly creating the stave, powers and opportunities will appear in your life that were previously absent. It is like a new scheme through which energy will flow, and this new scheme will produce a completely different effect than the old one. But the old pattern will not disappear, it will become more whole, more harmonious, and freer because the union of all the runes given to you by right creates what was previously inaccessible. Like a new neural connection, which becomes seamlessly integrated into the entire system of consciousness.

Creating the IRA is best done by the Lesser Ritual: closing the space with Thor's hammer, lighting a candle, and laying out a clean white sheet of paper before you. This white sheet is your Universe, a new world order ready to be born, and

ᚹ ᚨ

you are the demiurge in this Universe. As you write, so it will be. The closed space will protect the creation from external influences, preventing delusion from penetrating your mind. On this white canvas, you draw your new magical symbol, connecting all the runes of the IRC in a way known only to you. The energy of the runes begins to flow into each other, resulting in the birth of a third rune, seen only by you.

If you feel everything correctly and fully, if you can surrender to this process without fear and hesitation, your stave will be very harmonious. You will get a universal structure that does not diminish any of the bind runes' power, but rather gives them the opportunity to manifest themselves in a new and surprising quality, acquiring new, previously unimaginable properties in such a union. And of course, you will see in your stave those missing runes whose absence previously blocked your consciousness from particular worlds—worlds where you can achieve results previously unattainable in familiar spaces. You will also see the runes that will work later, runes you did not consider now but will be very much in demand by your altered consciousness tomorrow.

A harmonious, coordinated stave, as if reflecting off the paper, will be attracted to the only living being in this space—you. It will take its first breath, and the runes will start spinning within your consciousness, changing it not to how it should be, but to how it is right—for you, for your god, for your fate, for your common wyrd. This process aligns the process of minor creation with the larger processes, where the world doesn't need to expend much energy correcting egregore mutations because you did everything yourself. And from now on, you will do so, not accumulating invisible and unknown debts simply because "that's how you were drawn." Now you have drawn yourself, and

everything you do from now on will be from a pure mind, with full understanding and without debts.

ᛊ ᛞ

PRACTICE 3

Amulets and Talismans

Let's begin by briefly exploring the types of runic signs and their general functionalities. Traditionally, several types are distinguished.

The First Type: The Formula

A runic formula consists of runes written in a sequence. Their action is sequential, from left to right (unless otherwise specified). Another name for the formula is "runic script."

In a formula, the powers of each rune are sequentially transformed from one to another. Essentially, a formula is a command to action, a spell—clear, specific, with a pronounced final result. This is how it is read. Such a depiction of runes indicates that energy will transform sequentially within the formula, meaning each subsequent rune works with the already modulated energy received from the previous one. The final rune of the formula indicates the ultimate result. It is believed that an odd number of runes (3, 5, 7, etc.) executes a final algorithm, while an even number (2, 4, 6, etc.) executes a prolonged algorithm. So, if a formula is programmed for a one-time result (buy, meet, receive, give, etc.), an odd-numbered formula is used. If a prolonged result is needed (maintain health, ensure a steady financial flow, long-term relationships, etc.), an even-numbered formula is used. It should be understood that the effect of the formula may not be immediate, as each subsequent rune will engage only after receiving the "material for transformation" from the first one. It is important to remember that any formula requires energy to work. In the case of a final formula, this energy is taken once to activate the formula, just as much as needed to execute the command. In the case of a prolonged formula, energy is constantly drawn from consciousness, as it operates continuously. This is why prolonged formulas are justifiably considered more energy-consuming.

Healing runes. Formula-example

Let's consider the formula "Healing Runes" as an example: Kenaz-Perth-Inguz. This formula does not provide health "in general"; the runes here repair a malfunction in the body. Kenaz identifies the problem, Perth isolates it from everything else, as if placing it in a bag, and then Inguz brings it to a state of health, meaning normal functioning as per nature. Here, we see an example of sequential commands and transformation: find — isolate/contain — heal. Its final program will not operate continuously but only when a problem arises. Therefore, such formulas are typically activated as programs as needed.

FORMULA: EVEN NUMBER

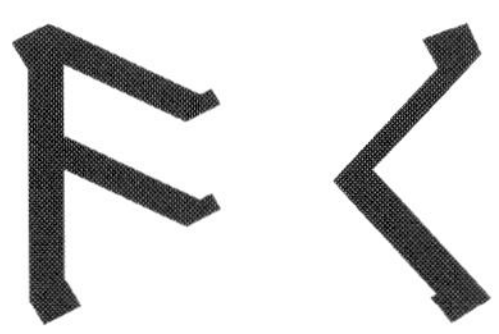

Formula of Awareness

Or consider another example: Ansuz-Kenaz. This is a formula for awareness.

It is an extended formula, meaning it works continuously and is not time-limited. However, it also operates sequentially: Kenaz — highlight with attention, Ansuz — understand. Thus, the formula will work as stated: what the bearer of this formula highlights with their attention will be understood. Whatever is illuminated by the torch of their interest will be comprehended. The formula will not indicate by itself what needs to be understood or where to look — it is a specific program but can work for a long time.

However, a completely different mode of operation is achieved if the runes are "linked" — that is, not written sequentially in a formula, but superimposed on each other. This will result *in a bind rune.*

The Second Type: The Bind Rune

A bind rune is a drawing composed of several runes superimposed on each other. Here, the runes form not a word but a concept. As one master-erilar accurately said: "A bind rune is a mage's combined mind capable of independent decisions and

ᛊ ᛞ

actions." This is a very precise formulation, in my opinion, and it can't be said better. A magical sign made of bind runes can evaluate a situation, instantly consider new circumstances, recalibrate itself, and give correct commands to consciousness and reality for action.

Examples of bind runes: Sons of Gefjon and Enlightenment.[148].

BINDRUNE

Sons of Gefjon

---

148 Read more about this stave in the chapters dedicated to the goddess Gefjon and the god Bragi.

ᚹ ᚨ

Bragi's Formula. Enlightenment

Here, it is important for the runes to have a common point of intersection, a junction of the rune flows. In this case, all the runes work not sequentially but in parallel, considering constant correlation and results. Due to this, the work proceeds faster but is less predictable. In a formula, one can see how the transformation of power flows from rune to rune, but the work of a bind rune is entirely invisible. A bind rune is like a symphony orchestra, and without being a professional musician, it is very difficult to determine which instruments and in what quantity are currently contributing their sounds to the overall flow. Such a bind rune possesses more power than just a formula, as it consists of runes connected in a single design.

A bind rune can be finite or extended, and this function is determined not by the number of runes included in the bind rune but solely by the task set before the bind rune. Such a task can be formulated as an "intent" — a clear verbal formula describing the task and conditions, or it can be simply an intention without any additional conditions — it all depends on the presence or absence of personal limitations and the skill of the erilar.

The meaning and essence of a bind rune is to connect the runes in such a way that they do not extinguish but amplify each other, transforming into something third that is not provided for in the familiar single runes of the Futhark.

Runes prefer decisiveness and will more likely follow the call of someone who clearly knows what they need. Therefore, for one-time and quick transformations, formulas are always preferable. When creating an Individual Rune Amulet, we will use a bind rune rather than anything else. In this form, the runes will constantly recalculate each other, and any slightest change in one rune will immediately cause changes in the others as well. This will make the transformation process more intense and effective.

The Third Type: Stave (or Galdrastafir)

A stave is a complex program that consists of several runes and/or bind runes. It can combine individual runes, formulas, and bind runes simultaneously.

An example of a very simple stave is the "Healing Formula: Cleansing the Fluid Media of the Organism"[149] (see the illustration on page 433, top picture). Here, the runes do not overlay each other but represent a looped scheme of infinite transformation, transitioning from one to another and back.

---

[149] The formula is used for kidney diseases, blood purification, or simply for removing fluids from the body.

STAVE

ODD FORMULA
TO HEAL

EVEN FORMULA
TO UNDERSTAND THE LAW

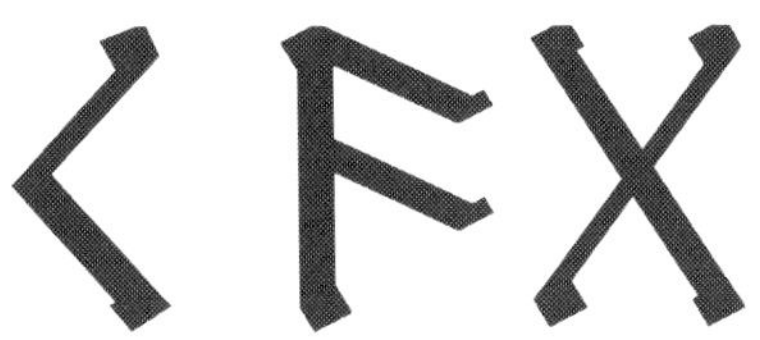

ODD FORMULA
TO MAKE A CHOICE

PALINDROM

In our world, the world of three manifested dimensions, three-rune formulas work especially well — quickly and accurately, but not for long. Four-rune formulas, considering the fourth dimension (time), have a more prolonged effect.

A variety of stave is the PALINDROME. This stave adheres to the mandatory rule of symmetry. Some formulas and bind-runes work better when arranged as a palindrome. A palindrome consists of several runes written in a column, cross, or square.

Example of a palindrome: harmony of sexual relations.

To understand how runes work not individually but within a stave, in combination, one must internalize them. Two or more runes combined into a single sign are like a family formed from different people. Each of them has their own temperament, character, abilities, and desires. All these properties of each are combined into a unified whole. In this unity, something additional is always born — through conflict, love, coincidences, or disagreements, but it is always born.

Some formulas explicitly define what should be born as a result of such a union, and then each rune begins to work in the form and volume necessary and sufficient for that specific outcome. Other staves, formulas, or signs do not impose a specific result, and in such cases, the runes will work as they see fit to express their free interaction. The skill of an erilar also involves understanding how the runes will behave, what effect can and should be expected from their combination, never forgetting that there will always be another element in play: the erilar's own mind, another person's mind, the mind of a god, or the face of reality. And sometimes, all together.

A magical symbol that the mage applies to the space becomes an integral part of that space. It completes it to wholeness, meaning that immediate and distinctive changes begin to occur in reality: previously it was completed in one way, now it will be in another. All the perceiving elements-minds of this reality will feel these changes (not necessarily consciously) and inevitably participate. The runemaster must foresee the coming changes, understand the consequences of the will's implementation, and know not only which elements-minds will be included in the process of changes but also how they might react—since every action generates a reaction. Seeing and being ready to work with this reaction and the initiated process of reality's flux is essential.

Runes always work. Even when it seems they do not. However, learning to see this, understand the causes and timing of the changes initiated by the mage, is mainly a matter of practice and developed magical vision, which also results from practice. Therefore, the more you practice, the more you will understand the runes, the effects of their combination, and the quicker you will learn to see the effects of applying your new skills.

The formulas you will work with further are not only for practice—they are meant to continue the process started in the first stage of learning the runes and to launch a new cycle of consciousness transformation. They will reveal certain caches in your mind, often in completely unexpected ways. Sometimes a simple formula for attracting money or harmonizing relationships, in addition to its intended purpose, unexpectedly unfreezes areas of consciousness that were previously de-energized and "dead." However, these effects are not uniform for everyone—each consciousness can perceive the energy of the runes uniquely and receive results that may be entirely unexpected.

Therefore, in the initial stages of work, it is recommended to conduct each step through runic diagnostics, constantly aligning with the runes and gods on the appropriateness of the initiated process of changes. Until this understanding forms in your mind automatically, and the consequences of magical impact in a given place, at a given time, and in this specific consciousness become entirely clear to you without additional questions. Achieving such mastery requires, I repeat, time and constant practice.

Keep a practice diary in which you reflect not only the formulas and staves you use but also all the effects that follow. This will help you quickly see and remember the mechanisms of cause-and-effect relationships, understand the intricate temporal effects of "start-result," which in magical influence on reality are not always linear and not always sequential. Additionally, honestly recording each step and all experiences in the process of magical transformation will help you avoid the terrible mistake that awaits anyone seeking their magical path—self-deception. Trying to present the desired as real, "forgetting" what you don't want to remember, hiding under your own fear when processes become incomprehensible and unclear. Mistakes are not terrible; lies are worse. Remember that in working with the northern gods, honesty is very important, sometimes even more than courage or valor.

ᛊ ᛞ

The creation of any object of power,
like any magical act, requires seclusion and secrecy.
If they are disclosed, they lose their power.[150]

For an Individual Runic Amulet (IRA), bind runes are used. The rules for creating bind runes[151] are as follows:

1. All runes in the bind rune must be clearly expressed.
2. Each rune must have at least one distinct line that is not part of another rune.
3. The orientation of the runes in the bind rune is considered (upright, reversed, mirrored), unless otherwise specified. If a rune is reversed or mirrored, it acts accordingly.
4. All unplanned runes that arise during the creation of the bind rune are considered, unless otherwise specified. These are called "secondary runes."
5. The bind rune should be compact and cohesive, forming a single, harmonious, balanced sign without "dangling" elements.
6. The sequence of runes in the bind rune does not matter.
7. It is better to create an amulet/talisman for the bind rune.

---

150 Agrippa of Nettesheim, "The Occult Philosophy."

151 These rules have been developed by many generations of runemasters and practitioners and are now universal and classic.

ᚹ ᚨ

Based on these rules, you should compose your own sign using your runic code and additional secondary runes chosen to enhance the stave.

As an example, let's take the bind rune SAR—Journey in Search of Power. It consists of three runes: Sowilo-Ansuz-Raidho.

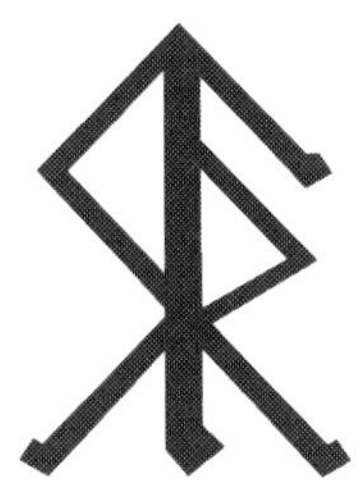

Secondary runes that appear when overlaying them will be significant if specifically mentioned: they carry an enhanced load, harmonizing the stave. These runes were not initially planned; they appeared as if "by themselves." But if they are needed to strengthen the stave, each newly appeared rune can provide additional enhancement. For example:

Kenaz—will allow you to highlight the main thing with attention. While journeying in search of power, don't miss the main thing and thus give your consciousness an additional task—not only to seek power but also to learn to see and understand its manifestations.

Isa—develop your will, always remember the main thing, no matter what happens.

Tiwaz— in search of strength, understand your truth. Do not let your consciousness be tempted by an easy form of power; resist the allure.

And so on.

ᛊ ᛞ

When creating your bind rune for the Individual Runic Amulet (IRA), it is very beneficial to layer the runes in a specific manner, allowing the harmonizing runes to appear almost by themselves. It's crucial that the necessary runes manifest naturally within the bind rune, rather than being forced or deliberately added to the already existing symbol. Such forcefulness would result in a corresponding backlash in your consciousness as a penalty for claiming what you do not initially have the right to. However, if the needed runes emerge in the bind rune, this is true magic, where with one stroke of the pen, one thing transforms into another — something essential. As swift as casting a spell.

Creating a bind rune is always a form of artistry. More precisely, it is a process of creation, akin to birthing something new, unique, and extraordinary, something that no one else can replicate. What one mind can create, another cannot.

When you have created the bind rune, and it is done perfectly tailored to you individually, you will feel it immediately. It doesn't matter if a lot of paper is wasted or if a lot of time is spent. It doesn't matter if you start dreaming about the intersecting lines of the runes. It doesn't matter if you reject many versions, drawing and discarding them with thoughts like "this is not mine, I don't want it, it's not beautiful."

But when the unique bind rune flows from your pen, you will know it instantly. It will be like Odin's Sleipnir, Freyja's Brisingamen, Thor's Mjolnir — a unique artifact created specifically for you. Connecting with your bind rune allows you to recognize, see, and feel yourself in it. Not as you are now, but as you have become your own ideal. It will be an overwhelming joy, like a dream come true, your deepest desire fulfilled when all hope seemed lost.

Once the bind rune is made based on your Individual Runic Code (IRC) and any necessary additions, you need to transfer it onto a physical medium — you need to create a runic amulet or talisman. An item of power for yourself.

ᛊ ᛞ

General Information on Creating Any Runic Talisman/Amulet

The difference between an amulet and a talisman is that **an amulet** is a power object designed to repel unwanted influences from its owner (e.g., protection, a guard).

A talisman is a power object designed to attract desirable influences to its owner (e.g., luck, power, money, etc.)[152].

Depending on the task and intention, the power object transforms into either an amulet or a talisman, repelling or attracting energy currents from or to the owner, respectively. Whether the created power object is an amulet or a talisman depends on the runes incorporated into the sign and your intention.

A power object is created in the form of an amulet/talisman (i.e., fixed on a permanent carrier) when its effect is intended for an unlimited number of people, an unlimited space, or an indefinite time. If the bind rune (stave, formula) is meant only for personal use (e.g., for one's internal transformation), making a physical power object might not be necessary: it's enough to write the runes on yourself or your reflection, imbue them with power correctly, and they will start working without a talisman.

For example, healing runes do not require the creation of an amulet for personal use — it's enough to apply them to the

---

152 In ancient times, it became natural to refer to a power object with the general term "amulet." Essentially, this is not a mistake but simply places emphasis differently: an amulet is an object with a magical purpose.

body, sleep with them overnight, and the need in the stave will disappear as the issue they were meant to address (healing) is resolved. However, if you need a power object, for example, to attract a current of money, then a talisman is necessary, and it should be on a suitable carrier, as it involves a process rather than a fixed result.

In an amulet/talisman, not only the power of the bind rune (stave) works, but also the power of the material on which the bind rune is displayed or integrated. Therefore, it is correct to use only natural materials for such amulets and talismans, and they should align with the task's magical characteristics.

Creating a power object is a magical process. The more time and mental effort you invest in it, the more it will give back to you.

When making a power object, it is essential to follow a specific sequence of steps and strive not to deviate from it.

Step 1. Attachment

If an amulet/talisman is of a personal nature, it should always be carried with you. The exception is for a power object that is consecrated with blood (or any other binding agent). Such an object has a very strong connection with the blood bearer and becomes permanently tied to them. In this case, the power object does not need to be carried constantly but must be kept in a highly secure place to prevent it from falling into the wrong hands. The reason for this careful protection is explained by one of the fundamental magical laws, which states:

Objects that have been in physical contact with each other continue to interact even after separation. Anyone you touch maintains a magical connection with you, albeit

weak, until the contact becomes sufficiently intense, prolonged, or repeated. Magical power is contagious.

If the power object is made for someone else, it is consecrated with the blood (or another binding agent) of the person for whom it is made. Under no circumstances should you use your biological material to consecrate an amulet or talisman if you are making it for someone else. The only exception is when creating a power object for your children under the age of 7.

If an amulet is made for home protection, it should be kept in the home. The best placement for it is the door or door frame.

A power object based on the Individual Runic Code (IRC) and created on a material medium will function in such a way that its influence will extend not only to its owner but also to the external world, attracting resources and circumstances according to the nature of the symbol embedded in the amulet/talisman.

The goal of the IRC is harmonization. It aims to harmonize the forces within consciousness and the surrounding world. A well-crafted bind rune can help consciousness draw energy and information from worlds it previously could not access. The reason for this inability is the specific frequency at which these worlds exchange information. In the consciousness of the receiving operator, there is simply no decoder capable of capturing, recognizing, and coherently integrating this information into their system.

Step 2: Cleansing the Medium and Charging It.

The material medium on which the power object will be created already has its own energy. For the amulet to work, it must integrate with the energy of the owner, enhancing it rather than weakening it. Therefore, the choice of medium (material) is given great importance in talisman creation.

Just as when you charged runic blanks with your vital rhythm before making a runic set, you need to charge any chosen medium: if the power object is made for yourself, then charge it with your own natural rhythms.

Wood and leather absorb energy quickly, while stone and metal require more time and effort to charge — hard materials remember longer but also retain the memory longer.

Even a simple sheet of paper on which you depict the bind rune should be attuned to you, containing a component of your natural power.

The medium can be cleansed and charged with the power of the elements. I will not provide this method here, as this topic is dedicated to a separate book.[153].

Step 3. Preparation for the Ritual

Runes like attention, especially from beginners. Therefore, the more seriously you approach the process, the more respect you demonstrate, the better the final result will be.

Creating a power object requires silence and solitude. No external interference from others' energy, advice, or distractions is permissible. Wives, husbands, cats, dogs, and other pets should be kept at a safe distance from the ritual site. Phones should be turned off, and all broadcasting devices should be shut down as well.

---

153 K Menshikova "The Power of the Elements".

Ideally, light candles and rely solely on "live" illumination.

Step 4. Conducting the Ritual

A ritual is an ordered sequence of actions that aligns the consciousness of the mage (erilar, operator) with the runic channel and the associated pantheon of Norse gods. This alignment of informational processes can only be achieved by performing the necessary and significant steps, which in magic are referred to as a ritual.

Ritualistic practices are present in every religious or magical system. They can be strict, such as in religious systems, or less so, but they are always necessary. The necessity of a ritual lies in two main aspects: firstly, the mandatory discipline of consciousness; secondly, the foundational conditions of the agreement between the gods (or god) and the cult that it generated. A well-established ritual is the result of the efforts of predecessors who invested significant time, energy, and possibly even their lives to build and solidify the channel. The more time invested in such construction, the stricter the ritual conditions.

In the northern tradition, there are two types of rituals: the grand ritual and the lesser ritual. The grand ritual is performed by the gothi during major solstice and equinox festivals at special sacred sites. Individually, the erilar works through the lesser ritual, which I will describe here.

The Lesser Ritual

1. Close the space. In runic magic, there is a universal method for closing the space using Thor's Hammer.

Thor is the Norse pantheon god responsible for safety. His weapon, the unique hammer Mjölnir, had a special feature — it always returned to its owner (Thor), and it could only be lifted with special magical artifacts — a belt and gloves that tripled the owner's strength. The Eddas[154] state that whoever possesses Mjölnir holds power and has the right to dictate terms to everyone else. Thor's function is protection, preventing any unwanted influence from entering where it is not expected.

Therefore, using the symbol of "Thor's Hammer" is a universal protective mechanism in any magical work, where it is necessary to eliminate both accidental and intentional disturbances induced by the system or enemies.

TO CLOSE THE SPACE:

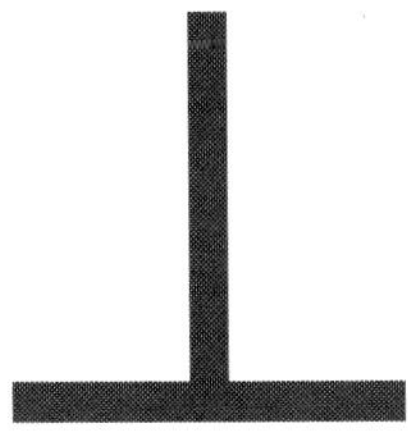

Thor's Hammer

This symbol should be drawn by hand on six sides while saying: "I close my space in the name of Thor, left and right, front and back, below and above."

This closing creates a spatial-temporal shell around the mage, in which they are invisible and unreadable. Within this

154 For more details on the magical functions of Mjölnir, read the chapter dedicated to the god Thor.

"shell," any work can be done as it will not cause field disturbances that the controlling system must respond to. With sufficient practice, one can even feel the current of forces within this closed space.

It is important to remember that Thor's protection will shield you from external influences but not from your own fears, which will remain with you inside the protective space. Also, remember that the magical artifact "Thor's Hammer" belongs to the god Thor, not to you. You should thank the gods for their assistance. More on thanking the gods will be written later.

Once the space is prepared, you can start working with the bind rune. The carrier should also be prepared and charged with the necessary power (your energy or the elements) in advance.

Now it is necessary to prepare what will be placed on the carrier—the magical sign itself.

No bind rune is ever inscribed directly on the power object without preliminary work. The consciousness must attune to the bind rune you will embed in the amulet and in yourself. This is the most crucial part, significantly more important than the creation of the material embodiment of your spell.

2. Take a white sheet of parchment (or paper). It must be white, not any other color. The white sheet represents your universe, but there is nothing in it yet. It is not even a primordial chaos; it is the Great Void. It is important to see this void, the abyss of infinite possibilities, absolute nothingness. The drawing you inscribe, trace, and depict is a map of events. In this process, the runemaster is a demiurge, a god, a creator of a new ordered reality.

3. Draw your bind rune on this white sheet. Do it meticulously and carefully, paying attention to each line and angle.

When the runemaster (erilar) traces the bind rune, they formulate the overall intention—for what the entire stave is needed.

"By the nature of this sign, let it happen…"

"By the power given to me, let it be fulfilled…"

"Let this runic stave create…"

There are many variations of the incantation; what's important here is to embed the main intention. At this stage, the naming is for the entire stave as a whole, not for each rune individually.

If a name for the stave comes to mind, remember it—it is yours. Some unexpected events or deviations from the planned path may occur at this stage—do not be afraid or think that the ritual is "ruined." The process of creation is unique every time, and it is not always possible to repeat the proposed ritual exactly, nor is it always necessary.

It should be noted that the Scandinavian tradition is very encouraging towards the creative process. Therefore, making improvisational changes, additions, insertions, and unexpected turns are viewed favorably by the gods, and they in no way punish their conductors for showing "creative madness," unlike in some other magical systems.

The initial tracing of the stave is a declaration of the intention to change the existing reality. At this moment, you are a programmer who has written an ideal program on paper, checked it, and is satisfied with the work. Now this program needs to be integrated into the system—to load it into reality so that it works according to the set task.

Runes alter form. The mage drawing the stave understands that they are creating a new form of reality. The way the runes are connected will determine the renewed reality, with the necessary rules and laws. With an understanding of what is "primary" and "secondary," important and not so important.

It should always be remembered that runes only set the vector of force but do not control it. Gods and systems that manage various currents of forces act each within their own range of frequencies and possibilities. Each frequency, each aspect of power belongs to a god (or a system that the god controls). When tuning your consciousness to a rune, remember that at this moment, you are manifesting a divine principle that these runes symbolically represent. It is no coincidence that certain runes are associated with specific gods—runes have their patrons. Using a particular rune in a bind rune, the runemaster essentially claims a part of the power that the god possesses, and through the rune, they draw energy into themselves, subsequently transferring it to the stave on the parchment.

This is why the parchment is white. You draw only these powers onto it, with nothing that can interfere with the purity of the flow, no foreign vibrations, no external information.

When the sign is ready, you need to feel it, let it into yourself. Feel how the powers of the gods enter your life. The clearer the weaving of the runes, the clearer you will see the result, the greater the currents of forces your runic talisman will possess.

4. Before inscribing on the chosen carrier, the next step is the *verbalization*, the *incantation* of the bind rune.

The *incantation* should be prepared in advance, at least in the beginning of your practice, do not hesitate to spend time learning to choose words and concepts precisely. Runes are a warrior's weapon. They love specificity and understandable results. Therefore, the more clearly you formulate the task for the runes, the faster and more accurately it will be fulfilled.

It is not advisable to burden the runes with the path to achieving the result—only the outcome. Because everything you say in the creative space of the ritual is taken as a mandatory command. Numerous details, reservations, and exclusions will only delay the result and may even repel the runes (there have been cases where this happened permanently).

"Let the runes act without harm... without affecting... excluding the influence..." — such formulations are disrespectful and incorrect. Why use a magical tool if you have so many fears, burdens, and conditions? Leave it and take a prayer, for instance, where such things are even welcomed. But runes as a weapon—they are either hidden or fired.

Runes will find the optimal path to the desired outcome themselves, and if not stopped or limited, this path will be the fastest and most successful. No human mind can grasp even a fraction of all the instantaneous calculations of situations that runes and the forces behind them can manage.

The mage says: "I need a result," and describes the result, not the path to achieving it. Only that. Therefore, the clearer the task is set, the faster you will get the result.

Take your time with the incantation. It is assumed that the mage fully understands the capabilities of their mind and can formulate tasks that align with expectations and assumptions.

Example: Masha wants Vasya to love her. Masha writes the formula "I want Vasya to love me"—and everything happens according to Masha's will—Vasya loves her. Every day he tells Masha about it in phone conversations, but he can't show his love in reality because he is three thousand kilometers away from her. Is Masha satisfied with this result? No, because by "love" she meant something else, but her inner prudishness prevented her from clearly formulating the task.

On the contrary, excessive specificity can also backfire.

Example: Masha found some runes for summoning and casts a spell: "I want Vasya to come to me on Tuesday at 8 PM and confess his love." Eventually, Vasya comes, but he is drunk because sober, he has his own will and other matters to attend to. Hugging a broom that once was a bouquet, he confesses his love to Masha—the spell is fulfilled. But Masha is again dissatisfied with the result because, as it turns out, she meant something else. Specifically: "I want to live with Vasya in love and happiness, marry him and have children." What could be simpler? But fears, prudishness, and ordinary human cowardice, the need to live for the moment without understanding tomorrow's consequences—all these are the results of the flawed practice of living "here and now" without looking beyond Midgard.

The incantation for the bind rune is usually done aloud. Not because the runes can't hear your inner whisper—they can. But when a person speaks the thought out loud, they can notice where they might have gone wrong, whereas with inner whispering, this can go unnoticed.

5. After speaking the general incantation-command, you need to assign tasks to each rune individually, especially in the case of bind runes, as we have seen that many secondary runes can appear in a stave. Sometimes, with enough skill, you might count half the Futhark. To avoid the inclusion of unplanned runes, and thus unplanned forces, you should name each significant (working) rune and give each a task within its capabilities, of course.

To do this, trace the working runes over the completed bind rune, both the main and secondary ones, while saying and assigning a task to each one:

"Let the rune Raidho pave the way from me to...", "Let the rune Gebo connect me with...", "Let the rune Kenaz show me..." and so on.

In this process, it is crucial to understand the runes and their traditional capabilities to avoid giving a rune a task it might misunderstand or misexecute. For example, it is foolish to ask the rune Hagalaz for love, as it has two functions — limitation and destruction. By its nature, it will destroy everything it touches and then say — choose from the debris of your life and others' illusions. If you find love there, it's all yours.

Thus, the bind rune itself does not change, but the emphasis and specifics of its action are clarified.

Drawing the symbol is just the beginning of creating an amulet/talisman. It is the most crucial part. The bind rune starts to work the moment it is drawn on paper — you will feel it. However, fixing it onto a material carrier will make it truly invulnerable, especially against your own human qualities — inattention, doubts, lack of willpower, fear.

6. The final step: open the space by removing the "Thor's Hammer," tracing it in reverse order with your hand on all six sides. Thank the gods for their assistance.

Depending on which forces the mage contacts and through which systems they work, they establish their ritual relationships accordingly. You too will interact with certain forces, possibly even from the Norse pantheon. Choosing a force is an individual agreement between a person and their guiding force. However, before choosing and being chosen, it is essential to properly acquaint yourself with the gods. This decision is solely determined by the soul and heart, not by rules and inevitability, which direct the mind, telling it who to believe in and why.

When working with runic magic, creating amulets and talismans will become a regular activity for you — this is inevitable. Therefore, all rules for creating bind-runes and staves, as well as the rules for conducting the lesser ritual, must be understood and accepted — they are fundamental. Try to approach this process with full respect, especially when creating a power object.

Any power object should work towards the specific task set before it, preferably as clearly and precisely as possible, not haphazardly. It should draw energy from the surrounding world and transform it for you to accomplish the set task. A power object changes something in the mind of the person for whom it is intended: it blocks certain areas of consciousness while activating others.

If you have experienced some imbalance in your life until recently, an individual runic amulet will correct this but always through lawful means — the path of honor. Honor, from the perspective of the Norse gods, implies that one must have the right to everything in this world: love, power, health, money, strength, magic — everything. These rights are determined not only by "divine favor" but also by rules that invariably exist in this world, as well as the strength of spirit and will that a seeker discovers by following the path of honor and dignity.

A properly executed individual runic talisman/amulet does not imply immediate free benefits but creates the most favorable conditions for the owner, offering them a chance to gain true rights to the flows of power. The Individual Runic Code, formatted into a bind-rune, supplements the consciousness with the necessary runes (qualities) that shift the perspectives within the consciousness: you begin to see things differently than before. This new perspective undoubtedly implies expanded thinking, making the mind more flexible, dynamic, and adaptive to rapidly changing circumstances in reality.

Therefore, for the power object to work efficiently and be seamlessly connected not only with you but also with the pantheon of Norse gods, it must be created according to specific rules, observing all essential ritual moments. The ritualism in this case symbolizes a tribute to the forces that will undoubtedly appreciate it. Both people and gods love respectful individuals. By investing your time, energy, and concentrating everything into a powerful bundle of intent during the creation of a power object, you open a channel to the minds of the Norse gods, which with each ritual, each acquired knowledge, and each formula used on this channel will become stronger and stronger, and your connection with it will become more and more solid.

PRACTICE 4

Introduction. Magical Formulas

Those who embark on the path of magical self-transformation through the mechanisms of runic magic must, above all, know, understand, and accept the runes. This acceptance must be absolute, without elevating some runes over others, without dividing them into "my rune" and "not my rune," or into "like" or "dislike." Such an approach was permissible in the initial stage of studying the Futhark, but not for long. It was a period when the childlike consciousness tested something new "by taste" and through such tactile contact attempted to comprehend the world. But at the moment when the final rune Dagaz draws all processes into one point, when the concentration of internal strength brings you to the awareness of an entirely different level of rights and possibilities, previously shown to you by the rune Fehu, there should, of course, be no preferences among the runes. Natural magic must flow through the runes in consciousness as a single stream, without stumbling or being limited by any rune, but rather, like water running over mountain rapids, only gaining strength at each stage of such a cascade.

If you have gone through this path, if you have reached runic initiation and entered the next stage of magical transformation, the absence of preferences among the runes should be natural for you. However, if you now realize that some runes are unclear to you, "didn't come to you," don't rush into the labyrinth; see your initial journey through to the end. The gods do not favor the doubtful, but they dislike even more those who harbor illusions about themselves.

What else is important for further work:

You must remember that you will be working with forces that will dictate the terms of their application to you. They to you, not you to them, and this should never be forgotten for a single moment. These terms must be respected.

God is a force that cannot be precisely defined. One can describe its characteristics and functions, but only as one understands them. A definitive description limits the perceived possibilities, which may mean that at some point you won't be able to fully receive the informational flow of a particular god from the northern pantheon without distortion or reduction to your own understanding. Therefore, each god has many names, each describing an aspect of their manifestation, but none covering all aspects. Each god has many facets, even within a single pantheon. In your case, the god may manifest with a particular aspect, but this depends entirely on your personality, not the god's capabilities. It's not about the mental definitions given within the tradition to a specific god, but about the specifics of the perceiver's personal consciousness. The god's informational channel refracts in the consciousness like through a series of mirrors, reflecting in a specific and defined way for each person. Note this point of reflection but remember that this image is not absolute; it is significant only for you.

To understand the informational power of each god and determine your capacity and limits for this perception, you need to "run" all the currents of forces generated by the northern gods' pantheon through yourself. Live in this current, allow it to transform you, understand it, and only then determine how much this current can be perceived by your consciousness without reduction. It is crucial during practice to identify "your" god, your power channel. This will be such a current and connection that can be fully and wholly received by your consciousness. The force that once created a person will enter even a consciousness distorted by the binary aggression of Abrahamic religions if the person seeks it instead of hiding in subconscious fear of retribution or punishment. The mind must connect with its primal source, and when that happens, the human mind no longer needs surrogate replacements for its power to overcome fear and doubt.

Fear and doubt are great assets for a person, which become weapons and strength if used for growth and development; however, they become a deadly poison if used for self-punishment. In magical training, these resources of the subconscious (fear) and superconscious (doubts) are used as fuel and opportunities for magical growth. But in the ordinary human mind, they become a slow-killing poison, causing a person to betray themselves, their force, and their gods.

Your further practice will involve learning to keep your consciousness on the informational channels of the northern pantheon gods. The formulas attached to each practice will serve not as a goal but as a means — a means to keep your consciousness on the channel for as long as necessary for you to feel and understand it more fully. The beneficial effects from using the formulas are a pleasant bonus but not the primary goal for those who aim to transform their consciousness in a magical way, and only then everything else. Remember this.

Also, be prepared that not every god's channel will "enter" your consciousness easily. You might resonate with some forces more than others. There's nothing wrong with this — everyone has their god, their channel, and their preferences. The main thing is not to miss yours, and this won't happen. You will feel it. An absolute frequency match, an absolute union of forces.

The story of your god is about you; it is your story. It is impossible to confuse and make a mistake.

ᛊ ᛞ

PRACTICE 5

God Odin

In the previous steps of practice, you directly experienced what it means to have limited freedom of choice. While creating your Individual Runic Amulet and crafting your magical bind rune, you encountered a rule stating that you couldn't include runes in your personal sign that weren't initially specified in your Individual Runic Code (IRC). You couldn't rely solely on your own desire to choose the missing runes; you had to follow certain rules. Firstly, the runes had to be *appropriate.* Secondly, they needed to *naturally* emerge from the overlaying of the given runes. Only if they emerged through overlaying were they considered yours. Of course, you still need to nurture, strengthen, and learn to make them work in conjunction with the other runes, but from now on, you can do so legitimately.

This task and understanding of the rule were a significant experience and practice in contacting the power of the god Odin — yes, that was it. The god's channel seemed to be saying: yes, you are free, but you are free within established constants — can you handle this? Not to break barriers or expand boundaries, but to achieve the desired outcome with the little that is given?

We are all bound by established constants — both humans and gods. We cannot ignore them, we cannot surpass them — doing so would violate the rules of the game, which threatens the destruction or damage of realities. However, the seeker is allowed to develop their consciousness to the point where constants stop being a limiting factor: as if they turn inside out, and what was a boundary suddenly becomes the core. And

ᛊ ᛞ

the space begins to work, not draining energy but, on the contrary, from within, feeding the newly formed core with the power of the worlds. This will happen with you when your understanding of the inherent and acquired constant-runes becomes absolute; when they no longer serve as a limitation or burden but develop your mind to the point where boundaries become the foundation and limits the core.

However, when working with the channel of Odin, it is crucial to correctly understand the meaning of what is happening: the channel does not so much insist that you have constant-runes imposing certain rules on you, but rather that there are rules being imposed. There are rules, and this is the basis of any system. There are rules of knowledge and following — and this is the basis of the northern system.

Working with Odin's channel will be connected with understanding his aspects as a mage-seer and a mage-warrior. Therefore, the practice itself will take place in two stages.

In the first stage, you will learn the science of foresight: reading information about formed situations. For this work, you will need your runes and the Yggdrasil Tree diagram. Here, we will look at the Tree of Nine Worlds as a structural scheme describing the program of reality construction, where changing one parameter immediately leads to changes throughout the system.

The purpose of this practice is to diagnose the current situation. Each world in the diagram is an informational block that, in response to a query, gives a specific result. This result is processed by other blocks, which, in turn, also provide an answer to the task at hand. As a result, a complex of answers appears, which together give a vision of the system's expected reaction to the presence of a particular consciousness. This reading and subsequent decoding of messages from the system is called

ᛊ ᛞ

diagnosis, commonly known as divination. But our task is not only to learn to read information from the system but also to interpret it correctly.

The practice of diagnostics involves forming a question and then randomly placing runes on the positions of the nine worlds in the Yggdrasil Tree diagram until all positions are filled. This way, you will draw nine runes from the bag; they do not need to be selected, they do not need to be reversed if they appear inverted; they should be placed as they are in the following order:

1st position — the world of Midgard. This represents a commentary on the current situation, showing how the issue that concerns you is manifested in the "here and now."

2nd position — the world of Jotunheimr. This reveals the past premises that led to the current situation.

3rd position — the world of Vanaheimr. This indicates the future development of the situation, showing what will follow and where it will lead.

This horizontal line essentially represents the well-known divination method of "past-present-future." However, the Yggdrasil Tree shows that events and situations do not form so simply. There are many more reasons and premises for the reality described by these three runes to take shape in this particular way and no other. Both the past, present, and future have their causes, and these causes, as seen from the world scheme, are not limited to one another.

4th position — the world of Svartalfheimr. This position highlights the mistakes and problems from both the past and the future that have allowed the situation to unfold in the manner it has.

ᚹ ᚨ

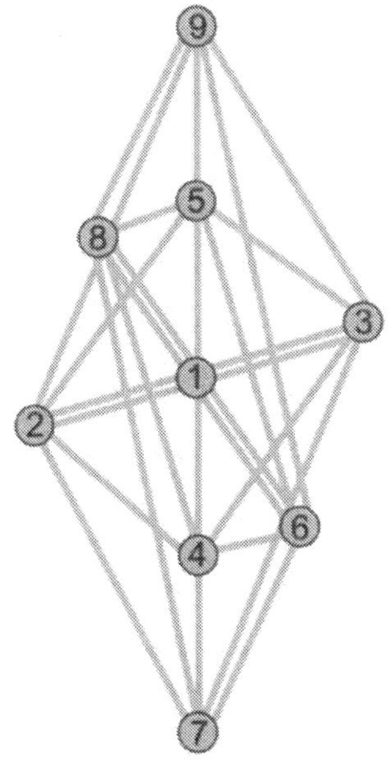

5th position — the world of Alfheimr. Conversely, this position shows the victories of the past and the desirable future developments, which have also influenced the formation of the "past-present-future" connection.

As we can see, the chain of probability is equally supported from both sides, and the algorithms of victory and defeat, hopes and fears equally influence how the mathematical past and mathematical future are formed. Moreover, the equal presence and influence of the worlds of Alfheim and Svartalfheimr show the situation from both favorable and unfavorable sides; it is both good and evil simultaneously—depending on how one looks at the situation and, more importantly, who is looking.

ᛊ ᛞ

6th position — the world of Niflheimr. This is the world of constants, darkness, and immutability. It reveals the constant of the person being prophesied about, around which the current situation has formed. This is the core of the problem, the program that dictated to reality what is paramount and what is not in this particular person's life. It is the root of the problem, the foundation of the issue, the true cause answering the question: why is it like this? Here it becomes clear that if the core remains unchanged, if the emphasis in the consciousness is not shifted, if this quality described by the rune continues to be the cornerstone of the entire program structure, nothing will fundamentally change: only some situational circumstances of life may be corrected, but the essence and outcome of changes will not.

7th position — the world of Hel. This world takes away what is no longer needed, what has lived its course, what goes into chaos for complete reprocessing, disembodiment, and becomes the building material for future realities. It is the price we always pay for acquiring something necessary—by the law of balance, we must simultaneously get rid of the unnecessary. In forming situations, this "unnecessary" is determined not by the human mind but by the system that creates the situations. It gives something but takes in return what occupies space in reality or consciousness, preventing the right circumstances (by the system's mathematical version) from arriving. What leaves is neither good nor evil but simply useless. In this position, you see the rune-sacrifice, what must be relinquished if the program reflected in the runes 2-1-3 ("past-present-future") is to work.

8th position — the world of Muspelheimr. This position, however, shows the potential for change. In the diagnostic spread, it acts as the triggering mechanism for the realization of an already written program, like the spark of a

ᚹ ᚨ

starter that ignites the engine, setting everything in motion. It is the rune of initiation and can indicate when the created situation will start unfolding into reality. However, the rune in this position has another function, which will be important and interesting in the next part of the practice.

9th position — the world of Asgard. The rune in the position of the world of gods indicates what is needed in this situation for the entire system, to maintain the law of balance, for the proper functioning of the program as a whole. Here, it is not about the individual and their personal wyrd, but about orlog—the collective fate of humans, gods, and worlds. It is a global program showing what such a weak and insignificant, on a universal scale, human fate program supports with its existence. It is assumed that the given situation under investigation is created under the aegis of a certain primary principle of the world of Asgard, and this primary principle is reflected by the rune (and its position) that fell on the ninth step for this world. It is also assumed that if everything is left as is and prepares for such an event's development, the event participant, the prophecy executor, becomes somewhat connected to this primary principle, and the rune reflecting it seals their consciousness. How "fortunate" or "unfortunate" this seal is for you personally, you can only determine yourself.

However, if such a global primary principle program were the only one (as, for example, in monotheism), there would be no point in thinking about changing it. But in a polytheistic system, in the world of Aesir gods, there are many such programs: each god or goddess themselves embody a universal constant (and sometimes more than one), each is a global program. This means that there is a chance for a person to change their wyrd, to reprogram the situation.

ᛊ ᛗ

The sluggard believes he shall live forever.
If the fight he faces not;
But age shall not grant him the gift of peace,
Though spears may spare his life.
(The Poetic Edda. Hovamol)

Such a chance is given to us by understanding the second aspect of the god Odin—the aspect of the warrior-mage. Here, the wide-brimmed hat of the wanderer-seer turns into a winged helmet, and the traveler's staff becomes the spear Gungnir. In this role, the god-mage, the warrior god, will never accept what is written and done and will fight fate as long as he remembers to fight fate. Under the aegis of Odin, we will use the protection of the Yggdrasil Tree and the boundless knowledge of the mage god. We will try to learn to rewrite an already created program based on Odin's lessons.

When analyzing the obtained spread, it is crucial to focus not on the rune that fell in the first position of Midgard as a commentary on the current situation. What is the current situation? In the blink of an eye, it becomes a situation of the past. Instead, attention should be directed to the third rune in the position of the world of Vanaheimr — the future.

Vanaheimr in the system of the Nine Worlds represents the ideal future, in our human understanding; the best outcome of the situation. Its prerequisites are the other eight runes located in the positions of the other worlds of the Tree. Under such conditions, says the rune in Vanaheimr, this will be the result. Under different conditions, something else will happen.

If you like what the world of Vanaheimr shows, leave everything as it is. But if something in the position of the Vanaheimr rune, in the future, does not suit you, then you can try to change everything. In this case, changes will be needed not

ᚹ ᚨ

only in the present but also in everything that led to this present. If there is a need or desire for changes, then also look at the rune in the 8th position of the world of Muspelheimr. The rune in this position shows the very possibility of reprogramming the given sequence. The rune that fell in the position of the world of Muspelheimr shows the chance. What can become the impetus for change and different development of the situation? Is there an opportunity to alter reality so that the life story unfolded in 9 positions will happen differently? Will the fire of Muspel agree to erase this program so that you can write another one there?

If feelings, beliefs, and signs show you the possibility of reprogramming this situation, then the knowledge and lessons of Odin will be invaluable to you. You feel the system, you understand it, you know how it works, and your intervention in this system is allowed by its knowledge.

The first thing to understand when undertaking the process of restructuring reality is that it has rules that are better not broken. This is precisely what was discussed at the beginning of this chapter. The wise do not destroy; the wise do not break. The wise seek advantage even in limitations. And if you, wanting to reprogram reality, do not want to be crushed by its response, then be attentive and act carefully.

Wits must he have who wanders wide.
But all is easy at home;
At the witless man the wise shall wink
When among such men he sits.
(The Poetic Edda, Hovamol)

Let me remind you of the rule you encountered when creating your magical symbol based on your Individual Runic Code (IRC): use only the given runes. The same rule applies here:

to change a situation, we use only the nine runes that were dealt in the spread. When creating your individual magical seal, you skillfully bypassed this limitation without breaking any rules, but rather developed it—you turned weaknesses into strengths and limitations into opportunities. Here, you will need to do the same. These nine runes are now your only tools, your resource. Only they can be used. The rest of the runes in the Futhark remain in the rune pouch, and you do not disturb them under any circumstances.

So, as we have already determined, on the Yggdrasil Tree, we are more interested in the outcome and the rune that will symbolize this outcome. It should be positioned in the world of Vanaheimr and determine the desired future. We will not break the rule if, to describe this future, we take one rune from the nine previously dealt—the one that, in your understanding, vision, and feeling, represents the desired result. You will place it in the position of the world of Vanaheimr.

We do not choose this rune blindly but quite consciously. Turn the rest of the runes face down and ritualistically shuffle them—they will be chosen "blindly." The rune pouch with the remaining runes should be set aside beforehand and not mixed with the others until the end of the work. The runes in the pouch are "foreign" runes right now; they have no relation to this spread, and you cannot use them to change the situation—this is the rule. However, the remaining eight runes are all yours. It is complete uncertainty how they will fall into the positions of the remaining worlds of the Yggdrasil Tree, what they will show as good or bad, what they will ask you to sacrifice, what memories of the past they will draw from you, and with which primary principle of the gods they will connect. All this you will discover further.

Next, you also lay out the remaining eight runes in the remaining eight worlds. As you do this layout, keep an eye on the initial diagnosis and observe the changes that the premises will undergo.

First, we again look at the "past-present-future" line: Jotunheimr-Midgard-Vanaheimr, where the final rune of Vanaheimr is already lying, but the other two are determined by the changed algorithms of fate.

The 1st position of the world of Midgard still describes the current present. But now there may be another rune there.

The 2nd position of the world of Jotunheimr still describes the past, just like before, but now you may see a different rune there. What does this indicate?

The future of everyone is determined by multiple factors. The events that occur are roughly formed on the strongest karmic algorithms of the past, but always in some informational environment. The overlay of these two factors determines the scenario of the current events[155] displayed. If one thing changes, everything else changes too. In this linear algorithm, the karmic indicator is changing—your personal internal algorithm that determines the most significant events in your life. This combination of runes Jotunheimr-Midgard-Vanaheimr will initiate changes within your consciousness. The nature of these changes and the transformation you are destined for will be revealed by the runes laid out and the difference between the initial and this altered spread. Sometimes one or even both runes remain unchanged, indicating that the changes will be introduced

155 This mechanism is described in more detail in the books by K. Menshikova "Karma - the Law of Cause and Effect" and "Egregores and the System of Controlling Reality".

not into you or your consciousness, but into the program forming the external world.

At this stage, you should have six runes left. Two of them, again blindly, are placed in **positions 4 and 5**, the positions of Svartalfheimr and Alfheimr respectively. Just as before, they will reveal the algorithms of good and evil that synchronously come into play from the change you are introducing into reality. The runes that fall into these positions will show which vulnerabilities of your consciousness will be exposed to reality and which victory algorithms you need to rely on to overcome these vulnerabilities, weaknesses, and past mistakes.

Remember, runes are the weapons of a warrior, not a weakling. They will not allow you to lie on the couch and wait for things to happen on their own. The runes in the positions of Svartalfheimr and Alfheimr unequivocally define for you the real actions you need to take to ensure things happen according to the correct algorithms (Alfheimr) and what to be wary of, which vulnerabilities to correct (Svartalfheimr).

Position 6 of the world of Niflheimr will also reveal the necessary constant of consciousness around which the new reality will be built. This rune will give the core of your mind new activity, find its analogue in the world of the ancient constants of Niflheimr, and align you with each other. This will allow you to see in ways you have not seen before and understand what was previously unclear.

However, everything done will require a price. And the more runes that have changed their old positions in the new spread, the more significant the sacrifice may be. What the "dark share of Hel" will be, is shown by the rune that falls into the corresponding world of Helheimr in **position 7**. This is what you will have to part with, what you will have to sacrifice for one thing to come in place of another[156].

Understanding the sacrifice can also be indicated by the rune that falls into **position 4** of the world of Svartalfheimr. But, unlike the sacrifice for Helheimr, the svartálfar insist on an active, not passive sacrifice, and the rune in the place of the world of Svartalfheimr shows what needs to be actively done to mitigate your vulnerabilities, while the rune in the position of Helheim describes what you will have to give up to achieve the result, even if only temporarily.

You have two runes left. The first will go to Muspelheimr and show exactly what it did before—the initiation of change processes. What needs to be done for the changes to begin? The rune you see in **position 8** of the world of Muspelheimr will indicate what can serve as the starting push for the changes to achieve your desired result.

The remaining rune will go to the world of Asgard, and its **9th position** in the spread will provide an understanding of the primary principle that will support the new life story, the scenario that will allow this "movie" to exist.

These runes can also appear in either upright or reversed positions—don't let this confuse you, just read the messages correctly.

156 For more details on sacrifices and offerings to the world of Helheimr, see the chapter dedicated to the goddess Hel.

ᛊ ᛞ

The described practice on the channel of the god Odin for reading information from the Yggdrasil Tree[157] system will be lengthy, and I highly recommend dividing it into two stages.

In the first stage, you will only perform readings without making changes. You need to develop the skill of not only flawlessly reading the information but also seeing all the cause-and-effect relationships described by all nine runes. To achieve this, you must perform many readings and observe their fulfillment. Runes are codes, programming codes, and they can manifest in the observable reality of Midgard in any form. You need to understand this multiplicity and clearly see the connection between the prophecy and its fulfillment. This requires time.

To make this stage productive and to avoid feeling embarrassed later in front of the god Odin for poorly grasping his lessons, consider the following:

1. Never do many readings in one day. Initially, do no more than one reading per day until you develop a stable skill in hearing the runes, seeing their manifestations in reality, and understanding the mechanism.

2. Always write down the question and document the reading in your journal. Analyze the day's events daily and correlate them with the diagnostic results. Record your thoughts and observations in detail.

3. To develop a stable skill in seeing and understanding, you need to perform many readings: a hundred, two hundred, even a thousand. Don't regret the time spent; it will be returned manifold, transformed into pure knowledge, and turned back into time in the volume and density you need.

---

157 This practice was first described by Master Liberty.

ᚹ ᚨ

4. In the first stage, I recommend using the knowledge from the previous practice and performing diagnostics through a lesser ritual, closing the space with "Thor's Hammer."

5. Use Odin's runes to enhance the understanding of the received information (formula to follow).

6. When working on changing the situation (the second stage of practice), always perform it through a lesser ritual and always close the space. You, like a programmer writing a program, must first complete it "in the cloud," then finalize it, and only then upload it to the general space. Otherwise, it may be destroyed before it is born. By closing the space with "Thor's Hammer," you create a timeless space around you where everything is possible because nothing is there yet. Until the work is finished, recorded in the journal, and the parchment with the new layout is protected or ritually activated (e.g., through fire activation), do not open the space or expose yourself to potential threats.

* * *

Odin is a teacher god for all of us. He not only tells us how things should be but also explains why. The practice of reading information from the Yggdrasil Tree is a valuable experience to learn from such a teacher who has experienced everything firsthand before teaching. He observes the learning process, which is very precious because he cares. And this, you will agree, is a great value — to have a teacher who cares.

For a deeper understanding of Odin's channel, you can use the formula "Help in Research".[158]"

---

158 Author — Master O. Shaposhnikov.

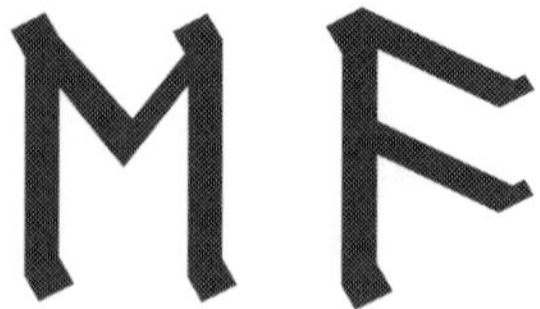

Odin's formula "Help in Research."

Let's break down this formula. An even number of runes implies that this rune stave involves a process extended over time. It does not imply a specific result expressed in a specific form, and in this case, this is true: knowledge is always a process.

ᛖ **Ehwaz** — a rune symbolizing consciousness

ᚨ **Ansuz** — a rune of knowledge, an informational current

This sequence of runes helps to include consciousness in the informational current. The command is given to the whole system (consciousness) to stay in the current, not to leave the current, and to constantly seek this current. When receiving such a command, the human mind stops scattering and concentrates only on the task at hand. With long-term use, it also starts to work as protection against external manipulations that can distract the seeker's consciousness from the search or switch it to a more "important" task. Two powerful runes, oriented more towards the inner world than its external projections, will slowly but steadily reprogram the mind, rearranging priorities: what is important for the mage and what is not.

It should be noted that the formula may be somewhat heavy for beginners. Working constantly, it does not allow the mind to relax, constantly keeping it in tone, "speeding up the processor." However, after some time, it becomes possible to get used to living in such a state, which, of course, leads to beneficial magical effects.

It is best to inscribe this stave on a permanent carrier and make a personal talisman, but it can also be written on yourself, especially during moments when you need to mobilize all the resources of your consciousness to search for information and, most importantly, to correctly understand what is found. It quickly accelerates, quickly brings the mind to the peak of its capabilities, and forcibly keeps it in this state, forcing the entire system of human thinking to mutate under magical capabilities.

Gratitude to the god Odin is desirable. However, the form of this gratitude will be indicated by the signs you receive. Odin’s power is everywhere, but I recommend paying attention to the behavior of ravens, dogs, and people.

I do not recommend rushing to the next practice. If you manage to "anchor" yourself on Odin's channel and comprehend it as much as possible for yourself, then understanding the channels of other gods in the Norse pantheon will not pose any difficulties for you.

ᛊ ᛞ

PRACTICE 6

God Thor

Working with the power of the god Thor, a seeker can learn much from him. First and foremost, one learns to rely on oneself for the future. If the help of the gods and their system is present today, it does not guarantee it will be there tomorrow, nor automatically. This is a crucial lesson and essential learning "from Thor": tomorrow will be a different story, everything will change, including those being protected. The need for protection is assessed by Thor in the given moment and does not have a prolonged effect into the future. With such a system of interaction with Thor's power channel, his lessons will always teach not to relax, to see the enemy now, to see the problem now, and to solve it now, not later. This is a lesson in vigilance and the ability never to rely on the assumption that tomorrow you will be protected the same way as today.

Understanding the nature of the god Thor reveals that he is the best protector against harmful witchcraft. Any interference in the established order of things falls within the interest of Thor and the realm of his power application. Thor is a destroyer of monsters, not humans. He does not interfere in human relationships but unmistakably sees the monster within a person or their surroundings. If Thor strikes a person, he strikes the monster living in them.

Anyone asking for Thor's protection can be confident that he will not seek the reasons for their problems nor investigate their past right or wrong actions. He evaluates the consciousness now, assessing it either as a system of order or a

ᚹ ᚨ

system of chaos. In the first case, one can count on Thor's help, but in the second — no.

Working with Thor's channel is always about working with protection. Partially, "entering Thor's halls" makes one akin to him: yesterday ceases to exist as a justification for one's inaction; tomorrow loses its importance as hope and as a right to do nothing today. Only the present moment matters, only what is happening now. No, the one channeling Thor will not become a defender of all the oppressed and insulted, but under Thor's aegis, a person will never become either oppressed or insulted.

The formula recommended for revealing and understanding Thor's channel is the classic protection formula, which can be said to be the seal of Thor — his Mjolnir.

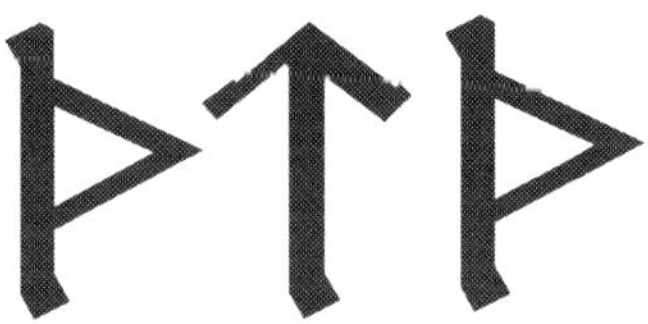

Thor's Formula: Thor's Hammer, universal protection

It consists of the runes Thurisaz-Tiwaz-Thurisaz, a double-edged battle axe[159].

Tiwaz awakens the inner truth, and the double Thurisaz protects it from all sides, shielding it from both external and internal threats. By defending against external influences, it reveals the true state of "here and now," showing inner strength as it truly is. This helps gather all internal resources for a decisive

159 Author is unknown.

ᛋ ᛞ

strike, stopping any energy drain if it exists (and the source of the drain will become very clear to you). Moreover, it will expose internal vulnerabilities: after all, something previously caused you to willingly give away energy, not resist theft, agree to loss without even attempting to fight. The formula "Thor's Hammer" will reveal all of this as well.

This formula will help you learn to live without looking back at the past, with maximum concentration in the "here and now," in the "present moment"; to live without seeking justification in the past and not relying on hopes for the future. It will allow you to feel the weapon in your hand, it will make you visible to the god Thor. It teaches solving problems as they arise, in a way that is worthy, honest, truthful, necessary, and sufficient.

This formula can be written on yourself or made into an amulet; it can be drawn on a photograph or visualized on the inner screen and a call sent to the god Thor in a difficult or urgent situation — anything is possible.

Thor's power will further strengthen the channel with the god Odin; if your connection with Odin needs protection, Thor will protect it. But if you step out of Odin's worlview, you will lose Thor as a protector. It's important to remember this: Thor is the defender of Asgard's interests, and he does not serve a person in their doubts and imperfections. Only the steadfast and loyal will feel the strength of the red-bearded giant as the power of a friend; others should not count on it.

ᚹ ᚨ

ᛊ ᛞ

PRACTICE 7

God Tyr

When exploring the power and specifics of the god Tyr's channel, you will not only work with his formula but also delve deeply into your memory and conscience through it. It is important, very important, to know the truth about yourself. To know and remember when dishonorable actions were committed, whether by you or your ancestor; to know when and how the bonds of Gleipnir were placed upon you; to know accurately and reliably who your personal Fenrir and your personal Garm are. If you can be honest with yourself, you will see the benevolent regard of the god Tyr.

However, remember that the god Tyr, as a teacher and the god of kings, does not provide protection, and it would be absurd to view his power as the help of a guide. His lessons teach that as long as you can manage without help, you should; as long as you can solve problems in a human way without involving magic, do so. Even a fool can do it with the help of higher and additional forces, but you try without them. If you succeed, that will be your valor, your rights, your power. This is the truth of a king.

This formula can be confidently regarded as the "Seal of Tyr[160]," as it embodies the true understanding of his power and the rules for its application: Nauthiz-Uruz-Tiwaz. The rune of need. The rune of strength. The rune of truth.

160 Author is unknown.

ᚹ ᚨ

The correct union of one's own truth and the strength needed for that truth. If there is a right to strength, the strength will be there. If there is strength, the right will manifest. If there is the strength to command, execution will follow.

Tyr's formula:
To obtain the desired, to gain rights

This formula can reveal the true right to power that you possess. The rune Nauthiz, being not only a mechanism for arousing true need, rather than desires and whims, is also a key to the world of Jotunheimr — the world of ancient memory, including ancestral memory. Combined with the runes Uruz and Tiwaz, it will awaken past memories in your consciousness, bringing forgotten or dismissed recollections to the surface, allowing you to remember. Uruz, as the force of the Mother, the force of the Earth, will help bring this memory to awareness of your own inner truth. Inner strength aligns with outer strength, and the Earth itself evaluates your rights, your position; it assesses you with its own measure, like a mistress evaluating her future spouse — the true king from a standpoint of impeccability.

If there is strength — the formula will reveal it. If there are vulnerabilities — it will show them too.

The three-rune formula is precise and acts as a single pulse that shakes the entire system of consciousness, pulling it out of stagnation, and forces the mobilization of all forces, as before the last battle, the final decisive exam. Here is memory. Here is strength. Here is truth. They must be adequate to each other, where based on one's own inner truth, memory and strength become equal to each other.

Tyr's formula, with such an intention, will unerringly show what you truly have a right to. Whatever it reveals — this knowledge is very valuable because it clearly defines the starting position, stripping away illusions. It is like that unknown force that shows the wolf Fenrir what the Gleipnir fetters truly look like, helping him to free himself from illusions. Thus, your strength, bound by a false understanding of yourself, through this formula, will be freed if you manage to see Gleipnir as it really is.

People often fail to reach their goals simply because they incorrectly determine their current position, making errors in their own positioning. But Tyr's truth says: it is better to know than not to know; better the sorrow of enlightenment than blind faith in illusions. If you don't command yourself to see the situation as it is, Gleipnir will bind you even tighter, making your consciousness an eternal torment for yourself.

A magical wound inflicted on a god never disappears. It cannot be healed, but the key mistake that led to the injury, which alters fate, can be corrected. Remember Tyr's experience, the experience of the god of kings. Mistakes do not need to be acknowledged; they need to be corrected. Remove illusions from your mind, as from Fenrir's paws, and the ultimate truth will prevail.

This formula can be used as a talisman or simply written on yourself or your photo. Be cautious about using this formula for another person: remember, the truth can be very painful, and for those not ready to hear it, it can be deadly. Not everyone is prepared to face their Garm right now. Therefore, use it only for yourself.

It should be noted that on Tyr's channel, all runic formulas work wonderfully, and not only them: spoken words, deliberate thoughts, and given commands all work, but only under one condition: if you know you are right. If you are wrong, the activation of the internal bonds of Gleipnir will not take long to manifest.

PRACTICE 8

God Heimdall

The lessons from the god Heimdall, if he chooses to teach you, can reveal how the constants of division in the human world still exist today. Perhaps the rules for classifying a person into one social stratum or another have changed, but the fact of such classification remains unchanged—there are castes in the human world.

How can one determine at a glance which caste a person belongs to? How can one avoid misjudging a person by identifying certain qualities and evaluating them?

The legend of Rig provides us with a way to understand this. First of all, remember, says the legend, that Heimdall does not teach just anyone. Jarl, his pupil and heir, produced someone who surpassed him in skill. For the god Heimdall to become your teacher, you must meet his requirements. You cannot deceive a god, but you can try to manifest the necessary qualities within yourself: what if you have them? If not, at least you can unerringly learn who you are, so as not to harbor illusions and become a Fenrir to yourself, to correctly understand your starting position. The constants of belonging to a particular stratum are embedded in everyone. According to the rule of Rig-Heimdall, they should not change over time during one's life—that is the law of this god. Whether you like it or not, that is how it is. If a constant is inscribed, the world's information system will read you according to it first, not based on what people think of you or what you think of yourself. For those seeking themselves in magic, it is always better to know than not to know, no matter what the truth is—it is more valuable than illusions. However, it should be remembered that a polytheistic system, unlike monotheism, consists of many forces, systems, and deities, filled with various algorithms for achieving results. Therefore, the formula "this way and no other" is not always applicable in polytheism. Rather, it is never applicable. However, now, while learning about Heimdall's channel, you will become acquainted with this very principle.

The god Heimdall is the guardian of boundaries. Heimdall's world is one of constants and compromises, where a compromise is an agreement about boundaries. Working with Heimdall's channel will help you understand your own boundaries and grasp the principle of the necessary presence of constants in consciousness as a system-forming factor. A person, as a system of various accumulations of feelings, emotions, opinions, desires, doubts, assumptions, misconceptions, and illusions, has great difficulty in recognizing the presence of constants in their consciousness as such, and even more so in identifying them by name. But the power of the god Heimdall can aid in this understanding. This power is like X-rays—they illuminate the skeleton, the framework; they show—here is the foundation, it is not visible under the accumulation of flesh, fat, and other biological compounds, but it is there—look at it.

It is very important to know and understand your foundation, but it is equally important to know what this foundation means in terms of the information evaluation of the system and the gods.

Whatever Heimdall's response may be, it is an algorithmic answer from the system to your query, "Who am I?" Knowing the system's answer offers a chance to understand it better, on one hand, and to learn how to apply a good magical mechanism, which states: if you cannot change something for now, then study this unchangeable thoroughly and make it your strength. You need to look at "Heimdall's verdict" from another perspective and see that if you do nothing with the constant he reveals, if you allow it to be prominent, it guarantees a right embedded in this stable property (perhaps the only one); it is a sword that will never break, a source that will never dry up. There is nothing unequivocally good or bad, successful or useless—everything depends on the area of application and can only be evaluated in that context, not in isolation from the result.

Who you are, according to Heimdall's constants, can be revealed through the following formula[161]:

Mannaz-Raidho-Ansuz. This three-rune formula means it is programmed for a specific result[162]. The formula should determine your social status (caste) and define the correct activity based on this determination. Using this formula means, on one hand, accepting your social fate, and on the other hand, receiving full support from the system for your activities. This formula, in such a revelation, will remove all obstacles and limitations imposed by unknown benefactors if they existed, but it will also exclude from your life path what, according to the system's rules, should not be in the life of representatives of your social layer. If you wholeheartedly accept Heimdall's paradigm and, like him, believe that constants are paramount and everything else is secondary, you can use this formula boldly.

---

161 Author is unknown.

162 It can be applied to oneself, to a photograph, or to an amulet.

Heimdall's formula:
The correct path from the perspective of higher powers

If you have doubts about correctly determining your caste affiliation, the following practice will allow you to accurately know the gods' opinion regarding you and your life's task. Moreover, this opinion will be quite detailed, as it will involve the already known information channels of the gods Odin, Thor, and Tyr, adding information received through the channel of the god Heimdall. This way, you will see if there is an alternative to Heimdall's strict definition, if there is a way to change your positioning in this world or, conversely, if no change is necessary or required. In the diagnostic spread presented below, the final word will be with All-Father in any case.

Spread "Speeches of the Aesir"[163]

In the spread, seven runes will be used. Draw them from the rune bag and place them rune-side up in the position as they are drawn: upright if upright, reversed if reversed. The position of the rune matters here.

---

[163] Author of the spread: Master Hadeken.

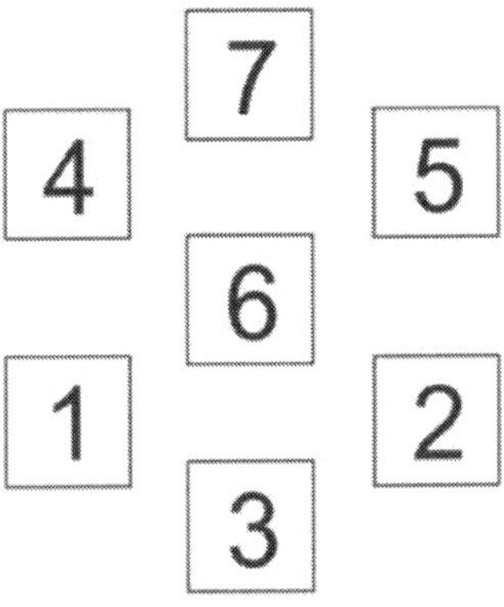

Speeches of the Aesir

Lay out the runes in the order described in the diagram, and they signify the following:

Position 1. Thor's Word. The god of strength evaluates your question from the "here and now" perspective and gives an assessment based on that. Thor's position evaluates the task on a simple basis: can you or can't you. Not legally, but physically; not potentially, but actually. Can you solve the problem now, by yourself, not later when favorable or simply different circumstances arise. Thor deals with concrete strength and evaluates what exists, not what might be or might not be.

Position 2. Tyr's Word. The god of justice looks at the issue differently, seeing the level of rights and the legitimacy of the querent. He assesses potential and opens or closes prospects based on truth. Tyr will unmistakably determine whether you are truly justified and if your demands are fair, without illusions.

Position 3. Heimdall's Word. The opinion of the White Aesir is based on all immutable circumstances. He sees what cannot be changed in resolving your issue and what can be changed. His word fixes those constants that must remain unchanged when solving your problem. He will indicate your position in reality as it is, which must be taken into account in further evaluations or transformations by the other Aesir.

Position 4. Odin's Response to Thor. The Allfather, who sees the situation unfolding and in perspective, assesses Thor's word in perspective: agreeing or disagreeing, laughing or getting angry — you will hear this yourself.

Position 5. Odin's Response to Tyr. Tyr's truth has judgment in Odin's eyes. He will express this to Tyr, and the rune in this position will show his word. Tyr's truth may dissolve in Odin's wrath or be strengthened by his wisdom.

Position 6. Odin's Response to Heimdall. Odin knows what immutable constants are, but he also knows there can be many. In his word, the Allfather will tell the White Aesir about this, either agreeing with him or highlighting alternatives if they exist.

Position 7. Odin's Word. His verdict, the result, the diagnosis that Odin gives considering all the factors expressed by the gods. This is the conclusion, and it must be accepted as given. Odin's final decision.

Each god expresses their position based on their principles of truth, existence, and possibilities. Odin, who encompasses everything found in the other gods, provides a personal opinion and a final general conclusion, as only he can consider all factors, both spoken and unspoken. He can connect everything, see additional opportunities, or deny them. That's why he is the Allfather; he speaks last.

This spread provides a comprehensive view of the senior gods of the Northern pantheon regarding the question or problem before you. The Aesir converse not with you but exclusively with each other, allowing you to simply hear their opinions. You do not participate as an actor[164] in this conversation. The conversation may proceed in an informal manner typical of close friends, so abandon any expectations that the gods will choose words convenient for you. Also, remember that none of your requests (clarifying or leading questions) are considered. This conversation is like a doctors' council, where you sit on a stool, listen to the verdict, and don't interrupt or interfere.

It is important to remind you not to rephrase or clarify your question multiple times. Do not make more than three spreads in one day, and certainly do not rephrase the same query in different words; you won't deceive the gods, and you risk earning the mark of a deceitful nag. Be honest and noble, and if you decide to ask the elder gods a question, have the courage to hear the answer. Remember, receiving this answer is a privilege, not a right.

It is also crucial to remember that this spread is diagnostic; it provides an opinion, not assistance. If the summary opinion of the god Odin opens a "green road" for you, it does not mean you can just lie on the couch. You will still need to walk your path, and the gods do not shield you from obstacles on this path. They will tell you there is a possibility, and then you must proceed on your own. Or they might say there is no possibility, but you still have to move forward on your own. Paganism is a system of action, remember that.

It is best to perform this spread using the lesser ritual, closing the space. Remember that it is customary to thank the

164 Actor — a significant subject playing a notable role in a particular process or under certain conditions.

gods for their help. You will understand how, when, and with what to show your gratitude after completing the ritual.

Even if the god Heimdall does not recognize your consciousness as an object of his systemic interest, simply being in the channel of this god can activate qualities inherent to Heimdall's power in your consciousness: to hear (perceive) everything happening in your environment, and through this, to understand people more deeply and accurately discern who is who. Any thought that suddenly comes to you in this channel about a certain person is a correct thought, and it determines who that person truly is, not who they wish to appear as in the eyes of others or themselves. Heimdall never makes mistakes in judging the children of humans.

Listen to the signs on Heimdall's channel.

PRACTICE 9

God Loki

In his lessons, the god Loki can be rough and cruel. However, a better teacher is hard to find. No one sees the key problem in the system more clearly than he does. There can be many problems in the consciousness, but there is always one key issue. Loki will highlight this key. He will show the stumbling block of the entire system of consciousness, the constant that forms the crooked structure. And he won't just show it; he will confront you directly with the main task: is this really the constant worth living for? Or is this value, this key in the system, something someone else lives for, while your life resources are used for someone else's ideals? Loki can reveal the problem in a very indelicate, rough, and cruelly mocking way. But if the result is more important to you than the process, you can endure anything for the sake of the result.

The channel of the god Loki dissolves everything in the consciousness that merely pretends to be a value, everything that only seems to be unshakeable constants of consciousness. Loki does not create mischief for no reason; he does so only where it is genuinely necessary, where there is a serious reason to see the problem, not for mere mischief. Though sometimes his lessons may seem like this, do not fall for provocations: if you have embarked on the path of knowledge, stay true to your intention no matter what.

Loki sees a person not as a social entity but as a projection of a god. If he sees a discrepancy between this and what you currently represent, he will correct it.

The formula proposed for working on this channel is the transformation formula[165].

Like Loki, it works quickly, harshly, and with maximum precision. It helps to get rid of fears, and by removing their veils, reveals your true essence, your genuine nature. Fears are the foundation of any illusion; if fear sneaks into the consciousness, the mind, affected by this virus, will easily build the illusion itself.

Loki's formula: transformation, getting rid of fears

The transformation formula is a bind rune of two runes: Dagaz and Eihwaz.

Eihwaz represents your fears, both small and big, deep and superficial. From the standpoint of the stave's task, these are the vulnerabilities that make the consciousness fragmented, weak, and sick.

Dagaz — the rune of transformation and change. Combined with Eihwaz, it helps turn weaknesses into strengths, fears into weapons, and inner imperfections into a concrete plan of action and self-transformation.

---

165 Author — Master Liberty.

You can inscribe this bind rune anywhere: on yourself, on a photograph, on your hand, on your leg, on your forehead, or even on a piece of sugar to eat — anywhere. It is very helpful for beginner witches and sorcerers who are fearful of everything but are eager to practice. It is also recommended for anyone who suffers from irrational fears of the external world, of the "powers that be," and of the unknown and the incomprehensible. This formula will help, and it will help quickly.

However, a word of caution. Do not apply this formula to other people, especially if they are dear to you. Not everyone is ready to face their own monsters, and not everyone is ready to see themselves without illusions. Remember, the god Loki is not a deity of gentleness and delicacy. His love and care are always specific and may not fit into the human stereotypes of what "divine help" should be.

Keep in mind that Loki will help you if you are truly ready to work on yourself. For those who believc that "everything should sort itself out," Loki does not help — he laughs at them. But if you manage to become strong through Loki's lessons, you will laugh together.

ᛊ ᛞ

PRACTICE 10

God Njord

The Vanir channel of power of the god Njord is not meant to bestow riches and resources indiscriminately on everyone. The gifts of the god of sea wealth are intended only for the strong and impeccable, only for the noble descendants of the Vanir tribe. A person with a noble soul will be able to enter the channel of the god Njord, and from that moment on, everything in life will increase. But if the soul is small and ignoble, if it is corrupted by the virus of envy and slander, instead of profit, there will be loss, and quickly at that. All gods of the ancient forces of nature judge a person precisely in this way; they cannot be prayed to, pitied, or frightened. Recall the Russian fairy tale "Morozko," and you will instantly understand what this is about.

"The King of Men," Njord does not judge "small" consciousness from the perspective of law, righteousness, or unrighteousness. The god of nature sees strength, and if it exists in a person—natural, noble strength—then there will be a connection, a response, and the right given by the gods. But if there is no such strength, the attempt to enter the channel of the god Njord will work strictly in reverse.

When approaching this channel, remember that the ancient gods have their own criteria for judgment, which do not conform to the current traditional social world and may seriously differ from human ideas about what constitutes impeccability and nobility. Remember that the Vanir magic of the god Njord absolutely and unmistakably determines the place that the nature

ᚹ ᚨ

of a particular person should occupy in the overall biocenosis. If a person occupies an incorrect place, the god Njord will determine this instantly. For him, such a person is like a cancerous cell, like fibrous tissue that spoils life for everyone around, taking resources from those to whom they are given and due by nature. But the reverse is also true: if Njord's power determines that the noble have been wronged, that the noble have been insulted by those who have no right to the resource, he will correct the situation—because such is his power, such is his nature: the whole world is one whole, and if one part of the world is in pain, all the others feel it.

Small people, alien people, those who do not love or understand nature's laws, will be at best ignored by the god Njord, and at worst (for them) stripped of their rights to resources and deprived of the ability to take these resources as they might have done before—thoughtlessly, maliciously, out of fear and hatred of the forces of nature.

His algorithms of goodness in this sense differ from the algorithms of the Aesir gods. The Aesir say: live by the law. The Vanir say: live by nature. Entering the channel of the god Njord will unmistakably show you how much you correspond to your nature, and if the power of the sea god of wealth deems it possible to enter your mind, he will correct injustice by nature if it exists. However, remember that the reverse is also possible: if the recognition algorithms of Vanir power see that what you have was not rightfully obtained, not by strength and not by ability, the excess will disappear. As an ancient law given by the gods to humanity states: do not demand justice—you might receive it.

This warning should always be remembered by modern social individuals, who often do not understand that they are not the masters of nature and that nature owes them nothing.

However, those who grasp this simple truth can find in the flow of the god Njord's power the very justice that has been violated and the restoration of their true natural rights. Njord determines unerringly: if it is due by nature — you will receive it; if you have the strength — take it; if you are impeccable — own it. What you should rightfully have from Mother Nature will manifest, but what you should not have will immediately disappear.

In addition to revealing such truth, much can be learned on this channel. For instance, to feel and understand your rights, to realize your strength. Never to encroach on others' rights, to understand unerringly where the boundary of permissible influence lies. To see clearly what place is destined for whom in this world by nature, where the realm of possibilities is located not only for oneself but for everyone else as well. This is the knowledge of the unity of everything with everything and the impeccable feeling of natural anomalies in the human world when they arise. To sharply feel unnaturalness, as children of nature instinctively sense impending natural disasters.

The formula recommended for use on this channel is called "Finding Your Path" [166]. The specificity of this formula is that the concept of "path" should be considered precisely from the perspective of the Vanir worldview of the god Njord, in the context of determining a place in the general world natural space.

Every person born has a predetermined place in nature, and this place, along with the right to live and sustain oneself there, is granted solely by the fact of birth. This applies not only to the physical manifestation of this place but also to the biological and social aspects: the people among whom you live, the function you perform, and the position you hold in your hab-

166 Author is unknown.

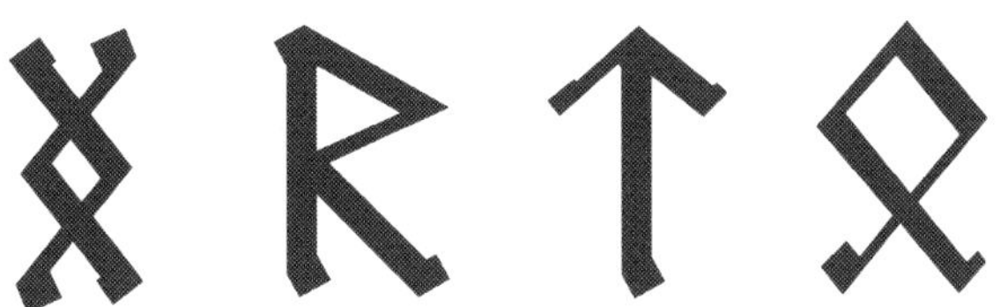

Nyörd's Formula. Finding your path

itat. This determination is somewhat different from the mechanisms employed by the Aesir's program, which defines a person's wyrd and designates their place based on existential volume, the fullness of consciousness, and familial caste affiliation, but not biology or nature. Njord's algorithm is different, and it does not operate with the concept of "existential volume." The Vanir algorithm accurately determines your natural function — why you were born, your contract with nature, and where and how you can be whole within the combined worlds. It determines the rhythm you need to exist in by nature and the task you must perform by nature. From this determination will depend your right to resources and the guarantee of obtaining them. The place, occupation, society, and regular results that the world expects from you — all this will help determine the "Finding your path" formula.

Since this formula extends over time, it is better to create it as a talisman on a permanent carrier or to apply it to your photograph. However, you should be prepared for it not to work quickly — the Vanir channel adheres to its own rhythms. It is also essential to understand that the purpose of this formula is not so much to provide you with information about the correct natural path for you but to lead you to this path, and this process takes time. So, relinquish any expectations that everything will happen immediately, but you can be sure that the process begins to work right away.

What ritual can you use when working with Njord's channel? The success of contact is more likely when you connect with the god's native element — the sea. Traditionally, to thank their god for help and involvement in their fate, Njord's followers feed seagulls, which he loves and delights in their cries.

Also, seers who travel with their minds through the worlds tell that Njord loves his halls, Noatun, but their constant expansion due to shipwrecks requires increased care. Therefore, Njord gratefully accepts gifts brought from distant travels by his devotees.

When working with Njord's channel, try to understand that the Vanir, here in the world of living nature, are the true masters. We humans are simply allowed to live here. If you can understand and feel this, interaction with the power of the Vanir gods and living "in the right" will become the foundation for you to fear nothing and lose nothing due to fear and misunderstanding of the true state of things.

As you begin to work with the channels of Vanir power, remember that the Vanir are a part of the world that, unlike the power of the Aesir, is not subject to analysis but only to feeling. This feeling requires not awareness but, on the contrary, a state of being without awareness, requiring a state of presence — and nothing more.

ᛊ ᛞ

PRACTICE 11

God Freyr

The story of the god Freyr teaches us that his power is great, but not all-encompassing. The development of his algorithm for achieving results, his victories, and his defeats show that his current of power leads to success in small or heartfelt matters. Although the god Freyr embodies the universal principle of infinite regeneration, according to the rule of reality construction, this principle cannot be applied to everyone and everything: the god's victory in the legend is an enhancement and expansion of the application of his principles and algorithms, while defeat and loss correspondingly diminish this application. The legend of the god Freyr's victory (love for Gerd) and defeat (the giant Surtr) indicates that his power can only be applied to his nature, the nature of Vanir interests, but he remains defenseless against "external power," and his affairs, his home, and his interests must be kept away from the "gaze of light": from the law, from excessive information flowing through light channels. His ancient memory must be applied to some specific occupation, not to the entire process of creation in reality. More precisely, find a task for yourself and direct yourself and your powers to this task. Do it for yourself, not for the whole world, not for other people — and Freyr will help.

Freyr's power does not provide protection — it is not intended for this. Protective formulas are not used on the Vanir channel, as the very concept of protection is opposite to the understanding of Vanir nature. The essence of protection is to reject, to exclude something from oneself. The Vanir are nature,

ᚹ ᚨ

where everything is connected to everything, and nothing can be excluded without harming the overall integrity. But Freyr's story shows how vulnerable nature is in its short-sightedness, and by living according to its laws, it does not see that an enemy, pretending to be an old friend, like Skírnir, can be very close.

Freyr's channel will allow the realm of your deep, true interests to manifest and only them to grow as fruits, like in the garden of the goddess Gerd. These interests should have already manifested on the previous channels of the Aesir gods, whose nature is primordial, like the ancestors of Freyr's beloved. Freyr's channel will show in what form you could manifest your true nature, what traces to leave behind as significant and necessary. The basis of these traces will be your deep essence, which the gods Odin, Thor, Tyr, Heimdall, and Loki have exposed. The exposed genuine essence becomes like a seed that Freyr will give life to, for he is the god of nature, but he allows only the strongest seed to survive. The goddess Gerd, with her long memory, will ensure that your seed is planted in such a way that it grows properly — without harming the seed or the garden. Freyr will show where your personal "herb garden" can be, where your area of application for your deep task lies.

The formulas that can be used on the channel of the god Freyr are generally associated with enrichment and prosperity. I will present a universal formula here: "Prosperity"[167].

---

167 Author is unknown.

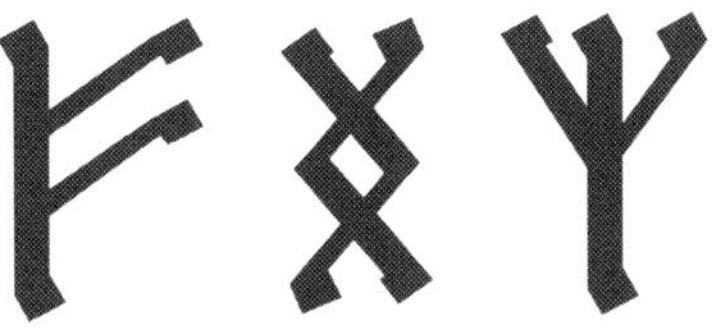

Freyr's Formula: Prosperity

A very simple three-rune formula: Fehu-Inguz-Algiz. Protected power of fertility.

This formula embodies the very essence of the Vanir channel, and its use will connect your consciousness with it very quickly and very naturally. It will highlight those values and needs associated with survival and well-being. It will activate the principle of natural selection at all levels of consciousness, from enhanced immunity at the physical level to a heightened sense of healthy egoism and a deep need to possess what is necessary and your own.

Using this formula will strengthen the Vanir component of your nature and make it visible to the Vanir gods, visible to the god Freyr himself. If the power of the gods of nature is initially strong in you, the contact with "your own" will happen very quickly. If the Vanir component is in an atrophied state, the formula will first try to revive it, initiate a drive for life, and repel parasitic Skírnirs so that resonance with the gods of natural forces and wealth occurs fully and without distortions.

Prosperity is the power of renewable resources, the ability to see benefit for yourself in everything, to see your habitat, to see how, where, and with whom happiness and well-being are possible.

ᛊ ᛞ

This formula can be made into an amulet, placed on an image (photograph), or simply applied to the body — it will work in any case. This formula and the power of the Vanir channel, if it enters you, can shatter the stereotypes in your consciousness that you have only one social path and only one socially approved (or familiar) purpose. It can erase from consciousness the program-belief that you can only receive resources from this world within the framework of this artificial image of purpose; it can erase the program that makes you blind to opportunities, that denies alternatives.

Freyr will manifest his power where he finds his Gerd — where she lives in your consciousness. He will find the most beautiful, the most phenomenal thing you have, and this will be "Gerd's herb garden," which you are destined to cultivate. This will be prosperity — prosperity in your own garden.

ᚹ ᚠ

ᛊ ᛞ

PRACTICE 12

Goddess Freyja

When working with the power of the channel of the goddess Freyja, you will have the opportunity to compare it with the previous channel of the god Freyr. Despite the fact that Freyja and Freyr are brother and sister, twins, and both are Vanir, these two currents are as different from each other as a man is from a woman.

The channel of the god Freyr is limited but constant. His light is warming, giving a sense of stability, in some ways calming. Freyja's channel is not like that. It is not confined to its own perception and is certainly far from stable — much like the goddess of Freedom herself. Soft and yielding now, in a second, it becomes fierce and angry. Just as quickly, it turns noisy and humming, and then again calm and gentle. Like a mountain river, like a spring wind, like the mood of a woman. Freyja's flow of power is never monotonous and never illuminates the same place. It is no wonder that Freyja is said to have four hats — four manifestations in which she reveals herself. Each hat has its own feature and unique property:

Spring hat — youth and joy, softness and kindness, the smile and ringing laughter of the goddess. This is not carnal love but love as a force of attraction, the desire to live and hope. This is the urge for change when it is not yet present but there is an anticipation of it. The power of this part of Freyja's channel is not for accumulation but for giving. Take and immediately give back. Inhale and exhale. It is the cycle of power in nature: if the goddess takes something, she immediately gives something

ᚹ ᚨ

equivalent back; if she gives something, she takes something in return.

The spring hat of the goddess Freyja will help you learn to feel this equivalence and understand: when something leaves, what comes in return? When something arrives, what will soon be taken in compensation?

Summer hat — this is the hat of the goddess of fertility, the hat not of a young maiden but of a mature woman. Here, goddess Freyja is a mother, and her flow is a nourishing flow. This flow is also not static, and the "summer hat" reveals the goddess as a Dis, a goddess of fate. According to legend, Disir are natural spirits who bestow certain strong and good qualities upon a newborn child (unlike the Norns, who weave the fate of the born). Freyja is sometimes called the "Dis of the Vanir."

The summer hat of the goddess Freyja will help you recognize those very strong natural qualities you are endowed with from birth; to highlight those special personality traits that can turn life into a full-flowing river, rich with fish, into arable fields, abundant with crops, into protected forests, teeming with game. The manifestation of these qualities will help you harvest the crops from the seeds you planted long ago, so long that you have forgotten about them, but they will suddenly yield fruit where you had lost hope.

Autumn hat — this is the power of reversal; the power not of giving birth but of killing. This hat is the winged helmet of a warrior. In this guise, Freyja's power is the power of a Valkyrie, a warrior woman. This flow takes away all that has lived its life and, like a tsunami, like a furious wave, sweeps away everything that has no roots from the environment. In her autumn hat, goddess Freyja takes the fallen warriors on the battlefield, taking them to her halls ahead of god Odin. She takes those who are destined to live in the world of Vanaheimr from now on, and first and foremost, these will be warrior women: those who, like Freyja, rely only on themselves in life, those who owe nothing to anyone.

In this guise, she shows her stark contrast to the goddess Frigg, the keeper of the proto-foundation Tradition, the creator of the hearth. Here, Freyja-Vanadis reveals herself as the true mistress of the diametrically opposite principle of Freedom: while Frigg, the mother of the Aesir, will save her offspring, Valkyrie Vanadis will kill for it. The autumn hat of the goddess Freyja will show you what freedom "as conscious necessity" is; it will show what exactly is needed to be free: what must be killed for this, what must be destroyed, what must be cleared. The autumn hat will also teach you never to rely on anyone.

Winter hat — this is the hat of a wise witch, Elder Mother, Frau Holle, old Gerda. All the qualities contained in all her previous hats seem to compress into this one, giving a dry residue — experience. Here, nothing bears fruit anymore; here, valuable things are preserved and frozen. In this hat, goddess Freyja is a teacher of magic, as she once was for Odin. Here she is a Völva-prophetess, a mad witch.

You can only put on the winter hat of goddess Freyja when all three previous ones are worn to the threads. Those who managed to be everyone and kept their freedom are worthy of the wise Freyja's teaching in this guise. The winter hat is her attribute as the mistress of Seidr.

Changing "hats" is not a chaotic trying on of someone else's wardrobe. It is the progressive development of oneself through life and maturation. But this is not necessarily a linear movement from youth to old age: one can come to Freyja's winter hat at sixteen, and one can keep the spring one until retirement. It is not necessary to be exclusively a woman to comprehend the power of Vanadis — her male followers can tell a lot about the Vanir magic.

The formula that should be used on the goddess Freyja's channel is, of course, her own seal. The formula is called "Freyja's Seal"[168]. It consists of two interconnected runes, Berkana and Inguz. Berkana is the rune of the goddess herself, and Inguz is the key to the world of Vanaheimr. Linked into a single sign, they show Freyja as Vanadis—the daughter of the Vanir, the mistress of Vanaheimr.

Freyja's Formula: Freyja's Seal

The use of this runic symbol will not only immerse your consciousness into the power channel of goddess Freyja but will also allow you to undergo the mystery of sequentially transforming your consciousness through all four of her hats. You should remain in each guise, in each projection for as long as necessary, without trying to change the hats at your own discretion. When the time for change comes, you will receive a sign. Each hat represents essential experience, a sequential

[168] Author: Master D. Voron.

passage through the four proto-foundations of consciousness: Love, Life, Hate, and Death, respectively. If you lack experience in one area, you will need to wear that hat for a long time; if you have ample or even excessive experience, the hat change will occur quickly. This is a highly individual process, but every witch or warlock will go through it: to achieve freedom, you must come to know everything and be everyone.

The "Freyja's Seal" stave is best made into an amulet and worn constantly, then it will act as a mechanism that triggers the mystical transformation. The drawn formula on oneself will simply enhance attractiveness, awakening natural innate forces. But to comprehend the power of goddess Freyja, to accomplish the Vanir transformation according to the rules of seiðr magic, you need to experience this power for a long time, to be in it, to live in it, to become it.

While living on this channel, strive to learn to be free and independent of obligations and debts. Learn to find strength within yourself and not to pay dearly for what is inherently a part of your nature.

ᛊ ᛞ

PRACTICE 13

Sif and Idunn

When experiencing the channels of the Vanir gods, specifically those of Njord, Freyr, and Freyja, you might find that one of the described Vanir qualities—altruism or egoism—has suddenly become pronounced. This doesn't mean these qualities were entirely foreign to you before, but the Vanir energy may amplify one more prominently in certain situations. It's as if your nature or character has unexpectedly shifted, revealing a new aspect that was rarely seen before.

There's no need to be surprised by this, especially now that you understand the specific extremes of the Vanir channel, represented by the goddesses Sif and Idunn. Falling into these extremes doesn't diminish your consciousness or intellect; it reflects the nature of your own power. The Vanir energies are more effective when channeled through this particular personality trait—this is your nature.

If you have recognized and understood the extremes of altruism or egoism in yourself, do not attempt to change if you envision natural magic and the Vanir power as the primary channel for your magical work and self-transformation. However, this approach should be different if the power of the Aesir is to become your main guiding force. In that case, seeking the golden mean and avoiding dangerous extremes is preferable.

Using the runic seals of goddesses Sif and Idunn, as provided further on, will help to reveal specific personal traits that keep your consciousness leaning towards a Vanir extreme — altruism or egoism. These traits may manifest differently in

ᚹ ᚨ

each person, so identifying your vulnerability is essential. Note, it is a vulnerability, even if it may not seem so. It is a vulnerability because "law and order" can easily control and manipulate your life and power through this trait.

If you already know your Vanir extreme — altruism or egoism — as pointed out by goddess Freyja or god Freyr, you can confidently use the seal of the goddess representing that extreme to study yourself. If you do not yet see this in your consciousness or align with the Aesir's power, try both seals to learn more about yourself. This aspect of your personality often goes unnoticed.

Egoism, as a Vanir extreme, sees no one but itself and refuses to understand or take others seriously. Altruism is similar, seeing everyone as equal or often superior. The commonality between these states is that both view everyone equally, uniformly, without hierarchy. The human world, the world of law, the hierarchical world, will continually prove the opposite if you are a descendant of the Vanir. The extremes of egoism and altruism are attempts to ignore the obvious. In our world, this is called "living in illusions." Even goddesses, with their incredible natural power, were vulnerable and dependent on the order of Asgard, let alone humans.

Natural witches and earthly people, learn to hide your Vanir extremes, either in the solitary tower of Trud or in the shell of Idunn's nut. Remember, you will benefit as long as others depend on you. But if you forget this for even a moment, Loki will quickly show you who depends on whom now. It is important to emphasize — you should never get rid of the extremes of Vanir nature. Gods forbid! Getting rid of them is like cutting Sif's hair or never receiving the hide of your totemic ancestor. Extremes are something to hide from prying eyes but cherish and study with pride — seek a connection with your magical roots through the uniqueness of your nature.

However, if in your personal magical mythodrama you seek not only self-knowledge but also development, you should remember the following. Your pronounced Vanir trait is not something that requires nurturing and strengthening (as doing so will only make it more visible and increase your vulnerability). Instead, you need to develop the opposite trait: altruism for egoists and egoism for altruists. By doing this, you will move closer to the power of goddess Freyja's channel, who, as you know, managed to preserve and even strengthen her freedom — this will be the quest for magical development for those who feel themselves descendants of the Vanir, natural witches, *seidkonas.*

The provided seals of the goddesses will also assist you in this development. To develop the absent trait, use the seal of the goddess that is not yet manifested in you. By developing the missing strength and balancing it with your natural trait, you will become stronger and freer, like Vanadís, the dis of all Vanir.

The Seal of Sif

ᛊ ᛞ

The Seal of Sif is a straightforward formula[169] consisting solely of Vanir runes—Inguz, Uruz, Berkana. Fertility—Strength—Growth. Uruz here is the sought-after rune. Placed between the runes of Freyr and Freyja, it denotes the essence of Vanir power. On Sif's channel, its application reveals the original mythological meaning—unveiling one's power. Beauty and fertility, growth, and abundance—in this formula, these are not effects but the desired state: only my power exists, and nothing else.

In practical terms, the formula acts to awaken female sexuality, make hair beautiful (if applied to shampoo or a hairbrush), and may also work to normalize the menstrual cycle and activate survival energies. However, these are pleasant side effects of the primary goal — to restore the connection with true nature and unite with the world of the Vanir.

Apply the formula to yourself, to a photo, or to a talisman — anywhere you like. Using this formula will enhance the Vanir's egoistic traits of the personality and increase your connection to the power channel of the goddess Sif. When fully aligned with the channel, the feeling of connectedness with the goddess, and sometimes even complete identification with her, occurs very frequently.

Idunn's Apples[170] are ordinary apples from any apple tree. They become magical and rejuvenating when the goddess Idunn imbues them with her Vanir magic, amplified by the ancestral craftsmanship of Ivaldi.

---

169 Author is unknown.

170 Author is unknown.

ᚹ ᚨ

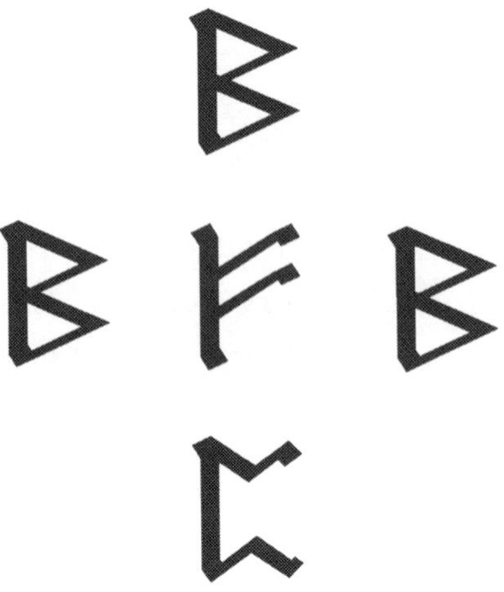

Idunn's Formula: Idunn's Apples

Triple Berkana, Fehu, and Perthro. Fehu symbolizes something already formed, already done—in this case, your consciousness. Three Berkanas initiate the development of what seems immutable, and if your mind turns toward the past, the three Berkanas will try to redirect it. Perthro here is the channel to the world of Vanaheimr, the force pulling forward into the future. The "Idunn's Apples" stave will help ensure that the natural quality of altruism and the zest for life, like in youth, stays with you for a long time.

For a lasting effect, it is better to create a talisman with this formula and wear it constantly. Avoid applying it to a photograph, as this may be perceived by the goddess's channel as an attempt to revive the past, and you already know what that can lead to.

ᛊ ᛞ

To achieve a rejuvenating effect, you can apply this stave to an apple (either by drawing or carving it) and then eat it immediately. This is not a one-time magic but a continuous practice to be performed every day from now on. This action is suitable for everyone: the old and the young, men and women, because Idunn's altruism does not distinguish between the worthy and the unworthy if the aim of her powers is the future and living in the future.

* * *

A deep immersion and study of the power channels of the goddesses Sif and Idunn is especially important for those who feel Freyja as "their" goddess. In this case, the depth of understanding all aspects of the manifestation of her extreme qualities becomes particularly significant and valuable. It involves grasping the reasons for their emergence and the real threat of forced stabilization and restriction of Vanir magic. The stories of the goddesses Sif and Idunn reveal the mechanisms through which the power of a natural witch can be destroyed or blocked with almost no resistance on her part.

ᚹ ᚨ

ᛊ ᛞ

PRACTICE 14

Goddess Frigg

The mistress of Asgard, the sovereign of destinies and guardian of tradition, goddess Frigg, sees every thread of fate in the fabric of reality she has woven. The thread of each person's life is interwoven into the pattern of the world order, and only she knows which thread belongs to whom. She sees your thread, your fate. The life line of each person in the world of Midgard is always reflected, taking into account the characteristics of the one fulfilling their destiny, their wyrd. These characteristics are found not only in the strengths of a personality but also in its vulnerabilities—everyone has their own mistletoe.

Presence on the channel of goddess Frigg's power will reveal both qualities: good and evil. The goddess's power can help you see your mistletoe before it begins to irreversibly change you. If this has already happened to your fate, the goddess has the power to guide you towards altering the "infected" destiny. This means embarking on the path of Baldr, repeating his mystery of healing, learning, and becoming.

Frigg's Formula

ᚹ ᚨ

ᛊ ᛞ

The formula[171] presented here can be used to open and maintain a connection with Goddess Frigg. It can be said that this is a call to her, a runic message to the goddess.

Kenaz-Perthro-Ansuz-Kenaz. This is a formula of search. The search for one's own vulnerabilities. The search for one's mistletoe. She who has suffered from it more than others, she who has lost the most precious because of mistletoe, will be able to recognize it everywhere.

But mistletoe is not just a vulnerability. Mistletoe is a deceit that occurred because at some point you were careless, you showed false magnanimity, and probably even prided yourself on it. This is a mistake you are currently unable to correct simply because you cannot see it. The power of Goddess Frigg will help you see the impossible, illuminating locally the problem in the affected part of consciousness, which for you is good, which is your true rights granted by the Earth itself. And it will reveal who or what, not having such rights, is parasitizing on your original strength.

The rune combination Kenaz-Perthro can be translated as "final choice," and Ansuz-Kenaz as "truth." The revelation of the genuine truth.

While working on this channel and comprehending the full informational power of Goddess Frigg, strive not to forget for a single moment that she is the supreme ruler, that Frigg is the queen of the gods. Remember the guidance you received at the very beginning: to know a god, you must become one.

---

171 Author is unknown.

ᚹ ᚨ

PRACTICE 15

God Baldr

Baldr, as described in myth, embodies both youthful and wise aspects. When you connect with the power of God Baldr, he will reveal the aspect that you need most. Do you need to be young or wise to understand your good? If his mother, Goddess Frigg, has shown you your personal mistletoe, her beloved son, God Baldr, will reveal what true good is for you and what light means for all. If you can combine these two insights—the good of Baldr and the mistletoe of Frigg—and see how one is vulnerable to the other, you will have the chance to understand the vulnerability of the most precious thing you have and what needs to be done to ensure it can protect itself.

Baldr's formula

The formula[172] that can aid in such understanding is the formula leading to victory: Sowilo-Dagaz-Mannaz.

---

172 Author is unknown.

ᛊ ᛞ

This three-rune formula implies a definitive result. On a psychological level, it pulls the mind out of a stupor and helps begin to understand what is happening. The Mannaz rune in the formula indicates that this understanding is not spiritually abstract but points to quite concrete social matters. All the success algorithms acquired through experience (Sowilo), and the realization of one's personal values—this "good" is related specifically to you and cannot be lost or changed. Dagaz transforms this knowledge to the level of mental understanding, and the mind finally begins to recognize what is right and wrong, successful or leading to failure for you personally.

This formula can be confidently called "Insight." In this state, the vulnerabilities of the personality become visible, but at the same time, the energies of the god Loki (through the Dagaz rune) activate what is called the "spirit of contradiction"—the strength and passion to heal and correct these vulnerabilities. It's not about changing your personality to fit your weaknesses but changing it to fit your strengths.

In the real world of the living, there are things you are never ready to lose. Do you understand this? Baldr was so familiar, and his presence so natural for the gods, that no one, except the goddess Frigg, tried to protect, strengthen, and enhance him. Similarly, people often treat important things as natural, forgetting that the main and valuable things require the utmost care and protection. But mistletoe can grow at any moment, and it will be too late to fight it if protection is not provided in advance.

Let the legend of the god Baldr and his lessons not be in vain and, together with this formula, teach you not only to see what is dear and valuable that you have but also to protect, develop, and multiply it correctly.

This formula can be applied to a photograph or made into an amulet. The story of Baldr and the presence of your consciousness on his channel should give you an important commandment for the rest of your life: what does not remain, decreases. If something you have is dear to you, don't let the process take its course. Everything should develop along with external life processes. Protection is not isolation; protection is constant development and acquiring strength. Let the myth of the god Baldr teach you this.

Understanding yourself, on the channels of Baldr and Frigg, it is very important to clearly and distinctly determine for yourself: what is your true value that you need not only to protect but also to develop? What could be the mistletoe in relation to your most important value—what should it be protected from and strengthened for?

ᛊ ᛞ

PRACTICE 16

Goddess Hel

The channel of the goddess, the guardian of the world of the departed, is very complex and powerful. Being in it, one can undergo the same process of liberation available in her realm only to those who have already died. One can sever attachments, give something up for destruction or preservation. While comprehending the power of the goddess Hel's channel, it is crucial to understand the principles and rules on which this mechanism of liberation operates and what needs to be done to use this gift without dying first.

Practitioners traditionally engage in cleansings on the channel of the goddess Hel—in the world of Helheimr, anything can be buried. Helheimr, connected with the world of Chaos, processes everything unnecessary, dead, and outlived, transforming it into the energy of the primordial creation. When we perform energetic cleansings on this channel, there is a high probability they will be done quickly and irreversibly. However, this is not the case with informational or programmatic cleansings. Information cannot be turned into chaos; it has different sources of origin and, consequently, different storage places. Information can be given to Niflheimr, but by law, Niflheimr stores only global and primordial information, information that must always remain unchanged. Information related to a human problem is unlikely to be classified as global, which is why it has no place in Niflheimr. For this reason, when giving Hel something more serious than a malaise, when sending her a problem of an informational nature, you must remember

ᚹ ᚨ

that this is not forever. Hel will take what is given for safekeeping and will take a fee for storage, and as long as you are alive, you must remember that what is given will have to be retrieved (only the dead can count on final liberation, but the living cannot).

The information given can not only be preserved but also undergo certain transformations. For example, if we relinquish a program for shaping destiny, it can be checked for correctness and corrected if the ancients find a bug that prevents it from working effectively.

In Hel, a program resembling mistletoe, which distorts the natural experience of events, can also be given. Despite being a harmful virus-like program, it will still be returned to you after the storage period expires—Goddess Hel always honors the agreement, and Niflheimr is not a place for storing mistletoe-like problems. Additionally, it is not the goddess's role to free a person from their fate inscribed by the Norns, nor to correct the mistakes that led to the mistletoe. By taking the virus program, she provides an opportunity to take a break, grow stronger, and after the allotted time, re-enter the battle with one's imperfections, understanding that the mistletoe is not an enemy but a provocation, not a disease but a vaccine against it.

However, it is important to remember that Goddess Hel is an autonomous force with her own understanding of who can contact her and who cannot. She will not provide explanations in case of refusal or agreement. The responses of the mistress of the Hel worlds are simply "yes" or "no," and they are final and unchangeable. We know this already from the described story with Baldr—the gods were powerless.

Therefore, before working with the power of the goddess's channel, perform a diagnostic using runes: simply ask if the goddess agrees to help you. Then formulate the task—what exactly you would like to get rid of—a quality, a personal trait, a failure program, lack of money, a disease, or another affliction. Be prepared for the fact that the response from Goddess Hel will not include explanations, only either agreement or prohibition. If you want to know the reason for your problem (the true cause), it is better to use other diagnostic methods (such as the "Nine Worlds" spread or the "Speeches of the Aesir," with which you are already familiar). If Goddess Hel agrees to your request for help, it is recommended to immediately understand the conditions: for how long she agrees to take your problem (extract the harmful program from your consciousness) and what you will have to give in return for this service.

A witcher is paid with iron coin, but the goddess Hel has no need for money. She requires life energy for her charges — it is in short supply there. Therefore, offerings to the goddess are made with animal food, something alive, not chemical. What provides energy to the living will also provide energy to the dead. In the past, bloody sacrifices were made to honor the dead, believing that only blood could satiate the departed. Nowadays, this isn't done, but traditionally, offerings include products that have not been processed either thermally or chemically — raw meat, liver with blood, and strong (very strong) alcohol.

Offerings are usually left at the borders of the worlds — under a dry tree, near a cemetery, in a ravine — one must either listen to the signs or follow their own feelings. Places where there is a high likelihood of contact with the goddess Hel have a reputation as "bad places" among the people. People reasonably avoid them since the energy of such places is incompatible with the energy of life, falling outside the usual range of energetic existence for the living. Signs that may guide you can be different from social "gifts of the universe": a crow cawing, a black cat crossing your path, showing where to turn, a madman approaching and saying something prophetic — these are all signs of where your contact might occur, where to take the offerings. It's crucial to listen, understand, and obey — as the mistress of Helheimr does not repeat herself.

Immersing yourself in Hel's channel can awaken quite strange sensations in those encountering her power and very specific chaos energy for the first time. It is quite unusual to feel layer after layer of all energetic accretions being removed, as if peeling an onion. This state is similar to what you experienced when forming the rune Hagalaz in your consciousness — a rune of both destruction and limitation. The association with the rune is no coincidence: Hagalaz is the rune of Helheim, the key to it. The reason for this "undressing" feeling lies in Helheim's rules — to strip away all artificial masks to reveal the dark hidden within. When identifying a foreign program, this action, as you can understand, is mandatory — what needs to be sent to Hel, even temporarily, must first be revealed. This means that all factors preventing this must be excluded. However, the feeling of purity and freedom that follows is worth it.

Any cleansing you do will always follow this principle: first, the energy is cleansed, and only then the informational system of consciousness. Traditionally, getting rid of problems (cleansing and reprogramming) always follows this algorithm:

Step 1: Diagnostics.

Step 2: Energy cleansing.

Step 3: Identification of the problem (informational component of the program).

Step 4: Isolating the informational part and separating it from the entire system of consciousness.

Step 5: Fixing the problem in Hel.

Step 6: Introducing a new program.

ᛊ ᛞ

The vulnerable part that you leave in Hel's world is similar to all those "inhabitants" existing in that realm — they too are vulnerable. It will live and develop like Baldr and Höd in the world of the dead. While you grow stronger without it, it will be stored in the timeless world, your mistletoe. But when the storage period ends, the goddess Hel will open the gates of her world, and it will return to you. You will need to battle this program again, enter your personal Ragnarök, and win. Currently, you are losing to it, since you can't manage without help. Hel can assist by hiding it within her realm, freeing you temporarily. If you use this time to work and develop your consciousness instead of resting on your laurels, you will not only overcome this problem but also make it your ally, your weapon. At worst, you will kill this problem, but let it die by your hand. Otherwise, it will consume you, as Fenrir swallowed Odin, and kill you, as the mistletoe branch killed Baldr.

Hel, the mistress of the dead, teaches us that nothing is ever eternal, not even death. Unresolved problems must be faced again, unfinished tasks completed, mistakes corrected, debts repaid. The goddess Hel can only grant you a reprieve, but Loki's daughter will not rid anyone of their problem forever — neither gods, heroes, the living, nor the dead. She knows better than anyone how unfairly those who are denied a second chance are treated.

What you send to Hel will look you in the eyes in the hour of Ragnarök. Remember this before asking Hel for help. If she agrees to assist you, from that moment, you are on the path to gaining strength because your existence depends on it — remember this.

ᚹ ᚠ

ᛊ ᛞ

Hels' Formula: Hel's Seal

Hel's Seal[173] — a classic formula for breaking ties. It consists of two runes — Perthro and Isa, intertwined. This stave seems to "seal" the flow of fate, blocking its program, halting inevitability. Breaking ties means severing energy-informational connections with anything and anyone at any level. This ranges from breaking ties with physical objects (things, items), breaking emotional ties with people, to breaking connections with egregores, systems, cults, and ideas. This formula is specifically recommended for you to work with while mastering the power channel of the goddess Hel.

This formula is aptly named "Hel's Seal" because it truly represents her signature: it encapsulates everything mentioned above. The final decision. The cessation of the process. The termination of the connection. You can mentally apply this formula to an object with which you need to sever the connection, to stop giving or receiving anything through this connection. Mentally, in writing, with a ritual or without one — it works quickly. However, remember that if you use this formu-

173 Author is unknown.

la to sever something, be prepared for the fact that it won't revert back, and if you later wish to restore this connection, you will have to start from scratch, as if it never existed.

"Hel's Seal" does not cleanse. But it cuts off what might be causing you to continually cleanse yourself with poor results.

Using this formula to establish contact with the goddess requires a more thorough approach, and in this case, it is best to perform a lesser ritual, preferably without outsiders present. The seal can be applied to parchment (paper), made into an amulet, or applied to a candle — here you should listen to your intuition and do as it suggests, not according to canon (what canon in chaos?).

When the channel opens, you will unmistakably feel it. It is on this channel that you should conduct your diagnostics for the cleansings you personally need[174], it is on this channel that you should speak with the goddess about getting rid of problems, even if only temporarily. It is precisely on this channel that you can ask the goddess for advice, and you will be very fortunate if the mighty goddess Hel grants it to you.

174 For ethical reasons, the cleansing formulas are not specified in this section, as the algorithm for cleansing is always built individually. The only thing that can be provided are the general rules for diagnostics, which have been outlined.

ᛊ ᛞ

PRACTICE 17

The Norns

Working with the channel of the Norn goddesses transforms the programmatic structure of consciousness. Connecting with the goddesses of fate and unlocking the related runes of the three lower worlds of the Yggdrasil Tree—Jotunheimr, Niflheimr, and Svartalfheimr—can restore the original destiny program before foreign corrective programs intervened. Continuing with the computer analogy, this process is like restoring the original version or reverting to factory settings.

Living in a dense informational space with numerous personal and egregorial connections inevitably mutates one's destiny program, adapting it to the environment. This "natural correction" undoubtedly aids survival but does not always guarantee success. Beyond natural mutation, destiny may be forcibly altered by informational energy damages: various severances, filters in the consciousness, programs of action/inaction (commonly known as curses), self-destruction programs (curses), and rights restriction programs, among others. However, remember that the correction could have been beneficial from a different perspective, such as protective measures. But good and evil are subjective concepts, and any program correction (regardless of intent) can lead to either good or bad outcomes, depending on one's perspective.

ᚠ ᚨ

However, distortions in the original program can become so severe that they not only divert a person far from fulfilling their basic task but also from understanding it in principle. In such cases, contact with the Norn goddesses is not only favorable but necessary, as the original contract still must be fulfilled.

Contact with the goddess Hel in the previous practice helped cleanse the energy layer that fed a possibly distorted destiny program, blocking inner strength and understanding. If so, returning your informational framework to its original state can help not only correct the life program but also understand the causes of past problems and the purpose of your existence in this reality.

Working with the Norns restores your destiny program to its original design. Personal achievements and mistakes remain, but if the foundation is unaltered, the personal thread will weave correctly into the overall pattern of reality. In this way, even the vulnerability of human consciousness can stop being a source of distortion, turning into a unique feature when perceived as such.

Working with the Norn goddesses primarily involves **diagnostics—gaining information. This is done through a simple three-rune spread: past, present, future**. However, the Norns' informational power penetrating the practitioner's consciousness allows you to understand this spread much more deeply, seeing it as a chain of cause and effect rather than a set of individual magical symbols. One event leads to another because of what preceded it, showing that nothing else could have arisen in that situation.

On the Norn channel, magical work often involves informational cleansing as a method of correcting the life program. Here, the goddess Urd unveils the life program, making it visible. The goddess Verdandi, wielding the rune Isa, compares this program with your standard, matching it with orlog—the destiny and strength of your ancestral god, which the Norns, unlike humans, can see immediately. The goddess Skuld removes the threads that distort the overall fabric of reality through your presence, severing informational connections that cause your time to be spent weaving a pattern that has nothing to do with you or your god. The Norns restore such justice, where justice means correctness.

Rest assured that if an intervention has distorted your destiny program, intentionally or unintentionally, you will find help and support from the Norns and other gods. A distortion in one person's wyrd inevitably affects the orlog of their god and, consequently, all gods of the pantheon. Therefore, everyone is interested in restoring justice as correctness.

If, on this channel, the Norns' power suggests a specific informational cleansing, they will likely lead you to the appropriate formulas for your case. This is typically how it always happens.

It's worth noting that the term "offering gifts" is not quite appropriate for the Norn goddesses. Understanding their nature and the experience of many practitioners shows that this term and the ritual it implies are poorly received by the mechanism that regulates universal processes, which operates more with the terms "correctness" and "justice." Therefore, it is more accurate to use the term "payment" when discussing compensation for informational correction of one thread in the overall fabric of reality. It's likely that the payment will be taken not from you but from the source of the problem, which distorts not only your personal wyrd but also the orlog of the gods. Thus, any gifts you might want to offer will simply go unnoticed—the goddesses of fate have a different understanding of right and wrong. However, if you bear any responsibility for the distortion (such as silent or cowardly consent made at some point), the Norns will quickly unpack this moment and take payment from you as well: according to the ancient law of justice, everyone must pay for themselves, but only for their own. The payment might involve a one-time or regular action, taking on a special geis, or something else that will correct the identified weakness in your personal mental strength.

Listen to the Norns, heed the signs.

ᛊ ᛞ

PRACTICE 18

God Mimir

Channeling the informational power of the god Mimir through your consciousness will allow you to feel like Odin, who "converses with Mimir's head." Mimir's power is the power of reason. It is the ability to understand one's memory and "sort" it correctly, separating the necessary from the unnecessary. Remembering that Mimir, in his current symbolism, is a head without a body, the effect of contact with this god will enable you to judge your past without personal attachment to it, allowing you to view your mind from an external perspective. This perspective helps to see all information in the consciousness not as tied to anything specific, but as simply forming a picture of the world. Like a construction set, from which anything can be assembled, not just the specific or what is suggested in the instructions.

All memory and experience, personal and others, have the right to be used, but only when the creator has no preferences. Mimir is understanding without flaws.

The formula that can be used to connect to the power of Mimir's channel is the attached stave, which practitioners have consistently named "Brain Cleanse[175]." It can confidently be called Mimir's seal, as it encrypts not only the god's name but also the function he carries.

---

175 Author — Master Vinany.

Mimir's Formula: Brain Cleanse

The stave consists of the runes Mannaz and Ansuz, which, when connected, generate the runes Thurisaz, Raidho, and Tiwaz. This stave "re-solders" the connections in the mental body "correctly," with Thurisaz breaking those that contradict truth, past knowledge, common sense, and/or elementary logic. Tiwaz activates the mechanism of recognizing true/false, and Raidho builds new logical connections. Mannaz symbolizes the mental body, and Ansuz represents the informational channel of communication with Mimir.

This stave can be used continuously, functioning as "Odin's Eye," or used once for a 3-9 day cleanse-transformation, akin to "drinking from Mimir's well." Here you can observe not only the process of changing the worldview but also another important aspect of your consciousness. And here it is.

As mentioned earlier, working with Mimir's channel will be similar to the connection between Mimir and Odin. Odin gave a part of himself to establish this constant connection, and you, during your work with this channel, will also transfer to Mimir something through which you will maintain contact with this god, if not permanently like Allfather, then at least for the duration of the work. And it's not an eye, so there's no need to be frightened in advance. It will be a strong part of your sensory abilities, which, during the contact, will not disappear or diminish but rather manifest strongly. Mimir will indicate this sensory part even if you do not know or are unsure of your strong point: since the natural is usually not considered phenomenal by a person. But Mimir, devoid of a living body but sensing yours, will do this unmistakably—his wisdom of recognition has no preferences, it sees the strongest and will point it out to you. For Odin, this strongest quality was all-seeing, but what is the strongest for you?

When Mimir takes part of this quality, he, on one hand, uses the already developed and habitual mechanism of forming a worldview, but on the other hand, allows you to see other sensory channels as functional and quite worthy of use. This method of interacting with the informational power of Mimir will help remove corrective filters from the mental body of consciousness, which are designed to block certain types of information, fearing for the stability and possibly immutability of a certain worldview. The extracted quality during interaction with Mimir is not a payment but a deposit. And it will certainly be returned, but this "extraction" is valuable because only in this altered state can one see and understand what was previously inaccessible to understanding.

The three channels you have successively explored now outline a very harmonious scheme for working with your consciousness:

Goddess Hel cleanses the energy of the living on clear and open terms; unburdening the subconscious from blocks and excessive tension, gaining freedom of action—at least for a while.

The Norns restore the informational layers of the superconscious to their original state, aligning them with the prescribed wyrd, bringing it in line with the correct design of orlog. This synchronizes your personal fate with the fate of the god whose small projection you are, which, in turn, will inevitably bring you closer to each other, uniting the small with the large.

God Mimir is the final step in the initiated transformation. He will cleanse the mental body, preliminarily isolating it from the influence of both the subconscious and the superconscious. If we use the analogy of the mental body and system computer processes, the connection with Mimir is a revision of all memory without the influence of life's processes, excitation and inhibition processes, personal evaluation, and personal preferences. Life goes on, but the worldview in the moment of alignment with Mimir's channel remains unaffected.

A worldview that has passed through Mimir's channel will be able not only to correctly unpack information coming from the gods and forces but also, importantly, to return the same accurate and undistorted information about what is happening in Midgard to the gods and forces.

PRACTICE 19

God Kvasir

In our further journey along the path of magical self-transformation, the channel of the god Kvasir is a milestone that must be passed. Kvasir in this context for the world of humans is an archetype of the ideal consciousness, in which the gods intended to fully and consistently combine all the capabilities of the gods of nature and all the strongest aspects of the gods of reason. Just as there were no winners or losers in the war between the Aesir and the Vanir, so in a human, by design, there should be no winner in the clash between nature and reason. Conducting your consciousness through the channel of the ideal program, you are as if testing it for compliance. The principle of such determination of compliance or non-compliance, the criterion of assessment, and the measurement scale are described in the myth of the god Kvasir, particularly in the part that speaks of his death. The cause of the failure of the ideal program was the same as the cause of Baldr's death—the inability to learn, the inability to gain other life experiences, but only to impose one's own. In Baldr's case, it was an impossibility, whereas, for the wise Kvasir, it was an inability. Baldr was intentionally shielded from impressions and knowledge, while Kvasir was simply "designed that way."

On the channel of the god Kvasir, all that is from the Vanir and all that is from the Aesir; everything that is in you now and already manifested, should unite. When united, they should achieve balance relative to each other, but only to the extent that both forces are available in your mind at the same time. But the wisdom created by Kvasir was enriched in his personal history with another piece of knowledge he gained by going through death—the importance of correctly manifesting oneself. This will be the lesson on the channel of the wise man Kvasir.

Maintaining balance between the nature of the Aesir and the Vanir can only be done through the correct application of these to reality. Understanding and mastery of this application come only with practice and experience.

The story of Kvasir teaches that if you come for experience and knowledge to take it, learn to be silent and listen. If you come to give experience and knowledge, learn to speak. If you do not know what the world needs from you, enter a state of balance and listen to reality—it will tell you what this home needs. But always remember that everything said in words must be confirmed by deeds. The reverse is also true: listening to words, make sure they find their reflection in reality, that the manifestation of these words and this experience truly exists and you can see it.

The power and wisdom of the god Kvasir will teach you not only to properly manifest yourself but also to see in the surrounding world what perhaps the master-dwarves Fjalar and Galar could see: when and who around you behaves just like the unfortunate Kvasir in Svartalfheimr; who gives out wisdom not backed by personal experience and knowledge; who teaches without learning; who believes without knowing; when the strongest thing in a person becomes his blood, and there is no person himself in the formed personality.

Wisdom must be compensated by proper behavior, then it will never be lost or diminished to today's needs of the environment. The state of the ideal program of consciousness will not leave you when transitioning to another informational channel if you can properly manage it and manifest it three times.

Consider that behind your back, never leaving, stand the masters Fjalar and Galar, and they see everything.

The ideal program will be able to manifest itself without dying beforehand if it gets rid of the vulnerability identified (and brutally eliminated) by the master-dwarves: the absence of measure and the lack of discernment of whom to give and whom not to give.

Therefore, the formula suggested for such recognition on the channel of the god Kvasir will try to test your already purified consciousness and, if needed, make a correction of the program through five algorithms of wisdom for spreading oneself in the world:

- What is needed.
- When it is needed.
- To whom it is needed.
- How much is needed.
- Where it is needed.

These are the rules for preserving, multiplying, and manifesting any talent, any ability, any genius (especially genius!). These are the rules for manifesting a gift—any gift, but especially a magical one.

Stave "Veda"[176]

---

[176] Author — Master Velya.

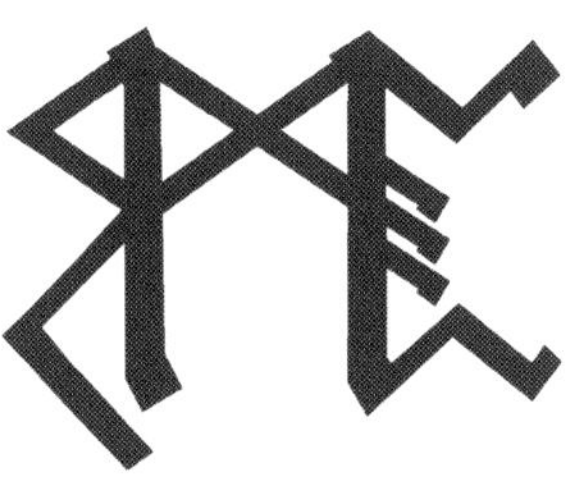

Kvasir's Formula: Veda

This stave consists of the following runes and combinations:

Mannaz + Perthro — this combination signifies a certain rebirth of the personality, the social persona. These linked runes unlock the mind and provide a larger operational volume for working with information. There must be predetermined free space in the consciousness to receive, but at the same time, nothing should prevent the information from being given away — everything as needed, which sometimes changes quickly.

Inside the Perthro rune, the Ansuz rune is inscribed. The combination of **Mannaz + Ansuz** symbolizes a confident shift in the assemblage point (AP), forming a new "format" of personality instantaneously. It helps always to stay on the same level of perception with the interlocutor, "viewing reality from the same branch of the universe." The Laguz rune included there enhances foresight and intuition. Additionally, the Nauthiz rune appearing in the background symbolizes necessity — the information coming to you is indeed needed, and the information leaving you is also necessary and sufficient for the state of correctness of what is happening.

On the opposite side of the Mannaz rune are the linked runes **Sowilo and Kenaz**. Sowilo nourishes the consciousness with algorithms of correctness, while Kenaz highlights what needs to be seen necessarily. Thus, the Mannaz rune represents a balanced consciousness, the ideal program of Kvasir, where on one side is the knowledge of what is right (good), and on the other side is the situation that needs to be balanced: to give or take something.

A side effect of using this stave may be the uncovering or greater manifestation of certain empathic or extrasensory abilities if your nature, your Vanir-Aesir connection, predisposes such abilities.

It is best to make this bindrune into an amulet and wear it constantly, at least while you are working on the channel of the god Kvasir. However, even on other days, when you need to behave correctly in unfamiliar society, this amulet may also come in handy. However, I hope that after three provocations by the dwarves on this channel, this ability will integrate into you as a stable algorithm for recognizing the environment.

Any gift, if innate, can lead to glory or to death. Therefore, those who have the "seed of genius" from birth should be especially attentive to the environment, the society they enter, and the people they interact with and live around.

If the god Mimir taught understanding, the god Kvasir can teach how to maintain balance between what is understood and what is necessary, teaching to feel the mechanism of equilibrium between what is taken and given, teaching to infallibly determine the possible area of application of what is understood. So that the inner genius can not only manifest but

ᛊ ᛞ

also not kill its bearer, you need to learn to work with this gift. Feel and understand your inner genius, but outwardly manifest not it, but the talent that will be acceptable to others. This is the quality of correctly transforming one force into another, without losing the properties of the first. This is indispensable for any poet, as our ancient ancestors believed: one must speak in a way that what is said is fully assimilated by the listener. The form of expression can be taught by the god of poetry Bragi, whom you will meet next. The god Kvasir can teach the essence of expression, and together they can teach to choose such a form that the essence is revealed but not distorted. Not how to say it, but what to say, to whom to say, at what time to say, in what place and under what circumstances to say, and whether it is worth saying at all if all the indicated threads do not converge at a single point of necessity. Kvasir is this point of necessity, and as everyone knows, any being, even a god, can only teach what he is himself—and nothing more.

ᚹ ᚨ

ᛊ ᛞ

PRACTICE 20

God Bragi

The gift of poetry almost never passes down through inheritance; it is always a gift from the gods. God Kvasir, embodying genius, was vulnerable, as any genius is in the external world—he does not see boundaries, violates others, changes the world without asking. The power of God Bragi considers these features of any talent and specifies them for those who manifest the gods' gift through words—it is important to know how to "sit in the middle of the bench," to have different relationships with loved ones, and to be resilient to the system's provocations.

What is needed. When it is needed. To whom it is needed. How much is needed. Where it is needed.

A poet must be free. He is a troubadour and a minstrel, a tumbleweed, and his task is to wander through the worlds, always feeling: where to take information and where to give it, when to be silent and when to speak, knowing how to say and to whom. While on the channel of God Bragi, it is difficult to expect that the gift of poetry will awaken, especially if it has not manifested before. But here, one can learn to handle words; one can feel how words can change reality and see how it happens. One can see the deep connection between words and the world, accessible to those on the path of magical transformation of themselves.

ᚹ ᚨ

ᛊ ᛞ

Skaldic poetry is a new form of beauty that appeared thanks to God Bragi and the "mead of poetry." Here is what is said about it in the Prose Edda:

The Signs of Poetry

Then said Aeger: In how many ways to you vary the poetical expressions, or how many kinds of poetry are there? Answered Brage: There are two kinds, and all poetry falls into one or the other of these classes. Aeger asks: Which two? Brage answers: Diction and meter. What diction is used in poetry? There are three sorts of poetic diction. Which? One is to name everything by its own name; another is to name it with a pronoun, but the third sort of diction is called kenning (a poetical periphrasis or descriptive name); and this sort is so managed that when we name Odin, or Thor or Tyr, or any other of the asas or elves, we add to their name a reference to some other asa, or we make mention of some of his works. Then the appellation belongs to him who corresponds to the whole phrase, and not to him who was actually named. Thus we speak of Odin as Sigtyr, Hangatyr or Farmatyr, and such names we call simple appellatives. In the same manner he is called Reidartyr.

The ability to weave words well, to feel the architecture of a phrase, is not innate but acquired. This gift is like the mead of poetry—it comes in adulthood based on much knowledge and experience. To write well, one needs to read a lot. To love words, one needs to understand them and always see for whom they are intended.

ᚹ ᚨ

Bragi's Formula: Bragi's Staff

The stave called "Bragi's Staff"[177] can also be considered his personal seal. The stave consists of two linked runes Ansuz and Kenaz, with the secondary rune being Naud. It is usually made as an amulet and worn constantly. This stave reveals the possibilities of the intellect. It develops the ability to listen to and speak words. However, on the channel of God Bragi, this ability will not be detached from reality, not a gift existing on its own, but applied correctly: what is needed, when it is needed, to whom it is needed, how much is needed, where it is needed.

The stave will help develop eloquence and add persuasiveness to words. Here, the rune Kenaz will highlight with attention what needs to be reflected; the information void that now needs to be filled with words. The rune Ansuz will gather the necessary current of knowledge that is appropriate or desirable in this direction. Naud will connect these runes with the principle of necessity.

---

[177] Author — Master Zigwult.

ᛊ ᛞ

PRACTICE 21

God Höd

On the channel of the god Höd, we typically work with what we lacked the strength to handle in previous steps of transformation. Here, his ability to multiply intention-action many times over comes into play, making what was previously inaccessible now available.

However, it is always important to remember that strength has two sides, where it is a benefit somewhere, it can be harmful elsewhere. To avoid becoming artificially blind, you should not wait for the effects of evil to manifest themselves "suddenly"; instead, turn to them and face them honestly and personally. Here, the work you began on the channel of the goddess Frigg will be useful, specifically — recognizing your mistletoe. This knowledge, combined with the strength of the blind Höd, will help you identify your personal mistletoe, acknowledging its threat; it will help you see it not as a weak sprout but in the full potential of the damage it can cause to your consciousness. A foolish warrior tries to see only the enemy's weaknesses while closing their eyes to their strength. The power of the god of darkness, blind Höd, if the warrior is brave and honest, will allow him to see his personal mistletoe in all its potential threatening possibilities for personal consciousness. It will seem as if this quality-mistletoe is magnified tenfold, becoming clearly and imminently threatening. This way, you will not overlook this vulnerability of yours or turn a blind eye to it. In the darkness of the blind, there is no possibility of comparison

ᚹ ᚨ

— light is needed for comparison. In darkness, everything is equal, equally unseen, and therefore equally dangerous.

In the currents of Höd's channel, within the force of blind primordial darkness, your own consciousness may present itself to you from a completely different perspective. It can show you the power of your own darkness, the strength of ancient memory not cloaked in any traditional garb. It will allow you to delve into depths you previously couldn't fathom. Now, with a cleansed and balanced consciousness from previous channels, darkness will appear before you as an opportunity to understand what was previously unthinkable as an object of knowledge. But it is precisely now that you need to engage in this process because if there is no balance between your own light and your own darkness, Ragnarök in a single consciousness becomes inevitable, and free creation of your magical destiny becomes impossible.

Only those who walk this path, those who not only recognize their inner darkness but also simply acknowledge its existence, begin to understand what specific light they personally need. Not a universal light for everyone, but precisely for themselves — for their own darkness. Knowing your Höd, you begin to know your Baldr better — how he should be, what needs to be learned, and what to strive for. The value of light is understood when there is darkness requiring manifestation; otherwise, the light only warms but does not teach or reveal. You can realize all your strength, your hidden magic, provided that the light is necessary and sufficient. Necessary and sufficient.

If Höd has his own seal, his own runic formula, it is hidden in darkness. And perhaps, it will manifest uniquely for each individual. I sincerely wish you to see it on the channel of the blind god — with your non-human vision.

It consists of the rune Inguz and four runes Ehwaz. The rune Inguz, stylized in the form of a diamond with a dot inside[179], symbolizes you as a living system, and the dot represents your goal, your inner intention, which, like a spark, leads you through life and gives meaning to everything that happens. The four runes Ehwaz around the rune Inguz symbolize the eight legs of Sleipnir, which can travel between worlds and carry the mind of its rider beyond the bounds of the probable.

The initiating power of this stave can only be what the god Hermod described in his myth—trust and love. Trust in the runes, trust in magic, and love for your dream. Unconditional love, without reservations or limitations.

This stave is designed for journeys between worlds. However, it is not limited to (or primarily about) traveling between the realms of Yggdrasil but also between realities and probabilities created by the breath of the Tree of Nine Worlds. These realities may initially seem only slightly different from one another, but this slight difference can turn the course of your personal probability in a completely different direction. The stave of magic, when applied, momentarily disables the inertia of the given reality, but this moment is often more than enough for the engine of your personal system to switch to the energy of love and change direction on the power of trust. Any of the many worlds becomes accessible to you, just as they are to Hermod and your companion Sleipnir if you can generate such an impulse of burning inner desire as contained in the original ancient form

---

179 This depiction of the Inguz rune is very ancient, one could say pre-runic. The diamond or circle represents the earth, and the dot inside symbolizes fire. This is the symbol of life, specifically "self-arising" life, the very principle of life as the primary creation.

of the Inguz rune—an impulse of inner creation, a dream stronger than pragmatism.

You can write the formula on a piece of paper (clean parchment, a symbol of an unborn universe) and, while drawing it, say: *"Carry me, my steed, eight-legged Sleipnir, through time, worlds, and spaces, to my goal. My goal is ..."*.[180] The shorter the continuation of the spell, the more precise the coordinates of the place of connection with your dream will be defined. Any reservation and condition "without harm" are shackles on the legs of the magical horse Sleipnir, fetters on the mind of his mother Loki. But there is another requirement. Sleipnir does not belong to you; he is Odin's horse. Therefore, rules dictate that before using the transfer formula, you must obtain Odin's prior consent, and this is crucial.

This stave works well in dreams when the criticality of consciousness is minimal. Therefore, you can place the inscribed stave under your pillow. However, to feel it fully, to recognize the winds of other worlds among the heap of smells and sensations, perform the first connection with this stave through a lesser ritual; visualize your dream in detail while looking at the point inside the Inguz rune — it is essential to concentrate the primary impulse of the strongest desire in yourself as much as possible, compressing the urge for the impossible into a single moment of being. Then, like a compressed spring, it will carry your consciousness along the shortest path to the reality of your true dream.

The activation of the formula is very individual — here too, the power of trusting yourself will help. Perhaps it should be activated by fire, or maybe stored in a secret place for a long

---

180 This wording is the recommendation of the author of the stave.

time; perhaps the formula will ask to be inscribed on the body and then washed off with water; maybe drawn mentally in the air and dissolve into it, invisibly but permanently changing the flow of your personal wind of change. All this is very individual and based only on your urge and love for the world and reality, without which nothing has any meaning, just as for Hermod nothing had meaning without the love of his mother.

The entire list of the impossible, which you wisely compiled at the beginning of the practice, becomes real if you connect with these forces — love and trust. This will help you understand and achieve results with the assistance of the god Hermod and the amazing Sleipnir. Driven by a wild desire for love-connection and the necessity to trust and be accepted in trust, this powerful engine can transport the seeker's consciousness anywhere, and god Hermod can connect the unconnectable with the power of this transfer. Trust is crucial. This ensures that the miracle does not collide with the wall of "common sense": *thinking that something can't be real.*

Since this stave is entirely magical, keep in mind that some effects may arise that will appear somewhat strange in ordinary reality. For instance, memories of certain events might change. Or you may begin to notice elements in the external world that previously did not exist for you (and if you mention this aloud, those around you will look at you with astonishment because these "new" elements will be new only to you, while for them, living in the reality you just arrived at, these elements have always existed). These effects are the most common when using this stave, and all travelers describe them, so be prepared for such astonishment. The same applies to memories: in the probability line to which Sleipnir transports you, something happened or was recorded as having happened differently. Here, more than ever, the moment of trust is crucial, so that the strength of your desire to live in your dream is not weaker than the force of sticking to the previous "loaded version" of the world—otherwise, you may easily be pulled back, and everything that happened will be perceived as a mirage or the echoes of a murky dream.

Trust and love are the foundations of magic. So desired and so impossible. Let god Hermod teach you to love the incredible more than the probable. Thank magic with your trust in it.

ᛊ ᛞ

PRACTICE 23

God Vali

God Váli's story will help you realize that a person can not only be perceived but also become more than just a one-time function created by the Norns for something specific. One must step beyond the limits of destiny, overcome grievances and experiences of past defeats. To see the reality of the future not from the position of a victim of global injustice, but from the perspective of someone who knows what injustice is and knows what it means to be a victim of others' violence.

You can view the world from various angles. You can see it from the position of the unjustly wronged, and then your fate is to be forever unjustly wronged. Or you can view it from the position of a fighter against injustice, but for this, you must know exactly what injustice is and see how it typically manifests in our world of reflections, in Midgard. Understanding that human consciousness is a program can be approached in different ways. You can fulfill your program and end your existence. You can resent the whole world and refuse to fulfill it out of principle. You can deny yourself as a program, or you can accept it. Or you can do as Váli did: not deny, but understand, fulfill, and change everything. This is the highest skill of the spirit that Váli shows us: his final appearance in the myth as a survivor says a lot—he managed to do what the fathers could not, and therefore did not perish in the battle of the gods.

To transform from a one-time program executing someone else's will into a reusable and constantly acting force of a new future reality, not perceiving this reality as an inevitable

ᚹ ᚨ

given but creating it, you need, on one hand, to connect with other building forces, and on the other hand, to be able to cut yourself off from realities that have nothing to do with yours. Those who make you a victim pull you into their reality into a game position that does not imply freedom of action. In such a case, your function is no longer the role of a player, but the role of a character in the game.

Váli managed to become a god of creation by recognizing the right of other gods to be gods of creation, and in this agreement, his ability to instantly detect system imbalance became an important part of execution, serving everyone but subordinating to no one.

The process of understanding the gods-builders of the new world begins with Váli because Baldr and Höd will enter this new reality system only when everything is formed. Váli and his kin are now starting to lay down new algorithms for building realities, linking them differently than Týr, Odin, Loki, Heimdall, Thor, and all the old gods did. Váli steps in first—to introduce the principle of achieving balance—instantly cutting off the unnecessary—cutting down the mistletoe, killing what exists without a pair, without a connection; closing access to those worlds that cannot interact with the new world on the principle of equality, but only on the principle of absorption—temporarily, until the wild realities go through their path of development and formation, and their presence ceases to be a threat to the balance of worlds.

In connection with what has been said about the channel of the god Váli, you can use the stave "The Axe of Death".[181]

---

[181] Author is unknown.

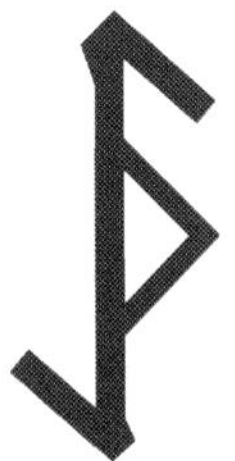

Vali's Formula: The Axe of Death

This stave consists of two runes — Eihwaz and Thurisaz. Instant severance, a swift blow. It is the breaking of connections, particularly those that support illusions. The principles of constructing reality dictate that everything must be balanced. If something disrupts the balance of personal reality, it must be eliminated. Vali's power quickly and immediately detects the disrupted balance, and the " The Axe of Death," like a sword in the god's hand, severs this illusory connection.

This stave is sometimes called "Anti-Morok," which is a very precise name: to see an illusion, you need to stop feeding it, primarily with your emotions. Eihwaz in this stave accurately determines the "evil" — what should not be present in your consciousness or life, and Thurisaz instantly cuts the energy-draining channel feeding this illusion. Realization of it can only come after the feeding connection is severed.

The use of this stave must, of course, be coordinated with the god himself and include divination to determine its necessity. The same rule applies to the method of its application for the best effect: on a photograph or poppet for long-term work, on oneself to sever physical and emotional ties, on a phantom or space to cut off spatial or temporal channels forming an illusion.

Those who realize themselves as avatars of the god Váli carry the "Axe of Death" within their consciousness from birth until the very end. This is a personality trait, a characteristic, and a life mission. Those who recognize this on the channel of the god Váli will see the projection of the myth about this god in their birth, destiny, and character, who was able to transform hatred into a weapon that is always within.

PRACTICE 24

God Vidar

After all that your consciousness has been through, and after severing the last connections with the help of God Vali, the power of God Vidar should logically lead you to naturalness. For this purpose, you can use the following very harmonious formula called "Initiation"[182].

Vidar's Formula: Initiation

This formula consists of the runes Thurisaz and Laguz, with secondary runes Ansuz and Eihwaz. Combined into a triangular form, the runes symbolize belonging to the familiar three-dimensional space, indicating their natural application to this physical projection and to you as a part of this projection. Here, all internal fears will manifest and be cut off in the process

182 Author — Master Espe.

of rotation on Laguz, and the sword of retribution will be directed at internal problems, not the external world. Ansuz will bring awareness, and the stable structure of the triangle and rotation on the flow will lead you to the one correct action necessary to manifest personal naturalness—the only one that requires deeds, not words.

Using this formula will lead you to a silent realization of the correct ritual action that is your natural form of good and an absolute tool of personal victory. This action is as ritualistic as the ancient ancestors offering a piece of leather for Vidar's shoe—how else could it be? This formula not only manifests but also partially cleanses internal flaws that may still remain in the consciousness but should not.

This stave can be applied to oneself, made into a talisman, or reflected on a photograph. Just do everything silently, showing respect to the silent Aesir Vidar.

Vidar's shoe can be sewn in different ways. You will also have your own ritual action. This is not a geis; it is more than a geis. It is naturalness, and it cannot be universal, but only yours. The silent Aesir hints that this action should be performed silently, understanding its correctness deeply but not explaining its meaning to all who wish to know. If the action requires commentary, and you provide it, it will no longer be the same. You cannot teach this action to your children, nor can you pass on its correctness as a tradition—it must be unique to each living person because each has their own strength and god. This action will not violate anyone's rights and freedoms, nor will it diminish your own. Those who understand and feel this will never impose their rituals on others and especially not on their children. Only those who have lost or never had a connection with their gods would attempt to establish a connection on borrowed energy and time resources.

God Vali, by cutting away the unnecessary, has also removed the slave collar if it was still there, and the other gods have eliminated the prerequisites for its appearance. Now nothing will prevent you from becoming naturally true and making this naturalness the norm. The action that signifies the acceptance of dedication is the acceptance of this norm and its establishment as a foundation in your consciousness.

Working on Vidar's channel is a test of honesty with yourself.

ᛊ ᛞ

PRACTICE 25

God Ullr

A great hacker can find a vulnerability in a system where no one else can—his function is unique and unparalleled. But Ullr is not only a great hacker; he is also a great programmer. After Ragnarök, he will build the new world alongside his distant and close kin. Here, the algorithm is the reverse of that of the forefathers: the older generation of creator gods acted on the principle of "task-solution." There is a task, and algorithms are selected for it. The necessary elements are introduced into the system, and the unnecessary ones are discarded. As we already know from the whole line of the narrative, a lot had to be discarded, and the world of Hel was overflowing.

The children act differently. They take everything that exists, discarding nothing and denying nothing. They lay the foundation on a completely different principle of existence, connecting everything with everything in such a way that everything finds its place and forms a holistic individuality. Such individuality will not depend on the system, and any connection is possible only by desire—mutual desire. There will be no place for violence and lies, no place for the parasitism of mistletoe. This is the work that Ullr will engage in—connecting everything with everything on the honest principle of individual manifestation. He is the only one who walked this path from a shaggy and seemingly useless being to the greatest god who, as

ᚹ ᚠ

ᛊ ᛞ

myths hint, even "replaced" Odin on the throne of power when he was condemned for violence against the goddess Rind[183].

The channel of God Ullr is very complex and completely unambiguous. Ullr is the classic embodiment of individuality, and consequently, in contact with each human consciousness, he manifests himself just as individually—to the point of complete disregard.

Entering the flow of Ullr's channel, we do so in the hope that reprogramming your consciousness now will seem like an interesting challenge to him. So that everything internal and external finds its place—after all, everything that hindered you, you have already removed yourself. Therefore, by this time, everything that is in your consciousness is needed by you—this is assumed, at least. And if Ullr takes you on, it's your luck.

Help yourself with the "Gaining Knowledge"[184] stave. It may not be very harmonious, but in a sense, it pays homage to Ullr—neglecting beauty and harmony for the sake of truthful results.

This stave can also be safely called a "lockpick" because this is the function it performs: to get on any channel—even if you were not invited to it. A purely hacker trick: "knock-knock, Neo." This stave can also be called "Ullr's Seal," and its activation kind of invites the god to solve a complex or simply interesting problem, which your consciousness currently embodies.

183 See the chapter about the God Vali

184 Author – Master Sam.

ᚹ ᚫ

Ullr's Formula: Gaining Knowledge

Many useful runes can be seen in this stave, but I want to highlight the functions of the following. The multiple Kenaz runes illuminate the area of application of the stave—your consciousness. They illuminate not only (and not so much) for you but for Ullr himself. It's as if saying: "Ullr, look at me." The Laguz runes symbolize the process—they represent the channel as a current. They also help to dose the volume of information so that the mind has time not only to accept the changes but also to comprehend them. The Gebo runes work as a re-coder, translating the program information into the understandable language of the Midgard mental realm. The Uruz runes help manifest the new system—Ullr's changes and reprogramming have an immediate visible effect. Eihwaz activates inner strength and simultaneously tests your readiness to accept Ullr's new program and to what extent to accept it.

This stave can be described as a test—are you truly ready to align with your desires? Understanding which reality suits such a level of desires will be aided by the god Forseti, whom you will meet later. But now, it is crucial to understand what you really need. The young gods and architects of the new reality first ask "what?", then "how?" and "where?". Not the other way around.

May the remarkable god Ullr show you that it is not necessary to die to be reborn as someone else. I sincerely wish you this.

PRACTICE 26

God Forseti

Connecting with the channel of God Forseti should logically continue from the work done on the channels of Hermod, Vidar, Vali, and Ullr. The mechanism of God Forseti should not only explain what your consciousness represents now but also what kind of reality will be built around such consciousness. All the rules, absolutely all of them, should be clear, transparent, and formed in the language you think in, without any Talmudic casuistry, Byzantine deceit, Zoroastrian dualism, or other Abrahamic intransigence.

Your consciousness is your reality, solely yours, with all its possibilities and impossibilities. This is what exists now, but the program of the young gods is written so that any changes in the inner world must manifest in the outer world, and this is also encrypted in "Forseti's Seal":

Forseti's Formula: Forseti's Seal. Connection to the God

"Forseti's Seal"[185] consists of two Mannaz runes superimposed on each other. Not placed side by side, not artificially connected by an additional rune, but one within the other. The social personality and the social reality. Contact, interaction. When superimposed on each other, they form a figure in which the harmony of interaction is inscribed—runes Inguz, Gebo, Ansuz, Fehu. Here we can also see Thurisaz, but turned inward, as determination and intention directed at oneself, not from oneself. The more and longer you look at this stave, the more you will begin to understand what harmonious interaction is. And the stave responds to you: the main thing in me is that each Mannaz remains a Mannaz. All changes will be in those runes that you see: the changes you see and accept will be the ones that occur. The most important thing is that any individuality in contact or connection with another individuality can change as much as it wants but remains an individuality. Always.

The use of this seal is a request to explain in detail who you are, in a comprehensible language; it is a request to provide the rules by which your reality exists—what is accessible to it and what is not, what will be in it and what will not.

Remember that Forseti is the god of justice and renders truly fair decisions: they must support your individuality, creating a personal reality, but at the same time, neither it nor you can infringe on anyone else's right to have their individuality and live by it, independently of you. Everyone must have the opportunity not only to be independent but also to bear clear responsibility for this independence—before the world.

---

185 Author – Master Forseti

Help God Forseti to formulate in clear words the law of the future reality—your reality. The justice of the new world is not the one that a person agrees with only because there is no other. It is the justice that he agrees with deeply. The power of God Forseti knows this depth—for he inherited the purity of perception from his parents Baldr and Nanna, which means nothing will prevent him from finding the same purity within you. This purity is your personal concept of justice. It is from this center that reality will be built for you.

NB! The purity will be clear to both you and Forseti if you have already gone through the entire path of awareness and purification, consistently moving through the algorithm of transitioning through the channels of the gods and have now reached Forseti. If not, then the application of "Forseti's Seal" will reveal you precisely, but will it be true purity? Therefore, use "Forseti's Seal" when you are ready to know the truth, not just guess at it.

ᛊ ᛞ

PRACTICE 27

Goddess Skadi

Every channel of a Norse god provides skilled practitioners with opportunities that are hard to access on any other channel. The channel of the goddess Skadi is no exception to this rule. However, its specificity is such that the presence of the power of the goddess Skadi in the mind will be detrimental and destructive to anyone who enters the channel with an unprepared mind. Therefore, even though the story of the goddess itself is not a logical continuation of the line of new gods-builders, but rather pertains to the gods before Ragnarök, contact with her is recommended only after passing through the path of Hermod-Vali-Vidar-Ullr-Forseti and the entire correction of the inner generator of future reality has taken place. Skadi now acts in the process of magical transformation as an incorruptible examiner, as harsh as the northern winter.

Goddess Skadi is the one who, following the algorithm, tests its strength. Inside, she is not what she seems. Her power will turn the core inside out, and what was inside will be outside, and vice versa. Although she formally acts only by traditional methods, she composes her testing algorithms in such a way that the result is completely different from what tradition expects. This is exactly what is needed now in the process of transforming consciousness in a magical key: what is inside must become real and form the reality of the future not from the mind, but in essence, even though all the elements through which such formation takes place remain the same.

Now, the task on the channel of the goddess Skadi is to make the final push and "turn inside out," melting into water and freezing again, but in a completely different configuration. The stave "Formula of Truth," [186] when used on the channel of the goddess Skadi, will work as a developer of liberated inner strength, which will shape the personality according to the true model. "

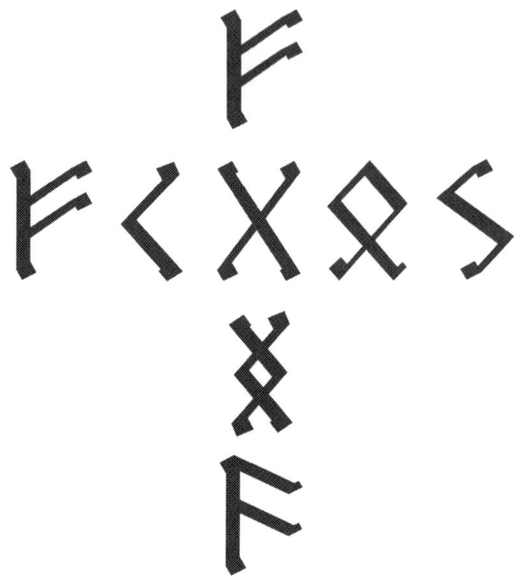

Skadi's Formula: The Formula of Truth

This stave consists of two intersecting lines. The vertical branch of Fehu-Gebo-Inguz-Ansuz represents the inner world. Here, in this line, the inner knowledge of one's rights (Fehu) is encrypted: the right to life (Inguz) and the right to know why this

186 Author – Master Irbis

life is needed (Ansuz). The horizontal line of Fehu-Kenaz-Gebo-Othala-Sowilo encrypts the outer world, the world of manifesting one's inner knowledge outward. This is the environment of communication, external connections, and agreements with the surroundings that God Forseti manifested in the previous step. In this horizontal line, the priorities are somewhat different than in the line signifying the internal world in this stave. Here, it also deals with the right of manifestation: the right to choose (Kenaz), the right to select and belong to a suitable community (Othala), the right to victory and wholeness (Sowilo). These two lines are connected by the rune Gebo, which is common to both and represents the agreement between the external and internal. In this connection, the internal plays the leading role: it is precisely from the vertical line that the drawing of this stave should begin. Gebo here acts not only as the keeper of the internal-external agreement but also as a delicate gyroscope that instantly detects any imbalance that might favor the external at the expense of the internal, and vice versa—it won't allow the internal to exert violence over the external or to use rights that the internal potential never had. This too is the justice towards which Forseti's power, familiar to you from previous practice, is directed.

The goddess Skadi teaches: whatever magic awakens within you, it must become what transitions from an internal representation and perception of self to a state of external power. The internal must become external, not by the will of circumstances, but by the internal drive to make your magical consciousness tangibly real and manifest.

This is the final step in the global transformation of oneself. On this channel, you must be attentive to provocations through laughter—they will definitely occur, as they should, with Loki always nearby. Remember this and never forget: you genuinely accept into yourself that which you sincerely laugh at. Some of what is accepted from the outside is indeed necessary for you, but some may be the poison that kills magic. By manifesting your true self outwardly through the provocations of the trickster god, learn to protect your magic from the mistletoe and the necessity of forgiving those who desperately need you to renounce your magic voluntarily. If something nonetheless penetrates you, at least understand—this is now the front line where your magical power will be tempered.

ᛊ ᛞ

PRACTICE 28

Goddess Saga

Starting from the channel of the goddess Saga and continuing through all twelve aspects of the goddess Frigg, you will need to test your magical consciousness, laying down various principles as its foundation. The consciousness of a mage is always built around a certain power; this power forms the tradition, and tradition, in turn, makes reality visible, dense, and protected. You might not yet know or be fully certain which cornerstone (or several of them) should form the basis of your personal magical reality. Conducting your consciousness through the channels of the twelve goddesses-projections of Frigg, as the keeper of the Tradition's foundation, will act as a litmus test to evaluate your consciousness for "magicality," determining its specificity.

The first channel into which you place your newborn consciousness is the channel of the goddess Saga. Will her power be the defining form that allows your magic to manifest, not dissipate in space, but concentrate around you firmly and for a long time? Only practice can reveal this.

Before her death in the battle of Ragnarök, "Saga" was one of the names of the goddess Frigg, and memory was one of her functions, working for tradition. After the battle, Saga became an independent name and, consequently, an independent program.

If the channel of the goddess Saga becomes central in the created reality, the main task of the creator of such a reality is to make the world truthful and filled with all sorts of

ᚠ ᚨ

information, without differentiating it into "good" or "bad." The magic of the goddess Saga reveals the truth, as if raising it from the depths of the waters. It is the Atlantis that surfaced in the middle of the ocean, a world where lies cannot exist because false words settle on the liar in dirty clumps, visible to everyone. A reality formed by the power of the goddess Saga is a reality where nothing can be hidden or forbidden, where the truth is visible and audible, where magic itself colors truth and falsehood in different shades, and where the world is built around the fact — an event either happened or it did not, and that's all there is to it.

Connection with the power of the goddess Saga will show you a reality without lies, filled with knowledge without white spots. You, in turn, will need to determine whether this reality is for you or not; whether you can live in it or not. In your reality, your manifestation will be absolute, and the magical power of the mind will reveal itself quickly and clearly — there will be no confusion. The configuration of consciousness that exists now is ready to activate its core, and you will need to understand with which channel your core will be absolutely connected.

The formula-stave "Discover the Truth"[187] will help you conduct such a test.

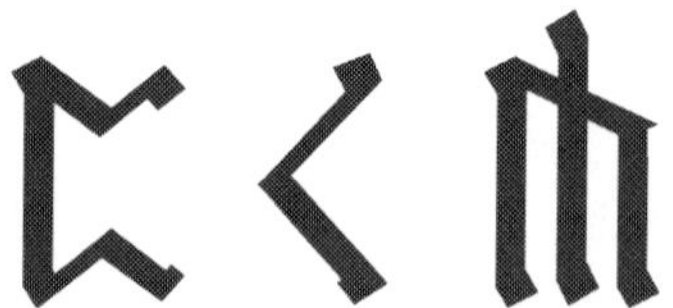

Saga's Formula: Discover the Truth

[187] Author is unknown.

Here we see a sequentially encrypted process of energy transformation using runes, where Perthro-Kenaz, the well-known "final choice" command, works to lift the veil, allowing everything to be seen clearly. The bind rune of Uruz-Naud represents the multiplied strength of the Earth, and in combination with Perthro-Kenaz, it reveals reality as it is. This acts like a second sight, which turns on the "X-ray" beam and allows you to see the hidden, exposing the foundation of reality rather than its illusion. This stave will be very useful for any learning and knowledge acquisition, and it is simply indispensable when immersing in myths. Myths are allegorical, and behind the poetic eloquence, one cannot always immediately see the core of the myth, its deep meaning. This formula helps to see everything differently than just from a human perspective.

However, the main goal of staying on the channel of the goddess Saga is somewhat broader than effective learning — here we are testing the strength of the core of our mind with the information flow of the goddess, where the manifestation of this flow should be reflected in the observed reality. Does the old reality melt under the new gaze of historical truth, revealing its skeleton? On the old bones in the new world, new flesh will grow, but it is necessary to scrape off the pieces of illusions from the bones of Ymir to see where the living is and where the dead is, where new knowledge is needed, and where it should not be touched because the living must live.

Raise from the "Submerged Bench" the true knowledge that is lacking and replace the false one that should not be. On the channel of the goddess Saga, you will be able to find out if this is your magical mission or not.

ᛊ ᛞ

PRACTICE 29

Goddess Eir

If reality were built on the principles and power of the goddess Eir, it would form itself based on the rule of biological preference dominance over all else. People would live where it is convenient for them, where they are a part of the world. People would live in harmony with the rhythm of the land they inhabit. People would live in such a way as to be an integral part of nature, not an extraneous part; they would live so that nature would see them as part of itself, not as an alien intrusion to be rejected. This would be the case if the foundation of tradition formation were laid by the goddess Eir. On this basis, the principle of "do no harm" would be fundamental, the main rule of existence for worlds, people, and all beings inhabiting these worlds. The principle of not harming each other.

In the practice of understanding the channel of the goddess Eir, this state is the most important thing she can reveal to you. If it is true that she is a "descendant" of the cow Audhumla, the nourisher of the primordial worlds, then the manifestation of her power will become clear and tangible while living in her channel: where your place is, there you should have everything you need: resources, health; everything is restored if you live in your world and reality. This presence not only satisfies basic needs but also adheres to the rule of "do no harm." That is, nothing and no one will harm you, but you will also harm nothing and no one. Worlds and realities will touch each other only if this obligatory rule is followed. That's how it is.

ᚠ ᚨ

The goddess Eir will not only help you restore your health but will also teach you to see that health is the most important indicator of the correctness of your place, time, and way of existence. Understanding this simple Vanir truth may not lead to the rapid development of industrial intellect or technological progress, but it may allow the quiet strength of natural magic to appear in your life.

To experience this, try using this bind rune[188]:

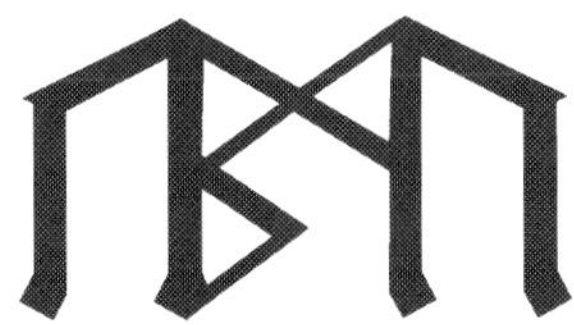

Eir's Formula: Seal of Eir. Universal Healing Formula

This stave can confidently be called the "Seal of Eir," and it is very convenient for activating a connection channel with the goddess. Here, Mannaz in the center represents a person, not as the center of the world and the focus of magical efforts, but as someone whose magical efforts are aligned with human nature and are in no way intended to harm it, even accidentally. This stave suggests that human nature requires careful attention to its specificities; what suits a jotun will not suit a human due to their different biologies. Berkana here symbolizes the restoration of life processes. Uruz represents physical health as a derivative of the power of the earth.

188 Author is unknown.

Through this formula, the goddess Eir seems to offer a suggestion: try it. Try to feel that the illness of your body is a dissociation within your own overall agreement. Something is out of balance, something is in conflict; nature fights with reason, emotions with logic, and good with evil. Try to understand this, try to feel it, reconcile everything within yourself, and perhaps everything in the world will come together for you as well. Conversely, if you harmonize yourself with the external reality, then perhaps everything within you will also return to its natural state and activate the power of eternal life restoration. Maybe the cause of your illness lies precisely in the need to perpetually maintain this internal conflict between biology and social behavior, between the internal speed of processes and the external speed of their manifestation?

ᛊ ᛞ

PRACTICE 30

Goddess Gefjon

The attribute and function embodied by the goddess Gefjon can become the center or core of your future individual reality if this value and foundation are essentially yours. The right to land, proven and secured.

The goddess Gefjon can determine whether you have the right to power by blood or not. Entering into resonance with the power of the ancient goddess can reveal the specific bloodline within the complex web of genealogies that holds the key to the transmission of rights by blood. If this line becomes the center of existence, everything else recedes to the periphery and must do so according to the ancient law of maternal right: the gifts of the Mother are inalienable; they either belong to her chosen one or return to the Mother. This is why ancient bloodlines still exist, and why true power belongs not to those whom people today mistakenly call powerful.

If the principle of the goddess Gefjon forms the foundation of your future reality, everything will be built around her.

Uruz is her rune. It characterizes the goddess Gefjon as a force capable of influencing and controlling the power of the earth, expressed in the rune Uruz (while human consciousness can only perceive this rune). The stave[189] to be used on the channel of the goddess Gefjon is based on the myth of her and

---

189 Author is unknown

her sons. By applying this stave, you seemingly elevate the power of the earth within yourself, and this power will identify and recognize within your blood and mind the ancient right that has been, is, and will be the defining true state of affairs.

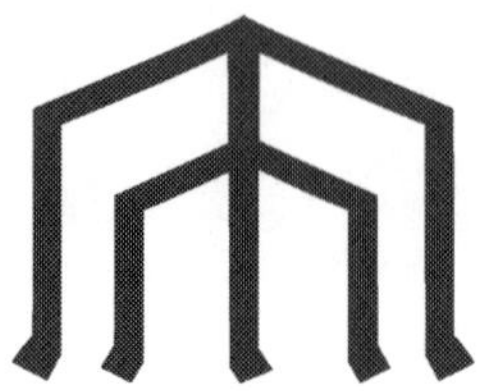

Gefjon's Formula: Sons of Gefjon

Four Uruz runes intertwined together quadruple the power of the earth. At the very least, this will boost your life force and health current exponentially. In relation to the channel of Gefjon, it also serves as an algorithm for recognition—whether there is royal blood or not.

Additionally, the power of this stave can give a clear indication of where your rightful land is. This effect is enhanced by the inclusion of the Tiwaz rune (twice), which appears in the background.

The stave "Sons of Gefjon" can be inscribed on yourself or on your reflection. You can also draw it on a piece of paper and place it under your pillow to seek an answer in a dream. Accompany this with a lesser ritual, asking the goddess to reveal the necessary quality, give a hint, or provide clear guidance.

The nobility of a true queen, the real mistress of the world, lies in the fact that she, the queen, never refuses a request. She doesn't fulfill wishes like the tooth fairy, but listening, understanding the problem, and freeing from guilt imposed by the patriarchal world of Abrahamic dominance is the sacred duty of the Mother of Worlds. Naturally, she has a special affinity for women, as each woman is a projection of the Mother.

ᛊ ᛞ

PRACTICE 31

Goddess Fulla

The independent power of the goddess Frigg, personified in the form of the goddess Fulla, aids in the re-establishment of tradition within the old core but under new conditions. The core of the tradition, while remaining unchanged, can reconfigure its internal connections so that the "tradition" program operates differently, yet retains its essential property—the core of tradition. In new conditions, tradition may no longer need to expend resources on embodying or maintaining old rules, but there is always something that must remain constant, for without it, the essence of tradition would die and cease to exist.

The core is hidden in Frigg's chest, guarded by Fulla.

The channel of the goddess Fulla can first reveal the incompleteness of your consciousness, identifying the unfilled gaps which become spaces for mistletoe (harmful elements). Nature abhors a vacuum, and if you do not fill it yourself, the space will do so inevitably. Additionally, the channel of the goddess Fulla can synchronize you with ongoing informational processes that flow continuously. Fulla's headband erases the boundary between the living and the dead—in tradition, everything is alive, only the forms differ. Fulla can assign your consciousness to undergo the necessary trials, lessons, and revelations, gaining the previously missed experience that resulted in the unfilled gaps in consciousness. The goddess Fulla will help you, residing in the world of the living, to synchronously undergo lessons along with Baldr and Hod, who do this in the

ᚠ ᚠ

world of the dead under the supervision of the goddess Hel. These lessons will help you make the power of your core invulnerable, and the tradition, which will unfold around this core after Ragnarök, capable of creating a complete reality, free of illusions.

The formula that can be used on the channel of the goddess Fulla is her seal, her name encrypted in runes.

The use of this formula[190] is possible with the goddess's permission, as it allows you to attract from the space those events whose experience you lack as quickly as possible. This is only possible and necessary when the diagnostic program of the goddess of Tradition's handmaiden reveals gaps in your consciousness that need filling. If you apply this formula without necessity, there is a high probability of cluttering your mind with copies of events you have already experienced in essence, just in a different time and scenario. However, for the essence of experience, the scenario is not as important as the core event itself. For this reason, a person's mind is filled with stories related to the same essence but executed in different scenarios. Unfortunately, for the essence of consciousness, scenarios are not important, the experience is recorded in the soul's structure only once, copies do not get recorded. Therefore, it happens that after living a long life, experiencing various events, a person leaves this world, like Baldr, with a minimal amount of true experience, even though their mind seems filled to the brim. But this is not experience; it's clutter, not only event copies but also copies of copies, simulacra, profanation, illusions of fullness. To prevent this from happening, under the tutelage of the goddess

---

190 Author is unknown

Fulla, you need to determine what events are necessary and what experiences are lacking and promptly fill in the gaps.

Fulla's Formula: Change the Level of Rights

The formula consists of two parts. The first part, Fehu-Uruz, means "basic rights," the initial fullness, what is actually in your consciousness now. The second part, Laguz-Ansuz, means "information flow." The colon between the parts of the formula signifies a transition—what we obtain as a result and what in mathematics is represented by the equals sign. Thus, it reads: basic rights = information flow. Information flow is not data or knowledge; it is the experience we undergo to fill the foundations of our mind not with copies but with entirely original data. Data and knowledge fill the mental, while the higher spheres of the mind are filled with condensed experience and conclusions drawn from it.

Using this formula on the channel of the goddess Fulla will be like quickly passing through an obstacle course, the opportunity to gain experience in a stream, quickly, intensely, not discretely, without rest or breaks. A small victorious war, a blitzkrieg with the system.

If your future reality, which your mind will begin to construct after Ragnarök, is based on the recreation of the old tradition where the goddess Fulla supports the core of reality with information, then it will become your direct duty not only to learn to receive stream events but also to produce stream events for reality and all who will dwell in that reality.

Diagnostic is mandatory, a lesser ritual is desirable, and the formula can be applied directly to yourself—and into battle.

ᛊ ᛞ

PRACTICE 32

Var and Vör

After the battle of Ragnarök, being separated from the maternal core of the goddess Frigg, all 12 of her projections are capable not only of performing independent functions but also of forming tradition anew, with different or varied emphases. The goddesses Vár and Vör are no exception. Their function is the fixation of spoken promises or oaths, even if they are whispered or said in secret.

In the world that existed before Ragnarök, the fate of gods and humans was woven by the Norns, forming the main tapestry that nothing could disrupt. After Ragnarök, the situation will change—gods and humans will become the architects of their own destinies, independent of each other. It won't be a preordained fate but rather one's own spoken word, verbalized intention, that should be the basis for the course of one's life, as declared by the initiator of the change. This was impossible in the old world, but in the new programmatic reality created by the young gods, their power and the skill of the god Ullr are capable of creating a decentralized destiny program with such fine-tuning that it can account for every spoken word and incorporate it immutably into the fabric of reality[191]. It cannot be removed, only

---

[191] Here's a prototype of blockchain technology. Blockchain (a chain of blocks) is a distributed database where the storage devices are not connected to a common server. This database maintains a continually growing list of ordered records, called blocks. Each block contains a timestamp and a link to the previous block.

ᚹ ᚫ

realized. The goddesses Vár and Vör ensure this: Vör reads the word, and Vár records it.

In the new world, humans will no longer be bound by the orlog of the gods but only by their own wyrd. This wyrd is woven not by the norns but by the individual themselves. The foundations of one's probable life path will be the vows and oaths, the promises, and assurances they speak aloud.

The ability of the goddesses Var and Vör to hear and account for everything spoken gains new power in the post-Ragnarök world. The world built by the young gods will not be as dependent on the karma of ancestors and gods, the karma of past actions. It will no longer rely heavily on the inevitability of what has been previously created, the obligations taken on by family or tribe members. The principle of collective responsibility for everything will disappear, as will the boundaries defined by orlog. Only the individual and their decisions, which do not extend to everyone else, will matter. The principle of responsibility for one's own words and actions will define the boundaries of possibilities and individual reality: the more fulfilled promises and truthful words, the larger this reality will be, with its boundaries of probabilities expanding each day.

The goddesses Var and Vör will teach you not only to take responsibility for your words but also to hear what others desire. In the new world, not only does the principle of individual responsibility reign supreme, but so does the principle that everything is connected to everything. The new program of reality building must account for everything without diminishing

---

The use of encryption ensures that users can only modify those parts of the blockchain that they "own" in the sense that they have the private keys necessary to write to the file. Additionally, encryption ensures the synchronization of copies of the distributed blockchain among all users.

anything, based on the principle of importance. Everything is important, and everyone has the right to manifest their own reality, but only within their own space. If two importances coincide in meaning, essence, and form, they have the right, if they wish, to merge their realities, but they are not obligated to do so just because of such a coincidence.

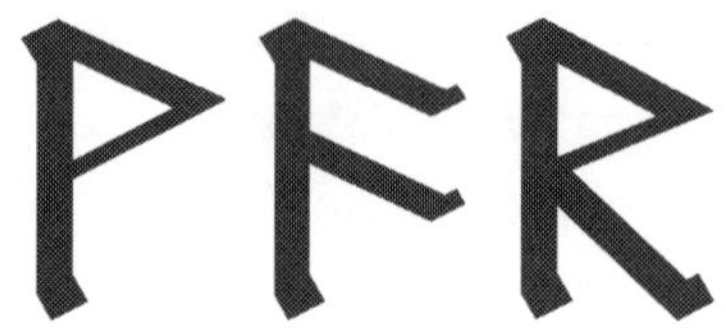

Var's Formula: Var's Seal

The formulas-seals of the goddesses Var and Vör will help you acquire the necessary qualities.

Using these formulas will show you how a program can function in the "cloud," where every word and intention is accounted for and realized instantly.

The names of the goddesses Var and Vör, recorded in runes, mean the following:

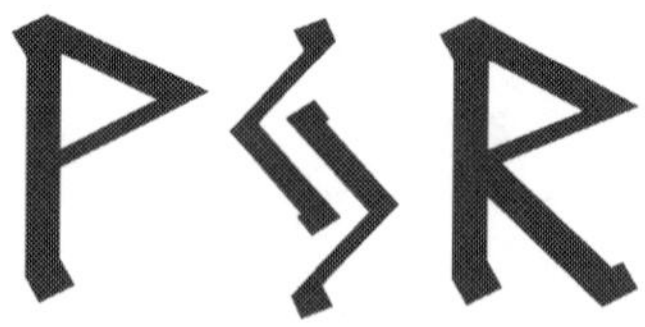

Vör's Formula: Vör's Seal

Var: Wunjo-Ansuz-Raidho. The integrated consciousness of one's information carves a path to the future; a channel on the fabric of reality.

Vör: Wunjo-Jera-Raidho. The integrated consciousness fills the channel with time currents, thus weaving itself and its decisions into the fabric of the future.

The difference between these two formulas lies only in the middle rune—Ansuz versus Jera, indicating: what is said is received; knowledge defines the future; the information stream with which the mind carves a path into the future determines the volume of time it can manage. It all depends on the integrated consciousness, and if it is truly integrated, the individual has the right to personal reality and responsibility.

You can use these formulas separately to understand each goddess's channel, or together to see how the program functions holistically. Joint use of the goddesses' formula-seals will balance and demonstrate how what is said and done today manifests in the future, even tomorrow. Even a mistake has the right to be accounted for, but you must ensure that your mistake affects no one but yourself.

If the core of your future reality includes the power of the goddesses Var and Vör, such a reality will foster the necessity for conscious participation in the programming process by every individual. You will need to see and understand how lies and deceit distort the fabric of reality and how reality limits such consciousness in its scope. Record changes in reality and understand why they occurred.

ᛊ ᛞ

PRACTICE 33

Goddesses Sjöfn and Lofn

The newfound independence of the powers of the goddesses Sjöfn and Lofn no longer serves a single tradition but instead becomes capable of participating in the formation of traditions themselves. In this sense, they become more closely associated with Forseti, the grandson and descendant of Frigg, the son of Baldr. However, while Forseti will establish voluntary decisions as law and necessary rules, the goddesses Sjöfn and Lofn define these connections: Sjöfn verifies the voluntariness, ensuring that two autonomous and free realities wish to establish mutual connections without any violence or coercion, and Lofn establishes such connections. In the new world, their power is unrestrained, unrestricted by boundaries, and free from obligatory caste rules. The key principle now is honest voluntariness. In this process, Lofn can determine the desired level of connections necessary for the merging realities, considering the needs and wishes of each party. While in the old tradition such binding of fates operated on the principle of "all or nothing," in the new world, levels of interaction can be chosen (like required options in a system): the main thing is that the agreement is mutual, without imposing conditions on the merging parties based on the principle of "if, then."

Programming the new world will be arranged in such a way that if the parties match, for example, on some subtle bodies and agree to communicate through them, no one has the right to force them to open all their consciousness and other subtle

ᚹ ᚨ

bodies to each other, to accept each other's fate, although in the old tradition it was exactly that way.

If a person wants to live in a particular reality but cannot achieve it, it means there is some special trick in their consciousness that tells them it is impossible or wrong, that it should not be. In the process of initiated consciousness transformation on the channels of the goddesses Sjöfn and Lofn in real-time, you will undergo a test that will not only reveal your true desire but also show the block in your consciousness that prevents its realization, entering into such a reality where it is not just possible but necessarily possible.

The power of these two goddesses can be strongly felt when using the "Path Convergence[192]" bind rune. Applying this bind rune in a training, playful form will bring you together with a person or people, introduce you to the necessary circumstances that will illustrate what you really want and why you cannot take the desired. It will show very brightly and prominently, so understanding the essence of your desires and realizing the prohibitive pattern will be simply impossible to miss.

Goddess Sjöfn will show you the old world patterns present in your consciousness that make reality static and lifeless. She will see not only the "true desire" but also what blocks both its manifestation and realization. If the urge to live in a new reality is very strong but you cannot achieve the desired, it is necessary to eliminate the reason that prevents two realities—yours and the desired—from touching.

192 Author – Master Orobas.

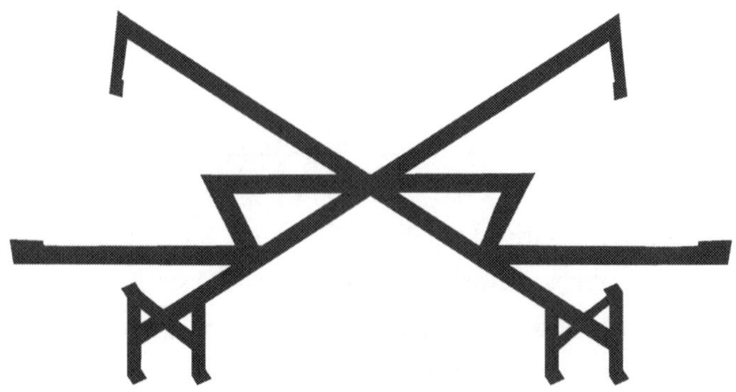

Sjöfn's and Lofn's Formula: Path Convergence

Goddess Lofn will connect two realities formed by each consciousness at the optimal convergence point needed for both—without diminishing oneself or the other, without imposing oneself where it is not needed, but also without the need to "accept everything else" in addition to the important.

The bind rune consists of two Raidho runes, somewhat stylized in this bind rune, but their stylization is not an artistic tribute but symbolizes the specificity of the paths, special channels for information designed to allow movement not only within the usual reality but also beyond it. The rune Gebo, on which the two Raidho runes are "suspended," shows voluntary and honest partnership. The two Mannaz runes represent people whose paths converge at the point of greatest favor and voluntary acceptance. The convergence should occur precisely at the level of realities acceptable to both. Two Laguz runes are the driving force that "carries" into the circumstances, directs the path through the channel to the meeting point. Such a test simulation will help you clarify not so much what is "wrong" in this world as what is "wrong" in you to enter another world.

This bind rune can be drawn on paper and activated in your usual way.

If the power of the goddesses Sjöfn and Lofn is at the core of the created reality, this can truly become a reality of magic—it will plastically change based on the emerging desires, and its stability will remain until the desires change. Not everyone will like living in such a world, but there are always those who dream only of this. If so, then such a reality should be programmatically possible because the power of these goddesses today may become your power tomorrow.

PRACTICE 34

Goddesses Syn and Hlin

In the world being programmed by the young gods, two forces represented by the goddesses Syn and Hlin, unlike the previous pair, are capable of protecting the new reality from unnecessary contacts and connections that could harm it. In this property, the most valuable quality of a person as a creator of reality becomes particularly significant, and this quality begins to be protected by all possible and impossible means.

The goddesses Syn and Hlin will find this quality without fail. In this function, they act oppositely to the previous pair of goddesses, who were capable of finding vulnerabilities that allow connections with the unnecessary and prevent connections with the necessary. Here, it is the opposite: regardless of the connections the new reality possesses, there is something that must remain unchanged; any stresses and cataclysms can be survived if the core of the new reality remains intact—this core must be preserved.

Previously, being connected to Frigg's foundation by rigid ties, the power of the goddesses Syn and Hlin worked to protect tradition. Now, separated from Frigg and oriented towards the new law-creator Forseti, they can protect not the collective but the strictly individual, preventing a personal newborn reality from dissolving into any aggressive and alien one. The following formula, "Seal of Justice," [193] will help you

[193] Author – Master Sam.

uncover your internal rules of justice, not imposed but natural and true.

The circle in this stave represents personal space and personal strength. Inside the circle, there is a stylized Kenaz, which, like a lantern, illuminates your true essence from above. Two Ansuz runes, one upright and one reversed, show "two truths"—your explicit and implicit truths—not only what is declared but also what stands behind it. The Tiwaz rune affirms that what is said and unsaid is the truth, and this is the foundation of justice, but only within the circle, within your own reality.

Syn's and Hlin's Formula: Seal of Justice

It is best to create this bind rune as a talisman and call upon the goddesses with a lesser ritual.

Recognize your inner sense of justice and let the goddesses Syn and Hlin teach you to protect yourself and your reality.

ᛊ ᛞ

PRACTICE 35

Goddess Snotra

This goddess, with the power of her informational might, can integrate all that has been learned and experienced on the channels of the goddess Frigg into a unified intelligence. In the new world, as you have already understood, there cannot be a single tradition for everyone, but there must be a tradition for each individual. The power of the goddess Snotra is meant to weld together all essential conditions and take into account the nuances of the program for building an individual reality. She will help combine all the essential distinguished qualities into a single program and prepare a ready image for inscription in the system of multiple worlds (this function belongs to the next goddess).

The combined main qualities of your consciousness and personality will predetermine not only the primary properties of the reality that will unfold around you but also the rules of permissible and impermissible connections with other realities that must also exist. However, such a combination is not static and tends to constantly evolve. This process is encoded in the bind rune of the goddess Snotra, called "Rebirth."[194]

---

[194] Author – Master Orobas.

ᚠ ᚨ

Snotra's Formula: Rebirth

The bind rune consists of five (!) Eihwaz runes, fastened together like a buckle by the Inguz[195] rune. The quintupled Eihwaz, symbolizing death and rebirth, like the ten channels you have already experienced as projections of the weaver goddess. Multiple stages of alchemical transmutation ultimately yield the sought-after Inguz — the symbol of life. It shows that this process, through the death of the old, binds new life, creating the philosopher's stone of ultimate rebirth. But you will go through it with open eyes, experiencing each alchemical stage, feeling death and rebirth with both your mind and body. In this process of multiple births and deaths, you will very clearly and sharply, as never before, experience the sensation of your own mind and restraint. This will form for you the right Inguz — your true nature. But its realization will be very different from the understanding of yourself in the old world system — now you

195 Unlike the traditional depiction, the already known stylized form in the shape of a rhombus is used here.

will neither need to prove it nor demonstrate it; understanding your true nature and its absolute acceptance is always associated with the state of mind and restraint.

When you want to "share" with others, this state is based on excess, on a subconscious feeling of having something extra. In the state of presence of what is yours, the desire to discard the excessive part through the process of sharing is absent.

To connect yourself to the channel of the goddess Snotra and activate her seal, use the power of a lesser ritual and invocation of the goddess. Your intention to enter the process of alchemical transmutation of yourself must be clear to you and free of any doubts.

ᛊ ᛞ

PRACTICE 36

Goddess Gna

Being a projection of the goddess Frigg, her assistant Gna fulfilled the role of a messenger and executor of the Great Weaver's tasks. However, as an independent force, she expands her functions of "disseminating information" not according to the vectors of Frigg's interests, but freely within the system of multiple worlds created by the young gods. The final force, describing the functionality of forming and spreading an individual program of reality construction, the goddess Gna, represents the final stage of projecting information about the completed program into all systems, worlds, and realities. Using the description of the blockchain system methodology, it can be said that the power of the goddess Gna allows for instant updates to the record of the reality program's state, which is then instantly copied (reflected) in all other records of other worlds with which your program is connected at any level or to any extent. The same happens with the fixation of changes in other realities—they are also recorded in your system of reality formation as data that is advisable (or necessary) to consider.

Thus, in this practice of transformation, the goddess Gna performs the final step: to write the new reality program into the entire system of worlds, bringing you "out of the cloud" and into life. For this purpose, you can use the seal "Request to the Subtle World[196]."

---

196 Author is unknown.

ᚹ ᚨ

This symbol is called a "galdrastafir" and has ancient Icelandic origins. There is no description for it; it is a holistic, not a composite sign. It was not created in the world of Midgard; it is a systemic function, and this function is encrypted in this stave—a function of communication, recording changes, and protecting them from external harmful influences. This sign can be fashioned into an amulet, inscribed on your reflection, or even on yourself. This stave will open up the space of other worlds, now programmatically connected to your new consciousness.

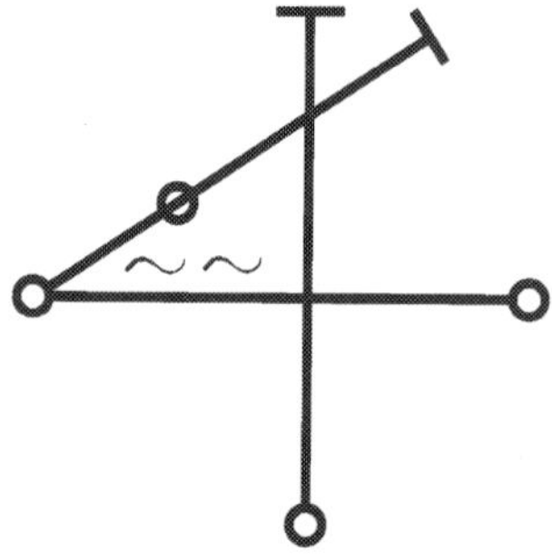

Formula of the Goddess Gna:
Request to the "Subtle World" for a Task

Building a personal reality on the power of the goddess Gna defines the creator of such a reality as a "messenger," a herald. Such a reality is akin to a registry where all records are protected and must be preserved even if all worlds perish and all connections between multiple realities are severed—everything can subsequently be recreated without distortions.

ᛊ ᛞ

PRACTICE 37

Valkyries

For the power of the goddess Frigg and her projections to be correctly implemented in the program of Ullr-Vidar, they might need assistance. The thoughts of Odin, having gained will and freedom, provide such assistance. In the new world, valkyries serve as guides. Their names are not random; they symbolize specific emotional powers that can accelerate the spread of one's reality through time and space, speeding up the "writing" of necessary new connections to bring personal reality to life and give it the right to manifest. To ensure that desires are realized immediately, not later, emotional strength is required.

When you read the names of the valkyries or hear the vibrational sound of a particular name, pay attention to your emotional response. This name and emotion can serve as an additional accelerating and expanding force that can function as a catalyst in your personal reality, hastening all processes. However, never forget that among Odin's thoughts, there is always a contradictory one that might act unexpectedly or strictly the opposite, leading your reality into unknown realms. But this program quirk can sometimes result in unexpected effects, not always negative. Even the most developed consciousness cannot calculate all possible event formations, all facets of multiple realities. At such times, the help of the valkyrie Sigrdrífa is invaluable.

ᚹ ᚨ

The proposed formula for further work is called "Brain Crash[197]." At this stage of the work, it will act as an instant destruction of internal blocks that restrain the force of fervor and those "correct" emotions which, for you personally, are not evil, but rather the catalyst that, like a big bang, will rapidly spread itself, forming new connections and manifesting a new reality. In combination with the name of the valkyrie that resonates with you personally, this formula will work in harmony with the tasks of the core of your future reality, ensuring you victory—at the very least over yourself and over those enslaving programs that previously bound your will.

The story of the valkyries, as thoughts of the god Odin, teaches us that power without will is a dangerous phenomenon. It can be captured by anyone, and your inner magic will work for the captor and occupier without you even realizing it. But when will controls power, the slavery of the Abrahamic world will not only be clearly understood but also impossible to endure ever again.

Valkyrie's Formula: Brain Crash.
Radical Removal of Conscious Blocks

This formula consists of two runes, meaning it has a prolonged effect rather than a one-time impact. When made into

197 Author is unknown.

a permanent talisman, it will work continuously, rapidly releasing the specific type of emotions that serve as the working fuel for your magic and your power to build a new reality according to your own algorithms, rather than being forced to participate in someone else's reality as an outsider.

The two runes—Eihwaz and Uruz—are runes of immense power. But Eihwaz is a cunning rune, a provoker. It can act as an enhancer or a destroyer. The subject of Eihwaz's work is Uruz, the true power of the earth, the source of all rights, the cow Audhumla, the nourisher of newborn worlds. If the power of fear, embedded in the rune Eihwaz, is greater than needed to awaken will and fervor, Uruz will quiet, and there will be no magic, no power in the program of personal reality construction. But if will exceeds fear, if fear only stokes the will, then Uruz's strength increases manifold and can only be directed toward the creation of worlds and the weaving of realities—its presence will be abundant, but necessary and sufficient for working with the team of young gods.

Working on the channel of the valkyries implies that during this period, you will be the valkyrie yourself. And you will test yourself to see how well your will matches your freedom.

PRACTICE 38

Ragnarök

Ragnarök is not a global battle between good and evil, as it might seem at first glance. Ragnarök happens in each individual's consciousness when the constants of the old system no longer correspond to reality. Ragnarök occurs when the choice is between two options: either to kill the constants and create new ones that match reality, or to kill reality and create a new one that matches the constants. All other compromise options have already been tried and have failed.

The Norse system was ingeniously designed but made with mistakes. There's no need to repent for mistakes; they must be corrected. Repentance changes nothing; it only diminishes the idea: any repentance is essentially a diminution and nullification.

Everyone will eventually enter their own personal Ragnarök. For each person, the time will come when there are three years of winter, where nothing grows and no idea bears fruit. When all your dead rise from Hel's gates, when the dog Garm — your personal nightmare — barks, when chaos floods your life, leaving nothing worth preserving, that's when Gjallarhorn's horn will sound, and only you will hear it. When the rooster crows, you will suddenly find yourself standing on the field of Vigrid.

This formula is the runic inscription of the battlefield Vigrid. Here, Wunjo-Isa-Gebo signifies unity with your god: in the final battle, you become them. Raidho-Inguz-Dagaz represents the path to new life. Thus, the formula contains the incantation of the god's rebirth into a new life, meaning you also rebirth with them — for you are part of them, and they are part of you. What was most important and valuable to your god should become the foundation of your personality, the core upon which you will build your new reality in the new world with the young gods, based on the value of life. A new reality in a new role, with a new status, a new function, but always in your true nature.

Apply this formula when you feel the time has come. You will meet your natural enemy, whom you will devour, and they will devour you. And when this happens, the joint rebirth will occur, just as the ancient gods once did to be reborn in a new quality, leading to your existence. Now, in the new reality with the young gods, it is up to you to build a new reality — honest and fair for yourself and for everyone.

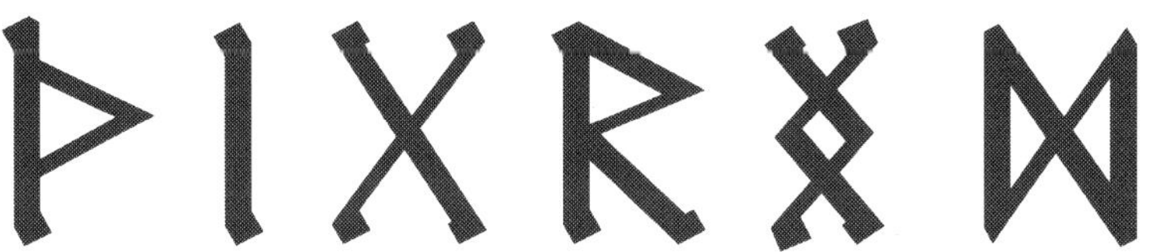

Formula of Vigrid: Let the Battle Commence

Let the battle of Ragnarök be not a battle to the death with the described outcome in the legends, but a knightly tournament where conflicting opponents come forth to honestly display their strength and truth. Let Ragnarök be the opportunity for you that the Norse gods did not have — to sort out your preferences, change the constants of consciousness, manifest the

main thing, and remove the unnecessary. If you succeed, then the honest tale of the Norse gods was not left to us in vain.

Copyright © 2024 Ksenia Menshikova
English Translation Copyright © 2024 STUDIO LABYRINTH Sp. z o.o., Poland
All rights reserved.

ISBN: 9798332112416

Made in the USA
Columbia, SC
11 June 2025